WINDS
OF
CHANGE

WINDS OF CHANGE

FINDING GOD'S DIRECTION IN TURBULENT TIMES

Warren C. Hamby

FLEMING H. REVELL COMPANY
OLD TAPPAN, NEW JERSEY

Scripture references identified KJV are from the *King James Version of the Bible.*

Scripture quotations identified as PHILLIPS are from *The New Testament in Modern English* translated by J.B. Phillips, copyright J.B. Phillips, 1958. Used by permission of the Macmillan Company.

Unless otherwise identified, the Bible texts in this publication are from the *Revised Standard Version of the Bible,* copyrighted 1946 and 1952 by the Division of Christian Education of the National Council of Churches, and used by permission.

Grateful acknowledgment is extended for use of the following material:

Murder in the Cathedral by T.S. Eliot is published by Faber and Faber Ltd., in London and by Harcourt Brace Jovanovich, Inc. in New York and is used by permission.

"Who Will Answer" by Sheila Davis-L.E. Aute © Copyright 1967 by L.E. Aute. Ediciones Musicales RCA Espanola, S.A. All rights for the U.S.A. and Canada controlled by Sunbury Music, Inc., 1133 Avenue of the Americas, New York, New York. Reprinted by Permission.

"Outmatching Defeat" by Cassius English Street was used as a motto by The General Electric Company.

SBN 8007–0449–5

Library of Congress Catalog Card Number: 78–149371
Printed in the United States of America

TO *my mother and father*

Contents

Blow, Wind of God! With wisdom blow
Until our minds are free
From mists of error, clouds of doubt,
Which blind our eyes to Thee!

Foreword

Not everyone can deliver clear, relevant, significant sermons—and then bring those sermons in essay form to the written page maintaining the same clarity, the same relevance, and the same excitement. Some people can do this, but not very many. They excel at either one or the other. Warren Hamby displays an unusual gift in being a part of that small number of people who can both speak and write brilliantly. He has displayed this unusual gift in *Winds of Change.* Warren C. Hamby is the product of the parsonage, and is himself a member of the North Alabama Conference of the United Methodist Church. He is now serving at an influential church in the city of Birmingham, Alabama—the Huffman United Methodist Church—having returned to his native North Alabama Conference from a distinguished pastorate at the Galloway Memorial United Methodist Church in Jackson, Mississippi.

The *old order* changes. We no longer need, if indeed we ever did, to argue this point. The winds of change have not only blown upon us, but they are constantly blowing all about us. Nowhere have they been more alarming and disturbing than in our beloved Southland. We are surrounded by unparalleled frustrations and by concerns deeper than we have ever experienced before. Many cry out for a return to the old fundamentals. All of us, in one degree or another, long for the old and the familiar. The thoughtful man knows that he cannot stop the world and get off, yet he is afraid, for the old seems to be leaving his sight. The religious man yearns for new strength equal to his tasks, and for a vital relationship with the gospel which might enable him to come to terms with the life of the new world. On every hand there are voices of despair, and prophets of doom seem to be a dime a dozen.

This book is not a reminder to us that we are living in a time of unprecedented change. It assumes at the very outset that we are intelligent enough to know this. It does assume —in truth, it believes—that God is within the winds of change and that He is not trying to say something to our generation, but that He is also doing something significant as He continues to make all things new. *Winds of Change* has to do with the author's own search for the basic landmarks of an authentic faith. With the ability of an artist splashing his colors upon canvas, Warren Hamby uses the Book of Jeremiah and the Word of God spoken *to* Jeremiah and *through* Jeremiah for his message to us in our time. He draws a meaningful parallel between the latter part of the seventh century B.C. in which Jeremiah lived, and the latter part of the twentieth century in which we live. He masterfully draws a parallel involving the turbulence of Jeremiah's time and the almost convulsive turbulence of our own day. Jeremiah was sent to call the country and its leaders back to the will and the ways of God. Like Jesus, Jeremiah sought religious reform in terms of inward cleansing and renewal, and, like Jesus, Jeremiah died a martyr at the hands of his own countrymen. It is nothing short of exciting to see the relevance of the Bible in our contemporary scene and to hear the Scripture as it speaks to our world.

The author does not allow the modern ministry to escape its responsibilities as he reminds us of Jeremiah's indictment of the priesthood for not fulfilling its role as the true spokesman for God; nor does he allow the Church—the institutional Church—to escape its responsibilities; nor does he allow the individual Christian to escape his. In his ancient writings Jeremiah indicted Israel for her unfaithfulness and for her apathy. Jeremiah was a weeping prophet because the people of God in his day did not seem to care. *Winds of Change* brings alive this ancient figure from the distant past and makes him a significant contemporary voice in the current struggle which is personal, social, and political.

One will not find in *Winds of Change* a recitation of the dynamics of change nor a nostalgic longing for the continuance of the old order and its plantation culture which seems to be slipping away. *Winds of Change* does not leave one depressed, for, after the change has been articulated, the author displays the authenticity of his faith by claiming that God is in the wind and He will use this change in His will—and for His purposes. *Winds of Change* is like the sound of a trumpet calling the professional ministry to a new understanding of itself, and at the same time reminding every person who has, in faith, entered into the covenant relationship and become a part of the Body of Christ, that he, too, is in the ministry.

One of the toughest administrative problems with which church administrators deal just now is ministerial morale. The minister will find in this book significant words on that point, as did this church administrator. The author does not pick the institutional Church apart and leave it lying in pieces, but he scrutinizes it carefully and leaves it hoping for its own renewal.

I recommend this book, I recommend it highly, and I am honored to write a word at its beginning. It represents the research—and finally the preachment—of one of the most gifted of the younger ministers in our Southland. He, like his fellow ministers, has been affected by winds of change, but he does not ask us to accommodate ourselves to change. He challenges us to direct change. This is a fine book. You will be the better for having carefully read it.

W. KENNETH GOODSON, *Bishop,*
Birmingham Area of The
United Methodist Church

Introduction

There have been few periods in history when earnest Christians were so deeply troubled as they find themselves in this generation. The frustrations involved in institutional renewal and reorientation of mission have in many places fragmented the church and sapped its spirit. The individual Christian struggles with perplexing personal choices and conflicting values. The underpinnings of the faith are awash in the undercurrents of uncertainty, and the general morale of religious leadership is drained of optimism.

There is great travail at practically every level of life. The whole of modern civilization appears to have broken its moorings. Everywhere there is upheaval and unrest. There is some evidence that man is fast becoming the victim of his own genius —that the massive complexity of interests, entities, and institutions which he has created to serve him, has become like a giant Gordian knot with a thousand entanglements, which he is hopeless to unravel, but from which he is also helpless to disentangle himself.

The individual, especially the man or woman of faith, yearns for a return to simplicity—a return to the fundamental truths and basic values which will restore the spiritual bearings of society, stabilize human relationships, and quiet the unrest of his own being. Overwhelmed by his own entanglements and frustrated by his personal inadequacies; yet, far too responsible to turn loose of the issues and demands confronting him, and far too sophisticated to rest in the panaceas of the past, the religious man of today yearns for new insights and fresh resources for faith and life.

The chapters of this book have received their cast from the matrix of this struggle. They reflect the author's own search for the basic landmarks of an authentic faith. They are shaped by daily encounter with others, clergy and laity, who share in the agony of our modern quest—who have unknowingly ministered to the author by allowing him to minister to them.

The basic premise of this writing is the viability of the Christian faith and the validity of the Bible—including the Old Testament—in a day when everything is up for reexamination and reappraisal. The premise should not be confused, however, with an appeal to traditional piety, or a throwback to the literalistic and legalistic pitfalls of so-called *fundamentalism.* Nor is it an effort to shore up the weak places of modern *liberalism* by window-dressing it with Scriptural reference.

There is an exciting timeliness about the Bible when it is approached with openness and receptivity. It is not the only resource of truth, to be sure, and the *Word* is not restricted to the Biblical record; but who will deny that we have too long muted its message, either through casual deference or distorted demand? Perhaps the author has not fully acquitted himself of duplicating these faults. He makes no claim to such an achievement. He has satisfied himself, however, that the Bible contains the *Word*—throbbing with life, fresh with relevance, and reassuring with authority.

The *Book of Jeremiah* provides the principal Biblical resource for the topics discussed in the ensuing chapters. In fact, the topics were themselves suggested as much by the incidents recorded in *Jeremiah* as by the circumstances current in our experience. While there is no effort here to prove a point, a good case could be made for the advantages of this approach in our modern search for the *Word.* One wonders if we don't often lose something through our tendency to skip around in the Bible, gleaning a bit of truth here and some inspiration there, but often denying ourselves the wholeness of the message which comes through exploring an entire book.

Our treatment of *Jeremiah* is more devotional than scholarly, however, and does not so much attempt to present a study of the book as to glean from it some of the insights and inspiration, which are there in such abundance for our help with today's issues and problems. Indeed, the principal significance of the *Book of Jeremiah* is in the resources it provides in this regard. In fact, the book appears to make no contribution to the theological development of Old Testament thought. It contributes nothing comparable to Isaiah's *suffering servant* concept of God, or Hosea's portrayal of *forgiving love,* or the idea of *justice* provided by Amos. Jeremiah adds to all of these, but he can claim no singular or revolutionary contribution of his own. The principal importance of the book is in its record of the life and preaching of this fearless and dedicated—though sometimes frustrated and complaining—man of God, who lived and preached during one of the most trying and crucial periods of Old Testament history.

In this regard, the book is a gem. Indeed, no other Old Testament writing provides such abundant biographical information about its central character. Baruch, the Prophet Jeremiah's private secretary and author of most of the book, can be credited with providing this good fortune. As a result of Baruch's care in setting down the record, we know a great deal about Jeremiah and the times in which he lived and preached.

Living as he did, in the latter part of the seventh century, B.C., Jeremiah was a man to match the times, and because of the amazing parallels between his time and our own, the prophet comes to us with a fascinating, almost unbelievable relevance. After growing up as the son of a priest in the village of Anathoth in the land of Judah, Jeremiah had a career which spanned one of the most turbulent periods in the history of the Middle East.

The little countries of Judah and Israel endured a constant buffeting by the crosscurrents of international politics, a situation acutely aggravated by their own internal problems and weaknesses. During Jeremiah's lifetime the balance of power shifted from Assyria to Babylon, and tiny Israel and Judah were caught in the military vise of these major powers. It was a struggle for the little nations to survive, and after a series of treaties and alliances they capitulated to Babylon and were reduced to the status of provinces in her spreading empire.

Religion, the one constant and stable support in the history of Israel, was also at low ebb. Religious practice had become little more than a matter of temple sacrifice and outward form. Jeremiah charged that neither the priests of Israel nor the official school of the prophets in Jerusalem were fulfilling the role assigned to them as spokesmen of God. Their leadership was compromised, they abdicated from moral and spiritual responsibility and bowed to the political power structure, with its shifting posture and increasingly precarious status.

Is there any wonder that Jeremiah's career was stormy? He was sent to call the country and its leadership back to the will and the ways of God. In that role, he was the most important man of his day at a most crucial time in the history of his people. From his initial sermon in the temple until the end of his life, Jeremiah was misunderstood, resisted, and rejected. In fact, his inaugural sermon met with a response quite similar to that of Jesus in the Nazareth synagogue, and the career that followed bore many interesting parallels to the later ministry of our Lord. Like Jesus, Jeremiah sought religious reform in terms of inward cleansing and renewal, and in the end, Jeremiah, too, died a martyr at the hands of his own countrymen.

One cannot read Jeremiah's book without sensing a dimension and depth which translate themselves into the authority of "Thus says the Lord." The man and his message are at once intriguing and inexhaustible, bridging the centuries and penetrating our modern defenses, bringing us the *Word* with a clarity for which we sometimes yearn, but which we are seldom ready to receive. Stanley Hopper summarizes it when he writes of Jeremiah:

> Overtures to his "greatness," while paying him conventional praise, would fail to adduce him. The man Jeremiah, the man "of flesh and bone," the man who was rejected by his family and local community, the man who was obliged to oppose priests, kings, prophets, and people, the man who stood at the last altogether alone, a coerced exile with the poor remnant of his people in Egypt, the man whose entire life was prolonged martyrdom to the integrity of his faith, the man whom Yahweh "hurled" into the most crucial and most tragic period in the entire history of Israel—this is the man who is too easily lost behind the protective barriers of the scholar's praise, or behind our unconscious resistance (though epochs removed) to the uncomfortably true (THE INTERPRETER'S BIBLE).

Five hundred years ago one of the world's greatest artists was commissioned by the reigning pope to paint the ceiling of a chapel in the city of Rome. The artist was Michelangelo, and among the more than three hundred biblical characters immortalized by his painting is Jeremiah, the "Weeping Prophet," the man from Anathoth, called to be a "prophet to the nations." Across five centuries, visitors to the Sistine Chapel have experienced a muted eloquence in Michelangelo's depiction of this rugged giant bowed low with inward distress. The head of the prophet is downcast and brooding, the shoulders are tired and slumped, the chin, resting in one hand, is square and determined, and the eyes are piercing and sad. Beholding it, one half expects the towering figure to spring to life, to voice the agony and the ecstasy, the weakness and the strength, so eloquently expressed in the prophet's life and so skillfully portrayed in the artist's work.

For half a thousand years visitors to that Roman chapel have been inspired by that painting. But at no time during this tremendous sweep of history—indeed, not since the time of Jeremiah himself—have the man and the message which inspired that painting been so relevant for the human family. It is nothing short of astounding to discover that this figure from the distant past and his ancient book could be so relevant to our current struggle—personal and social, religious and political.

This little book attempts to capture and express something of this relevancy. It is offered with the modest hope that its readers will discover a fresh and helpful sense of Biblical timeliness—a discovery which is sure to illumine the path and steady the step in the search for a viable Christian faith in a turbulent and troubled age.

WARREN C. HAMBY

WINDS OF CHANGE

1

The Impossible Imperative

Now the word of the Lord came to me saying, "Before I formed you in the womb I knew you, and before you were born I consecrated you; I appointed you a prophet to the nations." Then I said, "Ah, Lord God! Behold, I do not know how to speak, for I am only a youth." But the Lord said to me, "Do not say, 'I am only a youth'; for to all to whom I send you you shall go, and whatever I command you you shall speak. Be not afraid of them, for I am with you to deliver you, says the Lord." Then the Lord put forth his hand and touched my mouth; and the Lord said to me, "Behold, I have put my words in your mouth. See, I have set you this day over nations and over kingdoms, to pluck up and to break down, to destroy and to overthrow, to build and to plant" Jeremiah 1:4–10.

It is the task of the church in every age to find a fresh understanding and offer a relevant application of its mission and message to the times in which it is set. The fulfillment of this task in our time, as in every period of history, demands the effort and engagement of the whole church, both its ordained ministry and the larger ministry of the laity. Together they constitute the Body of Christ ("For the body does not consist of one member but of many" 1 Corinthians 12:14), and together they determine the life and effectiveness of the church.

In any consideration of the role of the church today, we must remember that we are not *one member* but many, mutually bound and crucially responsible to and for each other. To begin this consideration with an analysis of the ministry may suggest a bias in priority which I should like to disclaim. Neither do I wish to imply that ministry is the special function or private concern of the clergy.

To be sure, the effectiveness of the ordained ministry is crucial to the life of the church. If, however, those ordained to full-time ministry are to fulfill their ministry, that fulfillment must arise out of an understanding of and a commitment to the larger vocation of ministry, mutually assigned to both clergy and laity.

When Sylvester Horne spoke of the importance of preachers in history, saying, "They and not kings and prophets have been the moulders of history," he was describing a conclusion which most of us share in retrospect. For example, we recognize the important role of the Old Testament prophets, but who remembers their kingly contemporaries? The significance of those who occupied the throne during Jeremiah's time is pale in comparison with this flaming prophet and his preaching. However, Jeremiah and his contemporaries did not at the time recognize Jeremiah's significance. Actually, Jeremiah was the most important figure of his age, but it has been left to history to validate that assessment. It has been true of all the prophets—only history ascribed them greatness. Christopher Morley was right when he said, "Prophets were twice stoned—first in anger; then, after their death, with a handsome slab in the graveyard."

The place of the preacher in giving shape to history, particularly the history of religion, has indeed been one of singular significance. In every great period when the crosscurrents of historical circumstances have merged with human endeavor to forge the shape of values, to determine the character of institutions, and to give direction to man's destiny, not blind fate, nor kings and rulers, but great faith and relevant preaching have risen to the occasion, insuring much of whatever progress has marked the human enterprise.

Moreover, the preacher and his preaching are as significant today as ever. But we are just as loath as ever to see this significance. This is especially true of the preacher himself. He is often quite sure that he is about to be phased out and replaced.

One preacher, engaged in an active pulpit ministry, wrote: "All I can say and feel is that by the change of times the pulpit has lost its place. It does only part of that whole which used to be done by it alone. Once it was newspaper, schoolmaster, theological treatise, a stimulant to good works. . . . Now these are partitioned out to different offices, and the pulpit is no more the pulpit of three centuries back, than the authority of a householder is that of Abraham."

The complaint is quite modern and we would never guess that these words were written more than a hundred years ago. They were set down in the year 1851 by one of history's great preachers, none other than Frederick W. Robertson, and were recorded in *Life and Letters of Robertson* by Spofford A. Brooke.

Ministerial morale is a matter of some seriousness as it confronts the church in our time. There is the growing difficulty of maintaining an adequate corps of trained and capable ministers, particularly at the parish level of service. This difficulty is, in part, the result of an increasing deficiency in the number of those offering themselves to the ministerial vocation. The shortage of ministers thus incurred is alone enough to make the situation difficult. Add to this the high percentage of dropouts from the ministry, and the problem becomes one of acute proportions.

To describe this as a morale problem is not to dismiss it as unimportant; nor is it to conclude that the task of correcting it belongs exclusively, or even primarily, with the ministry itself. Its correction will come only as the whole church comes to a fresh and full understanding of the ministry, both in terms of the call to it and the fulfillment of it.

The opening paragraph of the *Book of Jeremiah* provides some helpful suggestions in this regard. There the prophet describes the nature of God's call as it came to him. He certainly considered the call fundamental to his ministry and important for the understanding of his readers, with whom he purposed to share the record of that ministry. Jeremiah begins his book with this preface: "Now the word of the Lord came to me saying, 'Before I formed you in the womb I knew you, and before you were born I consecrated you; I appointed you a prophet to the nations.' Then I said, 'Ah, Lord God! Behold, I do not know how to speak, for I am only a youth.' But the Lord said to me, 'Do not say, "I am only a youth"; for to all to whom I shall send you you shall go, and whatever I command you you shall speak. Be not afraid of them, for I am with you to deliver you, says the Lord.' "

THE CALL OF GOD

Every preacher can understand Jeremiah's reluctance, his unprevailing protest, and that because of his youth he does ". . . not know how to speak."

There is a certain audacity about preaching. "Preaching," wrote Karl Barth several years ago, "is an act of daring, and only the man who would rather not preach and cannot escape from it ought ever to attempt it. What can it mean?" asks Barth. "It means above all that we should feel a fundamental alarm. What are you doing, you man, with the Word of God upon your lips?

Upon what grounds do you assume the role of mediator between heaven and earth?"

A sense of imperative vocation, or the call to preach, is a fundamental requisite. The preacher must feel with basic certainty that God has called him to his ministry, and that he can do no other thing with his life. I wonder, however, if we haven't overstressed the mystical element of the call. Our tendency has been to literalize the dramatic incidents of the Biblical record and to expect that some approximation of those incidents be repeated in God's call today. Moses, removing his sandals before the burning bush; Isaiah, surrounded by angels in the smoke-filled temple of Jerusalem; Saul of Tarsus, speechless and blind as Jesus appeared to him on the road to Damascus—all, with the voice of God ringing in their ears, have become the ideal standard by which we measure the validity of the call.

Jeremiah's experience, however, provides a more realistic understanding of God's appeal. There is nothing dramatic or mystical about it. It is, rather, the voice of conscience born of heightened awareness or sensitivity. "For the wound of . . . my people is my heart wounded" (8:21), exclaims the prophet.

This quality of awareness—at any rate the capacity for it—is not the peculiar endowment of some special breed of men, however. It is God's gift to all, written into every life and basic to responsible living, whatever one's vocation.

The sense of vocation so basic to an adequate ministry is a matter of awareness—awareness both of the need and of the personal resources and equipment with which to meet that need. It also includes the awareness that God has chosen to work through ordinary men, whose gifts are often limited, in the accomplishment of His purposes in the world. The reluctance of Jeremiah, protesting the call of God by pleading his youthfulness, is a natural and essential quality of the kind of commitment that is useful to God. Martin Buber's comment on Moses' complaint that he was "slow of speech" (Exodus 4:10) fits Jeremiah, as it does all of us. "The tragedy of Moses," says Buber, "becomes the tragedy inherent in revelation. It is laid upon the stammering to bring the voice of heaven to earth."

DISENCHANTMENT AND DEFECTION

When the call to ministry is understood in terms of awareness, it follows that all men are potential ministers. Whether ordained or not, every person who in faith has entered the covenant relationship to become a part of the Body of Christ is in ministry.

This mutuality of ministry places the present problem of ministerial shortage in its proper context of responsibility. The object of the minister is to create a mutual awareness, a shared sensitivity, which is felt throughout the Body and results in the collective response of the church moving to meet the need. Mention was made earlier of ministerial morale and its implications for the whole church. Perhaps it is appropriate now to return to a consideration of the rather large scale exodus from the ordained ministry presently taking place across the church.

The most disturbing fact associated with this defection from the ranks of the ministry is the *disenchantment* and *discouragement* which are so decisively evident in it. The exodus includes many of the potentially fine ministers of the church—well-trained, dedicated people—who, after much soul-searching and painful discovery, have elected to seek some creative alternative. I know of numerous instances in which the decision to leave the ministry has been the ironic result of *dedication* and *honesty*—dedication to the full implications of the gospel for the modern church and society and honesty regarding personal frustration born of failure to evoke a practical application of the gospel on the part of those in the church.

Preaching, at its best, is an agonizing appeal for mutual awareness and collective response to human need, personal and social. It is sometimes a shattering experience for the preacher to discover the absence of visible results from his efforts in this regard. The act of preaching has been compared to the discharge of a pipette of eye medicine from a third-story window, in the hope that some of it will find its mark among those hurrying along the crowded street below.

The average preacher knows that this is a realistic comparison; yet he is loath to accept it as he goes, week after week, to his study and from there to his pulpit, fired with excited anticipation that some of the truth he has gathered will fall on good ground. Peter Berger identifies as the preacher's most common delusion the assumption that what he preaches on Sunday will have a direct influence on what his auditors do on Monday. Since the preacher is usually an idealist by nature, a discovery that his preaching does not meet with ideal results can be a traumatic experience.

If the preacher is gifted with creative ability, if in his preaching he makes the implications of the gospel so graphic and clear as to arouse the consciences of his people, it is likely that he will also arouse the resistance of some. Often this resistance is measured and mild, careful not to offend, but firm in its intent to discourage relevant preaching. Sometimes it is expressed in carefully couched criticisms, a word delicately dropped here or there to let the preacher know that he would be more popular if he didn't raise certain issues.

The criticism is not always mild-mannered, however, and the relevant preacher may at times find himself in open conflict of the kind that is unnerving and upsetting. Sometimes his plight will be akin to the fellow who took his grandfather clock to the shop for repairs. When the clock was ready, he put it under his arm, and hurried out onto the busy sidewalk. As he left the shop, a fellow pedestrian, apparently inebriated, came weaving down the sidewalk on a collision course. The impact sent the owner of the clock sprawling, as he tried vainly to hold on to the clock. Incensed by the indifference with which the other man regarded the whole affair, the victim brushed himself off, picked up his clock, and indignantly demanded, "Why don't you watch where you are going?" With bleary eyes, the drunken pedestrian sized up his challenger and indifferently responded, "Why don't you wear a wristwatch like everybody else?"

Relevant preaching sometimes results in upsets. The preacher who dares depart from business as usual in the pulpit will often be regarded as the sole cause of the ensuing conflict. If he would just wear a wristwatch like everybody else, if he would just go along, he would have no problem getting along. If he doesn't elect to do so, then the all-too-common assumption of many in the average congregation is that he has nobody to blame but himself.

Reinhold Niebuhr examined the role of the contemporary minister and gave a rather pessimistic report. "I'm not surprised," he said, "that most budding prophets are tamed in time to become harmless parish priests." I cannot agree that this happens to most of those entering the ministry. I must admit, however, that it is the happy medium of many. It is an all-too-common rationalization among those in the ministry that their vocation can be fulfilled by attending to the institutional demands of running a smooth ship. The preacher who decides that such is his calling will be delighted to discover that he has the approbation of most members of the average congregation.

Rationalizations, however, are seldom 100 percent. Consequently, the preacher who has so rationalized his calling is often unsure and defensive. Deep down, he knows that there is something more, something better to which he initially gave himself.

When there is this awareness, no amount of congregational flattery or denominational approval will satisfy the preacher's nagging sense of unrealized vocation. To be sure, a certain amount of institutional housework is essential and valid in doing the work of the ministry. However, when that routine becomes the all-embracing or even primary involvement, that is, when the best of his time, talent, and energy must be expended in keeping the congregation happy and the budget balanced, then something tragic happens to the preacher himself. Perhaps only in his better moments does he realize that his basic vocation as a preacher and the primary mission of the church itself have been compromised.

One evening a few years ago, a man by the name of Wahlstrom appeared on a major network television program to demonstrate a machine he had created. Wahlstrom had a genius for tinkering and had spent several years constructing his amazing machine. It all began when, wanting some recreation, he purchased an old bombsight and took it apart to see what made it work. When he started putting it back together, he discovered that he had some parts left over from other projects. He became fascinated to see how he could add these parts to the bombsight. The project grew into an intriguing hobby, as his friends brought him additional parts and pieces.

Ten years after he began the project, Mr. Wahlstrom appeared on television with this crazy and complex assortment of wheels, cogs, and belts—a total of ten thousand parts assembled together in what he appropriately called "Wahlstrom's Wonder." When he pressed the starter button, three thousand of those parts went into action. It was a marvel to behold! Wheels turned, lights flashed, bells rang, belts moved. The whole machine came to life, as the turntable on which it rested simultaneously revolved. It was nothing less than the work of genius. There was one small difficulty. It didn't do anything! It had no purpose! It didn't produce anything or change anything! It just ran!

It is hardly necessary to spell out the comparison of "Wahlstrom's Wonder" with the institutional machinery of the average church. The thought of creating and maintaining such a machine, whose only purpose is its own complex composition and smooth operation, has discouraged many a bright young man from entering the parish ministry. It has had a tragic effect on many potentially effective preachers whose sense of vocation has been dulled after entering the ministry. In many cases it has, understandably, prompted a reluctant decision to leave the parish ministry rather than to compromise the integrity of vocation.

AGONY AND ECSTASY

Many of those leaving the ministry would unquestionably summarize their rationale for doing so in terms of a failure to find happiness. Happiness is important. If, however, the minister's objective is defined in terms of popularity and personal happiness—an objective too often present at all levels and in all professions—then he will certainly be disappointed.

It will help to remember that some of the most important people of history have been those who suffered personal unhappiness along the route to greatness of living. Abraham Lincoln provides an illustration from recent history. Throughout his life, Lincoln struggled with his own inner emotional conflicts and personal unhappiness. In his early years he had within him all the makings of neurotic disaster. In 1841, he said of himself, "I am now the most miserable man living. If what I feel were equally distributed to the whole human family, there would not be a cheerful face on earth."

To be sure, happiness is a wonderful estate. But there are

other things of far greater importance, fidelity to which surprises us with happiness at its best. I think of the hundreds of ministers in the South (and not a few outside the South) who have been relieved of their pulpits during the last twenty years. They discovered what Jeremiah meant when he said, "For the word of the Lord has become for me a reproach and derision all day long. If I say, 'I will not mention him, or speak any more in his name,' there is in my heart as it were a burning fire shut up in my bones, and I am weary with holding it in, and I cannot" (20:8,9).

Many of these ministers, forced to leave their pulpits, have understood this word from the prophet. They had no alternative. They had to speak to the burning issue of race relations as to other issues. But in doing so, they paid the price of being prophetic. As a result, approximately thirty Methodist ministers left Mississippi in one year. I think they should have stayed, but who can say what their personal struggle was. Of this I am sure, they were not happy to take the stand they took—even less with its immediate consequences. They were modern Jeremiahs for whom there were more important considerations than personal happiness. There is little doubt, however, that should we poll them now, we would discover that genuine happiness has been their ultimate compensation.

GOD'S MAN

It is also salutary to remember that others have gone before us and have kept the faith. The similarities between Jeremiah's era and our own is suggestive of the challenge that has confronted those in every generation, especially those who have purposed to belong to God.

Almost twenty years ago, about two years before his death and following a ministry which spanned most of the first half of this century, my father retired. From some aspects of his ministry of an earlier day and of very different circumstances, I have gained help in my own understanding and commitment. Among other things, remembering his ministry has kept me from the false assumption that ours are unusually hard times.

During the early part of the 1920s, my father went into a little community in North Alabama and announced that he was going to hold a revival meeting and organize a church. The community was located just south of the Alabama—Tennessee state line. It boasted of its roughness. In fact, for a number of years there had been no religious services in the little frame church at the center of the village—only the unused building remained. The rowdies of the community had forced its closure years before. But the property still belonged to the Methodist Church, and my father, whose Methodist circuit was adjacent to it, was determined to make an effort at reactivating the congregation.

My father's announcement of the projected plan met with an interested but otherwise discouraging response from the few members of the church who came forward. From the hooligan element of the community, however, there came veiled warnings and open threats: if the preacher carried through with his plans, there would be trouble. When the announced time arrived, the services began with full attendance. Many came out of curiosity to see whether the preacher would keep his promise, and, if so, what the response would be.

There were various minor disturbances during the first evening service. It was summer, and the windows were open for ventilation as well as for emergency escape in the event of trouble. From outside came a continuous reverberation of noisy distraction and angry catcalls directed at the preacher and his congregation. When such strategy failed to dissuade the preacher, the offenders hurled missiles through the windows.

The preacher remained undaunted, and the services on the second night drew an even larger crowd. Halfway through that second sermon, the opposition became even more brazen than on the night before. Down the aisle of the church came a big bully, intoxicated, noisy, and profane. He sat down on the front pew and proceeded to heckle the preacher. It was impossible for the preacher to ignore or overcome the distraction. He, therefore, announced that there would be services again the following evening and forthwith gave the benediction. Walking down to the front pew, he made a citizen's arrest and—with the assistance of a friendly and physically well-endowed Methodist who volunteered to help—took his prisoner to nearby Huntsville, turning him over to the county sheriff. The man was placed in jail on the charge of disturbing public worship.

That night the preacher was deputized by the sheriff. The following evening the service began as announced. It must have been a memorable experience for the excited congregation that crowded into that little room. The altar appointments included two thirty-eight pistols, which the preacher gently tapped against the pulpit as he gave the call to worship. But they had a great revival. Before it was over, the man previously arrested and taken to jail but now released on condition that he attend the services with good behavior, was converted and joined the church.

During a recent six-year pastorate in the city of Huntsville, I often had occasion to drive past the little State Line Methodist Church. Once, when I was greatly discouraged and in need of personal renewal, I drove up there. After parking under the trees out front, I walked up the steps, quietly opened the front door, and reverently entered that simple little country church. From one of the pews I picked up a copy of a program used by those who had worshiped there the Sunday before. I walked down the aisle, skirted the little kneeling rail, and then climbed the two steps to the elevated platform. For a long time I stood behind that crude little hand-fashioned pulpit, behind which my father had stood so long ago and from which the gospel has been preached without interruption for almost half a century. For me it was the experience of Isaiah in the temple, Moses before the burning bush, Saul on the road to Damascus—all wrapped into a single experience; and, I hope, in some modest measure, appropriated to the same end.

It isn't always easy to be a minister of the gospel, but the fact of the matter is, it never has been. Many years ago, W. E. Orchard addressed a group of seminary students with this confession: "Gentlemen, I am 65 years of age. I have never been in prison; I have not been burnt alive, or shot at dawn; or stoned by the mob. You may guess that I have been playing my cards very carefully." He then concluded with an observation, even more haunting now than when he spoke it: "Every good man today has to explain why he is alive."

Through convulsive and constant change, where the issues are complex and confrontation is often characterized by conflict, where the signs are sometimes confused and the terrain is often rough, God is patiently, sometimes terribly, at work in His world. In such a world, God still calls us—often through profound but simple awareness—to be His ministers; some ordained, some not; but all bound in a common quest, and all given the same promise: "Be not afraid . . . , for I am with you to deliver you, says the Lord" (1:8).

2
Riding the Wind

"See, I have set you this day over nations and over kingdoms, to pluck up and to break down, to destroy and to overthrow, to build and to plant." And the word of the Lord came to me, saying, "Jeremiah, what do you see?" And I said, "I see a rod of almond." Then the Lord said to me, "You have seen well, for I am watching over my word to perform it." The word of the Lord came to me a second time, saying, "What do you see?" And I said, "I see a boiling pot, facing away from the north." Then the Lord said to me, "Out of the north evil shall break forth upon all the inhabitants of the land. For, lo, I am calling all the tribes of the kingdoms of the north, says the Lord; and they shall come and every one shall set his throne at the entrance of the gates of Jerusalem, against all its walls round about, and against all the cities of Judah. And I will utter my judgments against them, for all their wickedness in forsaking me; they have burned incense to other gods, and worshiped the works of their own hands. But you, gird up your loins; arise, and say to them everything that I command you. Do not be dismayed by them, lest I dismay you before them. And I, behold, I make you this day a fortified city, an iron pillar, and bronze walls, against the whole land, against the kings of Judah, its princes, its priests, and the people of the land. They will fight against you; but they shall not prevail against you, for I am with you, says the Lord, to deliver you" Jeremiah 1:10–19.

In a strange passage from the Book of Psalms, the psalmist refers to God as one whose chariot is the clouds, "who ridest on the wings of the wind, who makest the winds thy messengers . . ." (Psalms 104:3,4). In times of turbulent change, those caught up in it are seldom aware of the extent to which it is itself the manifestation of God. Indeed, God's work in history has often appeared strange to His earth-bound, security-conscious earthlings. This being the case, there was an understandable loneliness about Jeremiah's position that the chaotic, disruptive events of his day were themselves the messengers of God. Implicit in the prophet's message and running as a continuous thread throughout his book is the call for his people to recognize God in the changing order—to assume the challenge of riding the wind, to bring order out of chaos, to become partners with God in building a better world. Indeed, the prophet summarized his life engagement as the call ". . . to pluck up and to break down, to destroy and to overthrow, to build and to plant" (Jeremiah 1:10).

Change is an actuality of life which carries within it the dual potential for good and bad, depending upon the stewardship with which it is assumed. It can be overwhelming and defeating or it can be creatively channeled to serve the purposes of God. Moreover, the determining factor of good or bad in change is first and foremost one of attitude and understanding. The importance of the church's ministry in regard to change has established the thesis of this book, and succeeding chapters will relate directly and indirectly to the pivotal fact that God has lodged us in a time of vast and constant change.

NOTHING NAILED DOWN

The revolutionary turbulence of our present world situation is underscored by an apocryphal addition to a scene from Marc

Connelly's classic *The Green Pastures.* In the Negro dialect which Connelly uses so effectively in the play, the Angel Gabriel reports to "de Lawd" on conditions following Noah's flood: "Lawd, de're ain't nothin' nailed down any more. Ever'thing nailed down is comin' loose!"

How strikingly descriptive of the kind of world in which we live! I wonder, however, if those words wouldn't apply to almost any period of history. Sometimes we wrongly assume that change is the unique experience of our generation, that up to now the world has been static. Of course, this isn't the case at all. Since the beginning of time man has had to effect and assimilate change, and probably he has always felt that his particular generation has been more victimized by it than any other. Some wag imagines the day God drove Adam and Eve from the Garden of Eden, with Adam speaking words of reassurance to his mate as they left the garden, saying quite matter-of-factly, "These are changing times, my dear."

For many years, Methodists have prayed this prayer from their *Book of Worship:* "O God, we pray for Thy Church, which is set today amid the perplexities of a changing order, face to face with a great new task...." Such a prayer is certainly timely, but the very fact that it has been in the liturgy of the church for several generations reminds us that change and the church's concern with change are hardly new developments.

Only the proportion and pace of change have changed. It is here that the experience of modern man is singular. In contrast with the comparative isolation and relative slowness which have been characteristic of change in earlier times, change today is all-embracing and cataclysmic. It is universal and revolutionary. There is no isolationism that isn't finally touched by it, no ivory towers of immunity from it.

When one examines change with an eye to understanding its acceleration in our time, there seem to be at least three major spawning grounds from which it derives its hurricanelike character—*science, politics,* and *religion.* They are all interrelated and pervasive, affecting each other directly and indirectly. Collectively and individually they contribute to our present world revolution, producing change at a pace and with a proportion that is difficult for mere humans to assimilate.

Of course, the giant in this triad is science. A comparative newcomer, science has to a large degree been catalytic, provoking change far beyond the province of the purely scientific. Indeed, much of the dynamic for change arising out of the world's political and religious arenas is the indirect result of the scientific revolution of our time. Its effect is to sweep the world with new life-styles and restless expectations. Rich benefits and brand-new headaches have come with automated industry, computerized living, intercontinental missiles, lunar landings, pill-planned families, televised entertainment (and other unidentified flying objects).

The pace of what is happening is quite as consequential as its proportion. For example, someone has estimated that 90 percent of all the professional scientists who have ever lived are alive now. Moreover, they are busily rendering obsolete and old-fashioned as much of the present world as possible, and as quickly as possible. The so-called knowledge explosion is a case in point. It is overwhelming in its own right. Consider that it has been reliably calculated that in practically every technical discipline there now must be a completely new orientation of learning and proficiency every ten years. Such a reorientation is necessary just to keep pace with the new techniques and equipment which are constantly being created and made available in many technical professions. The old adage, "He who hesitates is lost," has never been more descriptive of realism.

Greatly influenced by the strides of science—but also making quite a splash of its own in the little pond of human existence

—is the explosive political activity of our time. The constancy and complexity of change in this area is of vast consequence—not only in its direct physical results, but perhaps even more significantly in its indirect spiritual and psychological effects. In this regard, it has infected the race with a mild form of paranoia. Everything is tentative, including the sovereignty of nations and the security of institutions; not to speak of the individual, who is the final and most important victim of it all.

Since the close of World War II, a rising nationalism of overwhelming proportions has swept the world. Its most signal effect has been on the continents of Africa and Asia, where colonialism had dominated the politics and exploited the people for centuries preceding this new era. With the breakdown of colonialism since World War II, however, approximately fifty new nations have come into their own as independent states. Nothing like this has ever before happened. Directly affected are an approximate seven-hundred-million people who populate these countries. The indirect effect is universal. For example, many of these nations are now full members of the United Nations. In the General Assembly of that organization, they enjoy an equal vote with the major powers. Consequently, in the global decisions confronting that body, these small nations exercise a power far beyond their size.

There is also the economic factor growing out of this rise of new nations. Those nations which were formerly in the position of colonial overlords have not only been depressed by the breakdown of colonialism, but they have also found the new nations—many of them beginning in virtual bankruptcy and under the necessity of seeking sources of revenue—vigorous competitors in world commerce.

The population explosion is an additional element in the political arena of our new world. In spite of such technological deterrents as the pill and the human decimation resulting from modern warfare, the earth's population grows by about sixty-five million a year—a number comparable to the present population of West Germany or Great Britain. Given a continuation of the present rate of growth it is only a matter of time until our planet will have standing room only. Someone has figured it out that by the year 2500, there will be only about one square yard for each person in the world, providing that deserts, mountains, and arctic regions are included in the distribution.

The rising expectation of the common man must also be taken into account in the assessment of political changes now in process. Long hot summers not only characterize the racial revolution in America, they are a part of the political climate around the world. There is a growing unrest on the part of little people everywhere. No longer will they remain docile and undemanding. The furnaces of life, stoked by proximity, inequity, and growing unrest, are seventy times hotter than ever before. There are the Koreas, the Cubas, the Biafras, and the Czechoslovakias of our time. There is rebellion in Santo Domingo, and there is war in Viet Nam. There are marches and murders. There is white racism, and there is black power. There is policed voter registration in the South, and there are race riots in the major cities of the east and west. Nothing is nailed down!

What is the place of religion in this world of change? Obviously, the church has not been unaffected. The so-called new theology and new morality—neither of which is really new, but both of which have enjoyed an attention and made an impact that are new—are the obvious products of change as it affects the church. At the heart of this change is a growing secularism which has, among other things, stifled interest and participation in the church.

But what about religion—the influence of the gospel, quite apart from institutional involvement—as an agent of change? It is impossible fully to assess the role of religion in this regard, except to say that much of what we have defined as *political* change is, in its essence, *religious*—if not in the outward form it takes, certainly in its underlying motivation and dynamic.

For example, God is at work in the racial revolution that history has witnessed and is witnessing in our day. Someone has said that slavery was destroyed by four words: "For whom Christ died." There you have it—four words, seeping down into the social conscience of mankind, although it has taken long centuries for the idea to be fully understood and finally accomplished.

The emancipation of the American slave was the result of long centuries in which the leaven of the gospel was at work in the loaf of human society. Finally, in the long patience of God, slavery became for man, as it had long been for God, an intolerable condition. There was a better way than that which our fathers chose, a better way than violence, and hatred, and war. Being more the sinner than the saint, however, man resisted the purposes of God. But the final result of God's plan for His creatures was a *new order;* and, through the awful means of war, emancipation became a reality, and the human family advanced another giant step in the direction of the kingdom.

The first stanza of Julia Ward Howe's "Battle Hymn of the Republic" expresses what always seems to be man's terrible hindsight in the on-marching truth of God.

> Mine eyes have seen the glory
>   of the coming of the Lord;
> He is trampling out the vintage
>   where the grapes of wrath are stored;
> He hath loosed the fateful lightning
>   of His terrible swift sword;
> His truth is marching on.

TO PLUCK UP AND TO BREAK DOWN

Perhaps there is no finer evidence that God is not finished with man than the widespread tensions under which we live in these tragic times. The Christian Church, including every Christian, is called to the same ministry which Jeremiah assumed in such terrible loneliness twenty-five-hundred years ago. It is still our purpose to ride the wind, "to pluck up and to break down, to destroy and to overthrow. . . ."

This suggests that the church must do more than respond to change; it must assume a responsibility for creating change. In the best sense of the term, the Christian must be a *revolutionary.* Change, even change for the better—which is the only change Christians are responsible for—often cannot await the slow and peaceful processes of evolution. It is, therefore, often born in conflict and social upheaval. Indeed, there is some evidence that Jesus saw this as necessary to the achievement of God's purposes. How else can we understand Him when He says, "Do not think that I have come to bring peace on earth; I have come not to bring peace, but a sword" (Matthew 10:34)?

The Roman Emperor Julian long ago saw the revolutionary character of this gospel and the Christ who is at the center of it. He called Jesus the greatest rebel that ever lived. To identify with Him at any period of history has been to be a part of the slow and patient, the deliberate and inexorable purposes of God —"to pluck up and to break down, to destroy and to overthrow" every custom, every system, every institution that holds man in bondage to something less than the image in which he is created. History teaches that God is patient but unrelenting in His purpose for a better world. Often the process is painful; many times the progress is slow, but God never abdicates His purpose.

TO BUILD AND TO PLANT

God calls us not only "to pluck up and to break down," but also "to build and to plant." Both are essential to the progress of history. Both are vital to the change taking place in our world today. Out of the rubble of our universal social upheaval, we must find the vision and the courage, the faith and the consecration for building a better church and a better world. We must remember, also, that both accomplishments can come only through better men. We must first be willing "to pluck up and to break down, . . . to build and to plant" within our own lives. We must become the kind of people who desire and who seek progress through creative change.

It is amazing that most of us as Christians are loath even to accept change, not to speak of creating it. This is especially true with regard to change in the church itself. This reluctance is a natural and understandable feature of institutionalism, and as such it is not peculiar to our generation by any means. Some anonymous poet has summarized it:

> All our fathers have been Churchmen,
> Nineteen hundred years or so,
> And to every new suggestion
> They have always answered No.

In our earlier reference to religion as one of the three basic sources of change, it was carefully noted that our reference was to the *leavening influence of the gospel,* often quite apart from institutional initiative or involvement. It should be pointed out here, however, that the church as an institution has been and continues to be essential. It is the principal agency through which the gospel is both proclaimed and demonstrated to the world. The institution has perpetuated the faith and provided a continuity, without which the gospel would have long ago dissipated as a rope of sand.

Moreover, it should be recognized that the reformers—those who have acted as the *avante garde* for progress and change in every age—have always been produced and inspired by the institutional church. While they have usually been rebuffed and resisted by the institution, they have also regarded it with agonizing love and undiminishing appreciation. One must include a host of men in this endless line of splendor, beginning with Jeremiah and the other Old Testament prophets. Jesus Himself epitomizes this relationship to the institutional church. Among those who have patterned life and ministry after His example are men such as Luther and the other sixteenth century reformers, the Wesley brothers, Walter Rauschenbusch, and numerous others. The effect of their work was "to pluck up and to break down, to destroy and to overthrow, to build and to plant."

I am sure that all would agree that the ideal is so to place oneself in the forefront of change and progress—within the church and through its institutional life—as to be an agent of God's purposes. Granting such an ideal, it would be a revealing exercise for us to imagine our positions had we lived in the time of those reformers. In the light of our personal attitudes, how would we have responded—perhaps *reacted* is more accurate—to those men and the causes they championed?

James Truslow Adams provides an analogy of limitless scope and relevance when he writes of the Daughters of the American Revolution: "Considering the extreme die-hard conservatism of the resolutions of the 'Daughters of the Revolution' today, it seems impossible to avoid the conclusion that very few of them would have been Mothers of the Revolution in 1776, when revolution meant riding the whirl-wind of social disorder."

How much more this applies to the majority of us in the church. Where would we have been in Jeremiah's time—with the prophet, or with the opposition? Imagine that we were in Jerusalem on that awful Friday when Pilate gave the people a choice. What would have been our choice? Would we have been Protestants in the early sixteenth century, when to do so meant riding the wind of change? When the Wesley brothers, George Whitefield, and others were projecting the new forms of the early Methodist movement, I wonder how many of today's Methodists would have joined the cause of those whose very name—Methodist—was given in derision.

Sometimes we treat today's call for *new forms* in the church with a caution which suggests that we may have forgotten that our *old forms* were once new. Somewhere, sometime, others have had to do what we are hesitant to do, namely, make the church and its message relevant to the times. John Wesley and his crew, most of whom were lay preachers, which was in itself a new form, were adopting new forms when they took the gospel into the open fields of England and America. It had long been assumed as canonical that only those with proper ordination could preach the gospel; and worship anywhere but in the church—and that with a proper liturgy—was considered blasphemous. And there went Wesley defying convention, bringing the wrath of the church fathers down on his head, taking the world for his parish and the gospel for his cause, riding the wind!

When I remember the new forms required in adapting the gospel to frontier America—camp meetings, brush-arbor meeting houses, and congregational testimony services interlaced with lusty hymn singing and sometimes a little shouting—I must admit that I probably would have resisted it all and come out in favor of keeping things as they were in the church. Sometimes today's talk of new forms of worship (string combos and ballad-singing folk choirs) and of needed new approaches to ministry which would take the gospel to the people where they are and at their point of need is nothing short of upsetting.

When I am honest with myself and realistic about the position of the average churchman through whom God is trying to bring renewal to His church today, I remember a story that comes out of London. During World War II, when the House of Commons building was bombed and heavily damaged, there was much talk about how it should be restored. Some people, including Winston Churchill, thought it should be put back exactly as it had been. Others contended for a wider view, for more room in it—at least enough space to seat its members comfortably. Then a reporter from a London newspaper was bold enough to remind the people of what had happened in the sixteenth century, when the great London fire had destroyed the central part of the city. The destruction had been great, but the people were encouraged by one thought. With the old city gone, there was the opportunity to rebuild it with a superior design prepared by the great architect Sir Christopher Wren. The plans had been enthusiastically approved and hopes had run high until they came to work out the practical details. It was then that many people—plain, common citizens—insisted that so far as their own houses were concerned they must be put back exactly as they had been. So the new London never happened, not because there was no plan, but because among the people there was no new mind to make the new London. One by one, they went back to build on the old foundations. How often by our resistance to change, our fondness for the old foundations, particularly in the church, God is stymied in His efforts for a better world.

DEDICATION TO GOD

But a willingness to effect change in the church and in society is not sufficient in itself. It must be accompanied by *dedication to God.* The ultimate will and goodness of God must be the standard for which we strive. We must measure our institutions and our behavior by Him.

In this regard, there is an interesting footnote to the record of John Wesley's personal struggle with some of the changes which his age forced him to implement. High churchman that he was, Wesley was reluctant to take the gospel to people where they were. The thought of preaching in the streets and fields, for example, was repugnant to him. Moreover, he wasn't sure such a ministry would be pleasing to God. His mother cleared the matter for him, however, when she remarked that she seemed to remember another Preacher of another age, who met the people where they were—by the lakeside and in the marketplaces and open fields of Galilee.

The standard of His life and the guidance of His Spirit must direct us as we seek to serve Christ in a changing world. We must believe that God Himself continues to lead His church and His people in the direction of a better world. Without this faith, we find history the mere record of a world spinning out centuries of meaningless nothing.

But at the heart of our faith as Christians there is a profound trust that God does not abandon His world to meaninglessness. Man's willfulness may delay the purposes of God, but His ultimate plan will not be defeated. A leading churchman once made a memorable statement in this regard. He said, "I don't know what the future holds. But I do know Who holds the future."

At the height of Israel's strife and confusion, when it seemed that nothing was nailed down and the future was hopeless, Jeremiah kept telling the people that beyond the chaos was God's purpose, and beyond God's judgment was His mercy. When it looked as if Israel would soon be only a matter of history, Jeremiah dramatized his faith in God and the future of

Israel by going out and purchasing a plot of ground (32:1–44). It was a symbolic act in which he invested in the future as a sign of his faith that God would insure that future.

In the year 1738, George Whitefield, a contemporary and sometime co-worker of John Wesley, came from England to America. Ocean travel in those days was both slow and dangerous, and on this particular trip the ship was caught in a storm. For days the situation seemed hopeless. During this time, George Whitefield made a notable entry in his journal: "Our allowance of water is just one pint a day, our sails are exceedingly thin and some of them last night were split and no one knows where we are. But God does, and that is sufficient."

In a world so filled with change and apparent chaos, when at times it may seem that nothing is nailed down and everything is out of control, we must ride the wind, believing that God knows where we are, and that that is sufficient. Into such a world He has sent us "to pluck up and to break down, to destroy and to overthrow, to build and to plant."

3
The People of God

Hear the word of the Lord, O house of Jacob, and all the families of the house of Israel. Thus says the Lord: "What wrong did your fathers find in me that they went far from me, and went after worthlessness, and became worthless? They did not say, 'Where is the Lord who brought us up from the land of Egypt, who led us in the wilderness, in a land of deserts and pits, in a land of drought and deep darkness, in a land that none passes through, where no man dwells?' And I brought you into a plentiful land to enjoy its fruits and its good things. But when you came in you defiled my land, and made my heritage an abomination . . ." Jeremiah 2:4–7.

"Behold, the days are coming, says the Lord, when I will make a new covenant with the house of Israel and the house of Judah, not like the covenant which I made with their fathers when I took them by the hand to bring them out of the land of Egypt, my covenant which they broke, though I was their husband, says the Lord. But this is the covenant which I will make with the house of Israel after those days, says the Lord: I will put my law within them, and I will write it upon their hearts; and I will be their God, and they shall be my people . . ." Jeremiah 31:31–33.

In the last chapter we discussed God's design for a better world, and how patiently He works through His people, as He waits for them to bring it about. We talked about rebellion, strife, and war. We must again stress that these are not a part of God's will. They are man's choice—the choice of sin, the choice of man's stubborn, historic resistance to moral progress. Why must it ever be so?

If God wants a better world, why doesn't He simply bring it about? He could, we suppose, but He chooses to pace His progress to the limitations of His creatures. There is insight in a remark once made by England's Lloyd George to the effect that the most dangerous feat in the world is to try to cross a chasm in two jumps. Someone has offered the additional comment that if the chasm measured a hundred feet and one could jump only fifteen feet, then one jump would hardly be a safe endeavor either. In that case, it would be wise not to jump at all, but to walk down and climb up the other side, one step at a time.

The chasms between *what is* and *what ought to be* in the world often exceed man's ability to jump. Sometimes his efforts are disastrous. He must then do what he should have done in the beginning: set out to bridge the gap, one step at a time. Certainly God could leap the chasms. But He has chosen to pace the moral and spiritual progress of history to the speed and distance of man—a creature whose leaps are limited, to say the least. It has been a long forward trek, one in which God has relied upon those chosen to be *His people* who have been faithful to His leadership, one step at a time, *plucking up* and *breaking down* the boulders of obstruction, *building* and *planting,* until the chasm is bridged.

Who are the *people of God?* When one examines the long march of historical progress, it is apparent that God has patiently worked through nations, institutions, and individuals. Sometimes He has looked hopefully to a generation or a group, only to be disappointed. In this regard, Leslie Weatherhead examined the world situation a few years ago and reflectively commented that God's workshop floor is littered with broken tools. The broken tools include nations, institutions, and individuals, which snapped in the hands of God and had to be discarded because they were no longer useful. Weatherhead soberingly concluded that we may be witnessing that moment in history when the free, so-called Christian nations of the Western world are snapping in God's hands, when God must put them aside for more workable tools.

The late H. W. Prentis, Jr. made the observation that history travels in a cycle which runs something like this: "From bondage to spiritual faith, from spiritual faith to courage, from courage to freedom, from freedom to a measure of physical abundance, from abundance to selfishness, from selfishness to complacency, from complacency to apathy, from apathy to fear, from fear to dependency, and from dependency back again to bondage."

Jeremiah's ministry found the Hebrew people in the final stages of such a cycle. Inspired to courage by the leadership of Moses, the people of Israel had broken the bondage of their Egyptian masters. At Sinai, God made a covenant with them and eventually led them into the Land of Promise, a land of freedom and relative abundance. As a matter of course, their history then took them through the balance of the cycle; and by the time Jeremiah came on the scene the chosen people, the tools of God's purposes, had snapped in His hands. Apathy had given way to fear, fear to dependency; and, at last they were about to go back into bondage, this time to the empire of Babylon.

It was a long process marked by the patient efforts of God. Approximately six hundred years had come and gone since the Covenant at Sinai. After Sinai there had been a period of ideal faithfulness, then the gradual apostasy and deterioration had set in. Israel had at last fallen, and Judah faced a similar disaster, if something were not done.

A CHOSEN PEOPLE—A BROKEN COVENANT

Shocked and appalled at the blindness of his people, Jeremiah addressed himself to the situation. Students of the Old Testament refer to the second through the sixth chapters of his book as "The Oracles." They contain the record of the prophet's concentrated attack on the problem. The problem, as Jeremiah saw it, was that God's *chosen people* had broken their covenant.

God directed Jeremiah, "Go and proclaim in the hearing of Jerusalem, Thus says the Lord, I remember the devotion of your youth, your love as a bride, how you followed me in the wilderness. . . . I brought you into a plentiful land to enjoy its fruits and its good things. But when you came in you defiled my land, and made my heritage as abomination. . . . Those who handle the law did not know me; the rulers transgressed against me; the prophets prophesied by Baal, and went after things that do not profit. Therefore I still contend with you, says the Lord, and with your children's children I will contend" (2:1,2,7–9).

The twenty-first verse of this second chapter summarizes the situation, as God affirms: " . . . I planted you a choice vine, wholly of pure seed. How then have you turned degenerate and become a wild vine?" But God had promised not to give them up; and much later, in the thirty-first chapter of his book, Jeremiah announces the promise of a *New Covenant:* "Behold the days are coming, says the Lord, when I will make a new covenant with the house of Israel and the house of Judah. . . ."

THE NEW COVENANT—THE CHURCH

Centuries later a New Testament writer picks up this promise, quotes from Jeremiah, and then speaks of Jesus Christ as "the mediator of a new covenant" (Hebrews 9:15).

The New Testament (the very word means *New Covenant*) records the institution of the Lord's Supper as a symbolic act of the New Covenant. "Now as they were eating, Jesus took bread, and blessed, and broke it, and gave it to the disciples and said, 'Take, eat; this is my body.' And he took a cup, and when he had given thanks he gave it to them, saying, 'Drink of it all of you; for this is my blood of the covenant, which is poured out for many for the forgiveness of sins' " (Matthew 26:26–28).

This New Covenant, promised in the Book of Jeremiah and fulfilled in the coming of Christ, is the *Covenant of Grace.* It provides what the *Covenant of Sinai,* or the *Covenant of the Law,* could not give. Pascal long ago said it: "The law imposed what it cannot give. Grace gives what it imposes."

Under the *Covenant of Grace,* God's chosen people are the people of His church, in every age and in every nation. As we seek to be the people of God, there is much in Jeremiah's book that is timely and relevant. The prophet describes the nature of the covenant, and records the sins which violated the relationship. We are thus reminded that we can break our covenant with God in many of the same ways.

FIDELITY

Mutual fidelity is the principal ingredient of the covenant relationship. ". . . I will be their God, and they shall be my people" (31:33). In return for His pledge to Israel, God demanded one thing above all—*obedience!*

This is the heart of the covenant relationship; and now as then, the greatest peril is not complete denial or abandonment of the faith, but weakening compromise. The people of Israel did not renounce their faith so much as they compromised it. When their forefathers entered the Land of Promise, they found the Canaanites relying upon a cult of agricultural gods known as Baals. It wasn't long before many Israelites were borrowing certain religious practices from their Canaanite neighbors. After all, they rationalized, every little bit of security helps. They weren't abandoning God; they were simply insuring the success of their crops. The innovations from alien cults had reached considerable proportions by the time of Jeremiah, and his choice of simile is apropos: "I planted you a choice vine, wholly of pure seed. How then have you turned degenerate and become a wild vine?"

D. T. Niles gives a modern version of the kind of compromise that often weakens the fidelity of our covenant relationship. He tells how a lady, who belonged to his church in Ceylon, once came to him with a problem. Her marriage had failed to produce children, which was a great disappointment to her. She had first consulted the doctors, but they had been unable to help her. Then she undertook a vow to the Virgin Mary at a Roman Catholic shrine, but still she had not succeeded in becoming pregnant. Finally, she took a vow at a Hindu shrine, and afterward she had a child. She came to Dr. Niles with the question, "Don't you think I must become a Hindu?"

He answered that, "in terms of what she wanted, it did not make any difference to what religion she belonged. If fertility or prosperity is to be the determining consideration, then the Christian faith is already compromised," he said.

This tendency to compromise, which Dr. Niles calls, "Jesus Christ and . . . ," is our modern Baal. Jesus Christ and nationalism; Jesus Christ and racism; Jesus Christ and materialism.

Unfortunately, the church in our day is no longer the tightly disciplined body of committed and practicing believers that it once was. The author Rufus Jones compared it to Robinson Crusoe's goat pasture—the fences are so distant and the fields are so wide, he said, that the goats on the inside are as wild as the goats on the outside. Often it is difficult to distinguish some aspects of the church from the country club or the political group whose members are also members of the church. Whether we like it or not, the church is to a large extent a cultural complex, reflecting the fallacies and the foibles of the culture in which it is set.

FLEXIBILITY

We are the *People of God* to the extent that there is fidelity to Him who sends us into the world to live and serve as His Body. This fidelity, this obedience, must not become so rigid, however, as to lose its dynamic capacity for change and adjustment. It must avoid the kind of rigid adherence to fixed rules which denies sensitivity and responsiveness of the church as a living, growing organism.

The church must be characterized by fidelity, within a flexible commitment, to a living God who reveals Himself in new ways and calls His people to new responsibilities in a world of change. Indeed, this is the pivotal difference between the old covenant and the new. The *Covenant of the Law* was written upon tablets of stone. The *New Covenant* is written in the heart of the believer. "I will put my law within them, and I will write it upon their hearts; and I will be their God, and they shall be my people" (31:33).

The fulfillment of this promise was affirmed by Paul in his correspondence with the Christians at Corinth. ". . . You are a letter from Christ delivered by us," said the apostle, "written not with ink but with the Spirit of the living God, not on tablets of stone but on tablets of human hearts" (2 Corinthians 3:3).

The church has been launched into a world of change, not to be buffeted or shaped by that change, but to create it and channel it toward an ever finer approximation of God's will. The people of God must, then, be constantly renewed. They are never in greater jeopardy than when they tie themselves to the past and become inflexible to the leadership of the Spirit—which is ever new and ever renewing. At Concord, Massachusetts, near the graves of some of the British soldiers who fell in that early conflict of the Revolutionary War, there is a marker which reads:

> They came three thousand miles
> To keep the past upon its throne.

This can happen to the church when it becomes inflexibly committed to the past. The late W. E. Sangster once told of an anxious matron, who, in speaking of a young lady who had been a party to loose company, remarked: "If I'm not mistaken, that girl's got a past in front of her." It is our constant peril that we let the past get in front of us. As sophisticated, intelligent people we accept the new in every other area of life, but we often stubbornly resist it in the church. Even a new order of worship, or a new hymn in the service of worship, produces a crisis for some of us. A new idea is often enough to throw us into shock when our covenant is written on tablets of stone.

But our covenant is with Christ, who says, "Behold, I make all things new" (Revelation 21:5). George Matheson, the blind English preacher and hymn writer of another era, was seeing what we must see, when he wrote:

Son of man, whenever I doubt of life I think of thee. Thou never growest old to me. Last century is old. Last year is obsolete fashion, but thou art not obsolete. Thou art abreast of all the centuries, and I have never come up to thee, modern as I am.

Great things are happening in the church today. But in many instances and in many places they are happening in spite of our resistance. The hope of the church is not in those who tenaciously hold on to the past, and whose covenant is written on tablets of stone. While many spend their time brooding over the fact that yesterday's institutionalism is crumbling, there is a new breed in our midst, and he is the hope of the future. He is old and he is young. He is male and female, preacher and layman, Protestant and Catholic, black, white, red, and yellow. He is disturbing to the Establishment because of the ideas he holds —ideas which he refuses any longer to keep safely wrapped in the grave clothes of creed and liturgy—ideas which are for him the living Word, grafted in the heart and validated in the struggle for a better world.

The church is the modern Israel with whom God has covenanted to bring about this better world. "But you are a chosen race," says the New Testament writer, "a royal priesthood, a holy nation, God's own people . . . called . . . out of darkness into his marvelous light" (1 Peter 2:9).

FAITH

We keep our part of the covenant by fidelity of obedience and flexibility of commitment, but what about God? Basic to the covenant is our faith in Him—faith that God will uphold His commitment to chart the course and lead the way across the wildernesses and chasms of history and of personal experience.

We have God's word that He will do this: "Therefore I still contend with you, . . . and with your children's children I will contend" (Jeremiah 2:9). Again He says, "I have loved you with an everlasting love; therefore I have continued my faithfulness to you" (31:3). As Christians we can add the word of Jesus, "I am with you always, to the close of the age" (Matthew 28:20). David Livingstone once remarked that the word of Jesus here is the word of a gentleman—it can be trusted.

In a fast-paced and fragmented world, where even the chosen of God are often the faithless breakers of the Covenant, there is one constancy which we can always count on—the integrity of God. Jeremiah, amidst the turmoil of his day, assured his people that God is faithful. Because of this faithfulness, he said, because of this alone, Israel shall again be built. And today it is because of this faithfulness, this alone, that the church can expect to find renewed life.

We must not despair of the future. We must entrust our lives and the life of the church to God. We must have faith in the integrity of His leadership, and we must be faithful followers of His leading. A few years ago, some unidentified Christian entered a Chicago church for Sunday morning worship, leaving behind an unsigned affirmation which wraps it up:

> I believe that the fulfillment of the teachings of Jesus is possible. But I believe even if I should be the only one, there is nothing for me to do but to fulfill them. There is no question as to whether many or few will act as I do, or what may happen if I do what I should do. I know that besides life and death, nothing can happen. And life and death are in the hands of God.

4
Cracked Cisterns

Has a nation changed its gods, even though they are no gods? But my people have changed their glory for that which does not profit. Be appalled, O heavens, at this, be shocked, be utterly desolate, says the Lord, for my people have committed two evils: they have forsaken me, the fountain of living waters, and hewed out cisterns for themselves, broken cisterns, that can hold no water. "Is Israel a slave? Is he a homeborn servant? Why then has he become a prey? The lions have roared against him, they have roared loudly. They have made his land a waste; his cities are in ruins, without inhabitant . . ." Jeremiah 2:11–15.

During a recent visit to the Holy Land I was impressed with the high premium the people of that semiarid part of the world place upon water. Late one summer afternoon in Jericho, I watched as hundreds of women and children made the trek of several miles down the dusty road from an Arab refugee camp to the community spring. With jugs and cans on their heads they came to take their places in the long line and return to their shabby dwellings with water for their family and household use.

Water has always been a scarce item and a prized commodity

in the land of the Bible. It is a parched land with seasonal and limited rainfall. Little wonder that water and thirst were among the most popular symbols employed by the Biblical writers, both in the Old and New Testaments. What could better describe the nature of God and of man's constant need for spiritual succor?

When Jeremiah describes the cause and effect of Israel's unfaithfulness, he searches for the most powerful symbol available and delivers this word from God: "For my people have committed two evils: they have forsaken me, the fountain of living waters, and hewed out cisterns for themselves, broken cisterns, that can hold no water."

Modern water systems have made both cisterns and wells practically nonexistent in our part of the world, especially cisterns. I can remember seeing cisterns a few times as a child. They were a kind of last resort, used to store rain water for family and farm use in areas where it was impractical to sink wells. At best they were poor substitutes. Their waters were breeding places for mosquitoes and other impurities which would rule out their use by modern health standards.

The cistern was a common sight in Jeremiah's world. Rarely was it feasible to sink wells or tap subterranean springs for fresh water. Because of the low water table and undesirable mineral and chemical character of the soil, wells were not practical; and it was, therefore, necessary to devise some means of catching and conserving water when it rained. The cistern was a large underground basin usually hewn out of the earth. Since the soil was porous and thirsty, the most effective cisterns were those hewn out of solid rock. When this wasn't practical, the inside of the cistern had to be lined with a primitive lime-based cement to prevent seepage. With age this liner would often crack and the cistern, although it looked good on the surface, would not hold water.

applied when assessing the greatness of the church.

To really care is a spiritual thing with dimensions of concern and motivation which determine the quality and character of its expression. Indeed, many times the outward act is spoiled by the inward motivation or attitude. Often behavior that is ostensibly humane and compassionate has motives that ruin its best effect. Recall the story of the farmer's wife who, as she came from milking, was asked how much milk the cow gave. She replied, "Nine quarts and a kick." There is often the kick, hidden away somewhere in the otherwise beautiful act, to spoil the overall effect.

In T. S. Eliot's *Murder in the Cathedral,* Archbishop Thomas à Becket describes that for which the human race is famous, when he says:

> The last temptation
> is the greatest treason:
> To do the right deed
> for the wrong reason.

One example of this is civil rights. Much of the outward progress in this area has missed the mark and fallen short of the Christian ideal which initially inspired it. Progress has been made to be sure, but the spoiler comes when one examines the motivation. For example, a great city finally removes some of its segregation barriers and begins to open itself and its services to all citizens. No one can question that the action is right—it is the motive that is wrong. After years of segregation, legal or *de facto,* the barriers are lifted not because other human beings had been penalized by those barriers, not out of genuine concern for people, but because removing the barriers finally became a political or economic practicality. Thus, the system is changed, not because the change is morally right, but because it is economically expedient to change it. Legal segregation is abolished, not because God or the church has spoken, but because the courts or the Chamber of Commerce has spoken—the right deed for the wrong reason!

Sometimes even the church has cared for the wrong reason. It is a matter of record that at the 1902 meeting of the General Conference of the Methodist Episcopal Church, a speaker appealed to the delegates in behalf of missionary support, saying, "It is the missionary who paves the way for your cotton, your lumber, and the output of your rolling mills"—the right deed for the wrong reason!

As incredible as it is to anyone of Christian conscience, there are still many white churches in the South where blacks cannot gain admission to worship. There are also cases where the doors have been opened on the basis of expediency rather than principle. Many congregations have been clever enough to open their doors in order to avoid confrontation. It is reasoned "The blacks don't really want to come [and who can blame them]; they just want to see if they can—and they'll create problems if they can't." From their counterparts in other sections of the country, many southern congregations have learned that they can officially open their services and still have segregation, without all the fuss—the right deed for the wrong reason!

The church must be *right* at the core of its motive as well as on the surface of its behavior. It must care for people more than for itself and place itself at the disposal of Him who called the church into being to carry on His work of compassion and concern—". . . to preach good news to the poor . . . to proclaim release to the captives and recovering of sight to the blind, to set at liberty those who are oppressed . . ." (Luke 4:18).

Eugene Debs, active in prison and labor reform in this country until his death in 1926, once said something which the church ought to be able to say: "While there is a lower class I am in it, while there is a criminal element I am of it; while there is a soul in prison, I am not free." To really care is to identify with men because they are men and because we are the church.

There are some churches that do care, where renewal is taking place, where the crying needs of people have awakened them to genuine mission and called them to servanthood. It is refreshing and encouraging to see this taking place in many congregations, North and South. Some are postponing building plans and redirecting monies raised for that purpose. They are going into the ghettos, urban and rural, with outpost Sunday schools, recreational facilities, medical clinics, job training, and other assistance. Most important of all, they are showing that they care.

What a time it is to be the church, to mend the cracks of self-centeredness, to care as God cares, to take the "fountain of living waters" to the inhabitants of the "dry and thirsty land" of our generation. Only in so doing will we be able to drink deeply ourselves and restore the church to life and health as the Body of Christ.

SELF-SUFFICIENT CHRISTIANS

Cracked cisterns are also the peril of our personal lives as Christians. Our great problem here is self-sufficiency. Modern secularism has infected most of us with some degree of assumed independence of God. Things seem to get along without Him.

Like the surface appearance of Jeremiah's empty cisterns, we often look quite adequate, even to ourselves, until there is some real test of faith. Jesus used a different analogy to describe this same self-sufficiency as he encountered it in his day, particularly among the Pharisees. The Pharisees were a proud lot. They were paragons of moral and religious virtue. But Jesus saw through their veneer of piety and compared them with whitewashed burial vaults that looked good on the outside, but were within full of decay and death.

Jesus illustrated the inadequacy of this self-sufficient, self-righteous position with the story of the Pharisee and the publican praying in the Temple. The Pharisee made his prayer an impressive enumeration of his virtues. In substance he said, "Consider the fine achievements I have made in moral character and religious respectability. I don't need you, God!" It was the contrast of attitude that Jesus approved in the poor publican's prayer. The publican is reported to have beat himself on the breast in an agonizing recognition of need, as he cried, "God, be merciful to me a sinner!" (Luke 18:10–14).

Nothing is so common or so tragic as the tendency to try to order our lives in conformity with Christian ideals, without at the same time seeing how empty and utterly inadequate we are. Our self-sufficiency looks good until we are faced with the deeper issues of life. It is often only then that we realize that such a faith is like cracked cisterns that cannot hold the life-giving refreshment of God. But hopefully, in some best moment of life we see our condition and make our confession of need—that without Him, life is empty and meaningless.

"For my people have committed two evils: they have forsaken me, the fountain of living waters, and hewed out cisterns for themselves, broken cisterns, that can hold no water." As the truth of this comes to us from the preaching of Jeremiah, another word takes up from the New Testament—a solicitous, hopeful word from Him who is our "fountain of living waters." Jesus says, "Whoever drinks of the water that I shall give him will never thirst; the water that I shall give him will become in him a spring of water welling up to eternal life" (John 4:14).

5
Crisis in Worship

My grief is beyond healing, my heart is sick within me. Hark, the cry of the daughter of my people from the length and breadth of the land: "Is the Lord not in Zion? Is her King not in her?" "Why have they provoked me to anger with their graven images, and with their foreign idols?" "The harvest is past, the summer is ended, and we are not saved." For the wound of the daughter of my people is my heart wounded, I mourn, and dismay has taken hold on me. Is there no balm in Gilead? Is there no physician there? Why then has the health of the daughter of my people not been restored? Jeremiah 8:18–22.

In his little book *The Problem of Pain,* C. S. Lewis says, "A man can no more diminish God's glory by refusing to worship Him than a lunatic can put out the sun by scribbling the word 'darkness' on the walls of his cell."

True enough—God is not diminished by our failure to worship him, but other things are diminished by this failure—things that are sacred and practical, values which greatly affect society and are profoundly determinative for individuals within that society. Much is currently being said or written regarding the *crisis in the nation.* This crisis, which we shall discuss more fully, reaches into practically every aspect of our national life, profoundly affecting every institution of our society. Perhaps more than we have realized, the overall crisis of the nation has its roots in another crisis—the crisis in worship.

More than a hundred years ago a Frenchman by the name of Alexis de Tocqueville came to America on a fact-finding mission for his government. He scouted the institutions, the government, and the people of this thriving young republic and reported back on what he considered to be the American genius. The greatness of America, reported de Tocqueville, was not to be found in her growing industrial complex, not in her legislative halls or her emporiums of trade, but in her churches, where Sunday after Sunday the nation's people gathered in devotion and worship of God.

The United States recently hosted another foreigner on a similiar, though unofficial, fact-finding tour of the republic. This time it was the highly regarded English historian Arnold J. Toynbee who examined the American people and their institutions, and then returned to England to write his analysis. Published in one of America's leading popular magazines, it was a rather dismal and distressing summary of a nation in crisis. Toynbee wrote of a nation that had lost the drive and optimism which a few short years ago had been its most apparent genius. He described a country in trouble around the world; and, more importantly, a country in trouble with herself, threatened by domestic problems which might very well prove to be her undoing—disturbances on her campuses, riots in her cities, and disenchantment and distrust among her people.

If religious faith has had the significant role in shaping America that has traditionally been ascribed to it, then certainly it becomes a prime suspect when the sources of the nation's present problems are sought out. Could it be that there is a direct correlation between the growing secularism in our society and the breakdown of stability and trust that presently plagues every institution within the society, including the church? I think so.

For a variety of reasons, Sunday mornings do not any longer find the churches of America filled with eager and devout worshipers. Church attendance peaked in the early 1960s, but for the last five years it has been marked by a more or less steady decline. The reasons for this decline are within both the American society and the American church. As American society becomes increasingly technical and affluent, it also becomes increasingly secular. Mobility has issued in anonymity, relationships are less personal, values have changed. Secular man has little conscious need for God and even less sensitivity to the presence of God.

"God has died in our time, in our history, in our existence," write Thomas J. J. Altizer and William Hamilton in their little book, *Radical Theology and the Death of God.* Such a pronouncement might very well say a great deal more about the church, and about the society in which the church is lodged, than it says about God.

The-Death-of-God theology is, to a large extent at least, a product of our age of secularism. In its more extreme forms this theology is much too radical to have any relevance for the average person. Indeed, to many people it makes very little sense. Theologians without a God—on its surface it appears to be a contradiction of terms, to say the least. It is comparable to oceanographers without an ocean. It has, nevertheless, provoked much discussion, causing widespread response and reaction. Indeed, this extreme expression of secular theology appears to have the unusual facility of being all things to all men. It is ridiculous, bizarre, shocking, satanical, threatening, exciting, intelligent, encouraging—depending on who is reporting.

Some have hailed it as the greatest thing for the church since the mimeograph machine. Many have been simply amused by it—it has aroused their curiosity, if for no other reason than its oddity. Others have been extremely agitated and unduly defensive. In some cases, people who never before evidenced much excitement in their belief that God is alive have become quite excited over the suggestion that He is dead.

Whatever its merit or lack of it, the Death-of-God hypothesis is the legitimate child of our age of secularism. It should be recognized that it is no new phenomenon, however. Friedrich Nietzsche gave scholarly articulation to the hypothesis seventy-five years ago.

Is God dead? It is, indeed, an old, old question. It is older than our generation, older than Nietzsche. Perhaps it is as old as religion itself. Its present form is but the modern echo of ancient doubt. The question even appears to have bothered Jeremiah twenty-five-hundred years ago. In the eighth chapter of his book he looks with a broken heart at the faithlessness of his generation. He is appalled at their trust in their own resourcefulness, their willingness to go after the gods of their pagan contemporaries, and their disregard for the God of their fathers. He finds it difficult to believe that God would permit such apostasy. Why doesn't God do something? Is He dead?

In one of the most familiar passages of the Bible, Jeremiah raises this question with his people. "The harvest is past, the summer is ended, and we are not saved," cries the prophet. "Is there no balm in Gilead? Is there no physician there? Why then has the health of . . . my people not been restored" (Jeremiah 8:20,22)?

Gilead was the medical center of Jeremiah's primitive world and was widely known for its doctors and medicines. It was the ancient counterpart of Hot Springs or Mayo Clinic. In Gilead there grew herbs, flowers, and trees from which the primitive doctors of the day extracted crude remedies for all kinds of common illnesses. The *balm* referred to by Jeremiah is believed to have been a popular medicine made from the resin of the styrax tree which grew in Gilead.

Gilead may have had additional symbolic significance for the people of Israel and Judah. Since it was across the Jordan and geographically to the east of the land of the Jews, some have claimed that Gilead was also a symbol of hope. It was over Gilead that the sun rose, bringing the light and promise of each new day. However this may be, it is apparent that Jeremiah was alluding to Gilead's fame as a center of healing. He saw Israel as a sick and dying man who had depended on a variety of inadequate remedies until, finally, the patient was in the throes of death.

WHEN FAITH DIES

"The harvest is past, the summer is ended, and we are not saved," exclaimed Jeremiah. His people had obviously done that thing so common to human nature. They had taken the position that, given time, everything would work out. They had assumed that time would fulfill their destiny, heal their condition, cure the ills of the nation, and bring them peace and security.

We are inclined to take this position in our own lives. We are often like Augustine, who, for years before his conversion, prayed, save me, Lord. But not now! We tackle life with vigor and enthusiasm, eager and determined to win success and find security. For a time the challenge of our work, the promise of success, and the advantages of affluence seem to satisfy us, but sooner or later we realize that all of these do not satisfy our craving. We discover that there is some deep, often unidentified, need that continues to gnaw at us. Success and affluence do not satisfy it, nor does the superficiality of nominal Christianity give us what we need and secretly crave.

In the early years of our lives it is not uncommon for us to assume that time will take care of the spiritual aspirations which stir within us. We postpone the surrender for which we are made, and the passage of time is often marked by additional delays and more complacent attitudes. Finally, in some moment of insight it dawns upon us that "The harvest is past, the summer is ended, and we are not saved." When such insight comes —regardless of our theoretical theologies—we realize that in the practical and personal world of our own faith and life God is dead! Religion becomes a dull round of creed reciting, moral resolution, and ecclesiastical bustle, without any healing of soul.

SECULARISM

Our fathers called it *sin.* We call it *secularism.* But whatever we call it, it is *alienation from God.* Our tendency to moralize about sin, when we dare discuss it at all, has been misleading to say the least. One may be basically moral, and yet sense an utter failure to fulfill his noblest yearnings for self-realization. Sin is a deeper and more subtle matter than moral misbehavior. It is a basic misalignment of life.

Secularism has performed a great service in turning man's focus away from other worlds and to this world and this time. Its great error, however, has been the tendency to assume the affairs of this world and this time independently of God. Reinhold Niebuhr's definition of sin as "even our best good corroded by egocentricity and pride," could just as readily apply as a working definition of much that is characteristic of secularism. In either case, it is the witholding of self and society from God. Individually it is the experience of that man or woman who is often both moral and successful yet unfulfilled in life. How often I have encountered these people in whom there is respectability, education, position, culture, money, but in moments of great honesty and trust they have confessed that something is missing.

The effect of this—"even our best good corroded by egocentricity and pride"—on society is frightening in the extreme. Many people today are understandably concerned about the future of our nation. If the nation continues on its present course of anarchy, crime, graft, self-seeking, hatred, suspicion, and distrust, what will be the outcome? Moral principles are pooh-poohed, and once cherished values are openly derided or violated. There is, indeed, cause for concern. In our seeming helplessness we sometimes ask, Why have we come to this? What has gone wrong? What has happened to our people? "Hark the cry . . . of my people from the length and breadth of the land. . . . The harvest is past, the summer is ended, and we are not saved. . . . Is there no balm in Gilead? Is there no physician there?" (8:19,20,22).

When one considers that 63 percent of the American people belong to the church, and that our churches, though seldom crowded, are far from empty on Sundays, then it becomes apparent that the problems of society may very well root in the failure of the church to secularize the gospel in the sense of making worship relevant to the world in which it is set.

Several months ago there was a nationally televised exposé of the Ku Klux Klan and its activities across the country. It was a horrifying revelation of hatred and violence, all mixed up with and dressed out in Protestant Christianity. The perversion of theological language and Christian symbol was incredible. By and large these people of the Klan are illiterate, unsophisticated, and culturally retarded people. I think we are inclined to take some comfort in that fact, but the sin that finds expression in the hooded night rider who burns crosses and shouts slogans of hatred is not restricted to those who engage in such display. It is not confined to poor people or those of limited intelligence and education. We don't have to look far to find the same basic attitudes, the same hostility and hatred, in the lives of many people—people who would never think of donning a hood or burning a cross. Many of these people are in our churches, often oblivious to the fact that such attitudes are a negation of everything the gospel represents.

It isn't that correcting our race problems would usher in the kingdom. The point is that this, like most of the problems besetting our generation, is symptomatic of an inner sickness of the soul. When this malignancy is so evident, even among church people, it is small wonder that some men can look at our world, examine the church, and conclude that God is dead.

What do we see when we look into our own hearts? The average churchman among us has concluded that it is enough to be an average churchman. Most of the preaching we have heard has been more moralistic than evangelistic. We have assumed that sin is a matter of immorality. We have believed that we can roll up our sleeves, blow on our hands, and build a better life, or a better world, any time we resolve to do it. In moments of honesty, however, we see what Jeremiah saw so long ago. "The harvest is past, the summer is ended, and we are not saved."

CALL TO WORSHIP

There is no way in which the church can better serve the present age than by calling its people to worship. Worship is the heart and soul of the church. It is also the source of healing and health for society.

During the darkest days of World War II, William Temple, who was at the time Archbishop of Canterbury, in a broadcast to America said this: "I am disposed to begin by making what many people will feel to be a quite outrageous statement. The world can be saved from political chaos and collapse by one thing only, and that is worship."

In this regard, as elsewhere, the Bible is a very practical book. Many of its admonitions, though spoken centuries ago, come to us with a moral force and relevance which transcend time. We find such an admonition in 2 Chronicles 7:14. The passage is addressed to a nation that was in trouble and a people who had become careless. God says to them: "if my people who are called by my name humble themselves, and pray and seek my face, and turn from their wicked ways, then I will hear from heaven, and will forgive their sin and heal their land."

This ancient call to worship becomes our own. It will not be met, however, by simply getting more people to attend church, whether by improved techniques of promotion or by appealing to their sense of duty. Most attendance promotion drives in local churches, however ingenius they may be, are short-lived in their effect. To remind church members of their vows also evokes a rather weak response. Indeed, vows are relatively meaningless apart from the values they symbolize. The word *worship* derives from the word *worthship,* and it is precisely at this point that the church must invest its efforts toward renewal.

WORTHSHIP

There is, for example, the value of identification and witness, a very basic need of the Christian regardless of his period in history. Through corporate worship the Christian is constantly reminded of his commitment. He is also reenforced in that commitment by the sense of community. He is thus reminded that he is a part of the church. The word *church* is the English word for the Greek *ecclesia* meaning "the called-out ones" or the assembly of the people of God.

Someone tells of an elderly man who never missed worship even though he was deaf. He couldn't hear the words of the sermon or the music of the organ and choir, but he never failed to be present. When someone asked him why, under those conditions, he bothered to go to church, he said, "I want my neighbors to know whose side I am on." Perhaps it is just a story, but it points up a value which worship should stress and reenforce—identification with those who are "called-out," the people of God, committed to doing His work in the world.

There is also the value of which Henry Sloan Coffin spoke when he defined worship as "adoration of God, appreciation of God, delight in God, . . . and offering up ourselves to God." Worship serves the need of man to express gratitude and praise to God for His goodness and love. It is both the reminder and the acknowledgment that "Every good endowment and every perfect gift is from above, coming down from the Father" (James 1:17). Genuine worship is the call and the commitment to a responsible stewardship of those gifts. Small wonder that secular man while he may believe in God (as 98 percent of the American people do, according to a recent Gallup Poll) does not worship. He has lost the sense of mystery and joy which recognizes that "The earth is the Lord's and the fulness thereof, the world and those who dwell therein" (Psalms 24:1).

Perhaps the paramount value of worship—especially in these days when life is so materially oriented and demandingly organized—is its provision of spiritual nurture. Even the pagan and the atheist recognize the need for a change of the mind's focus; and, denied this, life becomes a rather drab and monotonous affair. Man does not live by bread alone, and worship meets his need for spiritual nurture and renewal.

The claim is often advanced that this need can be adequately served by listening to great music, viewing beautiful art, or participating in wholesome recreation. The spiritual value of these things is unquestionable, and it is possible that one may experience a degree of worship by participating in them. The likelihood that one does, however, is remote. The man who says he worships on the golf course may find there some of the benefits of worship (I have difficulty even being moral on the golf course, let alone being religious), but he hardly worships in the full sense of its meaning.

Spiritual nurture comes only when worship is the shared experience of seeking and finding together that which could not be experienced singly or in isolation. There is, of course, no assurance that one's presence in church will result in his experience of worship. He must himself bring something to the orchestration, and if his own instrument is not tuned to the orchestra, it will strike no responsive chord.

IS GOD DEAD?

Theoretically, the people of America do not believe that God is dead. Numerically and proportionately more of the nation's people than ever before belong to the church. But as affluence and secularism affect their values, more and more of them are careless of religion and neglectful of worship. When we examine the effect of this at the level of the local church it is neither pleasant nor promising. One would much prefer to keep the discussion positive, but we can get at our problems only if we are honest and realistic.

Sometime ago, the *New Yorker* magazine carried a cartoon which showed a group of convicts huddled in a circle on the floor of their cell block. Spread out before them is a map of the prison grounds, and on the map is a detailed route for their planned escape. One of the prisoners turns to the leader of the group and says, "I wish you wouldn't keep saying, 'This is where we are now.' "

It isn't very pleasant to talk about "where we are now" in the life of the church. But if we are going to meet the crisis in worship, we must realistically and honestly take hold of it in our local churches. First of all, we must recognize that in most of our churches there is that large group—sometimes half the membership—who attach no value whatsoever to worship. Consequently, these people are almost never there for services—coming only on special occasions, such as weddings or funerals. Theoretically, these people are *theists*, they are among the 98 percent who believe in God, but practically they are *atheists*. God is dead for them; "there is no balm in Gilead. . . . there is no physician there." These people are lost to the church, and there is little hope for their recovery.

There is also another group of people in every church, representing from 20 to 30 percent, who are occasional in their attendance at worship. These people do a fruit-basket turn-over with each other—about half of them being in church half the time and the other half on a less frequent schedule, changing seats with each other from Sunday to Sunday. By and large these are good people, many of them holding places of responsibility in the organization, but they are the crisis people for whom the values of worship are tentative. On any Sunday, those values, though not completely dead, are up for grabs; they are played off against other values, such as sleeping in, entertaining guests, family recreation, and a dozen other things which are in themselves respectable and good.

With the present trends of affluence and secularism—increasing options for recreation, travel, and entertainment, and also money with which to exercise those options—many of these people will join that group in every church for whom the values of worship are nil. It is to be expected that even more of their children will discard these values. Not many of our bright young people are much sold on values that are tentative for their parents.

These people are not to be scolded, however; for while they constitute our crisis in worship, they are also our challenge. So long as these people are in church, even occasionally, there is the challenge and the hope of instilling in them those values discussed earlier—values held by that third group of people in every church, who worship in church somewhere every Sunday with the same regularity that they go to their jobs or their classrooms on Mondays. The challenge of both groups, however, is for the church to make meaningful its ministry of worship.

RENEWAL IN WORSHIP

The church must, first of all, analyze what it is doing with its worship opportunities. Some of the language and the forms still being used have come to us out of the past. They are meaningless to many of our people, but they have become sacrosanct, and we are very loath to reappraise or replace them.

It is said that there was once a Danish Protestant Church, built before the Reformation, in which worshipers maintained well into the nineteenth century, the custom of bowing when they passed a certain spot on the wall. No one knew why they bowed before the spot, until one day they removed the whitewash and found there a Roman Catholic Madonna. For three-hundred years the people had bowed before the place where the Madonna used to be. In most of our churches there are those forms and words used in worship about which all that can be said is that they used to be meaningful.

There is growing evidence, however, that the church is bringing a new honesty, creativity, and resourcefulness to its worship ministry. Some of the most spectacular changes in this regard are taking place in Roman Catholicism. In recent years, our Catholic friends have changed the language of the Mass from Latin to English. They have adopted the Protestant practice of congregational singing. The Folk Mass and the use of lay readers in their services are also new developments designed to enhance the meaning of worship.

Renewal of worship is also taking place in Protestantism. Sometimes the process is painful and the progress is slow; but as time passes, fewer eyebrows are raised and almost no backs are bowed as the choir sings calypso, or the minister reads from a new translation, or the congregation recites a modern creed. Religious drama, interpretive dance, and folk communion are gradually becoming meaningful forms, and there is more yet to come—for God lives, and His Church is being renewed.

In the words of the old Spiritual, "There is a balm in Gilead, to heal the sin-sick soul." Jesus Christ is the Great Physician, and in our worship He continues to keep the promise to be in our midst. A nineteenth century Englishman by the name of John Ruskin, long ago put into proper perspective the challenge of our present crisis. Ruskin said that the most precious hour in the week is that hour when a company of men and women, baffled and weary with the week's labor, have come in after six days exposure to the full weight of the world's atmosphere where the thorns and thistles have been springing up in their lives. And the minister has but sixty minutes to get at the separate hearts of a thousand people, to try by this way and that to open the hard fastenings of those doors where the Master, Himself, has stood and knocked saying, "if any man will open the door, I will come in."

Praise the Lord!
Praise God in his sanctuary;
  praise him in his mighty firmament!

Praise him for his mighty deeds;
  praise him according to his exceeding greatness!
Praise him with trumpet sound;
  praise him with lute and harp!
Praise him with timbrel and dance;
  praise him with strings and pipe!
Praise him with sounding cymbals;
  praise him with loud clashing cymbals!
Let everything that breathes praise the Lord!
Praise the Lord! (Psalms 150).

6

The Sacrament of Hope

For thus says the Lord: When seventy years are completed for Babylon, I will visit you, and I will fulfil to you my promise and bring you back to this place. For I know the plans I have for you, says the Lord, plans for welfare and not for evil, to give you a future and a hope. Then you will call upon me and come and pray to me, and I will hear you. You will seek me and find me; when you seek me with all your heart, I will be found by you, says the Lord, and I will restore your fortunes and gather you from all the nations and all the places where I have driven you, says the Lord, and I will bring you back to the place from which I sent you into exile Jeremiah 29:10–14.

For several years the laboratory of a great American company had this motto decorating its walls:

Have you got any rivers that are uncrossable?
Have you got any mountains you can't tunnel through?
We specialize in the wholly impossible,
Doing the things that no one can do.

Remember when this was descriptive of the American mood, when the national self-image was ten feet tall?

In the last chapter reference was made to Arnold J. Toynbee's recent visit to America and his report upon returning to Britain. His principal concern was our sagging morale. He spoke of our many complex and bewildering problems and then pointed out what he considered to be our greatest problem, the loss of optimistic drive and self-confidence.

Could it be that the American genius for achieving the impossible has succeeded in creating the ironic situation in which our genii have turned into devils to plague us? There seems to be no end to the snowballing magnitude of our domestic problems—spiraling inflation, a growing military-industrial-complex, decaying cities, rat-infested ghettos, rising expectations of the poor and disfranchised, black militancy, organized crime reaching into every facet of our national life, disillusionment and division with a hard-to-justify, frustrating, endless war half around the world—all these and more have stripped us of the dynamic optimism which once pervaded our outlook upon the future. Moreover, the problem of hopelessness has been compounded by a growing distrust toward the basic institutions of our society. The government, the economic system, law and order, higher education, the church—all are among the foundation stones upon which our society is planted; all are under suspicion or open attack.

Not since the Civil War has our country been in such deep and ominous internal trouble. Following that devastating conflict a hundred years ago, the country was confronted with problems that must have appeared insurmountable. Physically rent, financially bankrupt, numbed by suffering and sorrow, embittered by the experiences of the war, the country's future could have been lost to hopelessness and despair.

In Douglas Southall Freeman's *Robert E. Lee, A Biography,* one of the heroes of that period was a defeated, dispossessed, Confederate General from Virginia. He had lost everything in the war, including the cause he had espoused. But he held on to hope, the kind of hope that was to bind the nation's wounds and put her people on their feet again with faith in the future. When it might have seemed to a lesser man that the situation was hopeless, Robert E. Lee let it be known that he did not despair of the future.

Writing to Charles Marshall, General Lee said: "The truth is this: The march of Providence is so slow and our desires so impatient; the work of progress is so immense and our means of aiding it so feeble; the life of humanity is so long, that of the individual so brief, that we often see only the ebb of the advancing wave and are thus discouraged." Then Lee added this footnote of wisdom: "It is history that teaches us to hope."

What a word for us at this juncture in our national life. Near the end of the Johnson Administration, the president—sensing the need for a recovery of positivism in America—denounced the negative critics of the nation. He charged them with continually emphasizing what is wrong with our country and seldom giving credit or praise for what is right. His point might be well taken that there is far more that is right and good than there is that is bad. We might better serve the cause of patriotism by emphasizing the positive. But the perplexing paradox which bothers all our people—from those in the White House to the man in the street—is the contradiction between Providential gifts and human accomplishment, on the one hand, and the demanding restlessness of the human spirit, on the other.

Respect for the institution of law has been a basic foundation of our country—yet crime, lawlessness, and anarchy threaten to undo us. Ours is a government by the people and for the people, where freedom of expression is the cherished right and essential safeguard of all other freedoms; yet, we fear those who raise voices of dissent, and the effort to silence those who protest is not unknown among us. Because our country was founded on religious principles, we have long taken for granted that we are a Christian nation; yet money, sex, and violence are the stock-in-trade with which we entertain ourselves to the shock and amusement of the rest of the world. We enjoy unprecedented affluence; yet, 5 percent of our people do not have a living wage, and fifteen million of them live in slums. We genuinely love peace and sincerely seek its realization; yet no country has been involved in more war than we have known during the two-hundred years since we became a nation.

And now history has brought us to a point at which these contradictions are no longer academic. They can no longer co-exist side by side. World opinion and our own national conscience have delivered an ultimatum. We stand at the crossroads of our perplexing paradox, and it is as though God were saying to us again, "Behold, I set before you the way of life and the way of death" (Jeremiah 21:8). No generation has had such reason for hopeless despair and, at the same time, such exciting promise. So much hangs on our ability to be guided by the lessons of history. "It is history that teaches us to hope."

The twenty-ninth chapter of Jeremiah contains the prophet's "Letter to the Exiles." The people of Israel had come to the bottom of a long downward spiral. Inward deterioration and outward aggression had brought complete collapse, first to Israel and then to Judah. Their leadership had become captive, and their people had been exiled to Babylon. The future was gloomy. Everything depended on how God's people would now act.

Their greatest enemy was not Babylon, however, but their own despair and loss of hope. Jeremiah's "Letter to the Exiles" brought the counsel of hope. The letter peaks with the promise of the eleventh verse: "For I know the plans I have for you, says the Lord, plans for welfare and not for evil, to give you a future and a hope."

LEARNING TO HOPE

The point of comparison between our present situation and that of Israel and Judah is obviously not that of physical captivity and enslavement. In some respects their captivity is envious. It provided Jeremiah's day with a stimulus to determination and unity which solidified and strengthened the people in purpose and hope. Nevertheless, the loss of hope—marked by abandonment of positive purpose and direction—dogged them constantly. In this we find our point of comparison. When these incentives are lost, the future is gone. It was the great concern of Jeremiah that their loss possibly would constitute the final force of disintegration. He was fearful that the demands of the situation in which his people found themselves would be so great and the solutions so complex that they would yield to despair.

One does not have to search for our modern parallel. The voices of despair have seized the microphone and are loudly counseling the courses of hopelessness. They come from the left and the right and are equally ominous. "If we can't have our stake in this country, its wealth, its opportunity, its freedom, then nobody's going to have any of the cake! Burn, Baby, burn!" From the opposite corner comes the reactionary solution of suppression by force. Mace, billy clubs, and barbed wire are the solutions which great numbers of our people are ready to adopt.

Dietrich Bonhoeffer, who watched Nazi anti-Semitism destroy Germany in the thirties and forties, warns us against the stupidity of well-meaning people who become the tools of tyrants. In his book *I Loved This People,* he writes:

> Stupidity is a more dangerous foe of the good than evil is. It is possible to protest against evil, to expose oneself, and at times it can be prevented.... Evil always carries in itself the germ of a substitute for it, in that it leaves behind at least a feeling of uneasiness in men. Against stupidity we are defenseless.... reasons are of no avail; facts that contradict one's own prejudices simply do not need to be believed—in such cases the stupid person even becomes critical—and if [the facts] . . . are unavoidable, they can simply be shoved aside as insignificant, isolated cases. In this the stupid person, in contrast to an evil one, is completely satisfied with himself. Indeed he even becomes dangerous in that he is easily inclined to assume the offensive.

Stupidity is perhaps a stronger word than we should like. But Bonhoeffer makes a point which we would do well to consider as certain voices clamor to be heard in modern America. Jeremiah cautioned the exiles of his day against the dangers of false prophets. "Do not let your prophets and your diviners who are among you deceive you, and do not listen to the dreams which they dream, for it is a lie which they are prophesying to you in my name; I did not send them, says the Lord" (29:8,9).

It is apparent that Jeremiah referred to the voices of fear and negativism which were counseling reckless reaction to the conditions in which the people found themselves. The parallel is obvious. The voices of fear and negativism in our day have fostered a national mentality which sometimes borders on paranoia. A recent Associated Press release from the Southern Regional Council reports that there is a "disintegration" of American public life, involving "a tendency to anarchy, a willingness to destroy the good along with the bad of such basic institutions as higher education." The report describes the equally dangerous reaction from the other side as "a tendency to right-wing totalitarianism."

It isn't that there is that much wrong with our country. It is that we have been exploited by opportunists of various schools of thought who have created a dangerous imbalance of negativism and distrust. I am not suggesting that a responsible people should be uncritical either. Pascal once said, "The greatness of man is great in that he knows himself to be miserable." Dissatisfaction with things as they are is essential to human progress. It provides the creative tension that makes growth possible.

There is still a great deal of good in our country and its institutions, but we might fail to see it if we focus only on the negative. Two men were discussing New York City. One reported it to be an awful place, filled with cheap sensations, with morally degraded people, with sin on every corner. The other called it a splendid city, filled with art museums, great music, and stimulating lectures. New York was the city that each inwardly desired.

If we look we will see that not all of our campuses are in turmoil. Not all of our youth have dropped out. Not all of our politicians are demagogues. Not all Democrats are war hawks. Not all blacks are undependable. Not all white Americans are racists, not even in the South. Not all of our churches are irrelevant, and not all Christians are phonies.

If we look we will see that, with all that is yet imperfect, this is a great time to be alive and progress is being made. Consider the affluence of our people. It is often charged by our critics that we enjoy the luxuries of wealth while we look indifferently at the poverty that keeps great masses of our people, and other millions around the world, on the borderline of extinction. There is a great deal of truth in this criticism, but it isn't the whole story. Not all of our wealth is used to buy big automobiles, color TV's, and trips to Europe. No government in all of history has struggled more to do something about its poor. No country has given away more of its wealth in answer to the cries of human need and suffering around the world. And then what about the great foundations that private wealth has brought into being? What about the average man of this country in his support of the United Givers' Fund? What about the Heart Fund and Cancer drives? The critic will say it isn't enough. And I'll agree. But at the same time, there has never been anything like it in the history of man.

What about our young people? They're supposed to be on some kind of dropout jag, all taking LSD, and ready to tear down the Establishment. This just isn't so. A small percentage fits this description, to be sure. But what about the overwhelming majority? I say they are the most refreshingly hopeful generation of youth this country has ever produced. They're involved, and they're willing to pay the price of their involvement. They find phoniness and hypocrisy intolerable. In matters of race and war they represent the moral conscience of a nation that has nurtured them in the principles of democracy and the claims of Christianity. With all the pressures that swirl around them, they are the most heroic and hopeful generation this country has ever produced.

What about our racial situation? The inequities here have been so dramatized that much of the world has concluded that every white American is a night rider and every black man is a slave. True equality has not come, to be sure. At the same time, it has not been our critics abroad but the conscience of this nation that has dramatized the plight of the black. And the progress that has been made in the last fifteen years is incredible. Three major cities of this country now have black mayors. A black man sits on the Supreme Court. For the first time since Reconstruction a black sits in the Mississippi Legislature. A black bishop presides over a predominantly white conference of the Southeastern Jurisdiction of The United Methodist

Church. Some will say that's nothing to boast about; it is as it should be. I agree. But who would have thought it possible twenty years ago?

CREATIVE INVOLVEMENT

We haven't arrived, by any means, but we haven't gone to the dogs either. And if we take hold of the problems that are still around in abundance, these can be the most exciting times in all of history.

What Norman Cousins said in his book *In Place of Folly* of war and the threat of nuclear destruction can be said of every human problem. "Just think what we win if we win. No other age in history has had the same potential. About no earlier period in history could it be said that the earth could be made sufficient for the needs of all its people. The conquest of disease and poverty is clearly within reach. . . . Man has the potential sources of energy that can give him time to fulfill himself and develop his creative resources on a scale . . . that . . . (has) never before been possible."

"Just think what we win if we win." And the glory of life is the absence of guarantee. A better world is not going to evolve automatically out of our present situation. A speaker recently commented on the Genesis account of creation, saying that God brought order out of chaos; but, said the speaker, "God left a little of the chaos around and called upon man to join Him in continuing the creative process." This is both the tragedy and the glory of life.

The future is pregnant with hope. God still says to His lonely exiles, "For I know the plans I have for you . . . plans for welfare and not for evil, to give you a future and a hope" (Jeremiah 29:11).

Jeremiah's counsel to his people was for them to get involved creatively. He advised them not to listen to the voices of negativism—not to give up! He said, "Build houses and live in them; plant gardens and eat their produce. Take wives and have sons and daughters" (29:5,6). "Get with it!" he said in effect.

This is the hopeful thing about the church today. It is shaking off the shackles of cloisterism and saying to the people of God, "Get with it!" A clever quipster has taken the Biblical admonition for Christians to be *in* the world but not *of* it, accusing us of the reverse: the modern churchman is *of* the world but not *in* it.

It is still too much the case. But there is also a restlessness, a stirring of God's Spirit in the church of our day. There are a lot of laymen who are not satisfied simply to usher, or sing in the choir, or serve on a committee, as essential as these tasks are. The ministry of the laity has come to those laymen as a call for creative involvement in the world. And this is essential, too.

Sometimes, however, this restlessness for creative involvement, frustrated by the institutional restrictions of the modern church and despairing of any hope that the institution can be renewed, comes close to being a voice of negativism. A United Methodist Bishop hinted at this recently when he said, "The church is sick at the core, and no readjustments of organization will suffice" to make it well again.

Gordon Cosby—whose Washington congregation, The Church of the Saviour, represents one of the most vital and well known examples of renewal within the institutional church—recently confessed to a hopelessness regarding the church as it is presently structured. Cosby is quoted in *The Congregation in Mission* by George W. Webber as follows:

> The church as we know it in our time must go. This conviction has come to me gradually—I have worked with it consciously for the past 15 years and been disturbed by it for

> the past three. Just a few weeks ago I crossed a line in my thinking. Now I am on the side of feeling that the institutional structures that we know are not renewable. Even where there is renewal [and this goes on in many congregations] the stance of the church is almost always the same—a stance which is contrary to the very nature of a church committed to mission.

Such assessments by responsible churchmen are spoken with great sincerity, but they do little to encourage renewal within the church. The fact is, such comments help to generate a negative, reactionary, and iconoclastic mood, which serves only to impair and weaken the institutional church. As we have said, it is healthy and hopeful when an increasing number of laymen are not satisfied simply to usher, or sing in the choir, or serve on a committee—but it is reactionary and detrimental to the cause of Christ when these people move into a posture of complete denunciation, in which they are down on everything related to the institutional church. This is to throw the baby out with the bath water.

I have been over this route—vicariously, with a number of discouraged friends among the laity, and personally, in my own agonizing ambivalence regarding the institutional church—and when I look at the whole distance and try to anticipate the point at which it will come out, I keep coming back to the institution. As imperfect as it is, it is still God's best hope to get His work done in the world. Without it our noblest efforts at being the church will have limited longevity and restricted effectiveness. Do away with the institution, and we will have to create a replacement for it if the *Body of Christ* is going to have meaningful and continuing expression in the life of the world.

Gilbert K. Chesterton once told a parable which reminds me

of the more radical reaction to the institutional church. In Chesterton's story, a group of his countrymen are reported to have set off from the coast of England in search of a new land. They were tired and despairing of old England, so they thought to discover a new and better country. After a long and arduous voyage, they landed on the shores of what they believed to be the new and exciting place of their dreams. They pulled their boats onto the beach, raised their flag of conquest, and proceeded to examine the countryside. There was an uncanny familiarity about it all; and, to their amazement, further examination revealed that they had landed on the same coast from which they had departed. They were back in England. Trying to escape it, they had run square into it.

The parable, like all good parables, is self-explanatory. It certainly describes the inevitable result of any sincere search for the best structures through which the gospel can find expression in our time. The institutional church is not above criticism to be sure. There is much wrong with it, and this will continue to be the case so long as it is comprised of human beings. But with all of its faults, it still provides the best means for doing the work of God in the world.

A FUTURE AND A HOPE

"For I know the plans I have for you, says the Lord, plans for welfare and not for evil, to give you a future and a hope." How long God has waited for us to come to the place where we are now! How long He has waited for us to develop the resources and the conscience to build a better church and a better world!

Henry Van Dyke in "God's Message to Men" once put in a few simple verses God's great patience, and man's slow progress—how God patiently drops a hint, and waits for man to pick it up and do something with it.

> [One day] God said, "I'm tired of kings!"
> But that was a long time ago,
> And man kept saying, "No:
> I like their looks in robes and rings. . ."
> So He crowned a few more,
> And the kings as before
> Kept fighting and spoiling things.
> But at last man said, "I'm tired of kings!
> Sons of the robber chiefs of yore,
> They make me pay for their lust and their war,
> I am the puppet, they pull the strings!
> The blood of my heart is the wine they drink,
> I shall govern myself for a while, I think,
> And see what that brings."
> Then God (who had made the first remark)
> Smiled in the dark.

"It is history that teaches us to hope." While Nazism was at its worst in Germany and while Hitler threatened to wipe out the Jews and bring all of Europe under the cloud of the swastika, a beleaguered Christian professor, in prison awaiting his own execution, dared to believe in the future. Dietrich Bonhoeffer said, "I believe that God can and will bring good out of all things, even the most evil. For this he needs men who will let all things work for the best in respect to them. I believe that in every trial God will give us as much power to resist as we need. But in order that we will rely on him alone and not on ourselves, he does not give it ahead of time. Such faith must overcome all anxiety about the future. I believe that even our mistakes and errors are not in vain, and it is no harder for God to deal with them than with what we regard as our good deeds. I believe that God is no timeless fate, but that he waits for and answers upright prayer and responsible deeds."

"For I know the plans I have for you, says the Lord, plans for welfare and not evil, to give you a future and a hope."

7
Beyond Discouragement

And I bought the field at Anathoth from Hanamel my cousin, and weighed out the money to him, seventeen shekels of silver. I signed the deed, sealed it, got witnesses, and weighed the money on scales. Then I took the sealed deed of purchase, containing the terms and conditions, and the open copy; and I gave the deed of purchase to Baruch the son of Neriah son of Mahseiah, in the presence of Hanamel my cousin, in the presence of the witnesses who signed the deed of purchase, and in the presence of all the Jews who were sitting in the court of the guard. I charged Baruch in their presence, saying, "Thus says the Lord of hosts, the God of Israel: Take these deeds, both this sealed deed of purchase and this open deed, and put them in an earthenware vessel, that they may last for a long time. For thus says the Lord of hosts, the God of Israel: Houses and fields and vineyards shall again be bought in this land" Jeremiah 32:9–15.

When Benjamin Disraeli, twice Prime Minister of England, was asked by Queen Victoria to give his proof for the existence of God, he replied, "Oh, the Jews, your Majesty."

The *Book of Jeremiah* takes the roof off the house of this indomitable people and allows us to peer inside during a most significant period of their history. Inside we see the bad along with the good—inward deterioration of religious and national life combined with outward circumstances which at times threaten their continued existence; yet alternating with faith and heroism which make them invincible.

One of Daniel Webster's intimate friends once described Webster as "a compound of strength and weakness, dust and divinity." Such a statement readily qualifies as a biographical summary of any man. It also applies to men en masse. It is particularly accurate when applied to the Jews of Jeremiah's day. Collectively they were "a compound of strength and weakness, dust and divinity." Yet the Jewish people have survived all the trials of their history, and Disraeli was justified in pointing to them as signal proof for the existence of God.

The remarkable thing about the history of the Jews is their consciousness that they are a chosen people. During the period of The Old Testament this consciousness was kept alive by men like Moses, Isaiah, Amos, Hosea, Micah, and Jeremiah. The role of the prophet was to act as the voice of God to His people. Again, the *Book of Jeremiah* takes the roof off a period of history and permits us to view Jeremiah in his role as one of Judaism's greatest prophets.

Jeremiah's life and ministry are filled with paradox—at times, apparent contradiction. He loves his people, but he does not hesitate to lambast them. He commends them and he chides them. He counsels them to resist their enemies; and, when the word of God is to the contrary, he just as quickly advises surrender. He foretells their doom, and he talks of hope and restoration.

The paradox of Jeremiah's prophetic role can best be illustrated with a parable from recent history. When Admiral Richard E. Byrd and his party made their second trip to the region of the South Pole, they flew down the 180th meridian of longitude in the Pacific. As you know, this is the International Date

Line. To cross it is to add or subtract a day from the calendar. Later, when Admiral Byrd wrote about this flight, he said: "All the time we were continually flying as close as possible along the 180th meridian—it is obvious that no navigator could fly along a mathematical line. Consequently," he said, "we were zigzagging constantly from today into tomorrow and back again."

What a picture of the role of the prophet—standing as it were between two worlds, moving from today into tomorrow and back again. Jeremiah at times appears to be contradictory as he struggles with the problems of the present and holds out the hope of the future for his people. The people were "a compound of strength and weakness, dust and divinity"; and, as Jeremiah stood in the place of tension between them and their God, he had to relate his ministry to both sides of their nature. His greatest concern was to assure that their strength and divinity would prevail. It was a constant fight against discouragement—the struggle of living the circumstances of today without losing sight of the certainties of tomorrow.

The best appeal to the nobility of man is the appeal of noble example. It is reported that within hours after the first London air raid of World War II a meeting was held by the newspaper and radio executives of the city to determine what they could do to help the cause of Britain. It was decided that beginning with the next air raid they would appeal to the noble and heroic side of their people by reporting, whenever possible, examples of courage and heroism. Writing about it later one of them said, "It was established then and there how the people of London would behave while under attack."

Jeremiah was sensitive to this quality of human nature. When the people were ready to throw in the towel and surrender to discouragement, he announced to them that the future would bring them out of their present circumstances: "For thus says the Lord of hosts, the God of Israel: Houses and fields and vineyards shall again be bought in this land" (verse 15).

The greatness of the prophet, however, was not his word but his example. In this chapter we have the story of Jeremiah's purchase of a field in Anathoth from his cousin Hanamel. With witnesses he weighed out the silver, signed and sealed the deed. It was established then and there how the people should behave.

DEALING WITH DISCOURAGEMENT

Discouragement is man's greatest enemy. It has dogged his steps and deterred his progress throughout the human pilgrimage. In our time the human family confronts many perplexing problems. But the one big handicap, inherent in practically every problem—hovering like an ominous cloud, ready to rain down despair and disillusionment—is discouragement, the age-old, universal nemesis.

The black minority in America today must wrestle with a multitude of problems which stand as roadblocks to civil rights, full citizenship, and self-realization. White racism blocks the black's progress in a thousand subtle ways, including implacable personal and collective resistance, the cunning craft of legal maneuver and deceptive tokenism, and all the other numberless, nameless methods by which the system succeeds in keeping him locked into the physical and spiritual ghettos of cruel discrimination. Yet, white racism is not the black's greatest enemy. The greatest enemy is internal. The spiritual and psychological depression which seethes beneath the surface, awaiting the exploitation of militant black racism and ready to be ignited with explosive detriment, to the black community first, but with an ultimate effect that is shattering for our whole society—this is the real enemy of progress.

The nagging peril of those who are victimized by the cruelty systems and injustices of our society is discouragement. How do they avoid despair as they deal with the closed doors of discrimination? How does the leadership of the black minority keep them singing "We Shall Overcome" and hold in check the kind of discouragement that would set them back through recourse to hatred, bitterness, and reckless rioting?

Discouragement is also a real factor in the behavior of our youth. Caught up in the pressures of a dog-eat-dog materialism, living constantly under the cloud of a war that makes no sense to them, hopeless in their efforts to change an Establishment which often responds to their idealism with mace and billy clubs, the younger generation struggles endlessly with discouragement.

Discouragement is equally the struggle of the church in these days. So soon we have come from the booming popularity of the church in the 1950s and early 60s to the encroaching secularism of the present. Unable to deal effectively with the social problems which eat at the vitals of our society—a society disillusioned by an evangelical fundamentalism with its lack of relevance for life, or a society spiritually starved by a sterile liberalism which has too often substituted its own voice and its own way for the voice of God—the church suffers today from utter discouragement.

This discouragement manifests itself in many forms of negative and destructive reaction. Not least of these is polarization within congregations—a breakdown of community, in which the so-called liberal and conservative are equally distrustful of each other. Sometimes this is seen in the layman's suspicion of the clergy. If the minister is relevant he isn't spiritual; and if he is spiritual, he isn't relevant.

I frequently receive letters from an old gentleman who is completely disillusioned with the church. Sometimes he forgets that he is a gentleman. He is old, the church isn't what it once was, and he is discouraged. In his discouragement he has become bitter, suspicious, and caustic. He is sure that the church has gone to the dogs, and he suspects the integrity of its leadership. He is an extreme example of discouragement that has deteriorated into damaging suspicion. To a lesser degree, but just as dangerous in its potential, this suspicion lurks in the minds of many laymen. It fractures the community of faith. It is a destructive by-product of discouragement.

Laymen are not the only ones who struggle with discouragement, however. Every year, hundreds of fine, well-trained, talented men leave the ministry for other fields. They have become discouraged and disillusioned. They have come from the seminaries with ideals for the church—ideals which are soon shattered by those who are, after all, "a compound of strength and weakness, dust and divinity."

BEYOND DISCOURAGEMENT

It is the task of the church in our day to demonstrate a faith that we are the *people of God.* These are trying but tremendous days for the church. Our greatest peril is discouragement and its negative by-products—despair, suspicion, and polarization. It is time for us to stand together in the great cause of the future and to re-enact the role of Jeremiah by going out and purchasing the plot of ground in Anathoth.

First of all, let us be reminded that discouragement is nothing new for God's people. Jeremiah is called the "Weeping Prophet" because he was not always optimistic. If ever a people had reason to be discouraged—ravaged by war, weakened by faithlessness, encumbered by exile—the people of Jeremiah's day had reason.

There are many gloomy prophets around today, ready with

the postmortems to consign the church to the cemetery, referring to our time as the *post-Christian era.* Their predecessors frequent the pages of history, however, and in the light of past predictions and assessments we can take hope in the fact that the prophets of doom up to now have been dead wrong.

Consider the bleak assessment which Matthew Arnold offered more than a hundred years ago. The English critic, with melancholy sadness, stood one night on Dover beach and imagined the church to be like the tide, once full but now receding inevitably and permanently, leaving on the beaches of history only a few scattered pebbles to remind future generations of what once was. He saw the faith of his fathers being swept away by the ebb and flow of history, a fast-dwindling legacy of the past. With discouragement he wrote:

> The Sea of Faith
> Was once, too, at the full, and round earth's shore
> Lay like the folds of a bright girdle furled;
> But now I only hear
> Its melancholy, long, withdrawing roar,
> Retreating to the breath
> Of the night wind, down the vast edges drear
> And naked shingles of the world.

How many times the death of the church has been pronounced, only for history to give the lie to such pronouncements. In 1816, John Keats, observing the churches of his day, said of them, "They are dying like an out burnt lamp." He failed to take into account one factor, which someone described this way: "The first essential of a quiet funeral is a willing corpse." The church has never been that.

Indeed, the most singular historic characteristic of the people of God is that when things have been at their worst, God's people have been at their best. Who would have believed that those Jews of Jeremiah's day and the faith they held could survive the threat of Babylon? Who would have believed that those embattled, frightened Christians of the first century—hiding from Nero in the catacombs of Rome, being burned at the stake, and fed to the lions—would prove to be what they said they were, "more than conquerors"?

The New Testament is history's finest documentation of the power of the human spirit, reenforced by the grace of God, overcoming unimaginable hardship and discouragement to emerge victorious. Here is a book that opens with the massacre of the young and innocent. Its story centers around a life of perfect goodness, snuffed out by brute cruelty on a Jerusalem hillside. The book ends as it begins, with the drama of death and discouragement hammering away at the determined dedication of those dispossessed disciples while their souls cry out before the altar of their faith, "How long, O Master?" No wonder Jesus said to those who would follow him, "In the world you have tribulation . . ." (John 16:33).

It has been the continuing story of the church. In the hundred years since Matthew Arnold wrote his sad epitaph, the Church of Jesus Christ has experienced the greatest missionary thrust of its history, carrying the gospel to the darkened places of the globe, bringing healing and light and dignity to the forgotten and dispossessed peoples of the earth.

History is, therefore, on the side of believing that the very things which discourage us in these days will prove sacramental in the long haul of faith, leading us beyond discouragement to the dynamic of genuine renewal—renewal in terms of vision, dedication, and character.

The very darkness of present circumstances hopefully will serve to sharpen the focus and illumine the path where the light shines in darkness, providing a new vision of what it means to be the church. A wise man said long ago, "Where there is no vision the people perish" (Proverbs 29:18 KJV). In our own time, Scotland's James Stewart said the same thing to an American congregation, observing that if the world is destroyed it will be for want of imagination.

If we are to avoid being overwhelmed by the discouraging problems of our day, not to speak of the ossifying lethargy which characterizes nominalism, there must come a new vision in terms of imaginative venture. Perhaps nominalism is our greatest enemy—the tendency to be satisfied with a second-hand, creed-reciting, comfort-and-peace-of-mind understanding of religion. Such a religion turns adventure into security and becomes the ultimate threat to the faith, not by renouncing it so much as by simply sitting upon it.

A religion without adventure, a faith that is only a memory is worthless. Our commitment must be constantly fired with new vision and imagination, new understanding of the relevance of the gospel and the mission of the church to the world in which we live. It is the firsthand venture of following Christ wherever He may lead. Sometimes we are hesitant because we find the beaten path of past understandings familiar and safe. We are reluctant to put Christ at the center of our vision and follow Him into the strange, unexplored jungles of involvement in today's world.

E. Stanley Jones has a story about a missionary who once became lost in an African jungle. When the missionary finally came upon a primitive village and asked one of the natives to lead him out, he betrayed his lack of understanding of the jungle. After more than an hour of hacking their way through the maze of jungle growth, the missionary finally said to his native guide, "Are you sure this is the way? Where is the path?"

The guide answered, "Bwana, in this place there is no path. I am the path."

Is this not a picture of what it means to be the church in the world? The way is often strange and unexplored. There is no path, there is only one who keeps saying, "I am the way." He is the path and He bids us follow Him.

This calls for new dedication. We must get a new vision of what the church can be as it follows its Lord in these days, and we must completely place ourselves at its disposal in love and commitment. To do this will demand more of us than simply to believe in the church, as important as that may be. The nature of our needed dedication is suggested by a comment Robert Frost once made concerning the founding fathers of this country. He said, "They didn't believe *in* the future. They believed it *in.*" He went on to say, "The most creative thing in us is the capacity to believe a thing in, in love, in all else."

Where the church is concerned, some people are having trouble just believing in the future. That alone will be quite an accomplishment for some. But it will not be enough. We must believe the future in. If we don't, nobody else will. That's where the rub comes, isn't it? That's where the peril lies. We are all that God has to work with, and the future depends upon us.

All that God has—yet we are often half-hearted, complaining, criticizing, withholding, withdrawing! We look at the task before us and we look at ourselves, and we are discouraged. We seem hopeless. As someone said at the close of World War II, "How can we have a brave new world with the same old people?"

We can't! We can't get beyond discouragement, we can't catch the new vision or give the new dedication so necessary for church renewal in our time, until we become a new people. Again, it is Christ alone who can effect this in us.

Renewal of personal faith and life will enable us to bring our best efforts to the task before us; but, more important than that, it will anchor our efforts in God. Here is where the real difference lies, the difference between the old man, trusting his own resources and his own genius—which has been so characteristic of us modern westerners—and the new man of faith, who acts in the assurance that God is still in charge of His world. The late C. G. Jung put it this way: "The individual who is not anchored in God can offer no resistance on his own resources to the physical and moral blandishment of the world."

Such a faith will keep us plugging away with impatience of effort, but with patience of soul. It will look beyond the immediate and draw strength from the ultimate, recognizing that in the slow processes of God, setback is not defeat. Delay isn't easy for us, however, oriented as we are to instant results. But some things just cannot be done instantly. Adoniram Judson was seven years in Burma before he won his first convert. Many of the great cathedrals of Europe were hundreds of years in their construction. Each generation built upon the labors of those who had gone before. Like Moses, we may be able to view the Promised Land only from a distance, leaving its realization to others.

The Evanston meeting of the World Council of Churches drafted this statement concerning evangelism: "We must remember that evangelism is God's work in which we are His agents. It is not our work, and therefore we must wait upon Him in prayer and in meditation upon His holy Word, that we may learn what He would have us do." It will help if we remember this truth and apply it in the broad sense of the whole work of God which He has given to His people. More important than any measurable results is the faithfulness of our witness. Jeremiah must have been discouraged often with the results, but he knew the power with which God could work through the influence of his life—so he bought the field in Anathoth.

In a New York City church one Sunday morning a tired, discouraged student from Columbia University slipped into a back seat. He was not dressed for church. Throughout the night he had walked the streets of the city, struggling with his doubts about life, wondering if there was anything worth believing in or living for, tormented by a mood of depression not uncommon in students. When morning came he found himself in church, looking disheveled, not sure why he was there, not really in the mood for worship. During the prayers he did not bow his head. Instead, he looked around at the congregation, and across the way he spotted one of his teachers who was a professor of science and a man with many degrees and academic honors.

The discouraged student thought of the professor's great mind and spirit and reputation—and yet, there he sat in church with his head bowed. The thought flashed through the student's mind: "If a man like that can believe in God, surely I can." His burden was lifted, and he left church that morning with renewed hope and purpose. Some years later the professor learned of the incident when a medical missionary came back on furlough from his work in India. The first person he went to see was the professor, now much older and retired. Sitting in the professor's study, the missionary said, "I don't know what it was, sir. I think it was the look on your face, the fact that you were there. Something in your devotion set things right in my heart."

Purchasing the field in Anathoth may not seem to have much result, and if we apply our usual statistical measurements, we are likely to become discouraged, but our faithfulness is not to statistics or to results as such. Our loyalty is to Christ, and in this loyalty we encourage one another.

Herbert Butterfield writes in the closing paragraph of his book *Christianity and History:* "There are times when we can never meet the future with sufficient elasticity of mind, especially if we are locked in the contemporary systems of thought. We can do worse than remember a principle which both gives us a firm Rock and leaves us the maximum elasticity for our minds; the principle: Hold to Christ, and for the rest be totally uncommitted."

Our faith and devotion must not be tied to rules or results, but to a Person. Paul Tournier, in his book *The Adventure of Living*, illustrates such a faith with the story of a dear friend who rose from his knees one day to declare: "I understand now. What I have to do is put my signature at the foot of a blank page on which I will accept whatever God wishes to write. I cannot predict what he will put on this blank contract as my life proceeds—but I give my signature today."

To do this is to live beyond discouragement. "Houses and fields and vineyards shall again be bought in this land." It is not for us to question when; but, like Jeremiah, we must buy the field in Anathoth and leave the results with God.

8
"Who Will Answer?"

When Jeremiah had come to the dungeon cells, and remained there many days, King Zedekiah sent for him, and received him. The king questioned him secretly in his house, and said, "Is there any word from the Lord?" Jeremiah said, "There is." Then he said, "You shall be delivered into the hand of the king of Babylon." Jeremiah also said to King Zedekiah, "What wrong have I done to you or your servants or this people, that you have put me in prison? Where are your prophets who prophesied to you, saying, 'The king of Babylon will not come against you and against this land'? Now hear, I pray you, O my Lord the king: let my humble plea come before you, and do not send me back to the house of Jonathan the secretary, lest I die there." So King Zedekiah gave orders, and they committed Jeremiah to the court of the guard; and a loaf of bread was given him daily from the bakers' street, until all the bread of the city was gone. So Jeremiah remained in the court of the guard Jeremiah 37:16–21.

"I am a man!"
"Resist the draft!"
"Do your own thing!"
"Black is beautiful!"
Sometimes the voices are angry, denunciatory, militant. More

often they are plaintive cries for identity—arising out of a deep need for self-realization; a need that is often denied or frustrated by the structures and value systems of our society. The present so-called generation gap is the result of youth's effort to establish identity and achieve a measure of self-expression in such a society—a society that is dominated by the older generation.

A mother and father, accompanied by their eight-year-old daughter, recently stopped in a restaurant and ordered lunch. The mother placed the little girl's order for a hamburger, insisting that it be without onions. "But, I want onions!" protested the child. Like the mother, the waitress who took the order appeared to be oblivious of the child's plea. But when the hamburger came, much to the delight of the child, the onions were included. As the waitress walked away, the little daughter glowingly announced, "She thinks I'm real!"

The generation gap embraces a lot of things. Indeed, it defines a whole new life style for our young people. It is essentially their way of saying, "Look, I'm for real!" The resulting youth culture is characterized by peculiarities of language, dress, hairstyles, music, and a variety of behavior patterns. It is designed to express the complex and sometimes contradictory moods and mods of a generation of youth who are often confused and sometimes disenchanted with the direction and values of their elders.

The cry for relevance is certainly a dominant and dynamic factor in this youthful self-assertion. This cry is especially apparent in the music that is popular with the younger set. Ironically, the older generation is inclined to judge much of that music as a wild assortment of ear-splitting syncopation, set to the accompaniment of irrelevant, nonsensical lyrics. But what is nonsensical for their elders is often highly relevant for youth. Cryptic, incoherent words set to a wild beat are eloquent symbols of what many of these youngsters feel. Music of this kind is for them a kind of "cry in the wilderness," expressing the meaningless confusion with which many of our youth struggle.

Not all of the music popular with youth is cryptic, however. The folk ballad is a case in point. Its great popularity is, in part at least, its ability to clearly communicate a message. Many of these songs express the yearnings and frustrations of the younger generation. Most of the lyrics are issue-action oriented, and not a few of them are profoundly theological.

When Ed Ames, for example, sings "Who Will Answer?" the message comes through loud and clear. In fact, for many of our youth the song has more theological relevance than Handel's *Messiah* or Malotte's rendition of "The Lord's Prayer." Ed Ames' song eloquently expresses youth's search for identity and meaning in a complex and contradictory world.

The problem of war is the number one issue presently confronting youngsters of high-school and college age. The draft and Viet Nam dog them constantly, confusing their values, clouding their future, and distorting their decisions. Above all, war is for them a meaningless, immoral monster, spawned in the blunders of an older generation. It is for them devoid of the rationale of patriotism which was supportive and motivational for those of previous generations. How can they morally justify war? How can they be sure of life beyond it? How can they express their dilemma? Consider the song which Ed Ames sings for them.

> On a strange and distant hill a young man's
> Lying very still, his arms will never hold his
> Child because a bullet running wild has
> Struck him down! And now we cry:
> 'Dear God! Oh why, oh why!'
> But Who Will Answer?

With every passing year the endless round of madness, with its growing menace of nuclear disaster, becomes larger, more ominous, and more oppressive. The average person is concerned, but his helplessness soon relegates him to apathy or fatalism. He lives constantly with the common knowledge that one rash act, one careless mistake by those at the switch, could reduce civilization to a cinder heap.

The best that most of us can do is hope, hope that someone will come along with some answers; and, in the meantime, hope that what almost happened on November 25, 1959, will never happen. One shudders to recall the now-acknowledged, almost disastrous fiasco of that date. At 4:52 in the morning of that crisp autumn day, a green light flashed out on one of the control panels at the U. S. Strategic Air Command, near Omaha, Nebraska. Immediately, with the precision of a long primed readiness, things began to happen. It is reported that within twelve and a half minutes, at approximately 100 bases scattered over the world, some 750 planes taxied out on the runways and awaited the signal to take off with their deadly load of H-bombs. Only in the last tense moments was it discovered that the green light had malfunctioned because of an overheated motor. The order was given to cancel, and the world was spared the disaster of an irremediable blunder.

'Neath the spreading mushroom tree,
The world revolves in apathy as
Overhead a row of specks roars on,
Drowned out by discotheques. And
If a secret button's pressed because
One man's been outguessed,
Who Will Answer?

Perhaps it will appear strange to compare Ed Ames with an ancient King of Judah, described in the *Book of Jeremiah,* but there he is in the person of Zedekiah. Acting under comparatively tame circumstances, Zedekiah reminds us that our modern struggle for theological answers to human problems has ancient precedent. All of Jeremiah's book is crisis oriented, as the people of his land moved from one demanding dilemma to the next. The thirty-seventh chapter records such a period during the reign of Zedekiah. The city of Jerusalem was under siege by the armies of Babylon. Up from Egypt the armies of Pharaoh had come to the aid of the city, to break the siege and drive off the Babylonian attackers.

Just as King Zedekiah and his people were beginning to feel some relief in the situation, Jeremiah became a spoilsport. God sent the prophet to warn the king that the fight was far from finished, that Pharaoh's armies would soon return to Egypt, and the Babylonians would then come back to pillage and burn the city of Jerusalem. This warning was hardly the word which Zedekiah and his military advisors wanted to hear. Surely no patriot would want to mar the nation's celebration of victory with such a gloomy forecast. Poor Jeremiah—thought to be out of step with the national interests of Judah—was forthwith accused of sedition and thrown into prison.

Zedekiah, unable to dismiss the matter from his thoughts, quickly summoned his top military brass and laid Jeremiah's prediction before them. One can almost hear the Secretary of Defense advising the Commander-in-Chief to pay no attention to the dovish notions of a religious rabble-rouser such as Jeremiah. To give ear to the prophet would identify Zedekiah with the wrong people. It could be political suicide, and it certainly would be poor military strategy. Thus the king continued to listen to his advisors until finally he saw himself and his people on the brink of disaster. At last, he decided to turn to Jeremiah; but, fearful of being found out, he had the prophet smuggled in through the palace rose garden for a secret conference in the Oval Room. The shades were drawn and the king confessed that things weren't going too well. "The king questioned him secretly in his house, and said, 'Is there any word from the Lord?' "

> In the rooms with darkened shades,
> The scent of sandalwood pervades the
> Colored thoughts in muddled heads,
> Reclining on the rumpled beds of
> Unmade dreams that can't come true.
> And when we ask what we should do,
> Who Will Answer?

ANY WORD?

The questions being raised in our day are essentially theological, to be sure, but we kid ourselves if we think that those who are raising them are storming the church for the answers. By and large the church has been written off as an acculturated institution of the Establishment. In fact, the church is considered by many to be either too otherworldly in its orientation to be aware of the issues, or too shy of conviction and courage to act or speak to those issues with any degree of relevance.

There was more than humor in a recent column by Hal Boyle in which he had reported that he almost got into trouble with the parents of a certain youngster. The youngster had questioned Mr. Boyle about heaven. In his characteristic manner, the columnist said, "I did my best to explain to him all about this place where I hope someday to get my mail." He went on to say that, although he tried to answer the boy's questions with "the latest information available," a few days later the boy's father came and wanted to know what kind of ideas Boyle had been putting in the youngster's head.

"Our son," said the father, "has informed his mother that he never wants to go to heaven because it doesn't have an escalator. He says he would rather go to a department store."

The story says a great deal about the cry for relevance being raised by our generation. And the cry will not be adequately answered by a heavenly-oriented theology, even if we modernize it with celestial escalators. The church must speak to the pressing problems encountered by men in a secularized society—which Harvey Cox helps us to understand theologically. In his book *The Secular City,* Cox makes an important distinction between secularism and secularization. "Secularization," he says, "is man turning his attention away from worlds beyond and toward this world and this time." It is, thus defined, the essential and responsible stewardship of man in his world. It is what Dietrich Bonhoeffer in the 1940s called "man's coming of age."

Modern man is not anti-God. There is, however, much evidence that he is increasingly anti-Church. In many respects our youth are more Christian than they have ever been; but, ironically, they are less inclined than ever to identify with the church. Not a few intelligent, responsible, and dedicated people have left the church out of disillusionment, because it has failed to speak to the burning issues of our time. Someone asked one such person if his leaving the church meant that he no longer believed in God. His reply was that he believed in God, yes, but not in His "ground crew!"

In 1964, the Anglican Church of Canada attempted to come to grips with this attitude toward the church by getting at the cause of it. The denomination commissioned a brilliant newspaperman, who had himself dropped out, to do a study of the modern church and its relevance. In the choice of Pierre Berton, the church would have the view of an outsider, one who was capable of objective reporting. The resulting book, *The Comfortable Pew,* immediately became a best seller in this country as well as in Canada and England. It says a lot of disturbing things which need saying. It talks about the *Side of God* in the wars of recent history. The book asks such embarrassing questions as, "What Colour Was Christ?" Other chapter headings include—"Religion versus Christianity," "The Comfortable Pew," and "The Lukewarm Pulpit."

Pierre Berton still believes in God, but he has despaired of His ground crew. Listen to one of Berton's power-packed paragraphs: "In the great issues of our time," he writes, "the voice of the Church, when it has been heard at all, has been weak, tardy, equivocal, and irrelevant. In those basic conflicts that ought to be tormenting every Christian conscience—questions of war and peace, of racial brotherhood, of justice versus revenge, to name three—the Church has trailed far behind the atheists, the agnostics, the free thinkers, the journalists, the scientists, the social workers, and even, on occasion, the politicians."

It is an embarrassing admission, but honesty compels us to confess that the church has a long history of forfeiture. Franklin Littell, in his book *The German Phoenix,* recalls the failure of the church to proclaim the needed word at the end of the Civil War. He reminds his readers that when Bishop Matthew Simpson, a leading northern churchman, spoke at the funeral of Abraham Lincoln, his speech was a vitriolic call for revenge. At the bier of the man who had called upon his countrymen to "bind up the nation's wounds," Simpson called for vengeance against every Confederate officer; each of whom, he charged, was a traitor to his country. Professor Littell also reminds his readers that the identification of religion with special interests was no better on the other side of the Mason-Dixon line. As a result, millions have lived for decades in what Littell calls "the unresolved bitterness of the lost cause."

Dare we be honest enough now to confess similar failures of the church in our time? Dare we admit that with few exceptions the church, nationwide, has been timid, if not silent, concerning the great moral and social issues of our time. It has too often allowed other organizations and special interest groups—frequently of questionable character and sinister motive—to bring the Word.

If the soul is darkened by a fear it cannot name,
If the mind is bafflled when the rules don't fit the game,
Who Will Answer? Who Will Answer? Who Will Answer?

There are no easy or ready-made answers to the problems of our day, no simple solutions. We are, consequently, often as hesitant as King Zedekiah, either to turn to the Source of guidance or to follow that guidance when we receive it. The problems are so complex and our abilities so limited that we are often bewildered and perplexed. As Pascal once said, a part of the problem is man's realization that he is something but not everything.

What should we do about the war in Viet Nam? Should we get out, and abandon the people to Communism? Should we go for a military solution and widen the risk of world catastrophe? Should we continue the war of attrition and spend billions more in dollars and thousands more in lives—just to hold things together half-way around the world? And, in that event, how shall we escape the charges of colonialism, and how shall we handle the deterioration of morale at home?

What should we do with the racial situation in our country today? Send the black back to Africa? Buy him a bus ticket to take him from some poverty pocket of the South to some rat-infested urban ghetto of the North? Put him on a reservation? Yield to the demands of black militancy and black racism? Pass legislation for open housing, fair employment, and integrated schools? What, then, do we do about the angry passions of fear, resentment, separatism, and racism, black and white? The truth is, we don't have the answers, not the full answers. We, therefore, find ourselves crying with the words of the song—*Who Will Answer? Who Will Answer? Who Will Answer?*

GOD'S ANSWER

Jeremiah's reply to Zedekiah's inquiry was to announce that there is an answer. Finally, in the extremity of our helplessness we, too, will discover that only God can give the answer—and that He has, indeed, done so. Alvin Porteous, discussing the theology of the late Paul Tillich, writes in his book *Prophetic Voices in Contemporary Theology:* "This is the good news—that in this man Jesus of Nazareth, God, who is the ground of our being, manifests himself under the conditions of our estranged existence, conquering the destructive conflicts which have robbed us of the wholeness and health which God's creative purpose intended. . . . In this one who is 'bone of our bone and flesh of our flesh' . . . the destructive split between God and man, man and his neighbor, man and himself, is unambiguously overcome."

If we accurately perceive God's answer as given in Christ, we will also see that it is the answer of suffering love. We moderns don't easily grasp the meaning of this, however. We are too much like Zedekiah, who expected an answer in terms of power or force. We haven't much outgrown the Old Testament in this regard. Dietrich Bonhoeffer said, "Man's religiosity makes him look in his distress to the power of God in the world. . . . The

Bible however directs him to the powerlessness and suffering of God; only a suffering God can help."

Whatever else, this means that God has invested His answer in us—bungling, slow, and finite creatures that we are. Our solutions are often misguided; at best, they are partial and frustrated. We can manage only bits and scraps, and some are beyond our reach or control. We are "something but not everything." We often cannot see the end of the road, sometimes not even the road itself. In fear we draw back and seek the safety of noninvolvement. We often misunderstand discipleship and define it as being good, or being faithful at church, or reading our Bibles, or saying our prayers, or paying our pledges. But the answer given in Christ, tells us that Christian discipleship is more than these—more than some religious act. If Christ is to bring God's answer to our time, then He must bring it through our participation in the suffering love of God in the life of the world.

Such participation on our part cannot be done in security. When Jeremiah gave Zedekiah God's answer for that day, the prophet was human enough to want to avoid the demands which he personally confronted in giving that answer. But he couldn't give the answer free of the risk of personal involvement. For Jeremiah, this involvement meant prison. For many, it has meant this, or some other form of suffering love.

History and faith teach us that God is seeking to raise the level of humanity and that His way of doing it is through the redemptive process of helplessness and suffering. Our part is to participate, often through our own suffering and failure. Jeremiah goes to prison. Jesus goes to the cross. Those who attempt to bring conscience to bear in our world must often pay a price. Sometimes the contribution we can make appears to be of little consequence, hardly worth the price. But who can measure it in the service of God?

"Who Will Answer?" Two Russians recently gave their answer. They may not even belong to a church, but their answer was of the sort which must come to characterize the church if it is to be used of God in these days. Following the Russian invasion of Czechoslovakia, Mrs. Yuli Daniel and Mr. Pavel Litvinov dared to enter Moscow's Red Square and raise their voices against the action of their government. They must have known what would happen. Did they fail? They were arrested and sentenced to prison—she for four years and he for five. Did they fail? No! They had calculated the immediate result. They later said that they knew it would mean personal suffering, but they also knew they could not take the silent route of security.

American involvement in Viet Nam, while different in many respects from the Russian intervention in Czechoslovakia, was bound sooner or later to bring about a protest from the American people not unlike that of those two lonely, quickly hushed up Russians in Moscow's Red Square. Beginning with the youth of America—who are in many respects the nation's new moral conscience crying for a return to man's true sense of humanity—the war protests moved into a new dimension with the first nationwide moratorium on October 15, 1969. This new dimension brings the American frustration with Viet Nam into open and full expression, flushing from the security of silence a cross section of the nation's citizens, including students and housewives, hippie types and highly regarded leaders of the Establishment—men and women in respected religious, business, and government positions throughout the nation.

This war, the longest and costliest in our history, yet still not officially declared by the Congress of the nation, inevitably ran its course with the nation's tolerance and support. Morally unjustifiable, militarily impossible, and politically insoluble, the American involvement in Viet Nam has soured on the nation's stomach. The consensus of the nation, that it is time to extricate itself from this fiasco—consensus shared by the White House and most of the national Congress—was both strengthened and shattered by the moratorium. The shattering came not at the level of whether the country should, indeed, conclude the war; but at the level of how it shall be done, and how soon it can be accomplished. It is the frustration and divided opinion that comes of complex solutions and unclear alternatives confronting us in Viet Nam, as discussed earlier in this chapter.

What a tragedy if out of this frustration, this agonizing reexamination of our Viet Nam involvement, we fail to also reexamine our present national policy and our future role as peacemaker in the modern world. With biting humor, someone has said, "We have the 'hawks' who sanction war; the 'doves' who cry for peace; and the 'ostriches' who don't take sides. But one thing is certain, if there is an all-out nuclear war we are all 'dead pigeons'."

America is not to be blamed—any more than her enemies—for *creating* the conflicts and tensions that have led to the Viet Nam involvement. She is to be blamed, however, for a blindness of motive and method in her otherwise noble efforts to bring about peace. She is truly the world's best hope, and for the last twenty-five years she has expended great effort in the cause of world peace. But what has happened? "We looked for peace, but no good came, for a time of healing, but behold, terror." (Jeremiah 8:15).

It should be apparent to us, particularly those of us who are Christian, that there is something wrong with our methods—that, although our intentions have been good, the results have been poor. The one hopeful thing for America, and for the world, is that the United States will see the futility of its present policies and procedures, the helplessness of its wealth and its might, the apparent hypocrisy to the rest of the world of American generosity and goodwill, so long as she backs it all with force of arms. America has fallen into the trap of which Friedrich Nietzsche, of all people, once warned, when he said something about those people who fight monsters to be careful lest they become monsters themselves.

The only hope for mankind lies in the possibility that this nation will assume the risk of joining the kids of this country in crying, "Who will answer?" or an ancient king of Judah in asking, "Is there any word from the Lord?" The hope is also that we will now accept and respond to that Word, in a way and with a daring that no nation has heretofore been willing to. The words of Jesus, spoken to the people of Jerusalem at the outset of His final visit to that city, come now to modern man, and particularly to America, with moral force and urgent relevance. Luke reports that when Jesus ". . . came still nearer to the city, he caught sight of it and wept over it, saying: 'Ah, if you only knew, even at this eleventh hour, on what your peace depends—but you cannot see it' " (Luke 19:41,42 PHILLIPS).

PATTERNS FOR PEACE

We are certainly in the eleventh hour. "We looked for peace, but no good came, for a time of healing, but behold, terror." "Is there any word from the Lord?"

> Is our hope in walnut shells worn
> Round the neck with temple bells?
> Or deep within some cloistered walls
> Where hooded figures pray in halls?
> Or in old books on dusty shelves?
> Or in our stars? Or in ourselves?
> Who will answer?

The answer is in none of those questions raised by the song, but there is an answer. Perhaps we will not see it, even in the eleventh hour. But, from the New Testament, from history, and from our present dilemma, certain *patterns for peace* emerge. These patterns are radical and bold. They have implications far beyond the scope of this writing. In their simplest form, however, these *patterns for peace* can be distilled to three basic changes in our national approach to world leadership.

Perhaps the most primary of these patterns has to do with fear and faith. We can never become peacemakers until we become willing to trust what Jesus taught, until we begin to *replace fear with faith.*

What a devastating role fear has played in the history of warfare. How much it has had to do with getting us into our present predicament. Protracted fear has infiltrated every level of our society to do great damage to the American people and their government. Indeed, since the close of World War II, we have worked ourselves into a paranoiac fear of Communism. This fear has damaged our ability to trust each other, particularly our leadership at the highest levels of church and government. A decade and a half ago, this fear issued into a witch hunt in government that, left alone, would have finally destroyed us. The legacy of that era remains with us in certain extremist organizations, dedicated to the spread of fear and distrust as a matter of patriotic duty. The average man has been affected to the point of being afraid to even breathe out of conformity lest someone charge him with being a part of some strange, invisible but ubiquitous, "Communist conspiracy."

The true story of the Southern California high-school senior who was assigned to write a paper on Russia, could, without significant change of detail, be repeated a thousand times. She reportedly wrote to the Russian Embassy, requesting materials; but she wrote under an assumed name, lest someone link her with the enemy.

Robert Frost once said: "There is nothing I am afraid of like scared people." Our fear as a nation has led us to a world posture that has made America a source of fright to all but our closest friends (an ever smaller club) among the nations of the world. Fear has shaped much of our international policy and led us to military involvement around the world. We have justified the investment of billions of dollars and thousands of lives, dedicated to the containment of Communism. Fear has prompted some talk of a so-called preventive war. Fear has led us to a full-scale war of military intervention in Viet Nam, which, however much we may deny it or justify it, isn't too different from the role of the Russians in Czechoslovakia.

Because of fear, we have circled the Communist world with missile sites, yet we wonder why Russia attempted to place missiles in Cuba. Maybe she is afraid of us. Fear has divided the world into armed camps. Little wonder that we can't talk to each other. When we sit down together, we're like armed men with pistols drawn, cocked, and aimed at each others' heads, ready to pull the trigger upon the slightest false move; yet we know that there is no security in pulling the trigger first, for the uncontrollable, reflex action of the other fellow will also cause him to pull a trigger, and we are both dead.

The answer to this *fear* is *faith*—faith that we can put away our pistols, get rid of our bombs and missiles, and begin to act civilized. But for the average American, and, indeed, for the average churchman, such talk is judged to be highly irresponsible. And we wonder why the youth of this country are not looking to the church for the answers. Certainly, if we who say we are Christians are afraid to be Christian—afraid to trust that Jesus was right in what he taught—then there is absolutely no hope whatsoever that this country, or any other, will assume a Christian posture in the search for world peace.

We are in the eleventh hour, and we need something we don't have. As one leading atomic scientist expressed it, "We need a miracle." Then he added, "Maybe God will work a miracle, if we don't make it too hard for Him." One is reminded of a word found in Mark's Gospel. Describing the failure of Jesus in a certain place, the evangelist wrote, "And he could do no mighty work there, . . . because of their unbelief" (Mark 6:5,6).

If we are not willing to believe in, and to risk ourselves with, the teachings of the New Testament, then we will remain right where we are in the world—if we are lucky! Indeed, if we do not have this kind of daring faith, then the additional *patterns for peace,* which I am about to propose, are ridiculous in the extreme.

The second proposal is that we dare to replace narrow nationalism with world brotherhood. And what do we mean by narrow nationalism? Suppose we allow Mussolini, the Italian Fascist dictator of World War II, to define it for us: "The state!" said Mussolini. "Nothing beyond, nothing above the state."

Or, let Stephen Decatur, an American naval officer of a hundred and fifty years ago, define it for us. At a dinner meeting in Norfolk, Virginia, in April, 1816, Decatur proposed the following toast: "Our country! In her intercourse with foreign nations may she always be in the right, but our country, right or wrong."

Unfortunately, this kind of blind allegiance has become so confused with patriotism that anyone calling for an end of war, in the interest of humanity, is immediately suspect of being unpatriotic. If one is unpatriotic when he places the interest of humanity above that of country, then where does this place God? Certainly His one supreme and overriding interest is humanity. So, where do we place Him? Perhaps where Mussolini placed Him? "The state! Nothing beyond, nothing above the state"—not humanity, not even God!

Sometime ago a leading British statesman remarked: "Every succeeding scientific discovery makes greater nonsense of old time concepts of sovereignty. . . . I have been unable to see any final solution that will make the world safe from atomic power unless we all abate our present ideas of sovereignty. We have got somehow to take the sting out of nationalism."

Certainly the world is not going to believe in brotherhood until we who call ourselves Christians believe in it, in the sense that Jesus came to reveal it. If we do believe in that brotherhood, then on the basis of that belief we must move on to at least one more essential change. We must replace *force* with *love.*

But who is willing to listen to such dreamy-eyed talk? Not the men in the Pentagon, anymore than their counterparts in the Kremlin; not the people who serve on the Armed Services Committee of our national Congress; not the heads of the American armaments industry; not the members of our nation's veterans' organizations; sadly, not even the members of our churches—and thus the question turns from *who will answer?* to *who will listen?*

As a nation—indeed, as a people—we have come to believe in the unquestionable necessity of negotiating from strength—strength, in this case, meaning more of the wherewithal to kill the enemy than he has with which to kill us. Before leaving office as our nation's Secretary of Defense, Robert McNamara reminded us of the irrationality of this kind of national policy: "A full-scale nuclear exchange between the United States and the Soviet Union, lasting less than one hour," according to the former Secretary, "would kill almost 100 million Americans—the equivalent of over 300 World War II's. There would be little comfort," he added, "in knowing that over 100 million Russians would also be killed."

And what is the alternative? None! That is, unless we are willing to exchange *fear* for *faith,* and *narrow nationalism* for *world brotherhood.* If we aren't willing to make that exchange, then we had better stick by our guns, and hope that no one gets edgy at the trigger, grim as that prospect may be. But if in the first instance, we are willing, then love is the alternative. Admittedly, at the moment we're in pretty short supply of love around the world—and, come to think of it, we're not oversupplied at home.

"But," we are proned to reason, "if the world just understood us. . . ." Maybe the world does. That could be a part of the problem. Perhaps the world sees America as Paris must have seen Adolf Hitler when he overran that city during a triumphant moment for him early in World War II. With gusty emotion Hitler looked across Paris and exclaimed: "Great city! I have conquered her by force; I will now conquer her by love." But, of course, he never did. For, as someone has said, to overwhelm a people with arms does not bring them to your arms. It never has and it never will.

It isn't strange for Christians to talk about love as the alternative for force—after all, we have talked about such things for a long, long time. But it would be powerfully strange if we Christians ever became Christian in the full sense of love. The uncommitted millions of the world—and thousands in America—would be overwhelmed by such a sight. They might even take our Christianity seriously—if we did!

One such uncommitted person (at least he never consented to being called a Christian) was the late Mohandas Gandhi of India. Interestingly, Gandhi once replied to Stanley Jones, who had asked him the best way to sell the Indian people on the Christian faith, by saying: "I would suggest, first, that all of you Christians must begin to live more like Jesus Christ. Second, I would suggest that you must practice your religion without adulterating or toning it down. Third, I would suggest that you must put your emphasis upon love, for love is the center and soul of Christianity."

"Is there any word from the Lord?"

"Who will answer?"

"We looked for peace, but no good came, for a time of healing, but behold, terror."

"And as he came still nearer to the city, he caught sight of it and wept over it, saying: 'Ah, if you only knew, even at this eleventh hour, on what your peace depends—but you cannot see it'."

Must it always be so? Perhaps we don't have *always,* or, at least, not in the euphoric sense that we have been inclined to believe it. *Who will answer?* There is the more important question— *Who will listen?* The answer has been available for a long time. Are we willing to listen?

9
The Gathering Storm

Then all the commanders of the forces, and Johanan the son of Kareah and Azariah the son of Hoshaiah, and all the people from the least to the greatest, came near and said to Jeremiah the prophet, "Let our supplication come before you, and pray to the Lord your God for us, for all this remnant (for we are left but a few of many, as your eyes see us), that the Lord your God may show us the way we should go, and the thing that we should do." Jeremiah the prophet said to them, "I have heard you; behold, I will pray to the Lord your God according to your request, and whatever the Lord answers you I will tell you; I will keep nothing back from you." Then they said to Jeremiah, "May the Lord be a true and faithful witness against us if we do not act according to all the word with which the Lord your God sends you to us. Whether it is good or evil, we will obey the voice of the Lord our God to whom we are sending you, that it may be well with us when we obey the voice of the Lord our God." At the end of ten days the word of the Lord came to Jeremiah. Then he summoned Johanan the son of Kareah and all the commanders of the forces who were with him, and all the people from the least to the greatest, and said to them. "Thus says the Lord, the God of Israel, to whom you sent me to present your supplication before him: If you will remain in this land, then I will build you up and not pull you down; I will plant you, and not pluck you up, for I repent of the evil which I did to you. Do not fear the king of Babylon, of whom you are afraid; do not fear him, says the Lord, for I am with you, to save you and to deliver you from his hand. I will grant you mercy, that he may have mercy on you and let you remain in your own land. But if you say, 'We will not remain in this land,' disobeying the voice of the Lord your God and saying, 'No, we will go to the land of Egypt, where we shall not see war, or hear the sound of the trumpet, or be hungry for bread, and we will dwell there,' then hear the word of the Lord, O remnant of Judah. Thus says the Lord of hosts, the God of Israel: If you set your faces to enter Egypt and go to live there, then the sword which you fear shall overtake you there in the land of Egypt; and the famine of which you are afraid shall follow hard after you to Egypt; and there you shall die. All the men who set their faces to go to Egypt to live there shall die by the sword, by famine, and by pestilence; they shall have no remnant or survivor from the evil which I will bring upon them Jeremiah 42:1–17.

Worldwide, Protestant and Catholic, the church confronts a gathering storm in what has been termed a crisis of authority. Who is in charge? Who speaks for the church? How much shall the church address itself to the social problems and political issues of our time? Is there a common ground within the church for liberal and conservative, preacher and layman; or must there be increasing polarization and ultimate fragmentation of the Body of Christ? These are some of the cleavages which cloud the future and portend a growing crisis for the church.

In many local churches the storm has already struck with shattering effect. A few of these churches have been able to ride it out and emerge with a measure of purification, renewal, and resilience—by-products of confrontation and conflict, handled creatively. The exposure of these congregations to the crisis has, happily, issued into their becoming stronger, morc effective communities of faith and witness.

In June of 1966, I accepted the challenge of becoming the senior minister of one such church. I came to Jackson, Mississippi's Galloway Memorial United Methodist Church in the wake of its upheaval. For three years, prior to my coming, the congregation and my able predecessor had been riding the wind which had struck them with hurricane force in the early summer of 1963.

For more than a hundred years this great church had stood in the shadow of the state capitol and in the heart of Mississippi's leading city. The church had enjoyed the prestige of being the state's largest, wealthiest Methodist congregation. Like every other white Protestant Church in the state, however, segregation was the unchallenged rule of membership and attendance. It *was*—until that Sunday morning in the summer of 1963, when the congregation became the strategic target for a civil rights test.

The test was calculated to prove the already popular charge, "Eleven o'clock Sunday morning is the most segregated hour of the week." The stage was set in advance—with reporters and television cameras—so that the entire nation could witness the proof of the charge. The would-be visitors to the service, black and white, arrived on schedule, and, as they had anticipated, were turned away. That morning the beloved senior minister, who had served the congregation for more than seventeen years, resigned his pulpit with a broken heart.

The crisis precipitated that Sunday morning was the beginning of long months of conflict and tension, soul searching and frustration, redefinition of policy and fragmentation of unity. Three years later the Official Board at Galloway declared their church to be open to all people, regardless of color. The decision, born of great agony, was to cost the church several hundred members who promptly organized an independent congregation, free of denominational policies and committed to segregation as the *will* of God. Others departed for more suitable climes, within and without the denomination.

The Galloway congregation has made a start in purging itself of a situation that would have ultimately destroyed it. The more than two thousand members who remain are a lovely people; many of them have won a new understanding of the church; some of them have simply become tolerant toward the unavoidable circumstances of the situation. There is still that tension which sometimes threatens the remaining unity, but it is a healthy tension and progress is being made toward a growing posture of openness and servanthood. The dramatic and cataclysmic experience of this congregation is not typical to be sure, but the underlying causes of its experience are present in most congregations throughout the nation.

In a recent book entitled *The Gathering Storm in the Churches,* Jefferey K. Hadden, a sociologist, describes the larger crisis confronting Protestantism across the country. The opening sentence of the book expresses the seriousness with which its author assesses the situation: "The Christian churches today are in the midst of a struggle which has every evidence of being the most serious ferment in Christendom since the Protestant Reformation." The book describes the present crisis in terms of a widening gap between clergy and laymen and points to the growing acuteness of the gathering storm.

THE DEEPER CRISIS

There can be little question that such a gap exists between the clergy and laity, particularly in the major denominations of American Protestantism. The following statement from a pamphlet published and distributed by a Phoenix, Arizona, laymen's committee, is directed to the clergy when it says:

> We accept you as a specialist and authority in spiritual matters. However, we do not consider you as more wise, more informed, more adequately schooled in political and governmental affairs than we. We will study matters in these fields, prayerfully make our decisions, and then go forth as CHRISTIAN Americans to chart the course of our country. We feel that since we pay the salary of our clergy, build our churches and finance her general and missionary undertakings, that we should have just a little bit to say about what the clergy says in our name. We want you to so minister as to command our respect . . . as true disciples of Jesus Christ.

The widening gap between the people in the ranks and the professional leadership is a serious threat to the harmony and effectiveness of the church. If, however, this area of conflict is to be dealt with in a constructive way, avoiding the ultimate disaster it may otherwise bring, responsible clergy and laity must understand the deeper crisis out of which the strained relationship arises. On its surface the problem appears to be tied to the civil rights issue, which, since the Supreme Court ruling of 1954, has caused conflict and controversy throughout the country. But the real crisis in the church is at greater depth, and civil rights has merely served as the catalyst. The present crisis has roots in the basic theology of the purpose of the church and the inclusiveness of religious concern. In this sense the present problem predates the Supreme Court ruling and the whole issue of civil rights.

In its essence the gathering storm is a crisis of authority and is as old as religion itself. Across the centuries this crisis has taken many forms. Early in this century it came to a head in the Social Gospel movement and the attendant Fundamentalist-Modernist controversy in the church. Four-hundred-fifty years ago the crisis surfaced in the form of the Protestant Reformation. The story of Adam and Eve is the story of a crisis in authority. In one form or another, throughout the Old and New Testaments and at many points in the subsequent history of the church, this crisis of authority has been a problem for the faithful.

It is, therefore, no strange or alien story reported in the forty-second and forty-third chapters of Jeremiah. In Mizpah, the provisional capital of Judah after her fall to Babylon, a group of Jews, threatened with reprisals after a recent uprising, had decided to flee into Egypt. Before going, however, they went to Jeremiah, ostensibly to find out God's will in the matter—should they go as planned, or should they remain in Mizpah? They prefaced their inquiry with the pledge, "Whether it is good or evil, we will obey the voice of the Lord our God" (42:6).

With a responsible attitude toward the authority thus accorded him, the prophet asked for ten days, after which he announced to his inquirers that God wished them to remain in Mizpah. That did it! Their alleged willingness to obey the decision was quickly put aside. They had made up their minds already as to what they should do. They merely wanted God's blessing upon it, not His will in the matter. Incensed, they denounced Jeremiah, accusing him of merely consulting with his secretary, Baruch, and fabricating the whole report as coming from God. They were sure his recommendation that they remain in Mizpah was a plot to deliver them "into the hand of the Chaldeans." So they did what they had planned to do from the beginning—they went to Egypt. Interestingly, they forced Jeremiah and his secretary to accompany them into Egypt, perhaps under the assumption that if the prophet went along it would insure divine approval (a myth that is slow in dying).

The modern parallel of this incident may be found in many of our churches. *Thus saith the Lord* usually loses its forcefulness unless it fits our preconceptions of what the Word is to herald. Recently a minister of my acquaintance was visited by a parishioner who took exception to his sermon the previous Sunday. This in itself is not bad, but the manner in which it is done is important. The visitor accused the minister of dealing with some controversial issues, not because they merited speaking to, but because the minister, in the critic's opinion, wished to be sensational. The preacher was charged with trying to impress a distinguished visitor in the congregation on that particular Sunday—"You are telling a lie . . . Baruch . . . has set you against us. . . ." Such preaching will tear the church apart, said the visitor—"Baruch . . . has set you against us, to deliver us into the hand of the Chaldeans. . . ."

Sometimes influential individuals or groups within a congregation will contrive, in one way or another, to confirm their position by taking the prophet with them into Egypt. When a Columbus, Georgia, pastor was forced to leave his pulpit for speaking to the race issue, back in the 1950's, one of his former parishioners was quoted as saying, "Now we can get a preacher with the right sort of religion." This classic utterance reminds us that modern authority in religion is often questioned, unless it conforms to majority opinion.

THE WIDENING GAP

Majority opinion is, of course, a cherished rule of Protestantism and is to be protected. Majority rule is implicit in the whole concept of the priesthood of believers and is, therefore, basic to the Protestant faith. The principle becomes a dilemma, however, when coupled with another corollary belief—that the church is a voluntary association. This combination, basic as it is, makes Protestantism particularly vulnerable to the authority crisis. The very existence of some two-hundred denominations and sect groups within American Protestantism underscores the acuteness of this problem.

The churches most crucially affected by the present crisis are not the small sects or splinter denominations, however. It is, rather, the mainline, old, established denominations that are most crucially experiencing the widening gap between laymen and laymen—but, more consequentially, between laymen and clergy. Most of these denominations have within their memberships a wide disparity of education and sophistication and, more significantly, a highly trained clergy with seminary degrees. The resulting disparity of theological understanding of the nature and mission of the church is loaded with potential disaster.

The result is often polarization within the local body—a destructive deterioration involving conflict and shattering the religious community. The layman who does not agree with the broader mission of the church—its pronouncements and involvements in the social problems of our time—has several options open to him. He may adopt an attitude of tolerance or he may rigidly refuse to go along. Since he is usually in the majority at the local level, he can wield a powerful influence by boycotting the worship services or by canceling his pledge (both are effective ways of "getting at" the preacher). If these choices do not relieve his frustration sufficiently, he has the additional option of dropping out altogether, or of affiliating with a more compatible church.

The danger of polarization is present, however, only when a local church also has a proportionate number of laymen whose views demand that they contend for the larger mission of the church. There is a growing number of these laymen, whom Harvey Cox calls the New Breed, who insist that the church has a larger role than saving souls or dispensing balm to those within its four cozy walls. Because of their minority in most churches, however, they are often even more frustrated than the larger, so-called conservative group. The options open to this so-called liberal or progressive group are the same, though usually less viable, as those available to the other grouping.

These conditions for polarization are present in many of our churches today. At best, there is tension which can be creatively channeled. At worst, there is a polarization which can fragment the community and negate the essential nature of the church at its grass roots level. This internal conflict, therefore, often frustrates the mission of the church to the world in which it is set —a world that is today faced with unique problems and profound issues. The potential disaster of our failure to address the gospel to such a world has serious implications for the world and for the church. To summarize: the church is in crisis, and that crisis has its roots in the authority of theological understanding of *mission.*

THE MINISTRY

In such times, the minister finds himself in a role that is less than enviable. Often he finds that he must bear the burden of distrust and antagonism—*the widening gap*—regardless of his position. Certainly the issues are live and demanding. They will not go away. The minister must deal with the issues in one way or another. If he fails to speak to the issues, whether out of fear or theological conviction, he will be judged by many as irrelevant. George Buttrick, speaking at Yale University several years ago, said of such a preacher, "To many he is a pathetic figure, an anachronism, . . . wearing the expression of a scared rabbit." On the other hand, if, out of profound theological conviction, the preacher addresses his ministry to the issues of the day, he will be accused by many of sensationalism, apostasy, and radicalism.

The result is a loss of prestige for the profession, a loss which seriously erodes ministerial morale and crucially accentuates the growing shortage of clergy at the parish level. In 1967, a Lou Harris Poll showed the prestige of the clergy at an all-time low. Only 45 percent of the American public expressed confidence in the profession; whereas 74 percent voted confidence for physicians and 62 percent for educators. Politicians who have never enjoyed universal trust, ranked only one percentage point below the clergy. Little wonder that thousands of ministers leave the parish ministry each year for behind-the-lines positions, and hundreds of others opt out altogether. One major seminary recently reported that only 5 percent of its theological students plan to enter the parish ministry.

THE CHARACTER OF CRISIS

The great question is, What shall we do with the crisis presently confronting the church? The negative overtones of the word *crisis* may suggest a fatal attitude of defeatism. We may polarize, or drop out, or mark time while the gathering storm mounts to overwhelm us—or we may invest ourselves in the positive dimension of crisis. The dictionary defines the word as "the point in time when it is decided whether an affair or course of action must go on, or be modified or terminated—a decisive moment—a turning point."

Exactly so, and thus understood, crisis has characterized every great moment in the life and history of the church. The present crisis is also not peculiar to the church. Ours is a crisis-ridden era in which most of the basic institutions of society—government, law and order, education, economics, et cetera—are in the throes of crisis. The fact that the church shares this crisis is some indication that she is a dynamic, living organism, sensitive to the world in which she is set and responsive to the Spirit of God within her life. The church has the task of ministering to a new world—with new issues and problems, many of which have been thrust upon us with a rapidity unparalleled in history. The church can hardly minister to a world in crisis and at the same time be free of that crisis herself. In such times as these, a static, undisturbed church, tranquil and free of tension, has the mark of death upon it.

There have been few times in history when it has been more frustrating and tormenting to be a part of the church. On the other hand, there have been few times when the stakes were so high, or when there has been so much excitement and promise. We could lose! But we might also win—and just think what we win, if we win!

The challenge is ours, and the task belongs to the ministry and the laity together. We must close the gap, not by pitting position against position, or group against group, but in an openness to each other and in a transcending commitment to Christ. We must listen to the voice of God, even in our seeming contradictions. God does not say the same thing to each of us, but He seeks to reveal truth and love through all of us. There must be room in the church, and in our own tolerance, for varying points of view—for ministry to people where they are, within the church and without.

The minister must be willing to involve himself in reconciliation, without either feeling sorry for himself or adopting a martyr complex. He must learn, in such times as these, to carry conflict within his own soul. As he speaks the truth in love, he will more and more understand why Jeremiah took ten days to give his answer to the men of Mizpah. It isn't easy to take a position which is at odds with many whom one has come to love and whose approbation one would like. The minister must avoid any compromise of his understanding of the gospel as it is committed to the church—compromise that would carry him into some Egyptian exile of ineffectiveness, the compromise of getting along by going along. And yet, he must be understanding of those who dissent. He must find some place of integrity that will permit him to minister to those who are in Egypt, who are disaffected and adamant, who have refused to hear the Word or respond to the will of God for His church in these days. His aim, however, must not be to join them or affirm them in their Egypts, but to lead them out with love and patience.

There must also be a recovery of the excitement of preaching. Some are saying that preaching has had its day. I can no more agree with this pronouncement than I can agree with those who opt out of the church altogether. Only sterile preaching—preaching as entertainment, as moralizing character guidance, as irrelevant otherworldly spiritualizing—has had its day. Preaching that is humbled by the magnitude of its task and forced to agonize with the Word, as it struggles for fresh incarnation—such preaching has never been more possible nor more needed. Such preaching, like the life it seeks to evoke in its hearers, transcends both the preacher and his auditors. It is Biblical preaching—not shallow humanism—not narrow literalism—but truth, mirrored in the history of Israel and clothed in the wonder and mystery of the God-man, Jesus Christ. This kind of preaching is possible, and its promise for the church in these days excites those who have tasted its refreshing renewal, whether in the pulpit or the pew.

Together, minister and layman, must hear the *Word of God* as Jeremiah delivered it in Mizpah. The men of Mizpah were like many of us; they wanted to evade the hardships which the situation imposed and to run away into Egypt. We, too, can withdraw, but God's Word is still the call to remain in Mizpah—where there is frustration, disappointment, and danger.

Robert Frost once described his lifework as engagement in "a lover's quarrel with the world." Let us engage in this kind of quarrel—remembering that lovers' quarrels come out of common concerns and issue into greater unity. Lovers' quarrels seek to build instead of destroy. They are conducted in loyalty and are always aimed at reconciliation.

What a time to engage in such a quarrel! What an hour to remain in Mizpah and be God's people, His church! An unknown author has said what many of us feel as we look at the present crisis and decide where we shall invest our lives:

> Rejoice, whatever anguish rend your heart,
> That God has given you for a priceless dower
> To live in these great times and have your part
> In freedom's crowning hour.
>
> AUTHOR UNKNOWN

10
The Church Among the Dunes

In those days and in that time, says the Lord, the people of Israel and the people of Judah shall come together, weeping as they come; and they shall seek the Lord their God. They shall ask the way to Zion, with faces turned toward it, saying, "Come, let us join ourselves to the Lord in an everlasting covenant which will never be forgotten." My people have been lost sheep; their shepherds have led them astray, turning them away on the mountains; from mountain to hill they have gone, they have forgotten their fold. All who found them have devoured them, and their enemies have said, "We are not guilty, for they have sinned against the Lord, their true habitation, the Lord, the hope of their fathers" Jeremiah 50:4–7.

Arnold Toynbee, in his book *A Study of History,* writes of those living civilizations of history that have already broken down or are well along in the process. He reminds his readers that our Western civilization might well go the way of the rest unless some new creative factor is brought into play. In the hope that the Western world may make positive response to the modern situation, Toynbee says, "We ... are not compelled to submit the riddle of our fate to the blind arbitrament of statistics. The divine spark of creative power is still alive in us, and, if we have the grace to kindle it into flame, then the stars in their courses cannot defeat our efforts to attain the goal of human endeavor."

If that divine spark is to be kindled, the church must be the agent through which it is done, but there is no guarantee that she will rise to the occasion or meet the challenge. Many people have despaired of the possibility. Some are already speaking of our time as the post-Christian era.

We have discussed the crucial nature of some of the problems and issues which currently confront the church. In most cases, we have discovered that these problems and issues, though accentuated by the times in which we live and sometimes appearing in forms peculiar to our day, are not really new. Similar problems and issues confronted the people of God in Jeremiah's period of history, with all of the potential for *weal or woe* which presently inheres in our situation. Now, as then, the outcome depends upon the *faith-response* of prophet and people of God in a turbulent and troubled world.

"THE CHURCH AMONG THE DUNES"

"It is history that teaches us to hope." And from recent history comes an incident which accents the hope that the divine spark kindled in the faith of ancient Israel and Judah may still be alive in the human spirit. The time is early in World War II. The setting is a quaint little seaport not far from the Belgian border on the northern coast of France. There is significance even in its name, for it is called Dunkirk, which literally means *the church among the dunes.* For thousands of allied veterans, their families, and their nations, Dunkirk will always mean courage and heroism in the face of overwhelming odds.

The harbor of Dunkirk is separated from the town by wide,

sandy beaches and low bridges. In the Spring of 1940, the Belgian Army surrendered to the Germans, leaving the British and other Allied troops exposed to the full threat of the German effort to push them into the sea. The Allies withdrew to the beaches of Dunkirk, and the free world held its breath as the Germans surrounded our forces on three sides, and ships of the German fleet took up positions in the English Channel. It appeared that Dunkirk would be the last crucial stand of the Allies. The ensuing rescue of those trapped forces is an epic in strategy and courage. A fleet of almost 1,000 vessels took part. While the troops on the beach valiantly held the land approaches against the attacking Germans, cruisers, destroyers, minesweepers, gunboats, yachts, and even rowboats rescued 350,000 Allies and ferried them to the safety of the English coast.

The British people can be especially proud of their conduct in the outcome of this decisive confrontation of the war. Although it was a retreat, the determination and valor of our English allies represents a high-water mark in their history. When the war was over, Winston Churchill examined that history, matched Dunkirk with all their other proud accomplishments, and called it their *finest hour.*

Who would have ventured any hope for the future of Israel when Jeremiah concluded his book? The people of God were in captivity to Babylon—they were at Dunkirk with their backs to the sea. It could have been their grand finale, the end of the last act in a matchless drama. Who would have believed in the possibility of their survival? Only God and Jeremiah! In his valedictory, the prophet called upon the people of God to make it their *finest hour.* He spoke hopefully of their meeting the situation and of a time when they should say to each other, "Come, let us join ourselves to the Lord in an everlasting covenant which shall never be forgotten."

As we examine our present situation in the church, the analogy of Dunkirk is not strained. The church today is not threatened by physical captivity. No one is about to send it into exile or place its people behind bars. It is the victim, rather, of a more subtle captivity—captivity to the culture in which it finds itself. No one is presently threatening to push the church into some sea of oblivion. To our shame, it faces the greater threat of simply being ignored into oblivion—of seeking its own safety, and therein giving the kind of witness that is free of peril, but which, on the other hand, challenges no one to come with it in the cause of Christ.

Incredibly, in these demanding times when our faith ought to involve us daringly in God's efforts to set the world right, we have often continued to define an expound the gospel in terms which betray our own poor understanding of that gospel and insure its lack of appeal for many people. One local church reportedly posted this notice on its outside bulletin board: IF YOU'RE TIRED OF SIN, COME WITH US. A few days later it was discovered that some enterprising worldling with a lipstick had written this notice underneath that of the church: IF YOU AREN'T, CALL————!

A sidewalk comic with a lipstick thus upstaged the church and underscored how bland, cautious, unimaginative, and unattractive it can be in its appeal to the age in which we live. This evaluation isn't meant to suggest that the church should adopt the worldling's approach or appeal—we've been guilty of that, too—but that the church rediscover and winsomely and daringly proclaim the New Testament faith, which Dorothy Sayers calls "the most exciting drama that has ever staggered the imagination of man. We may call it relevation or we may call it rubbish," she says, "but if we call it dull, then words have no meaning at all."

THE PARADOX OF APPEAL

For both Jeremiah and Jesus, faith was a call to live on the cutting edge, to surrender self to the cause of their faith and be willing to risk all in the advancement of that cause. It was this kind of adventuresome, daring, and demanding proposition that appealed to the action people of their day.

Man is a paradoxical creature. Give him no perils to face, no hurdles to clear, and he becomes what Bertrand Russell cynically described as "a curious accident in a backwater." On the other hand, place him under stress, demand the impossible of him, and he becomes the embodiment of Robert Louis Stevenson's noble description: "To touch the heart of his mystery, we find in him one thought, strange to the point of lunacy: the thought of duty; the thought of something owing to himself, to his neighbor, to his God; an ideal of decency, to which he would rise if it were possible; a limit of shame, below which, if it were possible, he will not stoop."

A hundred years ago Giuseppe Garibaldi, knight errant of Italian unity, had experienced his third defeat and appeared to be a finished failure. Three times he had sought to liberate his beloved Italy. Three times he had failed and twice he had been forced to flee the country. Then, in 1860, Garibaldi, with a voluntary force which he proudly called his "Thousand Red Shirts," set forth for Sicily and from there to the mainland, conquering as he went. Volunteers poured forth from every town and village to join his cause. The red shirt of his volunteers became the proudest badge a man could possess. After repeated failures, Garibaldi's success was his appeal to the noble and heroic in Italian manhood. He addressed his followers in these terms: "Soldiers, what I have to offer you is fatigue, danger, struggle, and death; the chill of the cold night in the free air, heat under the burning sun; no lodgings, no munitions, no provisions, but forced marches, dangerous watch posts.... Those who love freedom and their country may follow me." And they did —by the thousands!

FAITH AT ITS FINEST

This same paradox characterizes the appeal of and response to the gospel. The New Testament is a call to find life by losing it. "Foxes have holes, and birds of the air have nests; but the Son of man has nowhere to lay his head" (Matthew 8:20). "If any man would come after me, let him deny himself and take up his cross and follow me" (Matthew 16:24). "Blessed are you when men revile you and persecute you and utter all kinds of evil against you falsely on my account. Rejoice and be glad . . ." (Matthew 5:11,12).

I wonder if the greatest peril to our faith is not our tendency to protect it and make it safe by accommodating it to the cultural and social context of our time, while we reduce the gospel to the vague and tired banalities of "heaven, home, and happiness." Many years ago E. Stanley Jones raised the question, "What are we doing?" He replied to his question: "As someone has suggested, we are inoculating the world with a mild form of Christianity, so that it is now practically immune to the real thing."

The church must return to the fundamentals of its faith and life—fundamentals which are admittedly somewhat confused and very much frustrated at this juncture. In its past eagerness to protect the faith by accommodating it to the prevailing culture, the church, over several generations, has gradually evolved into a condition of amnesia. We no longer know who we are. And our confused identity is increasingly frustrating and intolerable as we become more and more entangled in the web of a vast complication of conflicting interests, outdated institutions, dehumanizing value systems, and obsolete approaches—all of which are a part of the character of modern civilization. I believe that the time is coming, however, when the very frustration and intolerance of this entanglement will throw us back on the basic truths of the gospel and restore our sense of identity.

Moreover, I believe that the church must assume a primary role in this restoration of identity and that it is now urgently incumbent upon us that we recover the "everlasting covenant which shall never be forgotten"—that we break-out of our spiritual amnesia. The historical importance of covenant identity to the people of Israel is illustrated by modern Jerusalem's Yad Vashem, a memorial to the millions of Jews who were exterminated by the Nazis during the 1930s and 1940s. At an exhibition held in Jerusalem in 1966, the following quotation from the Baal Shem-Tov, Jewish sage, was written over the entrance way: "Forgetfulness prolongs the exile; remembrance is the secret of redemption."

Remembrance as the secret of redemption for the modern church is fundamentally a matter of what we believe. But to so assert it is to run the risk of oversimplification; for, to be sure, a great deal more is demanded of the Christian than mere assent to a creed. Genuine discipleship roots in belief—not simply as a matter of intellectual consent, but as a matter of commitment to an ideal, dedication to a purpose, and, most of all, surrender to a Person.

Simon Peter's confession of faith summarizes the simple yet profound base upon which the church stands and from which genuine Christian discipleship emanates. The confession, "You are the Christ, the Son of the living God" (Matthew 16:16), became the consummate faith, which not only claimed Peter but also determined the character and life of the infant church. It is in this sense that it represents the fundamental faith to which we must return in our time. To believe that Jesus was the Christ; to believe that God is uniquely revealed in that Christ; to believe that He lived and died for us; to believe that His Spirit survived the ordeal of that death to become a living, redeeming force in history; to believe that the church is the Body through which His Spirit is manifested in the world and that His Spirit is available to us here and now—to really believe these things is to return to the fundamentals, to find the dynamic of remembrance, to enter an everlasting covenant, which refuses to leave the future to some blind riddle of fate.

The Sacrament of the Lord's Supper, with the admonition of Jesus "... this do in remembrance of me" (Luke 22:19 KJV), has taken on heightened meaning for all who are involved in today's search for renewal of covenant. It speaks afresh of what it means to be the Body of Christ with faithfulness to Him who is the Head of the Body.

The sacrament signals anew the responsibility we must assume for the salvation of the world and the risk we must take in being His Body in such a world. It says different things in this regard to different ones of us, to be sure. But, hopefully, it will keep us mindful that our differences are a part of the genius of the gospel—that if we are to move responsibly and redemptively we must also move unitedly, with our "varieties of gifts, but the same Spirit" (1 Corinthians 12:4). There should be no cleavage between those for whom the sacrament is a call to deeper personal spiritual living and those who are called by its meaning to a greater involvement in the life of the world. This duality of appeal is not only possible and valid, it is also essential; ideally, the response of the church will be inclusive of both.

Hans-Ruedi Weber, in his little book *Salty Christians,* suggests that John Bunyan and Dietrich Bonhoeffer provide historic examples of two equally devout Christians who saw the work of the gospel in vastly different light from each other.

Bunyan, for example, in all his writings made little if any mention of the important secular events of the seventeenth century. He lived in their midst, but he had no interest in them, least of all did he see them as a concern of the gospel. In his best known work, *The Pilgrim's Progress,* Bunyan made it the clear and almost singular business of the Christian faith to rescue the individual from all worldly involvement, that he might thereby be brought into fellowship with God. Contrast this with Bonhoeffer, whose commitment to Christ resulted in an increasing involvement in secular affairs. He started out a pacifist only to become a militant participant in the underground resistance movement, including an ill-starred plot to assassinate Hitler. On the other hand, Bunyan began as a soldier and ended up a pacifist, becoming more and more religious with an emphasis on the devotional life of the gathered church.

The differences between these equally dedicated men do not render one right and the other wrong. Quite the contrary, they were both within the valid role of the gospel and the true work of the church, that of being "in the world but not of the world." A part of the task confronting us today is to reconcile the Bunyans and the Bonhoeffers of the church—who are often contemptuous of each other—fusing them into a unified and dedicated *Corpus Christi.*

Jesus is rightly understood by the Bunyans, the so-called conservatives or traditionalists, who see Him as a *man of the Spirit.* He was this indeed—a man of simple piety, a man of prayer, perfectly at home in the Scriptures and convinced that human fulfillment could come only in the pilgrimage of faith and spiritual living. But Jesus was also a *man of the world,* revealing a *worldly God,* whose love for the world caused Him to give His only Son to the world and for the world (John 3:16). In this regard, Jesus rejected many of those ecclesiastical forms and institutional hang-ups whose effect was, then as now, to grind the John-Smithness out of John Smith and reduce him to a religious robot. With this valid understanding of Him, many so-called liberal renewal groups, with an emphasis on servanthood, are finding new and exciting meaning in the Sacrament of the Lord's Supper.

Our peril is that of being only half-Christian, however, with a half-Christ, offered in a half-gospel, whether designed to meet only the moral demands of society or only the spiritual needs of the individual—as though either could be fulfilled without the other. In the past we have been more inclined to be Bunyans than Bonhoeffers, and the struggle to come into balance has produced no little agony for the modern church.

The *Black Manifesto,* presented in the Spring of 1969 by the militant James Forman and his National Black Economic Development Conference, demands that the long-established, predominantly white denominations of the United States pay an approximate 500 million dollars in reparations to the black Americans. The spirit in which the demand is made, and the demand itself, are open to debate. Indeed, many white and black churchmen, sympathetic with the conditions which evoked the *Manifesto* and conscious of the church's guilt in producing or at least condoning the system which produced those conditions, cannot go along with the Marxist rhetoric of the paper, and its threat of violent reprisals if the institutions of white capitalism—including the church—do not accept and respond to the demands. While the *Manifesto* has evoked a wide variety of response and reaction, it has had the salutary effect of bringing into focus the matter of the church's responsibility for the evils of our society, past and present. To this extent, at least, it has been good for us.

Indeed, we begin to be the Body of Christ only when we assume responsibility for the kind of world in which we live, repenting our failures and, whenever possible, making reparation. In this regard, Bonhoeffer certainly provides illumination. For example, when he examined the evils of Nazism in Germany, his prayer of confession for the church was not an irresponsible pointing of the finger. It did not charge a guilt that Bonhoeffer did not personally share. The prayer, which appears in the book *I Loved This People,* might well be our own as we American Christians seek to revitalize the church. "The church confesses," said Bonhoeffer, "that she has misused the name of Jesus Christ in that she was ashamed of Him before the world and did not oppose strongly enough the misuse of His name for evil purposes. She looked on while deeds of violence and injustice were done under cover of the name of Jesus Christ."

When we truly become responsible as a church, it may very well mean that we come to a literal acceptance of what has long been mere symbolism in the Lord's Supper, that we become the broken body, risking our security and assuming the fellowship of the cross in terms of suffering love. The risk is not only one of relationship to the world but of relationship to each other within the church, where great tensions are often created in the very effort of enlarged understanding and commitment.

We have gone through a period in which membership in the church has been at an all-time high. Unfortunately, too much of our popularity and its attendant growth of membership has been oriented to institutionalism and characterized by nominalism. Growth thus won now tends to accentuate the agony and frustrate the effort, as we endeavor to move into a posture of servanthood. Whatever the agony, however, we are going to have to come to see that membership is a poor substitute for discipleship. Dan Walker's book *Enemy in the Pew?* provides a helpful distinction in this regard: "Membership nails us down; discipleship pulls us loose. Membership draws us in; discipleship sends us out. Membership pays its dues and claims its rights; discipleship makes any sacrifice, asking nothing in return."

The modern church is reluctant to acknowledge this distinction and redefine her direction. She must, however painfully, continue to struggle with the imperative necessity of breaking out of long established institutional patterns. She must challenge and inspire her people to make faith a matter of life offered, and lead them into Christian discipleship in terms of responsible living.

The Church of the Saviour in Washington, D. C., is the outstanding example of a congregation that has gone far in the recovery of discipleship in terms of mission. Near the door of the main building is a sign which says a great deal about this dynamic church. The sign reads:

HEADQUARTERS OF
THE CHURCH OF THE SAVIOUR

A member-disciple of that congregation comments, "The sign is a reminder that we are also the church during all the hours of the week—in the neighborhoods where we live, in our homes, in our offices and factories."

Confederate General Nathan Bedford Forrest was one of the most colorful characters of the Civil War. Constantly in the saddle, overseeing and directing the forces under his command, General Forrest was once questioned about the location of his headquarters. His classic reply was, "My headquarters are wherever my hindquarters are."

This must be the posture of the church in these days, free of institutional encumbrances, not limited to the walls of consecrated buildings or historically defined prerogatives; but ready to move, speak, and act, wherever her word and witnesses are needed. Martin Niemoller, the German U-boat captain of World

War I, who as an evangelical Christian defied Hitler and went to prison during World War II, is an exciting kind of Christian. He is in this sense representative of the kind of faith and commitment which we all must seek in these days. While on a recent speaking tour of the United States, he gave the definition of faith that has marked the church at its best. In substance, he said that faith is not looking down from a balcony and watching Jesus bear His cross toward the city wall. Faith is not this—however sympathetic this may be. Faith leaves the balcony and joins Jesus in the street. It walks with Him toward the city wall. It is life offered.

The end of Jeremiah's prophetic career was marked by bleak prospects for the survival of Israel. The prophet was in exile and his people appeared hopeless in their faithlessness and confusion, overwhelmed by Babylon, a Godless and oppressive conqueror. The prophet's valedictory was one of hope and optimism, however, calling upon Israel to repent her faithlessness and reenter her covenant with God, to make the hour of trial her finest hour of faith. Had we lived in Jeremiah's time, perhaps we would have judged him irresponsible in this optimism, but history has vindicated his hope. Modern Israel is a fact, but there have been no Bonds-for-Babylon drives in recent history; nor have any of us lately bought clothing from, or seen a movie produced by a Babylonian.

Many oppressive circumstances and forces presently confront the church, God's modern Israel, as we have seen. Her new captivity is deceptively harmless in comparison with that of ancient Israel. The modern oppressors, though more subtle, are perhaps even more deadly than were the designs and devices of Babylon. There is reason to hope, however, that the divine spark of creative power is still alive in us, and if we have the grace to kindle it into flame, this may yet be faith's finest hour.

"Come, let us join ourselves to the Lord in an everlasting covenant which shall never be forgotten." Charles Wesley reflected on the meaning of Jeremiah's call and penned some words which, though sung by Christians for two hundred years, take on a new urgency and hope in our day:

Come, let us use the grace divine,
And all with one accord,
In perpetual covenant join
Ourselves to Christ the Lord.

Give up ourselves, through Jesus' power,
His name to glorify;
And promise, in this sacred hour,
For God to live and die.

V&R

Refo500 Academic Studies

Herausgegeben von
Herman J. Selderhuis

Band 76

Otfried Czaika / Wolfgang Undorf (Hg.)

Schwedische Buchgeschichte

Zeitalter der Reformation und Konfessionalisierung

Vandenhoeck & Ruprecht

Gedruckt mit freundlicher Unterstützung von MF vitenskapelig høyskole for teologi, religion og samfunn (MF Norwegian School of Theology, Religion and Society).

Bibliografische Information der Deutschen Bibliothek:
Die Deutsche Nationalbibliothek verzeichnet diese Publikation in der Deutschen Nationalbibliografie; detaillierte bibliografische Daten sind im Internet über https://dnb.de abrufbar.

Satz: le-tex publishing services, Leipzig
Umschlagsgestaltung: SchwabScantechnik, Göttingen
Druck und Bindung: Hubert & Co. Buchpartner, Göttingen
Printed in the EU

Vandenhoeck & Ruprecht Verlage | www.vandenhoeck-ruprecht-verlage.com

ISSN 2198-3089
ISBN 978-3-525-56497-4

Inhalt

Otfried Czaika, Wolfgang Undorf

Einleitung

Vorbemerkungen

Der vorliegende Sammelband bietet neun Beiträge, die sich mit der Buchgeschichte des Schwedischen Reiches in der Frühen Neuzeit auseinandersetzen. Während dieser Periode, d. h. seit dem Ende der Kalmarer Union, umfasste das schwedische Reichsgebiet hauptsächlich die schwedischen und finnischen Territorien zu beiden Seiten des bottnischen Meerbusens. Dies findet in dem Sammelband seinen Niederschlag darin, dass ein Drittel der Beiträge sich mit der Buchgeschichte im finnischen Reichsteil beschäftigen.

Der Begriff der Buchgeschichte ist dabei verhältnismäßig breit und interdisziplinär gefasst. Den Herausgebern ging es nicht nur um das Buch als Objekt an sich oder deskriptive Sammlungsbeschreibungen, um rein numerische Quantifikationen erhaltener Objekte oder die Zusammenstellung bibliographischer Angaben. Vielmehr inkludiert eine offenere Definition des Begriffes "Buchgeschichte" auch gerade eine tiefschürfende Beschäftigung mit einzelnen Textsorten sowie mit den dort verhandelten Inhalten und Diskursen. Aus diesem Grund widmen sich einige Beiträge ausdrücklich verschiedener Textsorten, u. a. der Geschichte des schwedischen Gesangbuches im 16. Jahrhundert, dem schwedischen Schuldrama der Frühen Neuzeit oder neulateinischer Poesie; wieder andere sind einzelnen Personen gewidmet. Dennoch sind es auch in diesen Beiträgen eben nicht nur die geistigen, theologischen, politischen oder aber auch staatstheoretischen Diskurse, die den einzigen Grund der jeweiligen Untersuchung ausmachen, sondern eben auch "buchhistorische" Fragen wie z. B. die hohen archivalischen Verluste, Nachdrucke, Neuausgaben o.ä., die als Teil der jeweiligen Studien tatsächlich zu einem umfassenderen Gesamtbild beitragen.

Wolfgang Undorfs Beitrag zum Buchhandel und Buchsammeln im Schweden des 16. Jahrhunderts eröffnet den Band und schneidet gleichzeitig ein Thema an, das gleichsam einem *basso continuo*, mal deutlicher vernehmlich, mal nur ganz leise im Hintergrund, alle Beiträge begleitet: Die transnationale Prägung nicht nur des gesamten schwedischen Buchmarkts der frühen Neuzeit, sondern gleichzeitig auch die transnationale Ausrichtung der gesamten Buchgeschichte inklusive der in den verschiedenen Werken verhandelten Themen. Wolfgang Undorfs Beitrag ist nicht nur ein thematisch, sondern *cum grano salis* auch eine chronologische Eröffnung des vorliegenden Sammelbandes, da er bis zu den Anfängen des schwedischen Buchdrucks im späten 15. Jahrhundert zurückreicht.

An diesen eröffnenden Ausblick schließen chronologisch die beiden eher personenhistorisch orientierten Beiträge von Remi Kick und Jason Lavery an. Remi Kick beleuchtet die während der Amtszeit des ersten schwedischen Erzbischofs Laurentius Petri (1499–1573, Erzbischof 1531–1573) entstandenen Drucke und in Sonderheit deren theologisches Profil. Jason Lavery zeichnet die volkssprachliche Reformation im finnischen Reichsteil nach, die untrennbar mit dem Namen des finnischen Reformators Mikael Agricola (ca. 1509/1510–1557, Bischof von Turku/Åbo 1554–1557) verbunden ist. Agricola ist nicht nur als Schöpfer der finnischen Schriftsprache und als Reformator Finnlands in die Geschichte eingegangen, er ist somit selbstredend auch der erste Finne, dessen Werke gedruckt wurden.

Die Druckgeschichte des schwedischen Gesangbuchs beginnt etwa um das Jahr 1530 und überschneidet sich somit mit dem Wirken von Laurentius Petri und Mikael Agricola. Die auf Grund der Überlieferungslage zum Teil nur in Bruchstücken zu rekonstruierende Geschichte des schwedischen Gesangbuchdrucks bis zum Ende des Reformationsjahrhunderts zeichnet Otfried Czaika in seinem Beitrag nach und unterwirft die bisherige Forschung einer kritischen Neubewertung. Diese ist nicht nur dank neuer Funde möglich; sie erscheint auch als der logische nächste Schritt im Hinblick auf die neuere buchhistorische Forschung, in Sonderheit mit Bezug auf die Frage nach den *Lost Books*, den verlorenen Büchern.

Während die Beiträge zu Laurentius Petri und Mikael Agricola sich mit der Buch- und Druckgeschichte im schwedischen Reich während der Reformationszeit befassen, gehen in der Geschichte des schwedischen Gesangbuchdrucks Reformation und konfessionelles Zeitalter organisch ineinander über. Kajsa Webers Artikel ist sodann ganz ausdrücklich ein Beitrag zur schwedischen Buchgeschichte im konfessionellen Zeitalter. Sie weist nach, wie ein von dem in Rostock ansässigen Buchdrucker Petrus Johannis Gothus herausgegebener Luthertext als „Statement" im schwedischen Konfessionskonflikt der 1590er Jahre Luthers instrumentalisiert wird.

Mit der schwedischen Buchgeschichte des 17. Jahrhunderts befassen sich die Beiträge von Elena Dahlberg und Martin Berntson. In ihnen werden auch zwei Textsorten in den Blick genommen, die bisher selten im Rahmen eines buchhistorischen Diskurses oder aber der Konfessionalisierungsforschung in den Blick genommen wurden: Die neulateinische Dichtung bekam in evangelischen Gebieten nicht zuletzt durch das Vorbild des Philipp Melanchthon neuen Schwung; ausgehend von Wittenberg als paradigmatischem Bezugsort ist sie in Schweden schon während der 2. Hälfte des 16. Jahrhunderts nachzuweisen.

Insbesondere blühte aber die neulateinische Dichtung im Ostseeraum während des 17. Jahrhunderts. Elena Dahlberg rekurriert auf die unter Gustav II. Adolf von schwedischen Truppen erbeuteten Bibliotheken. In den hier präsentierten Werken des Laurentius Fornelius und Jonas Columbus ist der Bibliotheksdiskurs eng mit der Frage der konfessionellen Wahrheit, der Verteidigung und Stärkung der *vera doctrina lutherana* verbunden. Als konfessionelle Literatur müssen auch die schwedischen Schuldramen der frühen Neuzeit verstanden werden. Bereits der schwedische Reformator Olaus Petri (1493–1552), der vermutlich auch Verfasser zahlreicher schwedischer Kirchenlieder war, hatte mit *Tobie Comedia* 1550 das erste schwedische Schuldrama publiziert. Während die erbeuteten Bibliotheken, die u. a. in die Sammlungen der Universitätsbibliothek Uppsala eingegliedert wurden, eher den gelehrten Funktionseliten des Reiches dienten, hatten die Schuldramen eine alle Gesellschaftsschichten durchdringende pädagogische Funktion. Martin Berntson zeigt auf, dass das Bild der „lutherischen Orthodoxie" als biblizistisch, dogmatisch verknöchert sowie lebensfremd nicht mit den Tatsachen übereinstimmt: Die schwedischen Schuldramen gehen relativ frei mit dem biblischen Stoff um und beinhalten zahlreiche humoristische Elemente.

Der vorliegende Band bietet also ein breites Spektrum: Eine in vieler Hinsicht transnationale Geschichte des Buches und der Druckkunst im schwedischen Reich nach der Reformation und reicht bis in das 18. und 19. Jahrhundert als, dank der durch die Reformation gesteigerten Lesefähigkeit, auch vermehrt alternative, in Sonderheit pietistische Deutungen der *vera doctrina lutherana* die Leseerfahrungen vieler Menschen im schwedischen Reich prägten. Neben der Orientierung an einigen für die schwedische Buchgeschichte bedeutsamen Gestalten sind es aber vielmehr ausgewählte Textsorten, die den vorliegenden Band prägen. Nur teilweise – etwa die Übersetzungen biblischer Texte durch Mikael Agricola ins Finnische – sind die hier präsentierten Texte Teil der kirchen- oder buchhistorischen Meistererzählung: Ephemere Lieddrucke, neulateinische Dichtung, Schuldramen oder aber auch pietistische Pamphlete werden nur selten im Kanon des kollektiven historischen Erinnerns aktualisiert. Wie die Beiträge zum Pietismus in Finnland aufzeigen, sind die Grenzen zwischen Manuskript- und Druckproduktion bis zum Ende der Frühen Neuzeit durchaus fließend. Noch bedeutsamer ist aber womöglich, dass viele der hier näher vorgestellten Textsorten die Grenze zwischen Mündlichkeit und Schriftlichkeit transzendieren. Wie u. a. Tuija Laine herausstreicht, war lange Zeit das Auswendiglernen von religiösen Texten im schwedischen Reich gang und gäbe. Damit war – auch wenn weite Teile der Bevölkerung sukzessive literarisiert wurden – Lesefähigkeit nicht zwangsläufig für die Teilhabe am gedruckten Wort erforderlich. Dasselbe gilt nicht nur für Kirchenlieder, die durch stetige Wiederholung im Zyklus des Kirchenjahres und dank der musikalischen Bindung sich auch allen einprägen konnten, die nicht des Lesens kundig waren. Schlussendlich waren auch die Schuldramen kein Lesestoff für eine individuelle Lektüre im stillen Kämmerlein, sondern zielten auf den öffentlichen Vortrag u. a. auf Marktplätzen ab. Insbesondere die Kirchenlieder und Schuldramen im 16. und 17. Jahrhundert, aber auch die pietistischen und z.T. separatistischen Leseerfahrungen im 18. und frühen 19. Jahrhundert weisen somit auf die Bedeutung des geschriebenen und gedruckten Wortes für breite Teile der Bevölkerung im schwedischen Reich hin: Selbst wer nicht des Lesens kundig war oder kein eigenes Buch besaß, partizipierte qua Gemeindegesang oder öffentliche Schauspiele an der Buchkultur. Kirchenlieder und Schuldramen beinhalten zudem multimediale Aspekte, Melodien, Orgelbegleitung und/oder szenischen Vortrag.

Esko Laine erinnert in dem den Band abschließenden Beitrag daran, dass nicht nur die Grenze von Schriftlichkeit und Mündlichkeit fließend war, sondern auch diejenige zwischen Manuskriptproduktion und Buchdruck. Es waren eben nicht nur gedruckte pietistische Werke einheimischer oder mitteleuropäischer, meist deutscher Autoren, die das religiöse Gefühl Vieler nachhaltig prägten und formten, sondern eben auch als Manuskript angefertigte und verbreitete Schriften. Wie schon Martin Berntson, so kann auch Esko Laine wiederum kritische Anfragen an die oftmals holzschnittartig verbreiteten Vorurteile gegenüber der lutherischen Orthodoxie und dem Pietismus stellen: Sowohl Lutherische Orthodoxie als auch Pietismus beschreiben den Sehnsuchtsort religiösen Erlebens als „Paradiesgärtlein“ und verwenden dabei zahlreiche Naturmetaphern.

Auch wenn dem (kirchen-)historischen Diskurs entlehnte Periodiserungen wie „Reformation“ und „Konfessionalisierung“ für diesen Band nicht bedeutungslos sind, so treten dennoch deutlich die Konturen einer *longue durée* zu Tage. Der Blick auf die Buchgeschichte enthüllt, dass seit der Inkunabelzeit bis an den Vorabend der Moderne sich religiöse Textsorten wie z. B. Schuldrama und Gesangbuch relativ stringent entwickeln. Der vorliegende Band kann somit auch als ein kritisches Korrektiv zur Periodisierungsdiskussion frühneuzeitlicher Geschichte gesehen werden: Möglicherweise legen die relativ fließenden, stringenten Entwicklungen und die Gemeinsamkeiten der sonst oftmals in Gegensätzen gekennzeichneten kirchenhistorischen Epochen nahe, dass der von Marshall McLuhan geprägte Begriff der Gutenberggalaxie auch für die Religions- und Kirchengeschichte der Frühen Neuzeit eine Operationalisierbarkeit für die Periodisierungsdebatte besitzt.

Zahlreiche Studien zur Buch- und Druckgeschichte des schwedischen Reiches sind nur in schwedischer oder finnischer Sprache zugänglich. Diesbezüglich will der vorliegende Band auch eine Lücke schließen und nicht zuletzt das wissenschaftliche Gespräch über die Barrieren der relativ kleinen nordischen

Wissenschaftssprachen hinaus ermöglichen. Während in Finnland der buchhistorische Diskurs zur Geschichte der Frühen Neuzeit in den vergangenen Jahrzehnten relativ lebhaft gewesen ist (was sich u. a. an dem Umstand ablesen lässt, dass eine aktuelle finnische Nationalbibliographie existiert, die alle zwischen 1488 und 1700 gedruckten finnischen Werke verzeichnet), trifft dies auf die schwedische Forschung nur in höchst begrenztem Umfang zu. Dies illustriert u. a. der Umstand, dass die schwedische Nationalbibliographie zum 16. und 17. Jahrhundert vor etwa achtzig Jahren angefertigt wurde und bisher keine neue Version dieses nun in Teilen veralteten und wenig aktuellen Standardwerkes existiert. Auch der Anschluss der schwedischen buchhistorischen Forschung an die internationale Debatte war in den vergangenen Jahrzehnten weitaus schwächer als in Finnland. Nicht zuletzt ist die buchhistorische Forschung teilweise noch immer stark nationalromantischen Vorgaben verhaftet, was sich u. a. an Isak Collijns schwedischer Nationalbibliographie ablesen lässt: Die Aufnahmekriterien eines Druckes als „schwedisch" in die Nationalbibliographie sind oftmals ein Spiegelbild des nationalen Diskurses im „langen" 18. Jahrhundert. Die hier hingegen oft ausdrücklich, oft aber auch eher nur zwischen den Zeilen verhandelte transnationale Komponente der schwedischen und finnischen Buchgeschichte dient als kritisches Korrektiv.

Erst in den vergangenen Jahren scheinen sich gewisse Blockaden, insbesondere der schwedischen buchhistorischen Forschung, zu ändern, zumal die jüngere Generation von schwedischen Kirchen-, Buch- und Profanhistorikern nun vermehrt den Anschluss an die international verhandelten Debatten vollzieht. Dennoch: Auch dieser Band kann selbstverständlich nicht die in den Nationalsprachen bisher veröffentlichten Publikationen ersetzen und auch nicht einen z.T. über Jahrzehnte gewachsenen Abbruch des internationalen Gesprächs überbrücken und auch nicht eine überalterte Nationalbibliographie ersetzen. Vielmehr ist dieser Band als ein Diskussionsbeitrag gedacht, der eine interdisziplinäre Dialogfähigkeit fördern soll.

Wolfgang Undorf

Buchhandel und Buchsammeln in Schweden zur Zeit der Reformation und Konfessionalisierung

Skandinavischer Buchhandel im 16. Jahrhundert

Im Schweden der frühen Neuzeit reicht die buchhistorische Spannbreite vom katholisch-europäischen Buchmarkt vor der Reformation und dem Einbruch um 1525 bis zur Re-Etablierung eines transnationellen, aber diesmal konfessionell lutherisch und geographisch mittel- und niederdeutsch geprägten Buchhandels in der zweiten Hälfte des 16. Jahrhunderts. Die wichtigsten Charakteristika der frühmodernen schwedischen Buchgeschichte beginnen mit den im Auftrag der bedeutenden Buchdrucker/Verleger in Mainz, Köln oder Straßburg reisenden Bücherführern der 1470er, mit denen leistungsfähige und stabile Verbindungen zwischen den Buchmärkten in Skandinavien und den wichtigsten Exportdruckern ihrer Zeit etabliert wurden.

In den 1490er Jahren hatte sich Lübeck als Hauptumschlageplatz für Bücher im Ostseeraum etabliert. Die Pfundzollbücher der Jahre 1492–1495 geben davon beredtes Zeugnis ab. Die Stadt wurde regelmäßig von Koberger aus Nürnberg und Drach aus Speyer besucht, die über die Buchmesse in Frankfurt auch die Kontakte zum Exportbuchdruck Venedigs und Lyons etablierten und aufrechterhielten. Stellvertretend für neue Exportzentren verweise ich auf Paris, das während der ersten zwei Jahrzehnte des 16. Jahrhunderts kurzzeitig zu einem der wichtigsten Buchexporteure nach Skandinavien aufstieg.[1] In dieser Zeit haben wir es nicht nur mit einem zum überwiegenden Teil verloren gegangenen Buchimport zu tun. Ein für gewöhnlich bibliographisch äußerst schwierig zu bestimmender lokal-regionaler Markt für Literatur diente der komplementären Grundversorgung mit pädagogischer und liturgisch-religiöser Literatur. Im Testament des Odenser Domprobstes Hans Urne sowie dem zwei Jahre darauf abgefassten juristischen Schriftstück über die Verhandlung seines Bruders mit einem unbekannten Buchdrucker treten in Odense gedruckte Bücher zu Tage, die von der dänischen Buchgeschichte immer noch nicht anerkannt worden sind.

Im Gefolge des Aufbruchs der Kalmarer Union zwischen Dänemark und Schweden sowie als Folge der Einführung der Reformation in den skandinavi-

1 Siehe Christiern Pedersen und die Malmö-Bücherliste.

schen Ländern brach der Büchermarkt kurzzeitig ein. Zwischen 1523 und 1526 wurde in Dänemark kein Buch gedruckt und in der Dombibliothek von Västerås fielen die Erwerbungszahlen in den 1520er Jahren auf ihren absolut tiefsten Wert seit 50 Jahren.[2] Allmählich etablierte sich ein wieder erstarkter transnationeller Buchhandel in Skandinavien und Nordeuropa. Zu dessen Kennzeichen gehört neben der Betonung neuer, konfessionell geprägter Grenzen (die Bedeutung Wittenbergs) aber auch die Persistenz gewisser überkonfessioneller Druckzentren, wie Basel und Frankfurt am Main im deutschsprachigen Bereich. Zeugnis davon geben erhaltene buchhistorische Dokumente, auf deren Basis Otfried Czaika Teile der Büchersammlung Sveno Jacobis (ca. 1480–1554), Bischof in Skara in den 1540er Jahren, rekonstruiert hat.[3]

Einheimischer Buchdruck im skandinavischen Kontext

Ausgangspunkt für die Beschreibung der Geschichte und Charakteristiken der skandinavischen Buchkulturen der frühen Neuzeit ist natürlich die quantitativ bescheidene regionale Buchproduktion. Es ist manchmal nicht einfach, die Anzahl der Druckereien in Dänemark und Schweden in der frühen Neuzeit zu bestimmen: Gewisse Buchdrucker arbeiteten an verschiedenen Orten, manchmal mit langen Intervallen zwischen den dokumentierten Aktivitäten. Kann man da von mehreren Druckereien reden oder von der ununterbrochenen Existenz ein und derselben Druckerei? Die folgende Statistik rechnet daher nicht mit Druckereien an sich, sondern basiert auf einer Auszählung der beiden Nationalbibliographien daraufhin, wie viele Druckereien sich jeweils in jedem Jahr nachweisen lassen.

---

2 Undorf, Gutenberg, 3.
3 Czaika, Sveno Jacobi.

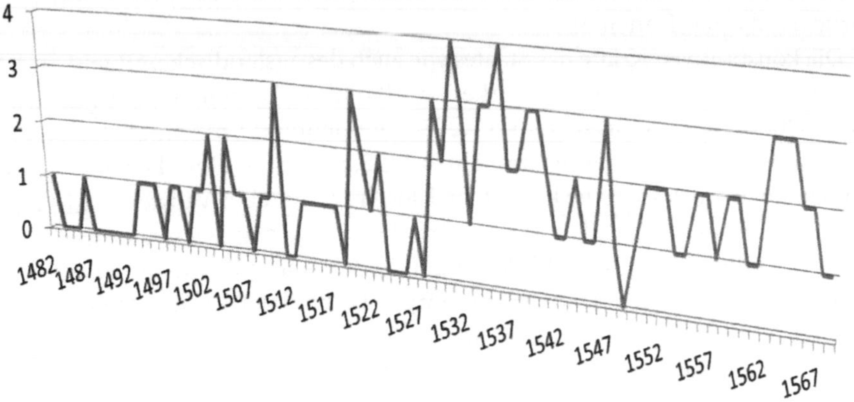

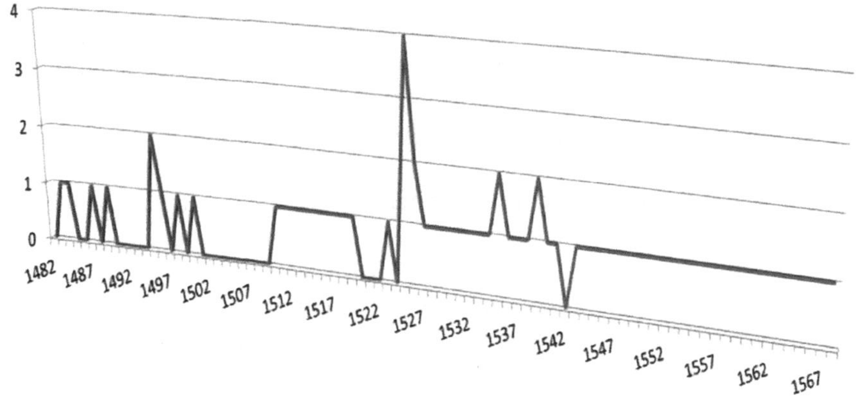

Druckereien tätig 1482–1568 in Dänemark (oben) und in Schweden (unten)

In Dänemark lassen sich bis zur Reformation jährlich im Durchschnitt ein Drucker bzw. eine Druckerei anhand datierbarer Drucke oder anderer Quellen nachweisen. Mehr Aktivität entfaltete der dänische Buchdruck zu Beginn der 1520er Jahre sowie im Jahrzehnt 1528–1539. In diesem für die Etablierung der Reformation entscheidenden Zeitraum registriert die dänische Nationalbibliographie im Durchschnitt 3 Druckereien pro Jahr. Danach pendelt sich die

Zahl der dokumentierten Druckereien auf zwei pro Jahr ein, ein deutliches Zeichen für die Konsolidierung, aber auch Monopolisierung der protestantischen Drucklandschaft Dänemark.

Die konstitutiven Kräfte des Staates wie auch des ausländischen Buchhandels waren in Schweden noch viel stärker spürbar als in Dänemark. Bis zur Mitte der 1520er Jahre versorgte der schwedische Buchmarkt nur höchstens einen Buchdrucker (mit Ausnahme des Jahres 1495, wo neben einer kommerziellen Druckerei in Stockholm die kurzlebige Klosterdruckerei in Vadstena tätig war). Für 1524 können möglicherweise 4 Druckereien nachgewiesen werden. Die Druckerei des Bischofs von Linköping in Söderköping wurde im Jahr darauf vom König geschlossen. Der Drucker Jörgen Richolff der Jüngere (1494–1573) war der Nachfolger Fabris in Uppsala und von einer vierten Druckerei wissen wir außer einem Druck nichts weiter. Im Jahr darauf hatte der schwedische König alle Konkurrenz für seine eigene königliche Druckerei aus dem Weg geräumt. Bis zum Ende des 16. Jahrhunderts gab es in Schweden dann wieder nur eine einzige Druckerei. Skandinavien gehört also in der frühen Neuzeit in vielerlei Hinsicht zu den von den großen kontinentaleuropäischen Buchexporteuren abhängigen Peripherien, zu denen auch die Länder auf den Britischen Inseln gehörten.[4] Allzu lange hat sich die nationale Buchgeschichtsschreibung in den skandinavischen Ländern aber auf die Darstellung eben dieses Buchdrucks beschränkt. Es gibt zwar einige Studien zu gewissen frühneuzeitlichen Buchsammlungen[5], aber man hat Buchdruck und Bücherbesitz (und damit auch Buchhandel) nie im Zusammenhang mit- und in Abhängigkeit voneinander gesehen.

Daneben existierte nämlich in der frühen Neuzeit noch eine für gewöhnlich bibliographisch äußerst schwierig zu bestimmende regionale, manchmal sogar nur lokal gedruckte und zugängliche Literatur, die der komplementären Grundversorgung mit pädagogischer und liturgisch-religiöser Literatur diente. Im Testament des Odenser Domprobstes Hans Urne sowie dem zwei Jahre darauf abgefassten juristischen Schriftstück über die Verhandlung seines Bruders mit einem unbekannten Buchdrucker treten in Odense gedruckte, aber ansonsten unbekannte Bücher zu Tage.[6] Im Unterschied vor allem zu Deutschland entfaltete sich über Jahrzehnte kein quantitativ nennenswerter Buchdruck in Dänemark und Schweden. Wenn auch die beiden Druckkulturen im Einzelnen abweichende Züge aufweisen können, zeigen sich doch in der Tendenz auch einige strukturelle Parallelen.

4 Undorf, Gutenberg, 313. Pettegree, Centre 105–106.
5 Siehe die umfangreich zitierte Literatur in Undorf, Gutenberg.
6 Ibid., 36–47.

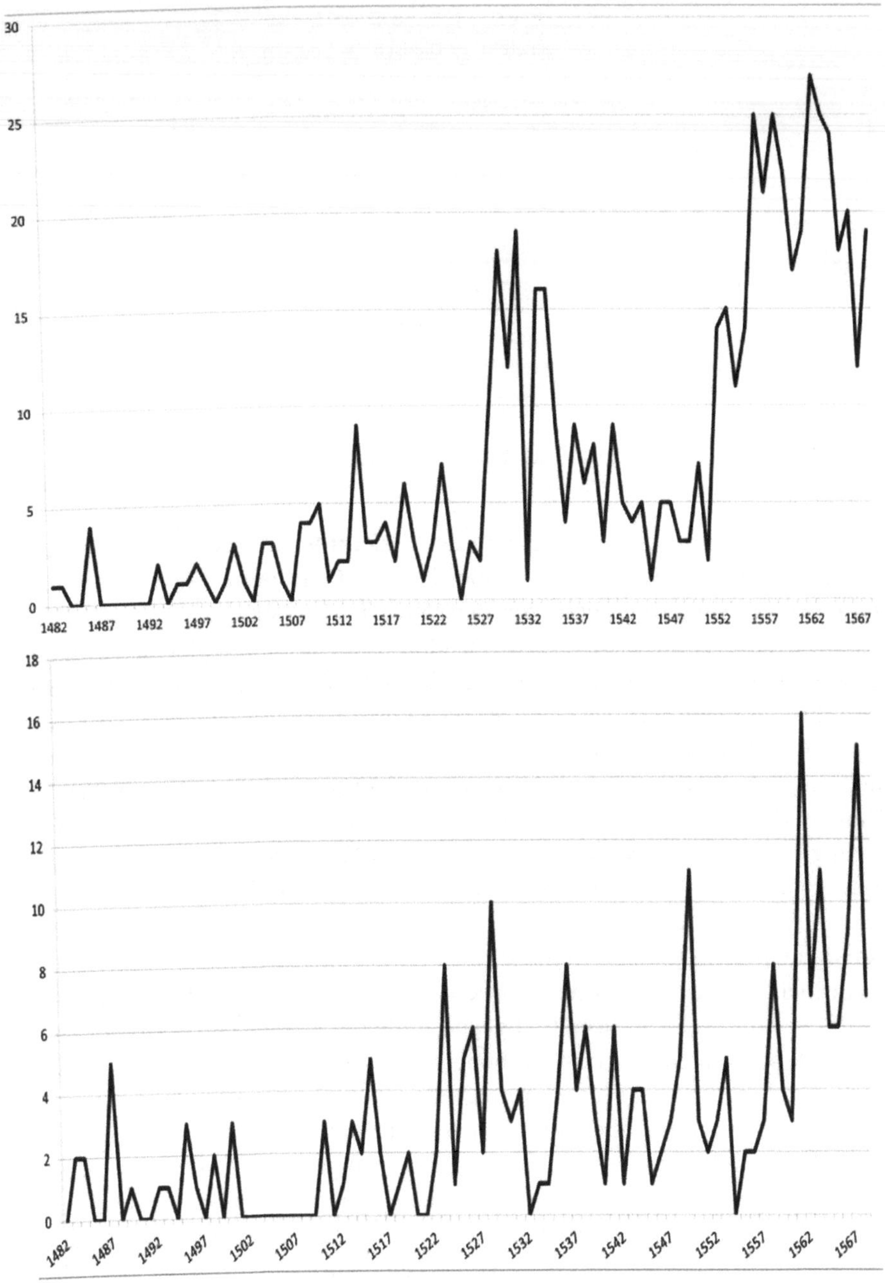

Anzahl der Drucke 1482–1568 in der dänischen (oben) und schwedischen (unten) Nationalbibliographie.

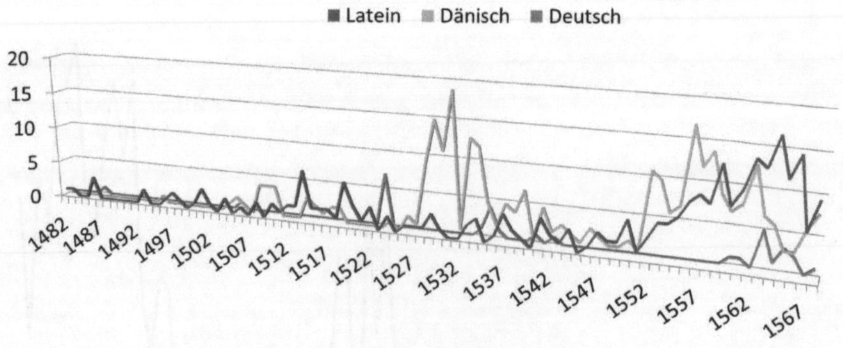

Drucke auf Latein, Dänisch und Deutsch 1482–1568 in der dänischen Nationalbibliographie.

In beiden Fällen steigt die Anzahl der (bekannten) Drucke erst im Laufe der 1520er bis zum Beginn der 1530er Jahre auf ein nennenswertes Niveau. In den etwa zwei Jahrzehnten von der Mitte der 1530er Jahre bis etwa 1550 bewegt sich die einheimische Druckproduktion in etwa den gleichen Dimensionen. Danach jedoch explodiert der dänische Buchmarkt förmlich. Auch der schwedische Markt wächst, aber die Fluktuationen sind viel stärker, was angesichts der wenigen Drucke, die jährlich die einzige schwedische Druckerei, die Königliche Druckerei, verlassen haben, nicht sonderlich verwunderlich ist. Thomas Kaufmann streicht in einem Artikel von 2013 deutlich heraus, wie wichtig Drucke in den Volkssprachen nicht nur für die Reformation als solche, sondern auch für das Entstehen einer breiten Lese- und Rezeptionsöffentlichkeit im Allgemeinen gewesen sind.[7] Diese Aspekte finden sich auch auf den skandinavischen Buchmärkten wieder.

Aus beiden Ländern kennen wir vereinzelte Drucke in den Volkssprachen bereits vor der Reformation. Erst gegen Ende der 1520er Jahre entwickelten sich volkssprachliche Drucke zur beherrschenden Druckkategorie. In Dänemark handelt es sich vor allem um Literatur religiösen und unterhaltenden Inhalts, in Schweden haben wir es mehr mit Verordnungen der Könige und religiöser Literatur zu tun. Bei den deutschsprachigen Drucken handelt es sich immer um politisches Schrifttum. Eine eindeutig reformatorische Ausrichtung hatten die in Schweden erschienenen Drucke in finnischer Sprache, die sich auf reformatorisches Schrifttum und die 1540er Jahre konzentrieren. In beiden Ländern spielt lateinische Literatur – abgesehen von den selbstverständlich zu

7 Kaufmann, Buchdruck, 13–34.

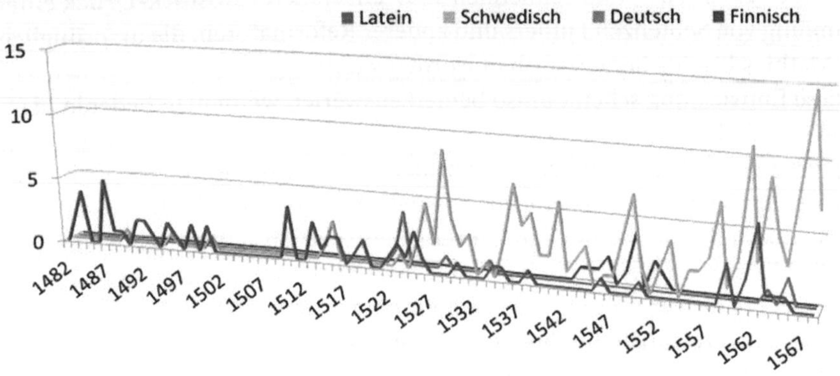

Drucke auf Latein, Schwedisch, Deutsch und Finnisch 1482–1568 in der schwedischen Nationalbibliographie.

erwartenden liturgischen Werken – vom Ende des 15. Jahrhunderts bis zum Ende der frühen Reformationsperiode in der Mitte des 16. Jahrhunderts keine wesentliche Rolle. Die Einführung der Reformation in den skandinavischen Ländern bis in die erste Hälfte der 1520er Jahre ist weitestgehend unabhängig von einheimischer proreformatorischer Buchproduktion.

Die Schriften der vor allem aus der Rücksicht der siegreichen Reformation auf ihre kanonischen Autoren, an erster Stelle wohl Martin Luther (1483–1546) und Philipp Melanchthon (1497–1560), tauchen in der frühen Reformation kaum in volkssprachlichen Ausgaben und gar nicht in Latein auf. Betrachtet man etwa die Schriften Martin Luthers als eine Art Leitfossilien der Reformation, dann ist der überraschende Befund, dass etwa in Schweden erst 1558 zum ersten Mal ein Text Luthers in vollständiger schwedischer Übersetzung unter dem Titel *Undervisning om Herrans nattvard* im Druck vorlag.[8] Danach dauerte es bis in die 1580er und 1590er Jahre, bis innerhalb von 10 Jahren immerhin vier weitere vollständige Übersetzungen von Schriften Martin Luthers auf Schwedisch im Druck erschienen: *Spörsmål och svar vid nattvardsgång* (eine Pseudo-lutherische Schrift, die eher Johann Mathesius zuzuschreiben ist) 1587[9], *Om man må fly för döden eller pestilensen* (Original *Ob man fur dem sterben fliehen muge*) 1588, *Ett sätt att bedja* (Originaltitel *Eine einfältige Weise zu beten für einen guten Freund*) im Anhang zu einer pseudo-anselmischen Schrift, die 1593

---

8 Originaltitel *Vermanung zum Sacrament des leibs und bluts unsers Herrn*, erste Ausgabe 1530; Collijn, Bibliografi, Bd. 2, 239–241.

9 Ibid., Bd. 3, 55–57.

in Rostock erschien[10], und schließlich 1597 ein weiterer Rostock-Druck einer Sammlung von Sentenzen Luthers und anderer Reformatoren, die ursprünglich von Mathias Flacius herausgegeben worden war.[11]

Diese Entwicklung scheint umso bemerkenswerter, wenn man bedenkt, dass schon sehr früh Luthers oder zumindest pro-lutherische Schriften in Schweden rezipiert wurden. Dabei handelte es sich allerdings zu Anfang um illegale Importe, später um offiziell importierte kontinentale Ausgaben. Der erste schwedische Druck, durch den sich milde kirchenreformerische Absichten manifestierten, war die Übersetzung einer auch in Dänemark verbreiteten Schrift Christiern Pedersens (1480–1554) unter dem Titel *Att höra mässan* 1523.[12] Für den Druck verantwortlich zeichnete Bischof Hans Brask (1464–1538), der zu diesem Zeitpunkt bereits ein eingeschworener Gegner Luthers war. Dies war einer der allerletzten Drucke aus der Brask'schen Druckerei vor ihrer Schließung auf direkte Anweisung König Gustav Vasas November 1526. Zu dem Zeitpunkt hatte nämlich schon die neue königliche Druckerei unter Jürgen Richolff aus Lübeck ihre Arbeit in Stockholm aufgenommen, nachdem sie zuerst eine kurze Zeit in Uppsala aktiv gewesen war.

Das Programm der königlichen Druckerei in Stockholm war von Anfang an reformkatholisch bis reformatorisch ausgerichtet. Hatte Jörgen Richolff d.J. 1525 in Uppsala, unter den Augen des Erzbischofs, noch ein katholisches Stundenbuch und vier Ablassgebete gedruckt[13], so druckte er in Stockholm ab 1526 fast nur noch reformatorische Schriften. Den Anfang machen drei katechetische Werke, von denen die ersten beiden mit dem Titel *Een nyttwgh wnderwijsning* zwei verschiedene Auflagen einer teilweise Übersetzung oder Bearbeitung von Luthers *Betbüchlein* und teilweise eine eigenständige Arbeit darstellen.[14] Die dritte katechetische Schrift aus dem gleichen Jahr 1526 trägt einen fast gleichlautenden Titel, *Een skön nyttugh vnderwisningh*, basiert aber auf einem Joachim Slüter zugeschriebenen Katechismus.[15] Die Arbeit, für die Richolff aber eigentlich ins Land gerufen worden war, war die erste schwedische Übersetzung des Neuen Testaments, *Thet Nyia Testamentit på Swensko*; der Druck ist datiert 15.8.1526.[16] Sie basiert vor allem auf Erasmus von Rotterdams lateinischer Übersetzung von 1526 und erst in zweiter Reihe auf der 1523 in

---

10 Ibid., Bd. 3, 157–158.

11 Ibid., Bd. 3, 256–257.

12 Ibid., Bd. 1, 286.

13 Die lateinischen *Horae de domina […] secundum ecclesiam Upsalensem* (Ibid., Bd. 1, 300–305) sowie einen Einblattdruck mit schwedischen Ablassgebete (Ibid., Bd. 1, 305–307).

14 Ibid., Bd. 1, 319–326.

15 Ibid., Bd. 1, 326–328.

16 Ibid., Bd. 1, 331–339.

Straßburg erschienenen Auflage der deutschen Übersetzung Martin Luthers. An der Straßburger Ausgabe orientiert sich die schwedische Übersetzung auch in typographischer Hinsicht und in der fast schon programmatischen Verwendung des Namens Jesu auf dem Titelblatt sowie in den Einleitungen der meisten Bücher des Neuen Testaments. Diese erste schwedische Übersetzung des Neuen Testaments fügt sich zum Teil natürlich ein in den allgemeinen Trend hin zur Emanzipation der Volkssprachen als Drucksprachen. Teile des Alten Testaments waren bereits im 15. Jahrhundert in schwedischen Klöstern übersetzt worden. An der kollektiven ersten vollständigen Übersetzung 1525–1526 waren Domkapitel und einige der Mönchsorden im Land beteiligt. Reformkatholizismus, Bibelhumanismus und Reformation hatten ein Interesse daran, die Bibel in die Volkssprache zu übertragen. Luther war, wenn auch anonym, in Schweden gegenwärtig, z. B. als anonymer Komponist und Dichter von Kirchenliedern im schwedischen Gesangbuch sowie im schwedischsprachigen Codex West aus den Jahren 1545–49. Wir haben es hier mit einer praktischen Reformation zu tun, die sich auf die Erfüllung der praktischen Bedürfnisse des Volkes konzentrierte und nicht auf die großen Namen und theologischen Arbeiten.

Wie 40 Jahre vorher, war also auch in der Mitte der 1520er Jahre wieder ein deutscher Drucker aus Lübeck nach Stockholm gerufen worden, um den eigentlichen Druck auszuführen. Und genauso wie in den Anfängen des schwedischen Buchdrucks in den 1480er Jahren fand auch dieser Drucker, Jörgen Richolff d.J., Zeit, einige kleinere Druckwerke in die Produktion des Neuen Testaments einzuschieben. Nichts beleuchtet besser das komplexe theologische Bild, das sich uns in Schweden in der Mitte der 1520er Jahre bietet als die Tatsache, dass Richolff in den ersten Monaten, in denen er in Uppsala, dem Sitz des Erzbischofs, seine Werkstatt aufgeschlagen hatte, katholische Drucke herstellte. Allzu spät hatte die altgläubige Partei eingesehen, dass auch sie sich in der Volkssprache der Masse der Gläubigen zuwenden musste. Ab Februar 1526 druckte Richolff dann in der Stockholmer Werkstatt aber dezidiert reformatorisches Schrifttum, Übersetzungen und originale Arbeiten von Olaus Petri. Dieses protestantische Programm und Olaus Petri als ihr publizistisch wichtigster Propagandist prägten noch mehr in den darauffolgenden Jahren 1527–1528 den literarischen Ausstoß der Königlichen Druckerei Richolffs. Knapp 15 Jahre später hatte sich die Reformation in Schweden durchgesetzt und der Druck der neuen Übersetzung der ganzen Bibel ins Schwedische 1539–1541 konnte diesmal in Uppsala ausgeführt werden.

Die Situation in Dänemark war eine wesentlich andere. Dort erschien bereits 1526 in Kopenhagen die erste Übersetzung eines Luther-Textes durch Hans

Tausen ins Dänische, *Een cristelig Vnderwyszningh paa the thy Gudz Budord.*[17] Zwei Jahre darauf wurde in der Stiftsstadt Wiborg die Schrift Her haffue wi bodhæ edt ønckeligt Klawaemooll gedruckt.[18] Insgesamt verzeichnet die dänische Nationalbibliographie bis zum Ende des 16. Jahrhunderts 44 Übersetzungen von Luthertexten ins Dänische. Selbstverständlich müssen wir in Anbetracht der großen Lücken in der archivalischen Überlieferung und Dokumentation der Reformation in den beiden Ländern, insbesondere was die reformatorischen Buchkulturen angeht, mit unseren Schlussfolgerungen vorsichtig sein. Der Buchdruck war zwar nicht die alleinige Vermittlungsinstanz der Reformation. Wie Czaika und andere deutlich gemacht haben, ist vor allem die frühe Reformation ein Transfervorgang, der das gedruckte ebenso einschließt wie das geschriebene oder das mündlich vermittelte Wort. Die gedruckten Werke der Reformatoren (weniger die ihrer Gegner) entfalteten aber die in diesem Zusammenhang ausschlaggebende Rezeptionswirkung. Pro-Lutherische Schriften wurden in den frühen 1520er Jahren über den Hafen von Söderköping in das Bistum Linköping geschmuggelt. Dabei wird es sich natürlich vor allem um im Norden leicht verständliche deutsche Schriften gehandelt haben.[19]

Reformatoren wie auch ihre Gegner versorgten ihre Anhänger mit Munition in Form von gedruckten Büchern. Viele, wenn nicht gar die allermeisten dieser Bücher sind heute verloren gegangen, das gilt sicher auch für den einen oder anderen einheimischen Druck. Wir müssen uns aber auch hüten, vom Ergebnis der Reformation und den kanonischen Autoren her den für ein einzelnes Land charakteristischen Vorgang der Reformation rekonstruieren zu wollen. Dazu zählt in diesem Fall die unvoreingenommene Analyse der entsprechenden Druckproduktion. Das Beispiel Schweden ist hier besonders aufschlussreich. Die Reformation war auch hier erfolgreich, aber eben nicht auf der Basis einer einheimischen Produktion von reformatorischem Schrifttum in der Form von Übersetzungen der Schriften Luthers. Seine Schriften fanden sich im Land, das wissen wir aus Briefen und Inventarien. Die frühe dänische Reformation war im Wesentlichen eine Initiative König Kristian II. Während seiner Regierungszeit erschien aber im Druck in Dänemark oder für den dänischen Markt lediglich die Leipziger zweite Auflage von Christiern Pedersens reformkatholischer Schrift *At høre Messe* (1517)[20] sowie Erasmus von Rotterdams Übersetzung des Matthäus-Evangeliums ins Lateinische 1522.[21] Erst im Jahr nach der Absetzung und Flucht Kristians II. ins niederländische Exil erschien die von ihm bestellte

---

17 Nielsen, Bibliografi, Nr. 163.
18 Ibid., Nr. 154.
19 Braunmüller, Semikommunikation, 35–70.
20 Nielsen, Bibliografi, Nr. 207.
21 Ibid., Nr. 167.

erste gedruckte dänische Bibelübersetzung bei Melchior Lotter aus Leipzig; der Druck wurde aber in Wittenberg ausgeführt.[22] Nach der Toleranzerklärung von 1527 erschienen in den Jahren 1528–30 eine ganze Reihe von reformatorischen Drucken, darunter fünf Schriften Luthers, 1531–35 weitere elf, 1536–1540 vier Schriften und schließlich 1541–1545 noch einmal fünf Arbeiten. Danach war das Interesse an Luther erst einmal gesättigt. Erst 1566 erlebte Luther, oder besser gesagt sein kleiner Katechismus unter dem Titel *Lille Katekismus* in Peder Palladius' Übersetzung mit 19 Auflagen von 1556 bis 1600 eine Renaissance.

Frühneuzeitliche Buchimporte nach Skandinavien

Erst seit kurzem ist man sich in Teilen der schwedischen akademischen buchhistorischen Forschung der umfangreichen, aber zum überwiegenden Teil verloren gegangenen frühneuzeitlichen Buchimporte nach Skandinavien bewusst. Dazu gehören neben den natürlich auch zu beobachtenden privaten Importen von reisenden Klerikern und Adligen, aber noch mehr von Studenten, auch Bücherversendungen an skandinavische Adressaten.[23] Speziell im Hinblick auf die frühe Reformation ist unter all diesen Gesichtspunkten der Aufarbeitungsbedarf noch groß. Die buchhistorische Spannbreite der frühen Neuzeit in Skandinavien reicht vom katholisch-europäischen Buchmarkt vor der Reformation und dem Einbruch um 1525 bis zur Re-Etablierung eines transnationellen, aber diesmal konfessionell lutherisch sowie geographisch hauptsächlich mittel- und niederdeutsch geprägten Buchhandels in der zweiten Hälfte des 16. Jahrhunderts. Zu dessen Kennzeichen gehört neben der Betonung neuer, konfessionell geprägter Grenzen (die Bedeutung Wittenbergs ist natürlich deutlich abzulesen), aber auch die Persistenz gewisser überkonfessioneller Druckzentren, wie Basel und Frankfurt am Main im deutschsprachigen Bereich. Zeugnis davon geben wenige erhaltene buchhistorische Dokumente, auf deren Basis Otfried Czaika aber immerhin wesentliche Teile der Büchersammlung Sveno Jacobis, Bischof in Skara in den 1540er Jahren, rekonstruiert hat. Bei Czaika findet man auch die Auflistung der vier Titel, die Mikael Agricola (1510–1557), der finnische Reformator, in Åbo/Turku in Finnland gekauft hat: Luthers *Enarrationes seu postilla* (Straßburg 1530, erworben 1531) sowie

22 Ibid., Nr. 270.

23 Reformatorische Drucke wurden von skandinavischen Studenten nach Hause geschickt oder sie trugen selber diese Drucke bei ihrer Rückkehr im Gepäck. Melanchthon selbst hat Exemplare seiner eigenen Arbeiten und der anderer Wittenberger oder ihm nahestehenden Theologen in den Norden geschickt; Czaika, Melanchthon, passim.

ein Sammelband mit je einem Druck aus Köln, Schlettstadt und Basel (gedruckt zwischen 1518 und 1525, erworben 1532).[24]

Die Reformation gelangte bis etwa 1530 auf vielfältigen, aber teilweise diffusen Wegen in den Norden, mit Hilfe von Briefen, gedruckten Büchern, dem gesprochenen Wort und den Gedanken der Menschen. Die Reformation breitete sich durch kulturelle Transferprozesse nach Skandinavien aus. Dazu gehört neben der Druckerpresse und dem Brief als Mittel zur Fernkommunikation natürlich auch die Anwesenheit skandinavischer Studenten in Wittenberg.[25] Die Offenheit für reformatorisches Gedankengut in gewissen Bevölkerungsgruppen in den beiden Ländern war fast unmittelbar, ebenso aber auch der Widerstand. Von Beginn an war natürlich der reformatorische Impetus getragen von Person, Wirken und Werken Martin Luthers, wenn auch andere Reformatoren in frühreformatorischen Buchsammlungen oft einen quantitativ prominenteren Platz eingenommen haben. Die expliziten Hinweise Bischof Hans Brasks auf die Anwesenheit lutherischer Schriften in Söderköping, der Hafenstadt seines Bistums Linköping, in der ersten Hälfte der 1520er Jahre sind Zeugnis des nicht sanktionierten, privaten Imports von Büchern. Auf der anderen Seite enthalten seine Briefe nicht wenige Hinweise auf anti—Lutherische Schriften. Ein Exemplar der 1521 in Rom gedruckten Ausgabe der *Assertio septem* Heinrich VIII. wurde Hans Brask direkt aus der päpstlichen Kurie zugeschickt. In einem Brief vom 20.7.1523 informierte er die Brüder im Birgittinerkloster Vadstena darüber.[26]

Wenn sich Brask auch über das Vorkommen lutherischer Schriften in seinem Bistum bekümmerte, war er gleichzeitig ein regelmäßiger Leser refomatorischer Literatur. Luthers Brief vom 21. Dezember 1525 an Herzog Georg von Sachsen lag Brask in einer niederdeutschen Version vor, die 1526 in Rostock gedruckt worden war. Weniger lässt sich über den Druck sagen, der Herzog Georgs Antwortbrief auf Luthers Brief enthielt und der ebenfalls Brask zugänglich war.[27] Während die Frage des Imports pro- und anti-lutherischer Schriften aufgrund der Quellenlage doch mittlerweile eindeutig positiv beantwortet werden kann, gilt das nicht für eine andere für die reformatorische Buchkultur in Schweden wichtige Frage, ob zur gleichen Zeit anti-lutherische Schriften auch in Schweden gedruckt worden sind. König Gustaf Vasa klagte Hans Brask in

24 Czaika, Plinius, 37.

25 Czaika, Melanchthon, 237–259.

26 „[…] *hiis diebus ex Italia receptum tractatulum per Illustrissimum regem anglie in propria persona editum contra luterianam heresim* […].“ Gunneng, Registratur, 182–183 Nr. 99. Beispiele für die Verbreitungeschwindigkeit gedruckter Bücher um 1500 im Norden Europas bei Undorf, Gutenberg, passim.

27 Stobaeus, Från biskop Brasks tid, 197–198.

mehreren Briefen vom Anfang 1527, der Bischof lasse in Kopenhagen „visor", also Flugschriften, drucken.[28] Brask bestritt diesen Vorwurf energisch. Die Wahrscheinlichkeit ist groß, dass Brask – in Übereinstimmung mit kontinentalen Verteidigern der alten Kirche – wirklich aktiv schwedische oder dänische Druckereien für seinen Kampf gegen die Reformation in Anspruch nahm, sich aber vor dem König, dessen pro-lutherische Tendenzen ihm nur allzu sehr bewusst waren, keine Blöße geben wollte. Da aber keiner dieser vermutlich für die schwedische Öffentlichkeit gedachten Drucke erhalten ist und uns auch keine gesicherten bibliographischen Informationen vorliegen, kann diese Frage letztendlich nicht befriedigend beantwortet werden.

Gleichzeitig beleuchten solche vereinzelten Quellen aber auch eine große Schwäche bei der Untersuchung der frühen Reformation in Skandinavien; die Quellenlage ist im Allgemeinen sehr unzufriedenstellend.[29] Quellen zur Buchgeschichte der frühen Neuzeit sind nur selten erhalten und geben immer nur punktuelle Einblicke in aktuelle Ereignisse und Entwicklungen. Das gilt nicht nur für Briefe und andere archivalische Quellen. Es haben sich auch kaum gedruckte Bücher oder Bibliothekskataloge aus dieser Zeit erhalten. Es fehlen etwa heute nicht nur die oben genannten nach Schweden geschmuggelten lutherischen Bücher, sondern auch die Vorlagen für frühe skandinavische protestantische Drucke.

Hogenskild Bielke

Bis zu diesem Punkt habe ich mich überwiegend der Frage des lokalen, nationalen und transnationalen Buchdrucks und -imports im Hinblick auf die Auseinandersetzung und Einführung der Reformation in Schweden und Dänemark gewidmet. Bei den aus dem Zeitalter der Reformation und Konfessionalisierung bekannten, dokumentierten oder auch erhaltenen Büchern handelt es sich auch passender Weise fast ausschließlich um gelehrt-theologische und praktisch-pastorale Werke in lateinischer, nicht so selten auch in griechischer Sprache. Doch wie sah die Literatur aus, auf die ein Nicht-Theologe auf verschiedenen skandinavischen Buchmärkten Zugriff hatte? Beispiele dafür finden wir in den Bucherwerbslisten und in der erhaltenen Bibliothek des schwedischen Adligen Hogenskild Bielke (1538–1605).[30]

28 Stobaeus, Från biskop Brasks tid, 206–209.

29 Czaika, Melanchthon, 240–241.

30 Walde, Boksamlare. Undorf, Hogenskild Bielke's Library für seine Bibliothek.

Er war 1538 in eine hochadlige schwedische Familie geboren worden. Seine Schul- und Ausbildungswege sind stark geprägt einerseits von regionalen Ressourcen, andererseits von seit einer Generation schon traditionalisierten lutherisch-skandinavischen Bildungswegen; symptomatisch ist die Tatsache, dass von seinen ausländischen Studienaufenthalten nur der an der Universität Wittenberg dokumentarisch belegt ist. Er besuchte in der zweiten Hälfte der 1540er Jahre die Kathedralschule in Åbo, die damals unter ihrem Rektor, dem finnischen Reformator Mikael Agricola auf ein hohes Niveau gebracht worden war. Neben Wittenberg 1551 ist ein weiterer Auslandsaufenthalt an der Lateinschule in Odense, Dänemark, (1554–1555) nicht eindeutig dokumentiert.[31] Zwischen der zweiten Hälfte der 1540er Jahre und 1568 liegen Bielkes Auslandsaufenthalte. Nach 1568 hat Hogenskild Bielke Schweden nicht mehr verlassen. Sein langes Leben verbrachte er zum größten Teil wegen seiner hohen Stellung im schwedischen Staat und auf Grund seiner zentralen Position in der schwedischen Politik in der turbulenten und dynamischen zweiten Hälfte des 16. Jahrhunderts ortsstabil in Stockholm. Die letzten 7 Jahre bis zu seiner Enthauptung 1605 hat er überwiegend im Gefängnis verbracht, was seine Möglichkeiten zum Erwerb von Büchern zwar erheblich beeinträchtigt, aber nie ganz unterbunden hat. Dieses Faktum macht seine Büchererwerbungen und den Inhalt seiner erhaltenen Bibliothek zu einem außerordentlichen Indikator vor allem für den Zustand des absolut wichtigsten schwedischen Buchmarkts im Zeitalter der Konfessionalisierung.

Erhaltene Briefe berichten davon, dass Hogenskild Bielke während seiner Schuljahre 1547–1549 (1550?) an der Lateinschule in Åbo/Turku im heutigen Finnland eine kleine Anzahl von Schulbüchern erhalten und durchgearbeitet hat. Als erstes begegnet uns natürlich ein Donat. Die Ausgabe kann nicht festgestellt werden; es gibt kaum bekannte skandinavische Ausgaben des Donat. Es hat sich daher mit an Sicherheit grenzender Wahrscheinlichkeit um einen Import aus Leipzig oder einer Druckerei in einer der deutschen Hansestädte an der Ostseeküste gehandelt.[32] Bei dem in den Quellen genannten Gesangbuch handelt es sich dagegen fast sicher um eine der bis dahin erschienenen schwedischen Gesangbuchausgaben, die von Stockholm aus natürlich auch nach Åbo exportiert und dort verkauft worden sind. Bielkes bekannte Schullektüre wird abgerundet durch eine unbekannte Ausgabe der Komödien des Terentius. Darüber hinaus könnten die folgenden beiden in der Universitätsbibliothek in Uppsala erhaltenen Titel, die zusammen einen Kolligatband bilden, gegen Ende

31 Berg, Hogenskild Bielke.
32 Siehe Malmö-Bücherliste.

seines Aufenthalts in Åbo erworben worden sein (falls es sich nicht um eine spätere, quasi antiquarische Erwerbung handelt): ein *Hortus Sanitatis*, Straßburg 1536, sowie Walter Hermann Ryffs *Anatomica omnium humani corporis*, Paris 1545. Der Einband dieses Kolligatbandes wurde vermutlich in Åbo hergestellt und kann auf um 1550 datiert werden.

Auf Grundlage der erhaltenen Besitzeinträge kann man erschließen, dass Bielke in der Zeit zwischen ca. 1550 bis ca. 1569 einige wenige seiner Bücher auf der Innenseite des vorderen Einbanddeckels mit „Her" oder „e" gekennzeichnet hat, was gerade für diese Periode charakteristisch ist, während das Kürzel „f:e" sowohl in den meisten frühen wie auch späten Erwerbungen anzutreffen ist. Es sind allerdings keine Titel/Bücher bekannt, die Bielke nachweislich 1551 in Wittenberg im Zusammenhang mit seinen Studien an der dortigen Universität erworben haben könnte. Ein paar der in seiner Bibliothek vorhandenen ältesten Bücher könnte Hogenskild Bielke während seines nicht überzeugend dokumentierten Aufenthalts 1554–1555 an der Lateinschule in Odense, Dänemark, erworben haben.[33] Es sind aber, das muss konstatiert werden, in seinen erhaltenen Büchern keinerlei Provenienzhinweise festzustellen, die irgendwie direkt mit Odense in Verbindung gebracht werden können. Lediglich vom Thema der Bücher her oder im Hinblick auf ihr Alter und ihren geographischen Ursprung könnte man argumentieren, dass einer oder mehrere der folgenden Titel unter diesen frühesten dänischen Erwerbungen gewesen sein könnten:

- *Acta der Disputation zu Flensburg*, Wittenberg 1529
- Bugenhagen, Johannes: *Wider die Kelchdiebe*, Magdeburg 1532
- Capito, Wolfgang Fabricius: *Ein wunderbar geschicht … so sich an eim Widertäuffer … zuotragen*, Straßburg 1534
- Tertullian, Quintus: *Opera*, Basel 1528

Die folgenden vier Kolligatbände sind nicht eindeutig zu datieren. Sollte es sich hierbei um Erwerbungen aus der ersten Hälfte der 1550er Jahre handeln, dann sind sie möglicherweise erst kurz vor Hogenskild Bielkes Ritterschlag 1561 als in seinem Besitz befindlich gekennzeichnet worden. Der älteste Band in Bielkes Besitz wäre der, der Guido de Columnas *Historia Troiana Guidonis*, Straßburg 1494, und Pelbartus Oswaldus de Temesvárs *Stellarium Corone benedicte virginis Mariae*, Hagenau 1502 enthält. Er ist ganze drei Mal mit „Her" bzw. „Herr" gekennzeichnet, Bielkes ältester bekannter Provenienz, und damit eindeutig der Zeit bis 1569 zuzuordnen. Der Einband ist im frühen 16. Jahrhundert entweder in Deutschland oder von einem eingewanderten deutschen Buchbinder in Stockholm hergestellt worden. Die Dekoration dieses

33 Walde, Boksamlare übergeht diesen Aufenthalt komplett.

braunen Schafsledereinbandes ist fast identisch mit der des weißen Schweinsledereinbandes, der folgende zwei Titel enthält: *Valerius Maximus cum commento Oliuerii Arzignanensis* in der Ausgabe Venedig 1505 sowie Caius Julius Caesars *[De bello Gallico] Commentaria Caesaris*, Venedig 1499. Laut Eintrag war er ein Geschenk des aus Finnland stammenden, späteren Erzbischofs Andreas Laurentii. Bielke selbst hat diesen Band erst einige Jahre später, nämlich 1564 als seinen Besitz gekennzeichnet, wiederum mit „Her". Der Einband ist einer der ältesten datierten in Bielkes Bibliothek.

Die beiden letzten Bände datiere ich aufgrund ihres jeweiligen Inhalts auf die Zeit vor 1560, obwohl sie mit dem erst ab 1569 üblichen „f:e" („friherre") gekennzeichnet worden sind. Der eine Band enthält sieben, zwischen 1548 und 1556 gedruckte Titel:

- Georg Meier *Trostschrifft*, Wittenberg 1554
- Johannes Freder sen. *Von dem Mißbrauch und Diebstahl der Kirchengüter*, Rostock 1556
- Veit Dietrich *Christliche … auslegung etlicher … Sprüche S. Johannis*, Wittenberg 1549
- Georg Meier *Zwo Predig vber das Euangelium johann*, Wittenberg 1552
- Remigius Albulanus *Exemplar eines Rechtgeschaffnen Christlichen Testaments*, Nürnberg 1550
- Martin Luther *Etliche Trostschrifften vnd Predigten*, Wittenberg 1548
- Leonhard Jacobi *Ein Christlicher lieblicher Trostbrieff… An die … Fürsten zu anhalt geschrieben*, Wittenberg 1554

Der andere Band enthält lediglich zwei Titel um die Mitte der 1550er Jahre gedruckt: das erste von zwei in Bielkes Bibliothek erhaltenen Exemplaren von Philipp Melanchthons *[Loci theologici Deutsch] Heubtartikel Christlicher Lere*, Wittenberg 1556, und Joachim Magdeburg *Epitaphivm Das ist Eine Grabschrifft … Johannis Aepini*, Hamburg 1553. Beide können daher sehr wohl Erwerbungen um 1560 darstellen.

Aus Anlass der Krönung des schwedischen Königs Erik XIV (1533–1577) im Jahr 1561 wurde Hogenskild Bielke zum Ritter geschlagen. Danach benutzte Bielke die Provenienz „Ridder" bzw. „Rit", jedoch nur in zwei erhaltenen Büchern. Das eine ist ein früher dänischer Druck, die Ausgabe der *[Expositiones circa leges Jutiae] Quedam breues expositiones*, [Ribe 1504] mit den Glossen Bischofs Knut von Viborg. Dieses Buch könnte Bielke in der Mitte der 1550er Jahre in Odense oder aber auch erst 1568 in Kopenhagen (siehe nächster Abschnitt) erworben haben. Es kann sich aber genauso gut um eine antiquarische

Erwerbung auf dem schwedischen Markt handeln.[34] Das andere ist eine weitere Inkunabel, ein Exemplar der *Chronica Mundi* des Hartmann Schedel mit früher Nürnberger Provenienz („*Liber Laurentij torst presbiteri norimbergensis partis orientalis*“) in einem Koberger-Einband. Bielke datierte seinen Besitzeintrag 1564 (*Hogenskildt Bielcke Rit Anno e 1564*). Aufgrund der Nürnberger Provenienz könnte es sich hierbei jedoch auch um eine frühere Erwerbung aus Deutschland aus den 1550er Jahren handeln.

Der Buchmarkt von Kopenhagen 1568

1567 übertrug der schwedische König Erik XIV. Hogenskild Bielke den Oberbefehl über eine Armee-Einheit im Krieg gegen Dänemark. Anfang Februar 1568 wurde er gefangengenommen und nach Kopenhagen gebracht. Dort verbachte er den größten Teil dieses Jahres. Während dieser „ehrenvollen“ Gefangenschaft hatte Bielke ausgiebig Gelegenheit, den Kontakt zu seinen dänischen Verwandten sowie zu anderen dänischen Adligen wiederaufzunehmen oder neu zu knüpfen. Gleichzeitig bekam er Zugang zum Buchmarkt in der dänischen Hauptstadt. Eine nicht unerhebliche Zahl von Büchereinkäufen dokumentiert eine von Bielke eigenhändig geschriebene Bücherliste aus dem Jahr 1568, von denen aber heute fast alle verloren gegangen sind.[35] Luthers *Psalter Deudsch* (Nr. 3) ist die einzige von Bielke dokumentierte Erwerbung des Jahres 1568, die sich bis heute erhalten hat, nämlich in der Bibliothek der Schule von Herlufsholm in Naestved, Dänemark. Die Liste umfasst insgesamt 43 Nummern, von denen die meisten aber Kolligatbände repräsentieren, womit die Anzahl der identifizierbaren Titel 112 beträgt, die meisten sind allerdings entweder gar nicht oder nur mit Vorbehalt zu identifizieren. Von diesen muss man ein leeres Malbuch abziehen, so dass 111 gedruckte Werke übrigbleiben. Von diesen hat sich kein Titel erhalten.

Außer eigenen Erwerbungen verzeichnet die Liste auch Geschenke an und von dänischen Adligen. Zu den solcherart dokumentierten Geschenken an die dänische Adelsdame Birgitte Göye gehört neben dem bereits erwähnten Psalter noch ein Exemplar von Johannes Manlius *Locorum communium* (Nr. 4–5).[36]

---

34 Zum antiquarischen Buchmarkt im östlichen Dänemark siehe die Malmö-Liste; Undorf, Gutenberg, 89.

35 Quelle zur Liste von 1568: Walde, Boksamlare.

36 Die Angabe bei Walde, Boksamlare, 205, ein Sammelband mit Spangenbergs *Der christliche Ritter* (Nr. 21:4) und einem *Würtzgärtlein für die kranken Seelen* (Nr. 18:2) sei von Hogenskild Bielke Frau Birgitte Göye zum Geschenk gemacht worden, ist eklatant falsch. Zum einen sind beide Titel Bestandteile verschiedener Kolligatbände, zum anderen fehlt in Bielkes Liste

Peder Tidemands Gebetbuch *En deylig Böne* war ein Geschenk an Susanna Jacob Bråkenhusses (10). Bielke erhielt auch selber Geschenke, so von Claus Glambek einen Kolligatband mit Wendel Schemps *Handtbüchlin Etlicher Trostreycher Gebet* (Nr. 17:1) und Johan Spangenbergs *Miles Christianus Von der Christlichen Ritterschaft* (Nr. 17:2). Nicht alle Erwerbungen aus dieser Zeit wurden aber dokumentiert, vermutlich weil sie erst nach Abschluss der Erwerbungsliste in Bielkes Besitz gelangten. Zwei solcherart undokumentierte, aber sehr wohl in der Universitätsbibliothek Uppsala erhaltene Buchgeschenke erhielt Hogenskild Bielke gegen Ende seiner Gefangenschaft von Folmer Rosenkrantz: Johannes Sleidans *Der erste[-ander] Theyl Ordenlicher beschreibunge* und das erste von zwei Exemplaren des *Sachsenspiegel.*

Der Büchermarkt Kopenhagens im Jahr 1568 war international, wenn auch eng begrenzt. Von den identifizierten Titeln auf der Liste kamen mindestens 70 % – zusammen mit den nicht identifizierbaren Titeln mehr als 80 % – aus Deutschland. Überraschender Weise stellen schwedische Druckerzeugnisse mit 9 % das drittgrößte Kontingent, danach erst gefolgt von dänischen Drucken (8 %). Spezialfälle sind die beiden Einträge, die vielleicht mit Exemplaren von Drucken der *Etliche schöne gebet vnd trostsprüche* der Elisabeth von Braunschweig-Calenberg, Königsberg 1561 (Nr. 19:1 und 22:2), identifiziert werden könnten. Aus Frankreich kam vielleicht nur das Exemplar der *Practica rerum criminalium* des Joost van Damhouder (Nr. 42:13).

Schaut man ein wenig näher auf die geographische Herkunft der erworbenen Titel, dann stellen neben all den Titeln, die keinem speziellen Druckort zugewiesen werden können, die Drucke aus Frankfurt am Main (10), Leipzig und Stockholm (jeweils 9) die größten Einzelkontingente dar. Geographische Faktoren haben mit Sicherheit keine wesentliche Rolle für die Belieferung dieses Buchmarktes gespielt. Das zeigt nicht nur das reichhaltige Angebot schwedischer religiöser Bücher, unter denen auch Übersetzungen Luthers (*Catechismus Item en liten Bönbok*) 1567 (Nr. 13:3 sowie Nr. 26) auftauchen, die also trotz des andauernden Krieges zwischen den beiden Ländern in Kopenhagen zum Kauf angeboten wurden. Größere Abstände zu überwinden hatten die in Süddeutschland gedruckten Titel. Aus Nürnberg kamen höchstwahrscheinlich Wendel Schemps *Handtbüchlin* (Nr. 17:1) und seine *Historia der heiligen zwölff Apostel* (Nr. 34:3) bzw. der *Widwe vnd Waisen Trost* (Nr. 15:2). Aus Straßburg stammen eine Ausgabe der *Chronica regnorum Aquilonarium Daniae Suetiae Noruegiae* des Albert Krantz (Nr. 2) und vermutlich eine Ausgabe des anony-

---

jeglicher Hinweis darauf. Stattdessen hat er Birgitte Göye zwei andere Bücher geschenkt, nämlich Martin Luthers *Psalter Deudsch* (Nr. 3) sowie Johannes Manlius *Locorum comunium* in zwei Teilen (Nr. 4–5).

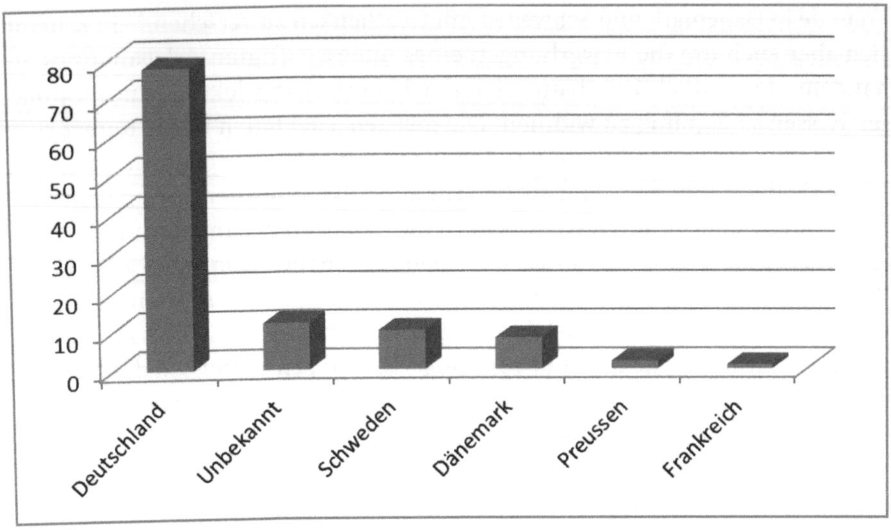

Druckorte und Anzahl der Erwerbungen Hogenskild Bielkes 1568 (verallgemeinert).

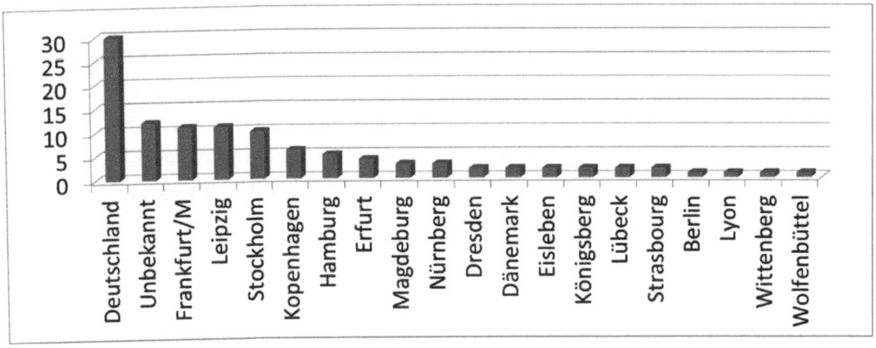

Druckorte und Anzahl der Erwerbungen Hogenskild Bielkes 1568 (aufgegliedert).

men *Rätherschbüchlein* (Nr. 39:2). Ansonsten präsentiert sich hier mit den Druckorten Leipzig, Hamburg, Erfurt, Magdeburg, Dresden, Eisleben, Lübeck, Wittenberg und Wolfenbüttel ein dominanter norddeutsch-lutherisch geprägter literarischer Einzugsbereich.

Das zeigt sich aber noch nicht im literarischen Spektrum der erworbenen Literatur. Die späte, theologisch so starke Bibliothek Hogenskild Bielkes ist hier noch nicht zu sehen. Stattdessen tritt das Bild einer Buchsammlung vor Augen, die laut Otto Walde (1879–1963) vor allem dazu dienen sollte, Verwandte und

Freunde in Dänemark und Schweden mit Geschenken zu versehen.[37] Es scheint sich aber auch um die Erwerbungen eines unbeschäftigten Adelsmannes zu handeln, der endlich Zeit hatte, sich der Unterhaltungslektüre und populärer Wissensaneignung zu widmen. Die meisten Titel fallen in die Kategorien Unterhaltungsliteratur, Erbauungsliteratur und praktisch orientierte Ratgeber. Mehr als die Hälfte der 111 Titel besteht aus Erbauungsliteratur im weiteren Sinne, von Gebet- und Gesangbüchern zu Psaltern und anderem (60 Titel). Jeweils etwa ein Viertel zielt ab auf Unterhaltung (26) beziehungsweise populäre Wissensvermittlung (21 Titel). Bei der Unterhaltungsliteratur dominieren natürlich die Ritterromanzen, bei den Ratgebern – ebenso wenig überraschend – praktisch-medizinische Literatur zum Aderlass und den Einflüssen des Mondes und der Sterne auf den Menschen. Die restlichen vier Titel verteilen sich auf die Fächer Theologie (2), Geschichte (1) und Recht (1).

Es kann nicht grundsätzlich ausgeschlossen werden, dass nicht doch der eine oder andere der Drucke, die Bielke 1568 in Kopenhagen erworben hatte, irgendwo erhalten geblieben ist. Einer der dort aufgelisteten Kolligatbände enthielt 12 deutschsprachige Komödien und Tragödien. Die Tastsache, dass Bielke diese Drucke hat zusammenführen und binden lassen, deutet auf eine gewisse Fürsorge um diesen Typ von Literatur. Als Einzelwerk wurden sie wohl in kürzester Zeit zerlesen und verschlissen. Gesammelt in einem Kolligatband sollten sie eine wesentlich größere Überlebenschance gehabt haben, falls sie nicht von übereifrigen Bibliothekaren des 19. oder 20. Jahrhunderts geschlachtet, systematisch eingeordnet, eventuell sogar neu eingebunden wurden und damit nun in irgendeiner Bibliothek ein anonymisiertes Dasein ohne erkennbare Provenienzen fristen.

Offen bleiben auch die Fragen nach der Identität einzelner Titel wie *Flores und Blanchefleur* (Nr. 33:1), Martin Luthers Predigt über das 5. Kapitel Hoseas (Nr. 37:2), der Liedersammlung *104 neue Lieder* (Nr. 33:3) und all der namenlosen Gebet- oder Aderlassbüchlein und astrologischen Schriften. Auch wenn die Identität vieler Schriften nicht geklärt werden kann, kann man doch davon ausgehen, dass es sich in vielen Fällen um Aktualitäten gehandelt haben wird. Michael Bocks Hamburger Drucke (Nr. 18:2 und 20:2), Hieronymus Wellers *Passional* (Nr. 21:1) und das Eislebener Liederbuch *Neun Schöne Geistliche Lieder* scheinen im Jahr ihrer Erwerbung durch Hogenskild Bielke veröffentlicht worden zu sein. Die meisten schwedischen Drucke stammen aus dem Vorjahr 1567, wie auch möglicherweise viele Leipziger Drucke. Eine schnelle Versorgung des Kopenhagener Buchmarktes mit aktuellen kontinentalen wie

---

37 Walde, Boksamlare, 204.

skandinavischen Ausgaben gewisser Literatur scheint also gewährleistet worden zu sein.

Dieser Artikel ist weit davon entfernt, ein vollständiges Bild der Buchgeschichte Schwedens im Zeitalter der Reformation und Konfessionalisierung als Medienereignis zu zeichnen, dazu reichen die erhaltenen und zugänglichen Quellen bei weitem nicht aus. Hier können aber bereits anhand von Beispielen einige der Dimensionen aufgezeigt werden, die man anhand der Frage nach Akteuren und Strategien der Verbreitung von Erzeugnissen des europäischen und skandinavischen Buchdrucks für einen schwedischen Sammler herausarbeiten kann. Das einheimische Druckgewerbe war teils nicht leistungsfähig genug, die skandinavischen Buchmärkte nicht bedeutend genug, als dass sich auswärtige Drucker ernsthaft dafür interessiert hätten, reformatorisches Schrifttum für Skandinavien zu drucken und dorthin zu exportieren. Die skandinavischen Drucker waren aber auch zu sehr politisch und kirchlich gegängelt, um einer eventuell vorhandenen eigenen reformatorischen Agenda physischen Ausdruck zu verleihen.

Wir wissen aus den Briefen Bischof Hans Brasks, dass bereits früh (höchst wahrscheinlich deutschsprachige) pro-Lutherische Schriften illegal nach Schweden importiert wurden. Das gleiche müssen wir auch für Dänemark annehmen. Czaika hat pointiert darauf verwiesen, dass die Reformation ein Transferprozess gewesen ist, an dem Theologie und Menschen, handgeschriebene Briefe und Drucke gleichermaßen Anteil hatten. Es ist aber leider so, dass der Anteil des Buchdrucks wie des Buchhandels nur sehr schwer zu umgreifen ist. Die Reformation in Dänemark und Schweden war viel mehr ein theologisch-politisches Projekt. Volkssprachliche reformatorische Schriften und insbesondere dänische oder schwedische Übersetzungen der Schriften Luthers sind in einem solchen Ausmaß abwesend in diesem Bild, dass man im Hinblick auf die Vermittlung der Reformation an breitere Volksschichten zumindest zu Beginn zu Recht von einer Reformation ohne Luther sprechen könnte.

Man muss natürlich hier sich der Gefahr bewusst sein, dass aufgrund der schlechten Quellenlage die eine oder andere Schlussfolgerung ohne Gewähr oder falsch sein kann. Aber einige grundsätzliche Erkenntnisse kann man doch ziehen. Die Einführung reformatorischen Gedankenguts erfolgte vermutlich über zwei Hauptwege, zum einen in Form illegal eingeführter deutschsprachiger reformatorischer Druckschriften, zum anderen in Form der Predigten in Wittenberg ausgebildeter skandinavischer Theologen. Charakteristisch scheint zu sein, dass sich in Dänemark und Schweden fast schon symbolhaft mit Übersetzung und Druck des Neuen Testaments auf Dänisch (1524) und Schwedisch (1526) zum ersten Mal offiziell reformatorisches Gedankengut manifestiert. Schaut man dann in erhaltene Bibliothekskataloge und andere Bücherlisten, so stellt man fest, dass der deutlich geringere Anteil sowohl einheimischen als auch

Übersetzungen ausländischen reformatorischen Schrifttums dem Siegeszug der Reformation in beiden Ländern keinen Abbruch getan hat. Besonders für die gelehrten Theologen stellte die Lage auf den einheimischen Buchmärkten kein Problem dar. Sie wurden eh brieflich, über Privatimporte, aber mehr noch über den transnationellen Buchhandel vor allem mit den großen Drucker-Verlegern Mittel- und Süddeutschlands ausreichend mit lateinischer protestantischer Literatur versorgt. Leider können wir aufgrund der Quellenlage keine einzelnen Akteure ausmachen, die mit ihren Handlungen diese Buchmärkte konstituiert und dauerhaft versorgt haben. Aber sowohl die quantitativen wie bibliographischen Ergebnisse meiner Untersuchung zeigen die Existenz und Leistungsfähigkeit dieses Buchhandels an. In vielerlei Hinsicht macht die frühe Reformation in Skandinavien den Eindruck einer Reformation ohne einheimisches Buch und eines Medienereignisses ohne Akteure, aber bei weitem nicht ohne Bücher und Resultate.

Nach 1568: Stockholm

Nach 1568 war Hogenskild Bielke wieder in Stockholm, der letzte seiner Auslandsaufenthalte war zu Ende. Von jetzt ab können wir anhand seiner Erwerbungen gewisse Einsichten darin bekommen, wie der Büchermarkt in Stockholm im letzten Viertel des 16. Jahrhunderts beschaffen war. 1569 wurde Hogenskild Bielke im Zusammenhang mit der Krönung König Johann III. zum Freiherren ernannt. Seit Beginn der 1570er Jahre bedient sich Hogenskild Bielke immer öfter – jedoch nicht ausschließlich – der Abkürzung „f:e" zusammen mit anderen Provenienzmerkmalen. Zu den Büchern, die Bielke aller Wahrscheinlichkeit nach zwischen 1568 und der Mitte der 1570er Jahre erworben hat, gehören folgende Titel:

- Petrarca, Francesco: *[De remidiis utriusque fortunae Deutsch] Das Glückbuoch*. Augsburg 1539. Erworben frühestens 1569 nach dem Tod des Baumeisters Paul Schütz.
- Ryff, Walter Hermann: *Der Architectur … bericht vnd verstendliche vntterrichtung*. Nürnberg 1558. Schwedischer Einband.
- Neubauer, Sebastian: *Über die Epistel S. Pauli an die Römer*. Elbingen 1562. Einband Kapsar Anglers in Königsberg (Haebler Bd. 1, 14).
- Caesar, Caius Julius: *[De bello Gallico] Warhafftige Beschreibunge*. Frankfurt am Main 1565. Ex. 1. Provenienz „Her Hogenschilldtt Bielcke e".
- Meurer, Noe: *Cammergerichts ordnung vnd Proceß*. Frankfurt am Main 1567. Provenienz „Her Hogenschilldtt Bielcke e".
- Meusel, Simon: *Postilla Das ist Außlegung der Euangelien*. Eisleben 1569. Provenienz „Her Hogenschilldtt Bielcke e".

- Pollicarius, Johannes: *Der heiligen XII. Aposteln ankunfft ... etc.* Wittenberg 1561. Provenienz „Her Hogenschilldtt Bielcke e".

Diese Titel, allesamt erhalten in der Universitätsbibliothek Uppsala, sind zugegebenermaßen zeitlich schwierig zu platzieren. Betrachtet man aber ihre Druckjahre und die vorhandenen Provenienzinformationen, so liegt es nahe anzunehmen, dass es sich um Erwerbungen nach Bielkes Rückkehr nach Stockholm handelt, also frühestens Ende 1568.

Aus der Zeit zwischen 1568 und 1578 lassen sich eine Reihe Erwerbungen festmachen, die in Hogenskild Bielkes 1995 rekonstruierter Bibliothek in der Universitätsbibliothek Uppsala erhalten sind:

- Alessandrini, Giulio: *Salubrium sive de sanitate tuenda.* Köln 1575. Einband Hans Düsterbach (1569–86), kein Supralibros.
- *Amadis de Gaula.* Bd. 4:2, Augsburg 1578. Bd. 5, Frankfurt am Main 1572. Bd. 10–12, Frankfurt am Main 1574. Bd. 13, Frankfurt am Main 1575. Einbände Jochen Ropers, kein Supralibros.
- Cassander, Georg: *De articulis religionis inter Catholicos et Protestantes controversis.* Stockholm 1577. Wurde anscheinend direkt vom Drucker an Bielke geliefert.
- Hondorff, Andreas: *Promptuarium exemplorum Historienn vnd Exempelbuch.* Leipzig 1572. Provenienz „Hogenskchildt Bielcke f:e Anno e 1572".
- Sabellico, Marco Antonio Coccio: *Opera.* Basel 1538. Erworben spätestens 1577 nach dem Tod König Erik XIV.
- Tertullian, Quintus: *Opera.* Basel 1528. Unbekannte Provenienz.

Diese sechs Titel können aus verschiedenen Gründen der Erwerbungsperiode vor 1578 zugeschlagen werden. Dabei handelt es sich um eine weitgefächerte Mischung von Genres, vom Ritterroman und einem medizinischen Werk über ein Geschichtsbuch, den theologischen Folianten als Memorabilium an den verstorbenen König Erik XIV. bis zu Georg Cassanders höchst aktuellem kirchenpolitischen Werk. Mehr Information zu Bielkes Büchererwerbungen gibt uns eine zweite erhaltene Bücherliste aus dem Jahr 1578, die punktartig auch ein hervorragendes Zeugnis für die Tätigkeit der in Stockholm ansässigen, wohl deutschstämmigen Buchhändler und Buchbinder Jochen Roper und Thomas Scheppe darstellt. Die von Thomas Scheppe selbst auf 1578 datierte Liste mit der Überschrift „*Item herr Hogenskilldt fan mir empfangen Anno 78*" verzeichnet 105 Einträge, davon nach Abzug eines Schreibbuchs mit leeren Seiten und einer Medizinhandschrift 103 Drucke.

Die Liste ist leider mehr eine Abrechnung von Buchbinderarbeiten und gelieferten Büchern als ein bibliographisch zufriedenstellendes Inventar. Daher lässt sich etwa ein Drittel der Einträge bibliographisch nicht zufriedenstellend identifizieren. Diese sind entweder unter einem Sammelbegriff aufgeführt (4 historien bücher, 6 Tabulen, 2 Tabulen, 2 klein Betbücher swedisch, 3 Psalmen bucher swedisch och 3 sma betbucher swedisch) oder unter materiellen Gesichtspunkten zusammengefasst, wobei Mehrfachnennungen auftreten können (6 bergamentt bücher, 8 octaua gebunden, 8 stucke in folio, 17 stucke in octaua, 2 in quarta, 1 in octaua). Unter den Historienbüchern könnte man sich möglicherweise noch am ehesten Volksbücher oder Ritterromane vorstellen und unter den Tabulen die beliebten Ephemeriden, die weitverbreitete Mischung aus astronomischen und astrologischen Tabellen. Auch hier gilt, wenn auch anscheinend nicht im selben Ausmaß wie hinsichtlich der dänischen Erwerbungen des Jahres 1568, dass sich wohl die wenigsten Bücher erhalten haben. Heute lassen sich nur noch 15 Titel in der Universitätsbibliothek Uppsala nachweisen:[38]

- Athanasius: *Opera*. Basel 1564.
- *Christliche Fragstück Von dem vnterscheid der zweien Artickel des Apostolischen Glaubens Bekentnis*. Wittenberg 1572.
- Chytraeus, David: *Onomasticon theologicvm*. Wittenberg 1571.
- Cicero, Marcus Tullius: *De officiis*. Straßburg 1574?
- Dietrich, Veit: *Annotaqtiones compendiariae in Novum testamentum*. Frankfurt am Main 1545.
- Dionysius Areopagita: *Opera*. Paris 1566?
- *Doctrina recte vivendi ac moriendi*. Basel 1577.
- Georg III of Anhalt: *Conciones et scripta complectentia summam verae doctrinae*. Wittenberg 1570.
- Irenaeus, Saint: *Opus Eruditissimum*. Basel 1571.
- Irenaeus, Christoph: *Prognosticon Aus Gottes Wort*. Wittenberg 1578?
- Matthesius, Johannes sen.: *Historia Vnsers lieben herrn vnd Heylands Jesu Christi*. Nürnberg 1572.
- Matthesius, Johannes sen: *Historien Von des Ehrwirdigen .... Martini Luthers anfang lehr leben und sterben*. Nürnberg 1566.
- Platina, Bartholomaeus: *Historia ... de vitis pontificvm Romanorvm*. Köln 1574.
- Plutarch: *Dvo commentarii ... Quomodo adolescens poetas audire debeat*. Basel 1566?
- Tertullianus, Quintus Septimius Florens: *Scripta*. Basel 1550?

38 Ein Dionysius mit der Nummer 59 scheint zu einem unbekannten Zeitpunkt nach Einverleibung der Bielke-Bibliothek in die Universitätsbibliothek Uppsala verloren gegangen zu sein.

Im Unterschied zu den Büchern, die Bielke nachweislich 1568 in Kopenhagen erworben hatte, handelt es hier sich bereits zum überwiegenden Teil um theologische Literatur, die das inhaltliche Profil der späten Bibliothek Hogenskild Bielkes entscheidend prägen wird. Gleichzeitig fällt aber auch wiederum auf, dass alle „leichtere" Literatur verloren gegangen ist, also alle die oben genannten Historienbücher, Tabulae und Gebetbücher. Was für einen Eindruck bekommt man nun auf der Grundlage dieser Bücherliste vom Stockholmer Buchmarkt um das Jahr 1578? Der Gesamteindruck ist im Großen und Ganzen vergleichbar mit dem von Kopenhagen zehn Jahre vorher, nämlich die absolute Dominanz des norddeutschen, lutherischen Einzugsbereichs (siehe Grafik unten). Die große Zahl an nicht identifizierbaren Titeln aus unbekannten Druckorten kann daher mit Sicherheit auch der Gruppe deutscher Druckorte zugerechnet werden.

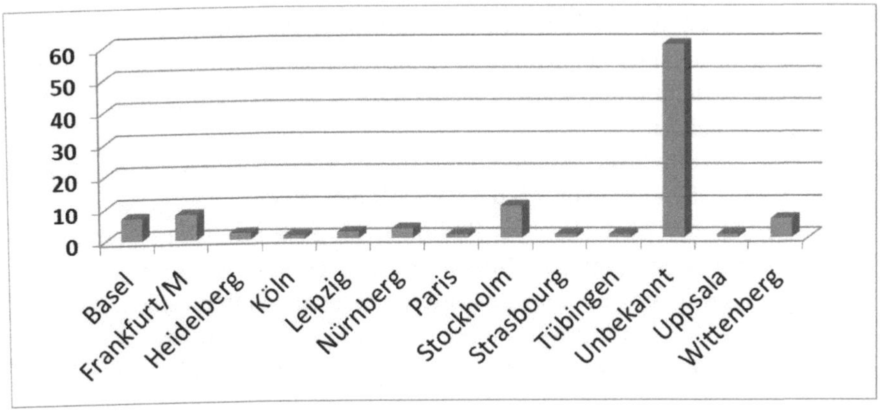

Einige wenige neue Druckorte findet man nach durchgeführter Titelbestimmung, aus denen Roper und Scheppe die folgenden Titel importiert hatten: aus Nürnberg Joachim Camerarius *De re rustica opuscula nonnulla* (1577), Johannes Matthesius sen. *Historia Vnsers lieben herrn vnd Heylands Jesu Christi* (1572.) sowie vom gleichen Autor die etwas ältere Biographie Luthers, *Historien Von des Ehrwirdigen .... Martini Luthers anfang lehr leben und sterben* (1566). Vielleicht kam die Ausgabe der *Opera* des Dionysius Areopagita aus einer Pariser Druckerei (1566?). Aus Köln stammt die *Historia ... de vitis pontificvm Romanorvm* des Bartholomaeus Platina (1574), aus Straßburg Marcus Tullius Ciceros *De officiis* (1574). Bei den „prutenica Tabule in quarta" handelt es sich anscheinend um eine der Ausgaben der *Prutenicae tabulae Coelestium motuum* des Erasmus Reinhold, gedruckt in Tübingen 1551 oder 1562. Gleich zwei Exemplare einer

Schrift „Contra Jesuitarum" wurden an Bielke geliefert, dabei könnte es sich um Wilhelm Rodings Buch *Contra Impias Scholas Iesuitarum*, Heidelberg 1575? gehandelt haben. Von diesen neun Titeln sind heute mit Sicherheit vier verloren gegangen, nämlich die beiden antijesuitischen Schriften und die Tabulae des Reinhold. Ein weiteres Buch, eine Cicero-Ausgabe, hat sich möglicherweise erhalten, falls wir annehmen, dass das heute in der Bielke-Sammlung erhaltene Exemplar, aber später neu eingebundene Buch dasselbe ist wie das in der Liste. Die restlichen vier Titel sind wohl identisch mit den entsprechenden in der Bielke-Sammlung der Universitätsbibliothek Uppsala erhaltenen Büchern.

Welche Art von Literatur bezog Bielke nun über die beiden Buchhändler/-Buchbinder von den altbekannten kontinentalen Druckorten? Aus Basel kam überwiegend theologische Literatur in Form von Ausgaben von Kirchenvätern (Athanasius, Irenaeus und Tertullian), aus Frankfurt am Main und Wittenberg kamen theologische Arbeiten lutherischer Autoren (Chytraeus, Luther, Dietrich, Heshusen). Auch die identifizierte Unterhaltungsliteratur kam von Frankfurter Druckereien (*Reinecke Voss, Grobianus et Grobiana*). Der lokale Stockholmer Buchmarkt garantierte lediglich die Grundversorgung mit Bibeln und Gesangbüchern.

Für die letzten zwei Jahrzehnte seines Büchererwerbs in Stockholm (1579–1598) haben wir lediglich das Zeugnis der in der Universitätsbibliothek Uppsala erhaltenen Bücher aus der Bibliothek Hogenskild Bielkes. Wir können also weder verloren gegangene Bücher im Großen noch verloren gegangene spezielle Literaturkategorien im Besonderen (Tabulae, Ephemeriden, Ratgeber, religiöse und Unterhaltungsliteratur etc.) abgreifen. Nur noch ganz wenige Bücher aus der Periode nach 1578 sind eindeutig als Geschenke gekennzeichnet. Der zweite und dritte Teil des *Wintertheils Der Kleinen Catholischen Postill* des Jakob Feucht war ein Geschenk des Jesuiten Antonio Possevino bei seiner Ausreise aus Schweden 1580: *„Och förährades mig af then Enfoldige Man Anthonio Posseuino 1580. NB Papistisch"*. Ein weiteres Geschenk ist datiert 1592. In diesem Jahr bekam Bielke von Bartill Folger sowohl das erste von zwei Exemplaren von John Cases's *Sphaera civitatis* (Frankfurt am Main 1589)[39] als auch Henri Estiennes *Principum monitrix* (Basel 1590) als Geschenke. Bei beiden Gelegenheiten wurden Schenker und Datum genauestens im Inneren des jeweiligen Buches verzeichnet. Das einzige Buch aus diesen Jahren, von dem wir wissen, dass Bielke es selbst verschenkt hat, ist ein Exemplar von Walter Ryffs *Schwangerer Frawen Rosengarten* (Frankfurt am Main 1569), ein

39 Ein zweites Exemplar aus Bielkes Besitz wurde später von der Universitätsbibliothek Uppsala als Dublette verkauft und befindet sich heute im Besitz der Stadtbibliothek Karlstad.

Einbandkennzeichnung	Anzahl	Periode
H*H*B	29	1577
H+H+B	23	1580–98 & undatiert
H H B 1584	18	1584
H H B 1590	1	1590
H H B 1595	1	1595
H H B	5	1698 & undatiert

Neujahrsgeschenk 1582 an seine Frau Anna Sture, das nichts desto weniger mit dem Rest seiner Bibliothek in Uppsala gelandet ist.

Die Datierung vieler der aus diesen Jahren erhaltenen Bücher wird durch die vermehrte Datierung der Einbände erleichtert. So wurden in den Jahren 1580, 1584, 1595 und 1598 schwerpunktmäßig die Einbände einer größeren Anzahl von Büchern mit den Initialen „H H B“ bzw. „H+H+B“ gekennzeichnet und vor allem 1584 auch mit der Jahreszahl versehen. In den 1580er und 1590er Jahren benutzte Bielke also immer öfter einen Bandtyp, bei dem seine Initialen und oft auch eine Jahreszahl in schwarzer Farbe auf den vorderen Einbanddeckel geprägt wurden. Diese Einbände erleichtern natürlich wesentlich die Datierung der Erwerbungen oder auf jeden Fall, wann der entsprechende Inhalt eingebunden wurde.

Zusammen mit dem Eintrag über die Schenkung Possevinos ist deren Einband mit den eingeprägten Initialen „H+H+B“ auf das Genaueste zu datieren. Dieser Typ des Supralibros taucht danach erst wieder in einer Gruppe von Einbänden auf, die dank handschriftlicher Eintragungen Bielkes auf das Jahr 1598 datiert werden können und damit das letzte Stadium seines Büchererwerbs darstellen. Eine größere Anzahl von Büchern wurde 1584 eingebunden und mit den Provenienzen „H H B 1584“ auf dem äußeren vorderen Einbanddeckel sowie ”f:e” im Buch versehen. Dazu gehören Werke zu Geschichte und Kirchengeschichte, sowie theologische, juristische und ökonomische Literatur. Aus dem Jahr 1590 liegt nur ein, mit „H H B 1590“ auf dem äußeren vorderen Einbanddeckel und „f:e“ im Buch datierter Einband vor, der ein Exemplar der *Epigrammatum libri sex* des Melanchthon, Wittenberg 1563, umschließt. Auch aus dem Jahr 1595 liegt nur ein, durch den Aufdruck „H H B 1595“ eindeutig datierter Einband vor. Darin verbirgt sich ein juridisches Werk, Johannes Oldendorps *Actionum forensium Progymnasmata* in einer Lyoner Ausgabe von 1577. Unter den absolut letzten Erwerbungen Hogenskild Bielkes aus der Zeit bis 1598 begegnen uns mit den Provenienzmerkmalen „H H B“ oder „H+H+B“ auf dem äußeren vorderen Einbanddeckel und „f:e“ im Buch wieder eine größere Anzahl theologischer und konfessioneller Schriften, aber auch wieder mehrere historische und politische Arbeiten.

Aus den 1580er und 1590er Jahren existiert eine ganze Reihe von Büchern, die von Bielke relativ konsequent auf dem inneren vorderen Einbanddeckel mit Namen und Datum versehen wurden. Repräsentativ für die Erwerbungen des Jahres 1585 ist etwa der Besitzeintrag in David Chytraeus' *Auslegung Der Offenbarung Johannis* (Wittenberg 1584): *„Hogenschilldtt Bielcke f:e Anno e 1585"*. Ein anderer Titel, der 1585 im Jahr nach seiner Drucklegung 1584 in Bielkes Bibliothek einverleibt wurde, sind die *Psalmi Davidis* vertont durch Orlando di Lasso und gedruckt in München. 1587 wurden nachweislich drei Titel in die Bibliothek aufgenommen. Dabei handelt es sich ausnahmsweise nur um naturwissenschaftliche Literatur, zwei Arbeiten zur Seefahrt – die natürlich auch einiges an geometrischem und mathematischem Stoff enthielten: Michiel Coignet *Nieuvve Onderwijsinghe op de principaelste Puncten der Zee-vaert* und Pedro de Medina *De Zeeuaert*, beide 1580 in Antwerpen gedruckt. Der dritte Titel ist Jakob Köbels *Geometrey*, Frankfurt am Main 1584. Auch in den folgenden Jahren, von 1589 bis zu den letzten datierten Erwerbungen 1598, überwiegt anteilmäßig die nicht-theologische Literatur, als ob die aktive Auseinandersetzung mit theologischen Fragen für Bielke zumindest zeitweise etwas an Bedeutung verloren zu haben schien. Unter den Erwerbungen der Jahre 1589–1591 überwiegen historische Arbeiten.

Erwerbungsjahr 1589:

- *Concordia .... Bekentnüs ... Augspurgischer Confession*. Magdeburg 1581
- Giovio, Paolo sen.: *Das leben Bapst Leonis des zehenden*. Leipzig 1584

Erwerbungsjahr 1590:

- Melanchthon, Philipp: *Epigrammatum libri sex*. Wittenberg 1563

Erwerbungsjahr 1591:

- Andreae, Jakob, sen.: *Acta des Colloquij ... zu Baden gehalten*. Tübingen 1590
- Andreae, Jakob, sen.: *Ein christlich Gespräch ... Von der Catholischen Apostolischen Christlichen Kirchen*. Tübingen 1590
- Baumgarten, Johannes: *Summarischer begriff der Magdeburgischen Stadt Chronicken*. Magdeburg 1587
- Caesar, Caius Julius: *[De bello Gallico] Warhafftige Beschreibunge*. Frankfurt am Main 1565. Ex. 2
- Curio, Caelius Secundus: *Thesaurus linguae latinae*. Basel 1576–1578
- Eytzinger, Michael: *Historica postremae relationis appendix. Das ist Ein Histörische veruolgung*. Köln 1588
- Eytzinger, Michael: *Niderlendischer Beschreybung der Ander theil*. Köln 1585
- Eytzinger, Michael: *Niederländische Beschreibung in Hoch teutsch*. Köln 1587

- Eytzinger, Michael: *Appendicis historicae … Ein weythere historische vervuolgung … 1589*. Köln 1589
- Horst, Jakob: *Das Fünffte Buch … Von den wunderbarlichen geheimnissen der Natur*. Leipzig 1588
- *[Kalender, Römischer] Notwendige … Bedenckhen Von dem … Römischen Kalender*. Heidelberg 1584
- Krafft, Adam: *Rettung Des Christlichen Tauffbüchleins Herrn D. Martini Lutheri*. [Unbekannter Ort] 1591
- Lauterbeck, Georg: *Regenten buch*. Wittenberg 1581
- Lindenbrog, Erpold: *Chronica Von dem Scheutzlichen Kriege*. Hamburg 1589
- *Niderlendischer Beschreibung der dritte theyl*. Köln 1587
- Richenthal, Ulrich: *[Das Concilium so zu Consstantz gehalten ist worden] Costnitzer concilium*. Frankfurt am Main 1575
- Selneccer, Nikolaus: *Von Heiligen Abendmal des herrn*. Frankfurt am Main 1591
- Sleidan, Johannes: *Ordenliche Beschreibung*. Straßburg 1587
- *Theatrum Mundi Das ist Der Welt Schawplatz*. Dresden 1588
- Weiße, Peter: *Meißnische Land vnd Berg-Chronica*. Dresden 1589–1590

Im Jahr 1598 sehen wir dagegen einen starken Einschlag von Arbeiten, die sich mit aktuellen politischen und jetzt auch wieder mit konfessionellen Fragen beschäftigen:
- Alber, Erasmus: *Christlicher nützllicher und vnd nohtwendiger Tractat von der Kinder Tauff*. Frankfurt am Main 1591
- Assum, Johannes: *Spiegel Deß Erkendtniß Gottes*. Frankfurt am Main 1590
- Bapst, Michael: *Artzney Kunst*. Leipzig 1592
- Beccadelli, Antonio degli: *De Dictis & Factis Alphonsi Regis Aragonum*. Rostock 1591
- Case, John: *Sphera Ciuitatis*. Frankfurt am Main 1589. Ex. 2
- Cicero, Marcus Tullius: *Epistolarvm libri tres*. Eisleben 1573
- Coler, Johannes: *Oeconomiae Oder des Hausbuchs …. Dritte theil*. P. 3. Wittenberg 1597
- Collibus, Hippolytus a: *Palatinus siue Aulicus*. Hannover 1595
- Crell, Fortunatus: *Isagoge logica*. Neustadt 1598
- Cuno, Johannes: *Anleitung Aller stende Spiegel*. Magdeburg 1583
- Cuno, Johannes: *Hoffarts Laster*. Wittenberg 1590
- Damhoudere, Josse de & Cavalcani, Borgnino: *Patrocinium pupillorum et viduarum nouum*. Frankfurt am Main 1586
- *Der Anhaldinischen Theologen Bedencken … des newich außgegangenen Concordienbuchs*. Neustadt 1581

- Engel, Andreas: *Kurtzer … Bericht von Johan Hilten vnd seinen Weissagungen*. Frankfurt/O 1597
- Erastus, Desiderius: *Varia opuscula medica*. Frankfurt am Main 1590
- Erich, Augustus: *Klarlige ac Visse Beskriffuelse Om … Christians den Fierdis … Kroning*. Kopenhagen 1598
- Gobler, Justin: *Chronica der Kriegßhändel … Maximiliani*. Frankfurt am Main 1566
- Gobler, Justin: *Chronica vnd Historien der Braunschweigischen Fürsten*. Frankfurt am Main 1566
- Gobler, Kaspar: *Wider die lesterliche Calumnia des … M. Flaschens*. Straßburg 1591
- Gregorii, Joachim: *Ein sehr nützlicher Tractat Vom ampte und eigenschafft der Richter*. Frankfurt am Main 1593
- Heilbrunner, Jakob: *Gründtliche vnd außfürliche widerlegung … vom heiligen Abendmal*. Lauingen 1593
- Herlitz, David: *Das Ander Buch vom Türcken*. Stettin 1597
- Hesshusen, Tilemann: *Extract oder Auszug aus einem Christlichen Sendbrieff vnd Warnung*. Eisleben 1591
- *Historia de vita … Viperti. Chronica Von … Wiprechten zu Groitzsch in Meissen*. Eisleben 1584
- Kittelman, Christian: *Zehen Grobe vnd schedliche Irrthumb der Zwinglianer vnd Caluinisten*. Magdeburg 1592
- La Ramée, Pierre de: *In Ciceronis orationes et scripta nonnulla omnes*. Frankfurt am Main 1582
- *Mandata Sigismundi*. Stockholm 1596. Ex. 1
- *Mandata Sigismundi*. Stockholm 1596. Ex. 2
- Polmann, Albert: *Gülden Rose des Bapsts … was von dem … Schreiben … zu halten sey*. [Unbekannter Ort] 1591
- Polmann, Albert: *[Handbuch Darinnen … was sich bey Gerichte zutregt] Handtbuch*. Wittenberg 1590
- Schlichting, Sigmund von: *Stambuch … das Christi Leib vnd Blut im Abendmal … warhaffftig vnd wesentlich zugegen sey*. Frankfurt/O 1593
- Schöner, Johannes: *Tabulae resolvtae astronomicae*. Wittenberg 1588
- Winter, Erasmus: *Specvlvm magistratvs politici. Die Erklerung des LXXXII. Psalms*. Eisleben 1592

Einzelne Bücher aus dem Besitz Hogenskild Bielkes haben eine geographisch wie chronologisch recht lange Reise hinter sich. Aus Venedig und Lyon, Zürich, Genf und Paris kommen die am weitest gereisten und zu den ältesten gehören drei Inkunabeln sowie einige frühe Drucke des 16. Jahrhunderts. Die ältesten Ausgaben stellen aber wahrscheinlich eher antiquarische Erwerbungen dar, die keine sonderliche Aussagekraft für den Buchhandel gerade zurzeit Hogenskild Bielkes haben. Unter den verbleibenden, über das evangelische Nord-Europa breit gestreuten Druckorten nehmen wie zu erwarten in absteigender Reihenfolge Frankfurt am Main, Wittenberg, Basel und Straßburg die vordersten Plätze ein. Frankfurt am Main versah den Stockholmer Buchmarkt und damit Hogenskild Bielke mit dem breitesten Angebot an Literaturkategorien, von Unterhaltungs- und historischer Literatur bis zu den Arbeiten von Paracelsus (5 Titel) und Ryff, juristischer und ökonomischer Literatur. Unter den theologischen Autoren stechen die Arbeiten Johannes Brenz (6 Titel) und Nikolaus Selneccers (3 Titel) hervor. Wie zu erwarten, übertreffen bei den in Wittenberg gedruckten Titeln die Arbeiten Melanchthons zahlenmäßig die Luthers (6 gegen 3 Titel). Quantitativ gesehen sind David Chytraeus (4 Titel) sowie Georg Meier der Luther-Rezeption mehr als ebenbürtig. Basel glänzt mit einer Reihe von Kirchenväter-Ausgaben. Von den Druckereien Straßburgs erwarb Bielke historische Werke und Klassiker-Ausgaben, an erster Stelle die Werke Ciceros, sowie eine Anzahl von praktisch orientierten Arbeiten zu Haushaltung und Medizin. Betrachten wir nun die erhaltenen Bücher in Hogenskild Bielkes rekonstruierter Bibliothek in der Universitätsbibliothek Uppsala und klammern dabei die Titel aus, die in den Bücherlisten der Jahre 1568 und 1578 erwähnt werden, dann ergibt sich in Bezug auf deren Druckorte folgendes Bild:

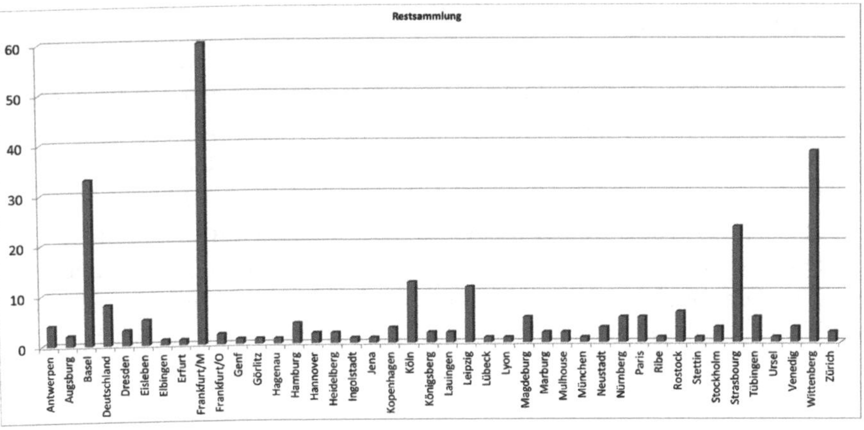

Selbstverständlich ist es möglich, auf der Grundlage der erhaltenen Zeugnisse eine recht aussagekräftige Zusammenfassung der Beobachtungen zum Büchererwerb und Bücherbesitz Hogenskild Bielkes vorzunehmen. Es ist aber fraglich, ob damit mehr als nur eine vorläufige und rudimentäre Charakteristik des transnationalen Buchmarkts in Skandinavien in der zweiten Hälfte des

16. Jahrhunderts möglich ist. Noch hat zumindest die schwedische Zunft der Buchhistoriker die neuesten Erkenntnisse und Erkenntnismöglichkeiten zur frühneuzeitlichen Buchgeschichte in Skandinavien und die Herausforderung durch das transnationelle Paradigma nicht angenommen. Immer noch geht man (mehr oder weniger stillschweigend) von der älteren Annahme aus, dass zu Hogenskild Bielkes Zeit ausländische Bücher hauptsächlich auf Reisen auf dem Kontinent erworben wurden.[40] Das Gespenst Otto Waldes liegt noch schwer auf der schwedischen Buchgeschichte, wonach „geordneter Buchhandel" ohne einheimischen „Verlagsbuchhandel" undenkbar und bestenfalls eine von Buchbindern oder Buchführern mehr oder weniger chaotisch ausgeführte Tätigkeit darstellt.[41] Die Analyse der Bücherlisten Hogenskild Bielkes aus den Jahren 1568 bzw. 1578 sowie seiner sonstigen Erwerbungen, so wie sie sich in der Universitätsbibliothek Uppsala und anderen skandinavischen Bibliotheken erhalten haben, spricht dagegen eine andere Sprache (siehe die folgende Grafik). Quantitativ stellt jede der beiden Bücherlisten jeweils mehr als ein Fünftel des totalen bekannten Buchbesitzes Bielkes dar, nämlich 22 bzw. 21 %. Fast die ganzen verbleibenden erhaltenen drei Fünftel wurden von Bielke während seiner sesshaften Jahrzehnte in Stockholm erworben. Verschwindend wenige seiner Bücher können während seiner in Wittenberg und andernorts auf dem Kontinent verbrachten Studienjahre erworben worden sein.

Walde erkannte zwar schon 1921 dieses Faktum im Prinzip auch an[42], jedoch hat weder er noch irgendein anderer schwedischer oder skandinavischer Buchhistoriker nach ihm daraus irgendwelche Konsequenzen für eine Neubewertung der schwedischen Buchgeschichte in einem transnationalen Zusammenhang gezogen. Konkret handelt meine Kritik davon, dass weder die Leistung des schwedischen Buchhandels noch die Bedeutung importierter Literatur für Manifestationen einheimischer Buchkultur bisher gehörig gewürdigt worden sind. Im Prinzip darf daher immer noch das Urteil unwidersprochen dastehen, das Ebbe Kock seiner Präsentation der zwei Listen, die Aufschluss geben über das Schicksal der Buchsammlung, die einst dem Leibarzt des schwedischen Königs Erik XIV., Benedictus Olai (1520–1583) gehört hat, vorangestellt hat: Olais Bibliothek könne nicht als Beispiel für schwedische Kultur gelten, da so gut wie alle Titel im Ausland gedruckt worden seien.[43]

---

40 Walde, Boksamlare, 197–198.

41 „*Någon ordnad bokhandel fanns vid denna tid knappast i Sverige.*" Walde, Boksamlare, 198. So auch noch im Winter 2015/2016 die Buchhistorikerin Lundblad, Föreställningar, 3.

42 Walde, Boksamlare, 199.

43 Kock, Bokkatalog, 146–147. Benedictus Olai ist Autor, oder besser Kompilator und Übersetzer, des ersten erhaltenen umfassenden Medizinbuchs in schwedischer Sprache; Lindroth, Lärdomshistoria 1975, 336–338.

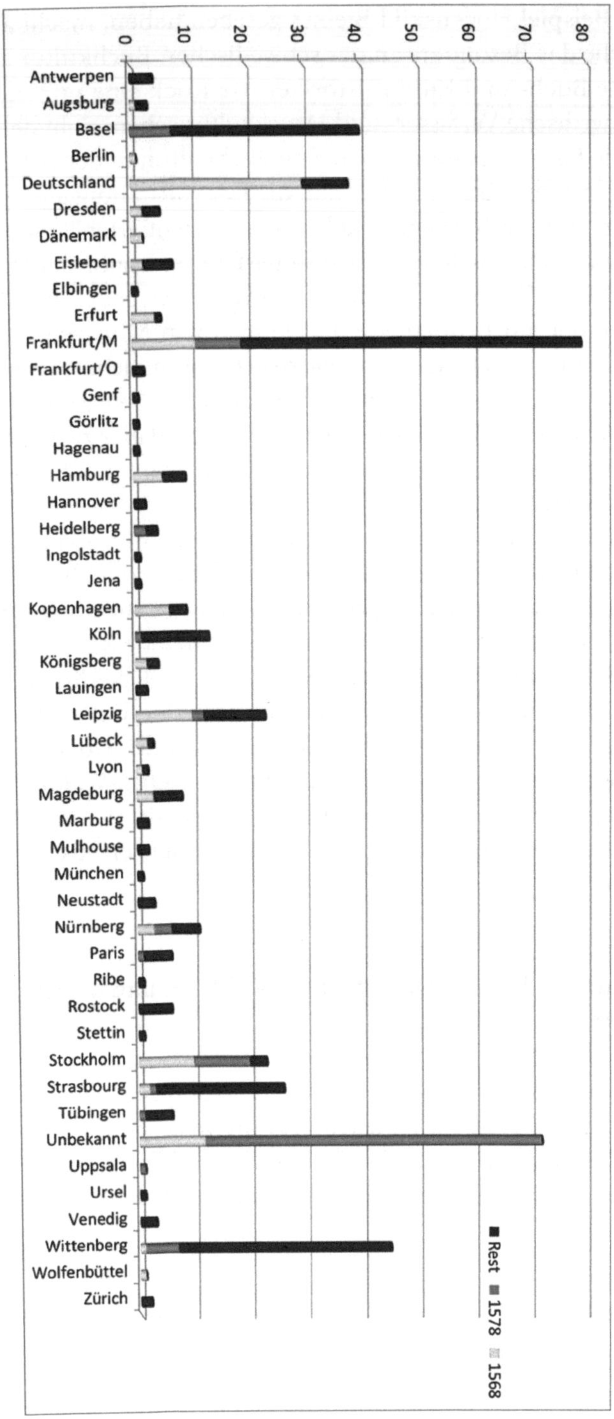
0
10
20
30
40
50
60
70
80
Antwerpen
Augsburg
Basel
Berlin
Deutschland
Dresden
Dänemark
Eisleben
Elbingen
Erfurt
Frankfurt/M
Frankfurt/O
Genf
Görlitz
Hagenau
Hamburg
Hannover
Heidelberg
Ingolstadt
Jena
Kopenhagen
Köln
Königsberg
Lauingen
Leipzig
Lübeck
Lyon
Magdeburg
Marburg
Mulhouse
München
Neustadt
Nürnberg
Paris
Ribe
Rostock
Stettin
Stockholm
Strasbourg
Tübingen
Unbekannt
Uppsala
Ursel
Venedig
Wittenberg
Wolfenbüttel
Zürich
Rest
1578
1568

Wie wir am Beispiel Hogenskild Bielkes gesehen haben, macht aber gerade diese Tatsache das Besondere an der schwedischen Buchkultur aus. Dort, wo schwedische Buch- und Kulturhistoriker wie Kock eine nur rudimentär entwickelte schwedische Verfasser- und Druckkultur sehen, sieht der transnational orientierte Historiker statt dessen eine Buchkultur, in der sich staatliche Kontrolle einheimischer Buchproduktion, die fast vollständig auf den Druck staatlich-bürokratisch sowie religiös-ekklesiastisch orientierter Texte ausgerichtet war, mit einem allen Anschein nach leistungsfähigen Importbuchhandel die Waage hielten.[44] Fast alle im 16. Jahrhundert in Schweden gedruckten Schriften antworten entweder auf Bedürfnisse und Fragen von Monarchie und Staat (politische und panegyrische Gelegenheitsdrucke, königliche Verordnungen, Mandate) oder von Kirche und Religion (Liturgica, Gebet- und Gesangsbücher, Erbauungsliteratur). Alle andere Literatur musste daher zwangsläufig aus dem Ausland importiert werden. Macht das den schwedischen Buchmarkt im 16. Jahrhundert ärmer?

Woran es mangelt, sind stattdessen zeitgenössische archivalische und Provenienzzeugnisse, die es uns wie im Fall Hogenskild Bielke ermöglichen, Schlussfolgerungen auf den Zustand des Importbuchmarkts von Stockholm zu ziehen. Wir besitzen zwar Dokumente, die uns einen Blick in eine Reihe von königlichen, adligen und anderen Buchsammlungen erlauben, Bücherlisten, Inventare etc. Wir wissen aber zu wenig über die Provenienzen der in diesen Listen verzeichneten Bücher, um die Frage beantworten zu können, wo jeder einzelne dieser Titel erworben worden sein könnte. Die von Otto Walde in seinem Aufsatz zu einigen der wichtigsten Büchersammlern aus der Familie Bielke erwähnten Bücher besitzen fast ausschließlich Provenienzen aus dem 17. und 18. Jahrhundert.[45]

Büchererwerbung in Schweden und Finnland im 16. und frühen 17. Jahrhundert

Von den Büchern im Besitz der Söhne Gustav Vasas besitzen wir auch Kenntnis durch einige zeitgenössische Bücherlisten. Das Inventar von 1563 der Besitztümer Herzog Johans, des späteren Königs Johan III. und seiner Frau Katarina Jagellonica (1526–1583) enthält auch einen Abschnitt mit der Überschrift „Här-

44 Das dritte Standbein einer Buchkultur, die Versorgung der lesefähigen Bevölkerung mit Populärliteratur, die es auch in Schweden in irgendeinem Ausmaß gegeben haben muss, ist noch nicht einmal ansatzweise angerissen worden.

45 Walde, Bielkeätten.

tugens böker", die Bücher des Herzogs.[46] Dieser Teil des Inventars verzeichnet 57 Schriften, oft bis zur Unkenntlichkeit verkürzt. In der Königlichen Bibliothek in Stockholm befindet sich der Entwurf eines Verzeichnisses der Bücher Johans III aus dem Jahr 1571.[47] Dieser umfasst 74 Einträge, wobei sich augenscheinlich 11 davon auf Bücher beziehen, die sich bereits 1563 im Besitz Johans befunden haben. Derselbe Schreiber Rasmus Ludvigsson hatte bereits drei Jahre zuvor den Bücherbesitz seines Vorgängers auf dem schwedischen Thron, Erik XIV., inventiert drei Tage bevor dieser auf den Thron verzichtete.[48] Die Liste enthält 221 Einträge, fast ausschließlich über gedruckte Bücher, aber deren Identität und damit eventuell auch Provenienz konnte in modernen Sammlungen bisher nicht festgestellt werden. Johan hatte als Herzog 1560 eine Reise nach England unternommen, während der er möglicherweise selbst die in den beiden Inventarien verzeichneten englischen Bibelausgaben erworben haben könnte. Von Erik XIV. ist kein solcher Auslandsaufenthalt bekannt. Demnach sind die Bücher in seiner Bibliothek entweder in Stockholm oder über Mittelsmänner im Ausland erworben worden.

Die Situation hinsichtlich der Bücher aus dem Besitz König Sigismunds (III.) (1566–1632) ist grundsätzlich gesehen ebenso unsicher wie bei seinen Vorgängern auf dem schwedischen Königsthron, aber gleichzeitig wesentlich verworrener, da es sich bei diesen Büchern viel öfter um Sekundärbesitz handelt.[49] Folgt man den Ausführungen Otto Waldes erscheint es als fraglich, ob Sigismund überhaupt in nennenswertem Umfang aktiv Bücher erworben hat. Walde nennt zahlreiche Beispiele dafür, dass Sigismund zum einen zahlreiche Bücher aus nach der Reformation konfiszierten schwedischen Klosterbibliotheken seiner eigenen Bibliothek vereinnahmt hat. Dazu zählen unter anderem eine größere Zahl von Inkunabeln[50] aus schwedischen Klöstern oder mit anderen schwedischen Provenienzen des 16. Jahrhunderts, die sich alle in der königlichen Bibliothek und damit später in der Schenkung an die Universitätsbibliothek Uppsala aus den Jahren 1620/1621 nachweisen lassen. Zum anderen enthielt Sigismunds Bibliothek zahlreiche Bücher, die ursprünglich seinem Onkel mütterlicherseits, dem polnischen König Sigismund II. August gehört hatten und Sigismund III. über seine Mutter Katarina Jagellonica, die Schwester Sigismund II. Augusts, als Erbe zugefallen waren.

Über diese königlichen Buchsammlungen hinaus kennen wir neben Hogenskild Bielke nur noch ein paar wenige andere schwedische Provenienzen aus

46 Hausen, Förteckning, 37–38.
47 Lindberg, Boksamling.
48 Concept.
49 Walde, Sigismund.
50 Undorf, Catalogue.

dem 16. Jahrhundert. Diese sind jedoch überwiegend, ebenso wie Bücher aus dem Besitz anderer Mitglieder der Bielke-Familie, aus in schwedischen Bibliotheken erhaltenen Büchern bekannt. Johann Copp (1487–1563) war ein aus Oberbayern stammender Arzt, der gegen Ende der Regierungszeit Gustav Vasas aus Prag nach Schweden gekommen war.[51] Walde hat 50 Titel in 10 Bänden aus Copps Besitz identifiziert, die er in schwedischen Bibliotheken gefunden hat, in der Universitätsbibliothek Uppsala ebenso wie in den Stiftsbibliotheken in Skara, Västerås und Strängnäs. Nach Copps Tod vor 1563 waren seine Bücher erst in den Besitz Herzog Johans übergegangen, spätestens 1563 aber war die Auflösung seiner Bibliothek bereits in vollem Gange. Für die Geschichte des schwedischen Buchhandels im 16. Jahrhundert sind Copps Bücher aber bedeutungslos, da es sich mit größter Wahrscheinlichkeit ausnahmslos um Erwerbungen vor seiner Einreise nach Schweden 1555 handelt.

21 Titel aus dem Besitz von Bischof Erasmus Nicolai Arbogensis (gest. 1580) in Västerås sind bekannt.[52] Zwei Drittel dieser aufgrund von Provenienzeinträgen und/oder Einbanddekor identifizierten Titel stellen Erwerbungen aus den Jahren 1558–1562 dar, als Erasmus Nicolai sich an der Universität in Wittenberg aufhielt. Die meisten der verbleibenden sieben Titel sind vier antiquarische Erwerbungen aus dem Besitz aufgelöster schwedischer Klöster, womit also nur noch drei Titel übrigbleiben, die möglicherweise Erwerbungen auf dem schwedischen Buchmarkt darstellen. Was Informationen zum Bücherbesitz des finnischen Reformators Mikael Agricola (1507–1557) angeht, sind wir voll und ganz auf die 16 in 11 Bänden erhaltenen Titel angewiesen.[53] Ungefähr ein Drittel stellen Erwerbungen aus Finnland dar, alle anderen wurden von Agricola während seines Aufenthalts an der Universität in Wittenberg 1537–1539 erworben. Auf dem einheimischen Buchmarkt standen ihm immerhin Werke folgender klassischer wie moderner Autoren zur Verfügung: Martin Luther, Erasmus Roterodamus, Hermannus Torrentinus, Valerius Maximus, Sebastian Münster und Johannes Bugenhagen.

Archivalische Zeugnisse liegen uns nur noch zu den umfangreichen Büchersammlungen des Arztes Benedictus Olais, des Bischofs von Skara Sveno Jacobi sowie des königlichen Sekretärs Henrik Matsson Huggut (1540–1617) vor, wobei es sich um Verzeichnisse handelt, die zu jeweils ganz speziellen Anlässen angefertigt worden sind. Die frühere der drei ist die Bibliothek Benedictus Olais, eines weiteren Arztes und Nachfolgers Johann Copps als Hofarzt.[54] Die 255 Titel in 324 Bänden, die sich nach seinem und dem Tod seiner Mutter

51 Walde, Johann Copp.
52 Walde, Erasmus Nicolai.
53 Czaika, Plinius.
54 Kock, Bokkatalog. Walde, Benedictus Olai. Hult, Benedictus Olai.

Herbst 1586 noch in Stockholm befanden, wurden Mitte Oktober jenes Jahres aufgelistet. Fast eine Generation später musste deren Erbe Nils Chesnecopherus von den verbliebenen Büchern 81 Titel an seinen Cousin Nicolaus Sabancorus abtreten. Über diese Bücher wurde am 2.4.1611 eine entsprechende Liste angefertigt. Die Einträge beschränken sich auf ein oder ein paar Autorennamen und/oder Titelstichworte, weswegen sie keine wesentlichen Schlussfolgerungen zur Erwerbungsgeschichte der Bibliothek ermöglichen. Benedictus Olai hatte sich von 1542–1560 in Deutschland und Italien aufgehalten und viele Titel können in dieser Zeit auf dem Kontinent erworben worden sein. In den Fällen, in denen klar ist, dass ein Titel erst nach Benedictus Olais Rückkehr nach Schweden Anfang 1561 im Druck erschienen ist, können wir einigermaßen sicher sein, dass er wohl in Schweden, hauptsächlich bei Stockholmer Buchhändlern erworben wurde. Dies ist bei 85 Titeln der Fall.

Drei Wochen nach dem Tod Bischof Sveno Jacobis in Skara wurde am 22. August 1554 ein Inventar erstellt, in dem unter der Überschrift „*Thette effterschriffne är titeln på alle hans böcker*" 40 Titel erfasst wurden. Darüber hinaus sind nicht nur weitere 14 Titel namentlich bekannt, die bereits vor 1554 aus der Bibliothek ausgesondert worden waren. Sveno Jacobi hat natürlich zu seinen Lebzeiten noch mehr Bücher besessen, als nach seinem Ableben vorgefunden wurden; sein Amtskollege Nicolaus Canuti, Bischof in Växjö, schrieb ihm 1551, er habe ihm eine (leider nicht näher spezifizierte och namentlich genannte) Anzahl von Büchern geschickt.[55] Sveno Jacobis Aufenthalt in Deutschland hat sich natürlich konstitutiv auf die Bildung seiner Buchsammlung ausgewirkt; 11 der insgesamt von Czaika zusammengetragenen Titel sind aller Wahrscheinlichkeit nach zwischen 1508 und 1510 in Rostock erworben worden. Die überwiegende Mehrzahl, nämlich weitere 40 Titel, wurden aber erst nach seiner Rückkehr nach Schweden erworben.

Ein charakteristisches Beispiel dafür – sowie für die einem Mann der Kirche und Akademiker mit Kontakten zu anderen Studenten seiner Alma mater zugänglichen informellen Beschaffungswege für Bücher – ist die Anwesenheit von zwei Exemplaren der lateinischen *Loci communes* des Philipp Melanchthon. Zwischen 1521 und 1531 erschien die erste Ausgabe, von der Jacobi 1554 noch immer ein Exemplar besaß, nämlich *Loci Communes Philippi the förste* (Nr. 21 a). Von der 1535 zum ersten Mal im Druck erschienenen völlig umgearbeiteten zweiten Ausgabe besaß Jacobi das Exemplar, das ihm ein Student aus Jacobis eigenem Bistum Skara in Wittenberg, Benedictus Olai Scarensis, mit Brief vom 18. Juli 1536 übersendet hatte, *Loci communes Philippi the […] se-*

55 Czaika, Sveno Jacobi, 69.

derme vtgongne (Nr. 21 b).[56] Wie bereits vorher erwähnt, erhielt Bischof Hans Brask in Linköping 1523 ein Exemplar der zwei Jahre zuvor in Rom unter dem Namen des englischen Königs Heinrich VIII. gedruckten Ausgabe der *Assertio septem* direkt aus der päpstlichen Kurie zugeschickt. Diese beiden Wege des Büchererwerbs prägen zusammen mit dem Erwerb direkt vor Ort immer noch das allgemeine Bild der Teilnahme schwedischer Leser an der europäischen, im Druck überlieferten literarischen Kultur in der frühen Neuzeit.

Die Reformation war ein komplexer Transferprozess, der vor allem da seine größte Bedeutung für informelle Buchverbreitungswege erreichte, wo reformatorische Schriften noch illegale Druckwerke waren oder wo die schwedischen reformatorischen kirchlichen Strukturen noch nicht voll etabliert waren. Im Laufe des 16. Jahrhunderts wuchs die Bedeutung des Buchhandels im Takt mit seiner Professionalisierung und der Etablierung der Reformation im Norden Europas. Das Beispiel Hogenskild Bielkes gibt uns wenigstens ein paar Anhaltspunkte für die Entwicklung der Buchmärkte in Kopenhagen 1568 und Stockholm ab 1578 weniger als Ersatz als vielmehr ein stetig an Bedeutung und Umfang gewinnendes Komplement zum informellen Buchhandel.

Noch schwieriger wird die Rekonstruktion der schwedischen Buchhandelsgeschichte, wenn es sich bei dem frühneuzeitlichen Buchbesitzer weder um ein Mitglied des Adels noch um einen Mann der Kirche handelt. Augenscheinlich passt diese Charakterisierung auf Henrik Matsson Huggut (ca. 1540–ca. 1617), Sekretär und Vertrauensmann Herzogs, später König Johan III.[57] Aus seinem Leben ist kaum etwas bekannt. Kiiskinen gibt an, Matsson Huggut hätte in den 1560er Jahren am Dreikronenkrieg (oder Nordischer Siebenjähriger Krieg) teilgenommen und sei 1568 als Assistent in der Kanzlei Herzog Johans, des späteren Königs Johan III., genannt worden. Danach habe er bis 1599 verschiedene hohe Positionen in der königlichen Verwaltung bekleidet, bis er vor der Bedrohung durch Herzog Karl (später König Karl IX.) aus Finnland erst nach Reval (Tallinn) und im Jahr 1600 weiter nach Polen floh.[58] Sein in Reval zurückgelassener Besitz fiel 1601 in die Hände Herzog Karls und wurde konfisziert. Im Zusammenhang damit wurde auch Hugguts Bibliothek von 292 Titeln in 314 Bänden erfasst, von der augenscheinlich kein einziger Band erhalten geblieben ist.[59] Die Liste der konfiszierten Bücher selbst gibt keinerlei Hinweise auf ihren Erwerb und Kiiskinen spekuliert lediglich an einer Stelle sehr kurz darüber,

56 Czaika, Sveno Jacobi, 64–66.

57 Kiiskinen, Henrik Matsson.

58 Kiiskinen, Henrik Matsson, 10–12.

59 Diese Bände waren in drei Kisten untergebracht. Undorf diskutiert die Bedeutung der Kapazitäten dieser und anderer bekannter Bücherkisten, bezieht sich aber, was Hugguts Bibliothek angeht, auf Kiiskinens Angabe von lediglich 309 Bänden; Undorf, Gutenberg, 118–121.

ob Hugguts Bücher aus der königlichen Bibliothek stammen könnten, z. B. als Ersatz für ein eigentlich in barer Münze auszuzahlendes Gehalt.[60] Falls dem wirklich so wäre, dann wäre die buchhistorische Frage nach der Herkunft der entsprechenden Bücher an sich ja lediglich um eine Stelle weiter gerückt und würde lauten: woher haben dann die schwedischen Herzöge und Könige ihre Bücher bezogen?

Wie dem auch sei, nach der bibliographischen Bestimmung der 1601 verzeichneten Titel lässt sich jedenfalls etwas sagen über das Datum post quem des möglichen Imports nach Schweden/Finnland und/oder Erwerbs durch Huggut oder andere. Bei der Herkunft der allermeisten Bücher bietet sich das gleiche Bild wie bei der Bibliothek seines Zeitgenossen Hogenskild Bielkes: Frankfurt am Main (15 Titel), Basel (32) und Wittenberg (20) sind die wichtigsten identifizierbaren Druckorte. Regional bedeutende Druckorte waren Rostock (8) und Stockholm (4 Titel). Eine Handvoll Titel kamen aus Paris (7), Köln (10) und Straßburg (6 Titel). 22 weitere Druckorte sind mit jeweils 1–3 Titeln repräsentiert, darunter aus skandinavischer Perspektive ansonsten so exotische Städte wie Dortmund, Grätz, Lemgo oder Posen.[61] Der absolut größte Anteil der verzeichneten Werke lässt sich allerdings aufgrund des Mangels an zusätzlicher Information leider keinem spezifischen Druckort zuweisen. Wenn wir aber davon ausgehen, dass die bisher herausgearbeiteten und bestätigten bibliographischen Analysen zu frühneuzeitlichen schwedischen Buchsammlungen auch für die Huggut-Sammlung Bestand haben, dann handelt es sich dabei hauptsächlich um Importe aus deutschen Druckorten.

Wenden wir uns nun dem buchhändlerischen und Provenienzbereich zu. Es ist auf der Basis der erhaltenen archivalischen Zeugnisse anzunehmen, dass Huggut spätestens ab 1568, seit er in der Kanzlei Herzog Johans fest angestellt war, Schweden, d. h. Stockholm und die zentrale Landschaft rund um den Mälar-See sowie Finnland, in dem Huggut als Gouverneur und Richter hohe Verwaltungsposten innehatte, nicht mehr verlassen hat. Die Erwerbungen von Büchern, die 1568 und später erschienen sind, wird sich also vor allem auf zwei Wegen abgespielt haben, zum einen direkt als Erwerbungen auf dem einheimischen Buchmarkt, zum anderen indirekt durch Zusendungen von Personen vor Ort auf dem europäischen Kontinent.

Auf der nächsten Seite wird gezeigt, wie sich die in seiner Bibliothek vorhandenen Werke entsprechend dem Jahr der Erstausgabe verteilen.

---

60 Kiiskinen, Henrik Matsson, 26–27.

61 Vorausgesetzt, dass die bibliographischen Identifizierungen, die der Autor hauptsächlich auf der Basis der Datenbank *Heritage of the Printed Book* und VD16 vorgenommen hat, korrekt sind.

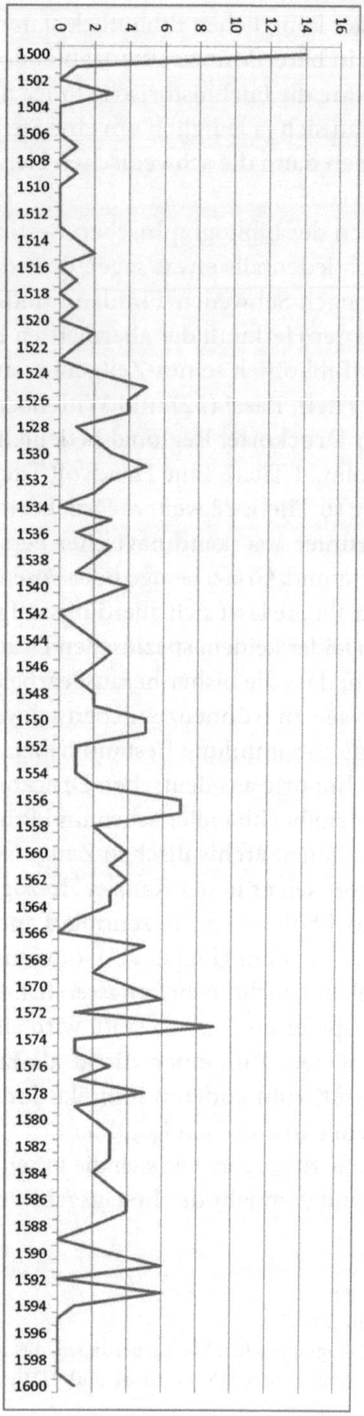
0
2
4
6
8
10
12
14
16
1500
1502
1504
1506
1508
1510
1512
1514
1516
1518
1520
1522
1524
1526
1528
1530
1532
1534
1536
1538
1540
1542
1544
1546
1548
1550
1552
1554
1556
1558
1560
1562
1564
1566
1568
1570
1572
1574
1576
1578
1580
1582
1584
1586
1588
1590
1592
1594
1596
1598
1600

Es können keine Titel identifiziert werden, deren Erstausgaben aus den Jahren 1589 sowie 1595–1599 belegt werden können. Das deutet darauf hin, das Huggut in diesen Jahren schon größere Schwierigkeiten oder gar nicht mehr in der Lage war, neue Literatur zu erwerben. Zwischen 1567 und 1594 erschienen aber jährlich 1–9 Titel in seiner Bibliothek, entweder in der Erstausgabe oder in der einzigen im Druck erschienen Ausgabe des 16. Jahrhunderts überhaupt. Es lässt sich quellenmäßig natürlich nicht eindeutig belegen, aber es ist nicht auszuschließen, dass der gleichmäßige Erscheinungstakt mit einem analogen Erwerbungstakt parallel geht. Ein ähnlicher Befund begegnet uns in der Erwerbungsgeschichte Hogenskild Bielkes aus den Jahren nach 1578. Gleichzeitig wissen wir aber aus der Rechnung der beiden Buchbinder/Buchhändler, die 1578 Hogenskild Bielke beliefert haben, dass größere Bestellungen auch punktuell durchgeführt werden konnten. Es ist aber die Frage, ob bei einer solchen Gelegenheit nicht in erster Linie Neuerwerbungen erfasst wurden, wie Bielkes Erwerbungsliste aus Kopenhagen aus dem Jahr 1568 nahelegt.

Charakteristisch für alle diese Beispiele für schwedische Buchbesitzer aus der zweiten Hälfte des 16. Jahrhunderts ist zum einen das fast komplette Fehlen schwedischer Literatur. Diese kann sowohl von ihren frühneuzeitlichen wie auch späteren Besitzern als von so geringem Wert angesehen worden sein, dass man sich weniger darum gekümmert hat, sie mit Provenienzen zu versehen oder sich um ihr Überleben und ihre Verzeichnung Gedanken zu machen. Zum anderen macht gerade das internationale Profil, die fast völlige Konzentration auf lateinischsprachige Bücher das wahre Merkmal dieser wahrhaft transnationalen Buch- und Schriftkultur aus, deren Produkte diese Bücher sind. Man las und korrespondierte eben zu einem überwiegenden Teil in der gelehrten Lingua Franca. Charakteristisch ist die Erkenntnis, das Bücher in anderen Sprachen als Latein entweder auf besondere Wissensbedürfnisse (Bücher in Griechisch) oder auf besondere Lebensumstände verweisen (Herzog Johan hat die englischen Bücher, die in zwei erhaltenen Bücherlisten erwähnt werden, aller Wahrscheinlichkeit nach während seines Aufenthalts in England als Brautwerber bei Elisabeth I. für seinen Bruder Erik XIV. erworben). Dagegen sind die ebenso massenhaft wie illegal nach Schweden eingeführten pro-lutherischen Schriften in deutscher Sprache, auf die in den Briefen Bischof Hans Brasks aus den 1520er Jahren immer wieder hingewiesen wird, wieder aus unserem Blickfeld verschwunden. Es sind dem Autor keine zeitgenössischen schwedischen Provenienzen bekannt. Dies stellt die schwedische Buchgeschichtsschreibung vor nahezu unüberwindliche Schwierigkeiten. Die Tatsache, dass es nicht einmal Ansätze zu einer Provenienzverzeichnung von Drucken des 16. Jahrhunderts gibt, die der Verzeichnung von Provenienzen von Inkunabeln oder bis 1525 erschienenen Drucken das Wasser reichen kann, verschärft noch den Widerstand, mit dem jeder Versuch zu rechnen hat, dieser Epoche gerecht zu werden.[62]

62 Undorf, Catalogue. Undorf, Gutenberg; die dieser Arbeit zugrunde liegende Liste zeitgenössischer skandinavischer Provenienzen ist online zugänglich als Teil 2, 543–1094 der Doktorarbeit des Autors unter http://edoc.hu-berlin.de/dissertationen/undorf-wolfgang-2012-01-05/PDF/undorf.pdf.

Remi Kick

Erzbischof Laurentius Petri und die Buchgeschichte der schwedischen Reformation

Thema dieses Beitrags ist die Präsentation und die buchhistorische Bewertung eines ehemaligen Studenten in Wittenberg, Laurentius Petri (1499–1573), von 1531 bis zu seinem Tod Erzbischof von Uppsala und damit im Zentrum der schwedischen Reformation.

Vorgeschichte

Laurentius wurde 1499 in Örebro, der Hauptstadt der schwedischen Provinz Närke, geboren. Seine Kindheit und Jugend fällt mit den Jahrzehnten zusammen, in denen die Kalmarer Union von 1397 zerfiel und Schweden, in einem zum Teil heftigen und blutigen Konflikt mit Dänemark, seine Eigenständigkeit wiedererlangte.[63] Laurentius' sechs Jahre älterer Bruder Olavus war zwischen 1516 und 1518 Student in Wittenberg gewesen, wo er auch zum *magister artium* promoviert wurde. Nach seiner Rückkehr wurde er in Schweden Sekretär des Bischofs von Strängnäs, Matthias Gregersson. Gregersson war einer der ersten, der beim Stockholmer Blutbad am 8. November 1520, seine Unterstützung für die Selbstbestimmung Schwedens mit dem Leben bezahlte.[64]

Gustav Eriksson Vasa (1496–1560) wurde im August 1521 in Vadstena zum Reichsvorsteher ernannt und auf dem Reichstag zu Strängnäs 1523 zum König gewählt. Als König duldete Gustav Vasa die Befürworter einer Kirchenreform.[65] Eine schwedische Übersetzung des Neuen Testaments erschien im August 1526 in der einzigen damals aktiven schwedischen Druckerei zu Stockholm. Dieses Neue Testament 1526 war das dritte schwedische Druckerzeugnis, das einem „reformatorischen" Geist Ausdruck verlieh (Fig. 1).[66] Nach dem Reichstag von Västerås im Juni 1527, der die Verkündigung des reinen Gotteswortes forderte, verfasste König Gustav am 25. Juli ein Empfehlungsschreiben an

63 Westman, Genombrottsår, 49–74 & 120–140. Metcalf, Scandinavia.
64 Holmquist, Reformationstidevarvet, T. 3:1, 80f. Westman, Genombrottsår, 118.
65 Westman, Genombrottsår, 133 & 144. Holmquist, Reformationstidevarvet, T. 3:1, 86 & 89.
66 Holmquist, Reformationstidevarvet, T. 3:1, 112 & 120.

Martin Luther für drei schwedische Studenten.[67] Laurentius Petri schrieb sich am 23. Oktober 1527 an der, wegen der Pest, nach Jena verlegten Universität Wittenberg ein.[68] Erst am 13. April 1528 kehrte die Leucorea vollständig nach Wittenberg zurück.[69]

In einem Brief vom 20. Januar 1563 berichtet Laurentius Petri, dass er Luther, Melanchthon und Bugenhagen sowohl als Universitätslehrer als auch als Prediger gehört habe.[70] Alles deutet darauf hin, dass Laurentius wohl von 1528 bis 1530 Student in Wittenberg war, ansonsten hätte er kaum sowohl Luther als auch Melanchthon und Bugenhagen vorlesen und predigen hören können.[71] Bei seiner Weihe zum Erzbischof 1531 galt Laurentius Petri, dem päpstlichen Legaten Johannes Magnus (1488–1544) gemäß, als „unerfahren, gerade von der Schule und der Rute der Lehrer befreit."[72] Man findet Laurentius' Namen nicht auf der Liste der neunundzwanzig Schweden, die zwischen 1517 und 1561 Magister geworden sind.[73]

Zur schwedischen Buchgeschichte

König Gustav errichtete 1526 de facto ein Monopol für den Buchdruck in Schweden; es gab nur noch eine Druckerei im Land. Von 1526 bis 1573 erschienen in Schweden 215 Titel, deren Umfang sehr unterschiedlich war: vom großen Folianten bis zum kleinen Oktavband. Ein Großteil der Produktion waren Drucke in der Kategorie Bibelausgaben, Liturgien, Rituale und Gebetsbücher. Schweden musste in sechzehnten Jahrhundert sowohl das Papier, wie auch die Druckausrüstung importieren.[74]

---

67 Holmquist, Reformationstidevarvet, T. 3:1, 156–157. Carlsson, Wittenbergsstudier, 43.

68 Carlsson, Wittenbergsstudier, 43. Foerstermann, Album, 130–131.

69 Foerstermann, Album, 129.

70 "[…] non ab ullo praestigiatore aut fanatico anabaptista, quales revera (ut liquido apparet) fuerant praeceptores huius mei criminatoris, sed a viris probatissimis foelicissimae recordationis doctore vidilicet Lu- thero, per quem Deus puram evangelii veritatem hoc seculo mundo restituit, et D[octore] Philippo Melanthone[!], Pomerano [Bugenhagen], etc. Quos viros ut aliquandiu publice legentes, disputantes et in ecclesia concionantes meis auribus presens audierim." Laurentius Upsalensis. Christiano Lectori. s. d. [20.1.1563], Linköpings stiftsbibliotek, T 235, Bl. 36r–v; Kungliga Biblioteket, Rålamb Bd. 40 4:o, 357.

71 Bornkamm, Luther, 527, 548, 562, 576–577 & 582. Maurer, Melanchthon, T. 2, 471 & 486. Lohse, Melanchthon, 405–406. Holfelder, Bugenhagen, 357.

72 Laut Johannes Magnus „rerum inexpertum et nuper a schola et ferula magistri subductus", zitiert nach Kjöllerström, Kräkla, 20. Lindroth, Johannes Magnus.

73 Callmer, Wittenberg, 6.

74 Kick, Book.

Nur siebzehn Werke von Laurentius Petri wurden zu seinen Lebzeiten gedruckt.[75] Zwanzig seiner insgesamt siebzig bekannten Schriften sind noch heute nur als Handschriften zugänglich und liegen also nicht einmal in einer neueren Ausgabe vor. Der Wunsch der Pfarrerschaft beim Konzil von Uppsala 1593, das die Schriften der schwedischen Reformatoren gesammelt und herausgeben würden, ist für das Werk von Laurentius Petri bis heute noch nicht erfüllt.[76] Die Handschriften des Erzbischofes waren seiner Zeitgenossen bekannt und hatten auch als solche eine breite Wirkung und Verbreitung. Der Schwiegersohn und Nachfolger von Laurentius Petri, Abraham Andreae Angermannus (1540–1608) gab drei Schriften des Erzbischofes in Deutschland posthum heraus.

Das Werk von Laurentius Petri umfasst, sowohl kurze schwedische und lateinische handschriftliche Briefe, als auch umfassende, gedruckte Predigtsammlungen. Von Amts wegen war Laurentius Petri auch für die Herausgabe der schwedischen Bibel 1541 und der nachfolgen Neuübersetzungen einzelner biblischer Bücher zumindest mitverantwortlich. Der Erzbischof war, wenn auch nicht immer klar ist in welchen Umfang, an der Herausgabe von Liturgien und Gebetsbüchern beteiligt, oder hat sie beaufsichtigt.[77] Die Bibliothek von Erzbischof Laurentius Petri wurde sehr wahrscheinlich, mit einem Großteil der Bestände der Königlichen Bibliothek, ein Opfer des Stockholmer Schlossbrandes von 1697.[78] Es ist uns kein zeitgenössisches Bildnis von Laurentius Petri erhalten.

Laurentius Petris Werk

1. Unter König Gustav I.

Für eine kurze Zeit hatte Laurentius Petri die „praebenda scholastria“ des Domkapitels von Uppsala inne.[79] Für die bevorstehende Hochzeit von Gustav Eriksson mit Katharina von Sachsen-Lauenburg war es nötig, nach langer Vakanz, einen schwedischen Erzbischof zu wählen.[80] Laurentius Petri wurde vor Ende

75 Collijn, Bibliografi. Zur Problematik, dass bis dato keine aktuelle schwedische Nationalbibliographie vorliegt, siehe auch den Beitrag von Otfried Czaika in diesem Band.

76 "Meniga presterskapets besvär framstälda på mötet i Uppsala 1593", Riksdagsakter, 115.

77 Nur der Brief an Georg Norman vom 12 November 1540 belegt die Teilhabe von Laurentius Petri an der Herausgabe der sog. Gustav Vasa-Bibel (1541). Zu den Teilausgaben der Bibel siehe Collijn, Bibliografi, Bd. 2, 43–49, 168–177, 182–183 & 287–290.

78 Lundstedt, Bibliotek.

79 Kjöllerström, Striden, 50.

80 Holmquist, Reformationstidevarvet, T. 1, 214–215. Åsbrink/Westman, Ärkebiskopar, 205. Kjöllerström, Kräkla, 19–20.

August 1531 gewählt und am 22. September von dem, in Rom konfirmierten Bischof von Västerås, Petrus Magni (†1534) im Gråmunkekloster, dem Kloster der „grauen Mönche" (also der Franziskaner) zu Stockholm geweiht.[81] Ein Vertrag vom November 1533 regelte die Einkünfte des Erzbischofs von Uppsala und bestimmte, dass er nur mit königlicher Erlaubnis Reformen unternehmen durfte.[82] Laurentius Petri hat wohl in diesem Zusammenhang seine ersten, uns bekannten, Schriften verfasst: Kommentare zu dem Rezess und der Ordonanz des Reichstages von Västerås 1527, welche die Rolle der Kirche neu bestimmten.[83] Das schwedische Reichsarchiv verwahrt vier Briefe der Jahre 1535, 1537 und 1539 von Laurentius Petri an den Bischof zu Skara Sveno Jacobi.[84] Leider haben wir keine Spur der Briefe von Sveno Jacobi an den Erzbischof. Die, zum Teil schwer lesbaren, Handschriften geben ein Bild von den Debatten zum Verständnis und der Geltung des Kirchenrechts in Fragen der Verantwortung von Geistlichen vor weltlichen Gerichten und des Eherechtes. Eine Debatte die sowohl die Bischöfe wie auch die jeweiligen Domkapitel befasste.[85] Die Herausgabe der Psalmen, Sprüche, Weisheit und Prediger Salomo und Jesus Sirachs im Jahr 1536 belegen, dass die Arbeit mit der Übersetzung des Alten Testaments bereits im Gange war.[86]

Die Synode von Uppsala im Oktober 1536 verpflichtete die Kathedralen und soweit wie möglich die Hauptkirchen im Lande, die schwedische Liturgie zu gebrauchen. Aus diesem Grunde wurde eine Neuauflage der schwedischen Messe (*Then Swenska Messan*) im Jahre 1537 gedruckt.[87] Dieselbe Synode hob das Priesterzölibat auf und stellte die Pfarrer vor die Alternative entweder in keuscher Ehelosigkeit zu leben oder ehrlich zu heiraten.[88]

Das erste im Druck erschienene Werk von Laurentius Petri war ein Traktat über das Weihwasser (*Een forclaring om wijgdawatn*, 1538). In dieser Erklärung betont der Erzbischof, dass das Weihwasser nicht mit der Heiligen Schrift zu begründen ist und dass dessen Missbrauch nur durch eine friedliche Abschaffung beseitigt werden kann.[89]

---

81 Kjöllerström, Ärkebiskopsvalet, 237. Holmquist, Reformationstidevarvet, T. 1, 217. Åsbrink/-Westman, Ärkebiskopar, 206. Piltz, Månsson.

82 Holmquist, Reformationstidevarvet, T. 1, 231. Andrén, Introductorium, 52–53.

83 Laurentius Petri, Recess. Laurentius Petri, på Ordinantien. Åsbrink/Westman, Ärkebiskopar, 209. Hellström, Laurentius Petri.

84 Laurentius Petri, Visitationis virginis matris (1535), Vigila omnium sanctorum (1535), Domino d: Svenoni (13. 2. 1537), Ders., Eternam in Domino salutem (4. 1.1539), Riksarkivet, E 5702.

85 Czaika, Sveno Jacobi, 243–262.

86 Collijn, Bibliografi, Bd. 2, 43f.

87 Collijn, Bibliografi, Bd. 2, 50f; Kjöllerström, Förarbeten, 8.

88 Holmquist, Reformationstidevarvet, T. 1, 46–247.

89 Collijn, Bibliografi, Bd. 2, 60–61.

Die Politik von König Gustav I. in Kirchensachen war von 1529 bis 1539 geprägt vom Prinzip, dass die Reformation zuallererst im Unterricht und in der Predigt geschehen sollte, und erst danach in den Formen des Gottesdienstes. In einem Brief vom 24. April 1539 betonte der König, dass der Erzbischof für eine gute Ausbildung der Pfarrer sorgen solle und nur zum Predigen taugliche Personen berufen werden sollten.[90] Das lateinische Handbuch zur Pfarrausbildung, das Laurentius Petri in diesen Kontext verfasste, das sogenannte *Introductorium theologicum* verblieb ein Manuskript.[91] Die Wirkungsgeschichte dieser Handschrift wirft viele Fragen auf.[92] Im selben Jahr verpflichtete sich der Erzbischof gegenüber dem König dafür, zu sorgen, dass keine Fehler oder Mängel bei der unternommen Bibelübersetzung geschehen würden.[93]

In einem Brief vom 12. November 1540 an den vom König für die ganze Kirche eingesetzten Ordinarius und Superattendent Georg Norman, bedankt sich der Erzbischof für die geliehene Literatur und die königliche Unterstützung für die Übersetzung der Vollbibel.[94] Laurentius Petri und seine Mitarbeiter konnten diese Arbeit 1541 abschließen. Die sogenannte Gustav Vasa Bibel (*Biblia, Thet är, All then Helga Skrifft på Swensko*) erschien 1541 ist mit ihren 762 Folio-Blättern und sechzig Holzschnitten das prächtigste Werk des schwedischen Buchdruckes in Schweden zu Laurentius Petris Lebzeiten.[95] Für diese Ausgabe überließ man dem deutschen Buchdrucker Georg Richolff die Leitung der königlichen Druckerei. Er importierte die Holzschnitte aus Deutschland. Am Ende des Vorwortes zum Alten Testament wird ausdrücklich darauf hingewiesen, dass man eher Luther als der Vulgata für die Übersetzung wie auch für die Vorworte und Glossen gefolgt sei; als Grund hierfür wird Luthers größere Treue zum Urtext angeführt.[96] Jede Kirchengemeinde im Königreich wurde verpflichtet die Bibel für zehn Mark zu erwerben.[97]

Mit ihrer vierten erweiterten Auflage wurden die Messe in schwedischer Sprache (*Then Swenska Messan*)[98] und die Agende (*Een Handbook*)[99] von 1541 zu offiziellen Ausgaben für den Gebrauch der Gemeinden in ganz Schweden. In seinem posthum erschienen *Dialog zur Veränderung der Messe* (*Dialogus*

90 Andrén, Introductorium, 52–55.
91 Andrén, Introductorium, 165–203.
92 Andrén, Introductorium, 161–163.
93 Collijn, Bibel, 4f.
94 Laurentius Petri, Superattendij.
95 Collijn, Bibliografi, Bd. 2, 88–104.
96 Biblia, Bl. a6r.
97 Collijn, Bibliografi, Bd. 2, 103.
98 Collijn, Bibliografi, Bd. 2, 106f.
99 Collijn, Bibliografi, Bd. 2, 104ff. Holmquist, Reformationstidevarvet, T. 1, 294.

Om then förwandling medh messone), der dem Herausgeber Abraham Andreae Angermannus zu Folge aus dem Jahr 1542 stammt, erklärt der Erzbischof die Entwicklung der Messliturgie anhand von vier Dialogen zwischen Petrus, dem Alter-Ego des Erzbischofs, und Simon, dem Verteidiger der lateinischen Messe.[100] Die Dialogform deutet auf ein mögliches öffentliches Vorlesen des Werkes als Wirkungsform hin.

In den Jahren 1543 und 1544 erschienen Gesangbuch ([*Then Swenska psalmeboken*]), Katechismus ([*Catechismus*]), Evangeliar und Passionsgeschichte ([*Evangelia och Epistlar. – Passio Wårs Herres Jesu Christi Pina*]) auf Schwedisch.[101] Sie sind allerdings nur fragmentarisch erhalten. Ende 1544 hatten alle Bistümer in Schweden eine der Reformation zugetane Leitung.[102] Auf dem Herrentag zu Arboga 1546 stellte Laurentius Petri ein Kirchenordnungs-Projekt vor, das uns leider nicht erhalten ist.[103] Ab dem Reichstag von Strängnäs 1547 war es deutlich, dass König Gustav keine Kirchenordnung approbieren würden, so dass der Erzbischof und die leitenden Personen in den Bistümern selbst Kirchenstatuten verfassten, um verschiedene Aspekte des Kirchenlebens zu ordnen.[104]

Spätestens 1548 heiratete Laurentius Petri Elisabeth Didrikdotter, eine Kusine des Königs.[105]

Der 1549 an die nordischen Königreiche ergangenen Aufforderung Kaiser Karls V., zum Interim Stellung zu nehmen, erteilte eine Versammlung schwedischer Geistlicher noch im selben Jahr eine Abfuhr.[106] Die weltlichen Vertreter folgten dieser Haltung ein Jahr später.[107]

Eine neue Ausgabe des Neuen Testaments auf Schwedisch (*Thet Nyia Testamentet*) erschien 1550, vermutlich unter der Aufsicht des Erzbischofes.[108] Die Bücher der alttestamentlichen Weisheit-Literatur (*Jesus Syrach. – Salomos Ordspråck. – Salomos Wijsheet. – Hiobs Book. – Judiths book. – Esthers. Book.*)

---

100 Collijn, Bibliografi, Bd. 3, 65.

101 Collijn, Bibliografi, Bd. 2, 124–133.

102 Hellström, Laurentius Petri, 378. Holmquist, Reformationstidevarvet, T. 1, 305–309.

103 Andrén, Introductorium, 161. Kjöllerström, Förarbeten, 10.

104 Holmquist, Reformationstidevarvet, T. 1, 340. Kjöllerström, Kräkla, 25. Zu den Kirchenstatuten siehe Kjöllerström, Förarbeten.

105 Hellström, Laurentius Petri, 376. Åsbrink/Westman, Ärkebiskopar, 222.

106 Petri, Laurentius, Betenkiande om Interim (1549), in: Kungliga Biblioteket Rålamb, Bd. 40, 4:o, 13ff & 50ff.

107 Holmquist, Reformationstidevarvet, T. 1, 330.

108 Collijn, Bibliografi, Bd. 2, 182-183. Thors, Nya Testamentet, kann nachweisen, dass es sich hierbei um eine Neuübersetzung handelt.

wurden mehrfach neu übersetzt und herausgeben.[109] Eine Handschrift aus dem Jahre 1551 mit der Überschrift „*Endrecteligen skicka* [...]" („Folgende Punkte müssen die Pfarrer befolgen um einträchtig zu handeln")[110] sammelt Richtlinien zu Predigt, der Feier der Taufe und der Messe und beinhaltet auch sehr ausführliche Bestimmungen zur Beichte und zur öffentlichen Kirchenzucht.

Ein Großteil des Jahres 1552 war Laurentius Petri mit den Fragen zu der dritten Eheschließung von König Gustav beschäftigt: ist es dem König erlaubt, die Nichte seiner verstorbenen Ehefrau zu heiraten?[111] Am 21. August 1552 heiratet Gustav I. Katharina Stenbock, die am folgenden Tag vom Erzbischof zur Königin gesalbt wurde.[112] Die Aktensammlung, die der Erzbischof zu dieser Frage zusammengestellt hat, gibt einen Einblick in die Verhandlungen, aber auch, was selten ist, in das tägliche Leben des Laurentius Petri. Die Artikel von Vadstena, eine Vorarbeit zur Kirchenordnung, wurden 1552 nach den Verhandlungen zur dritten Ehe des Königs verfasst.[113]

Laurentius Petri konnte 1555 mit königlicher Hilfe seine das ganze Kirchenjahr umfassende Postille veröffentlichen. Das Werk greift zwar auf Vorlagen zurück, ist aber mehr als eine bloße Übersetzung. Die Predigten wurden dem schwedischen Kontext angepasst. Mit seinen 776 Blättern ist die Postille (*Postilla för öffuer Winterdelen. – Postilla öffuer Sommardelen.*) das umfassendste Werk aus der Feder des Erzbischofes.[114] Die Postille beinhaltet hundert Predigten, eine Mahnung zum Gebet nach der Predigt, ein Sündenbekenntnis und zwei Texte zur Sündenvergebung. In der Predigt zum dritten Sonntag nach Epiphanias (Mt 8.23–27) wird die Kirche so beschrieben:

„Wer immer, wie in einem Spiegel, das rechte und eigentliche Bild der heiligen Kirche sehen will, muss an ein Schiff inmitten der wilden See denken, wie vielen Gefahren es ausgesetzt ist, insbesondere wenn der Hauptsturm tobt, sowohl Wind wie auch Wellen es so fürchterlich anfallen, dass niemand anders vermuten kann, als dass es jeden Augenblick kentern und untergehen wird."[115]

---

109 Collijn, Bibliografi, Bd. 2, 114–118, 168 & 287–288. Collijn, Bibliografi, Bd. 2, 169–171 & 290. Collijn, Bibliografi, Bd. 2, 172 & 288–289. Collijn, Bibliografi, Bd. 2, 172 & 316–317. Collijn, Bibliografi, Bd. 2, 173–175. Collijn, Bibliografi, Bd. 2, 175–177.

110 Kjöllerström, Förarbeten, 40–50 (Übersetzung des Titels durch den Verfasser).

111 „Acta circa Matrimonium (1552)", Linköpings stiftsbibliotek, T 131 Bl. 197r–224r; Laurentius Petri, Acta, 10–49.

112 Laurentius Petri, Acta, 29.

113 „Pro uniformitate (1552)", zwei Varianten in: Kjöllerström, Förarbeten, 60–72; Holmquist, Reformationstidevarvet, T. 1, 343–344.

114 Collijn, Bibliografi, Bd. 2, 216–220; Holmquist, Reformationstidevarvet, T. 1, 350.

115 „Hoo som helst lust haffuer til at skoda/ lijka som uthi en speghel/ then heliga kyrkios retta och egentliga beläte/ han tencke på itt skep/ som stadt är uthi willende haffuet/ huru margahanda farligheet thet undergiffuit/ serdeles när en hoffuud storm är uppå/ och bådhe

Das Bild ist kennzeichnend für die Sicht von Laurentius Petri auf die Kirche, in der er und für die er vierzig Jahre gearbeitet hat.

Auf Betreiben des Königs wurden 1557 die sieben Bistümer der schwedischen Kirchenprovinz in fünfzehn kleine Einheiten unter der Aufsicht eines sogenannten *Ordinarius* gegliedert.[116] Im selben Jahre erschienen auch die zweite überarbeitete Ausgabe der Agende (*Een Handbook*) und der schwedischen Messe (*Messan på Swensko förbättrat*).[117] Laurentius Petri veröffentlichte in diesem Jahr das Werk *Emoot Dryckenskap*, eine schwedische Übertragung von Matthäus Friedrichs Schrift *Wider den Saufteufel*.[118]

Der Ordinarius des Bistums Skara, Erik Falck (* nach 1510, † 1570) gab 1558 *Een kort vnderwijsning* (*Ein kurzer Unterricht über einige der vornehmsten Artikel des christlichen Glaubens*) heraus, eine schwedische Bearbeitung von Johannes Spangenbergs *Margarita theologica* (1540).[119] Dieses Werk, das vom Erzbischof sehr geschätzt wurde, wertet die Kirchenbräuche und Ordnungen in einer eigenständigen Weise aus und auf.[120] Laurentius Petri gab im selben Jahr seine Schrift *Förmaning til Clerkerijt samt medh meninge man om Boot och bättring och almenneliga böner* heraus, eine schwedische Fassung von Martin Luthers *Vermanung zum Sacrament des leibs und bluts unsers Herrn* (1530).[121] Der Tenor dieser Schriften ist ein Aufruf zur Ehrfurcht vor Gott.

Das handschriftliche Statut zum Priestererbe aus dem Jahre 1559 zeigt, dass die Lebensumstände der Pfarrschaft sich geändert hatten, und man nun mit Witwen und Kindern von verstorbenen Pfarrern rechnen musste.[122] Im selben Jahr verfasste der Erzbischof eine schwedische Fassung von Justus Menius *Oeconomia Christiana*, die das christliche Leben in Familie und Gesellschaft behandelt.[123] 1560 erschien eine neue schwedische Übersetzung des Psalters (*Dauids Psaltare på nyt öffuerseedd*).[124] Drei handschriftliche Statuten wurden im selben Jahr von Laurentius Petri mitverfasst: die *Artikel vom Herrentag in Stockholm* 1560 sowie *Eine kurze Instruktion zur öffentlichen Buße und zur*

---

wädher och wåg så grefeliga anfalla/ at man intet kan förmodha uthi all ögnableck/ än thet skal jw omstielpa eller löpa i qwaff." Petri, Postilla Winterdelen, Bl. P4v–P5r

116 Holmquist, Reformationstidevarvet, T. 1, 354.

117 Collijn, Bibliografi, Bd. 2, 231–232.

118 Collijn, Bibliografi, Bd. 2, 232f. Friderich, Sauffteuffel.

119 Falck, Vnderwijsning. Siehe auch Collijn, Bibliografi, Bd. 2, 243-244.

120 Eckerdal, Förbättring, 110–112.

121 Collijn, Bibliografi, Bd. 2, 241-243. Luther, Gesamtausgabe Weimar, Bd. 30:II, 589, 595–626 & 691–693.

122 „Statuta om preste arff (1559)", in: Kjöllerström, Förarbeten, 18–19 & 38–40.

123 „Œconomia Christiana (1559)", in: Laurentius Petri, Oeconomia 1897.

124 Die Titelseite schmückt das schwedische Reichswappen. Collijn, Bibliografi, Bd. 2, 265–267.

Ehescheidung.[125] Diese Teilstatuten wurden in die spätere Kirchenordnung eingearbeitet. König Gustav I. verstarb am 29 September 1560.

2. Das Werk des Erzbischofes unter Erik XIV.

In einem Patent vom 5. März 1561 bot der Nachfolger von Gustav I., Erik XIV. (1533–1577), denjenigen, die das Evangelium und eine reine Religion bekennen, in Schweden Asyl.[126] Auf dem Reichstag zu Arboga im April 1561 stellte Erik an den Klerus Fragen zur Abendmahlsliturgie und einer Revision des Landesgesetzes in Bezug auf die Kirche.[127] Ein Entwurf oder eine Zusammenfassung der Antwort des Klerus ist handschriftlich überliefert.[128]

In schwedischen Archiven finden sich heute mehrere Abschriften einer Beschreibung der Krönungszeremonien vom 29. Juni 1561, die *Inauguratio Erici decimiquatri Regis Suecia*, die Laurentius Petri zuzuschreiben ist.[129] Der Erzbischof konnte eine erweiterte Fassung seiner Krönungspredigt *Een Christeligh Predican om werldzligh Öffuerheet* (*Eine christliche Predigt zur weltlichen Obrigkeit*) im Druck erscheinen lassen.[130] Es ist erstaunlich, dass sowohl die Predigt, die Laurentius Bruder Olavus anlässlich der Krönung von Gustav I. verfasste (*En Christelighen formaning til Sweriges jnbyggiare*),[131] und die, die der Erzbischof bei der Krönung von Erik XIV. hielt, im Druck herausgegeben wurden. Diese Texte bieten eine Betrachtung des Staatswesens, die die biblischen und mittelalterlichen Aussagen zum Obrigkeitsamt neu interpretieren. Die dänischen Krönungspredigten, der gleichen Zeit, sind uns nur durch Handschriften und viel spätere Quellenausgaben bekannt.[132]

Während des Sommers legte der Erzbischof einen Kirchenordnungsvorschlag dem neuen König vor.[133] Erik XIV. stimmte dem Projekt nicht zu, was in der Forschung als ein Zeichen für den wachsenden Einfluss gewertet wird, den Dionysius Beurreus, ein französischer Kalvinist, auf den jungen König ausübte.[134] In Schweden tobte zwischen 1562 und 1565 eine, zum Teil sehr heftige, Auseinandersetzung um die Kirchenbräuche und das Abendmahlsverständnis.

---

125 „Articlar siste herredagh (1560)", in: Kjöllerström, Förarbeten, 51. Laurentius Petri, „Om uppenbara scrifft" (1560), Uppsala Universitetsbibliotek, N 1772, Bl. 67r–71v. Ders., „Om åtskillnad i äktenskap" (1560), Uppsala Universitetsbibliotek, N 1722, Bl. 75r–81v.

126 Kjöllerström, Striden, 267ff.

127 Kjöllerström, Striden, 78–81. Eckerdal, De Officiis, 125.

128 „Suar på the puncter (1561)", Linköpings Stiftsbiblioteket, T. 131 Bl. 24r–24v.

129 Janzon, Kröningsritual. Yelverton, Laurentius Petri, 16.

130 Collijn, Bibliografi, Bd. 2, 274–275.

131 Collijn, Bibliografi, Bd. 1, 343-344. Siehe auch Hesselman, Skrifter, Bd. 1, 313-329.

132 Münter/Werlauff, Aktstykker. Bruun, Kong Frederik. Olden-Jørgensen, Kroningstale.

133 „Hwadh och hurudann Stycker" (1561), Linköping Stiftsbiblioteket, T 131, Bl. 75r–136r.

134 Holmquist, Reformationstidevarvet, T. 1, 358–386. Kjöllerström, Förarbeten, 31.

Dieser, von den erschwerten Importen u. a. von Abendmahlswein sowie anderen Auswirkungen des Nordischen Siebenjährigen Krieg begünstigte Streit, wurde zu allermeist mit Handschriften ausgetragen.[135]

Im Jahre 1562 konnte Laurentius Petri drei Schriften im Druck veröffentlichen. *At the är rett och Christelighit bruka Exorcismum widh Döpelsen (Dass es recht und christlich ist den Taufexorzismus zu gebrauchen)* ist eine Übertragung eines Werkes von Justus Menius zur Verteidigung des Taufexorzismus.[136] Das wiederum in Dialogform verfasste Werk *Om Något stycker wårs HERras Jesu Christi Nattward (Einige Stücke die das Abendmahl unseres Herren Jesus Christus betreffen)* durchleuchtet die Auffassungen der Radikalen und ‚Sakramentarier' um sie nacheinander zu verwerfen.[137] Das Alter-Ego des Erzbischofes Christophorus begegnete Gregorius, der am Ende des Werkes gesteht, die Argumente der Radikalen und ‚Sakramentarier' nur vorgetragen zu haben, um von Christophorus zu lernen, wie man sie widerlegt. In *Een Predican emoot mandråp (Eine Predigt gegen den Totschlag)* stellt sich der Erzbischof gegen eine Verrohung der Gesellschaft, die für Diebstahl harte und für Totschlag milde Strafen fordert.[138]

Die Nationalbibliothek Islands in Reykjavík besitzt das einzig erhaltene Exemplar der im Jahr 1562 gedruckten Ausgabe eines für das Leben der Kirchengemeinden wichtigen Sammelbandes, der Gesangbuch, Katechismus, Evangeliar und Passionsgeschichte umschließt.[139]

Der König erließ am 29. August 1563 ein Mandat, das die Verbreitung von Irrlehren unter dem Volk verbot und die Gewissensfreiheit schützte. Die Debatten zu Abendmahlslehre und Kirchenbräuche sollten die öffentliche Ruhe nicht stören und nur von Beauftragten geführt werden.[140]

Eine neue schwedische Übersetzung vom Buch Hiob erschien 1563.[141] Der 45-zeilige Hirtenbrief (*Lavrentivs Episcopvs Vpsalensis* […] *Parochis ac toti Clero* […]) aus dem Jahre 1563 ist der erste Hirtenbrief eines schwedischen Erzbischofs, der im Druck herauskam.[142] Es ist jedoch möglich, das Werke dieses Genres schon früher als Handschriften verbreitet wurden und uns nicht erhalten sind. So erschien 1564 der Hirtenbrief (*Lavrentivs Episcopvs Vpsalen.* […] *Viris ac Dominis, Ecclesiarum per totam Vpsalen.* […]) vom 14. Februar

---

135 Kjöllerström, Striden. Ahlberg, Nattvardsuppfattning.

136 Collijn, Bibliografi, Bd. 2, 298-299. Menius, Exorcismo.

137 Collijn, Bibliografi, Bd. 2, 299.

138 Collijn, Bibliografi, Bd. 2, 300.

139 Malmgren/Kroon, Reformationsskrifter. Dahl, Reykjavikfyndet. Siehe hierzu auch den Beitrag von Otfried Czaika in diesem Band.

140 Kjöllerström, Striden, 176–177.

141 Collijn, Bibliografi, Bd. 2, 316.

142 Collijn, Bibliografi, Bd. 2, 316.

für das ganz Bistum Uppsala im Druck[143], während der Hirtenbrief für die Gemeinden des Fjärdhundra vom 8. Juli nur handschriftlich verbreitet wurde.[144] Der erste Brief ermahnt die Pfarrer, das Volk zur Buße aufzurufen und deutet den Weinmangel als Gottes Strafe für den mangelnden Eifer zu am Abendmahl teilnehmen zu wollen. Der zweite Brief warnt die Pfarrer des Fjärdhundra, den Darstellungen des Ordinarius von Västerås, Johannes Offegh zu folgen, die dieser von den Beschlüssen eines Treffens der Bischöfe aus dem Mälartal im Februar 1564 gegeben hatte.[145]

Die Auseinandersetzungen über das Abendmahlsverständnis, bei denen Offegh kalvinistischen Lehren Vorschub leistete, gingen 1565 mit polemischen Handschriften weiter. Erik XIV. ließ sein Mandat vom 18. April 1565 drucken. Dies gebot den schwedischen Pfarrern, nur der Norm der Schrift gemäß zu predigen; er ordnete darin auch Visitationen der Pfarreien an.[146] Am 20. Oktober 1565 gebot der König den Bischöfen, im ganzen Land Gebetstage feiern zu lassen. Der Erzbischof entsprach dem Befehl mit seinem handschriftlichen Hirtenbrief vom 19. November mit der Ordnung für die Gebetstage.[147]

Bei der Synode für das Bistum Uppsala vom Juli 1566 konnte der Erzbischof einige Texte vorlegen, die vorerst handschriftlich blieben, darunter eine lateinische Fassung eines Kirchenordnungsvorschlags, die *Hypotiposes*.[148] Es ist wahrscheinlich, dass diese Synode auch der Rahmen für die Präsentation des im selben Jahr gedruckten Werkes *Von kirchlichen Statuten und Zeremonien* war. In diesem Werk, das erst postum herausgegeben wurde, stellt Laurentius Petri seine Haltung zu kirchlichen Regeln und Gebräuchen dar; er prägte somit die Identität der Schwedischen Kirche entscheidend mit. Das Werk unterscheidet mit Hinblick auf die kirchlichen Regeln und Gebräuche drei Gruppen von menschlichen Satzungen. Die erste Gruppe, die die Kirche nicht ohne Schaden entbehren kann. Diese Satzungen und Ordnungen fördern die gute Ordnung und die Ehre Gottes. Die zweite Gruppe sind die Satzungen, die geduldet werden

---

143 Collijn, Bibliografi, Bd. 2, 320.

144 Laurentius Petri, Fiedrundiam P:positis ac Rectoribus (8.7.1564), in: Kungliga Biblioteket, Rålamb Bd. 40, 799–830. Riksarkivet, Kopiesamling, n° 42 343–378. Linköping Stiftsbibliotheket, T 131, Bl. 255r–266r.

145 Das Fjärdhundra ist der Teil des Bistums Uppsala, der an das Bistum Västerås grenzt; Kjöllerström, Striden, 197–211.

146 Collijn, Bibliografi, Bd. 2, 325. Zu den Visitationen siehe Kjöllerström, Striden, 231–237.

147 Erik XIV [Brief vom 20.10.1565] in: Riksarkivet, Kopiesamling, n° 43, S. 379–382; Laurentius Petri, „Honorabilis“ (19.11.1565) in: Riksarkivet, Kopiesamling, n° 44, S. 382–387; Ders., Ordo caeremoniarum, 1565 in: Riksarkivet, Kopiesamling, n° 45, S. 388ff.

148 „Hypotiposes“, 1566, Linköping Stiftsbiblioteket, T 131, Bl. 7r–24v. Kjöllerström, Striden, 259ff. Kjöllerström, Förarbeten, 32f.

können, aber nicht notwendig sind. Die letzte Gruppe sind die menschlichen Satzungen, die in der christlichen Kirche nicht geduldet werden können.[149]

Der Hirtenbrief des Erzbischofs vom 20. Oktober 1566 (*Laurentius Episcopus Vpsalensis* [...] *Parochis ac toti Clero Diocesis Vpsalen.* [...])[150] erschien in der Stockholmer Druckerei, die Herausgabe dieses Werkes wurde durch ein handschriftliches königliches Schreiben veranlasst.

Die Universitätsbibliothek von Helsinki hütet das einzige bekannte Exemplar der Ausgabe in einem Sammelband überlieferten Ausgaben des Gesangbuchs, Katechismus, Evangeliars und der Passionsgeschichte, die 1567 in Stockholm erschienen.[151] Eine neue Übersetzung des Propheten Jesaja erschien 1568 trotz Krieg und innerer Unruhen.[152]

3. Die letzten Jahre unter Johan III.

Der Aufstand der Herzöge Johan und Karl, gegen ihren Bruder Erik XIV., führte 1568 zur Absetzung des als verrückt geltenden Königs.[153] Aus dieser Zeit stammt Laurentius Petris Manuskript *Quaestiones aliquot circa magistratum*, das auf die Frage des Widerstands gegen die Obrigkeit detailliert eingeht.[154] Der Erzbischof krönte am 10. Juli 1569 den neuen König im Dom zu Uppsala.[155] Johan III. (1537–1592) sprach in seinem Krönungseid von den Ämtern in der Kirche, und bekundete somit seinen Willen, das klassische Episkopat in der schwedischen Kirche wiederherzustellen.[156] Johan hatte, während seiner Gefangenschaft auf Schloss Gripsholm 1563–1567 wegen seiner ohne Zustimmung des Königs am 4. Oktober 1562 eingegangenen Heirat mit der polnischen Prinzessin Katharina Jagiellonica (1526–1583), intensiv die Kirchenväter studiert.[157] Er wollte die Kirche, dem Ideal der ersten sechs Jahrhunderten entsprechend in ihrer Einheit wiederherstellen.[158]

Der Friede von Stettin im Dezember 1570 gewährte Schweden eine gewisse Selbstständigkeit. Der Nordische Siebenjährige Krieg und die Absetzung von

---

149 „Om kyrkio stadgar och caeremonier" (1566) in: Linköping Stiftsbiblioteket, T 131, Bl. 149r–195r.

150 Collijn, Bibliografi, Bd. 2, 335f.

151 Collijn, Bibliografi, Bd. 2, 343–355.

152 Collijn, Bibliografi, Bd. 2, 373ff.

153 Holmquist, Reformationstidevarvet, T. 1, 442–443.

154 „Quaestiones aliquot" (1568) in: Linköping Stiftsbiblioteket, T 131, Bl. 65r–70v; Holmquist, Reformationstidevarvet, T. 1, 444.

155 Holmquist, Reformationstidevarvet, T. 1, 449. Kjöllerström, Kräkla, 53.

156 Kjöllerström, Kräkla, 53.

157 Holmquist, Reformationstidevarvet, T. 1, 374. Holmquist, Reformationstidevarvet, T. 2, 15–16.

158 Lindgren, Kyrkomålningar, 24. Ahlberg, Traditionen, 195.

Erik XIV. hatten aber das Land und die Kirche verarmt und isoliert.[159] Der König und der Erzbischof teilten eine abweisende Meinung in Bezug auf die Heirat von Erik Gustavsson Stenbock mit seiner Cousine Malin Sture, einer Verwandten des Königs. Die Hochzeit wurde 1571 in Dänemark gefeiert und von einigen Geistlichen und der Universität Rostock gutgeheißen.[160] Laurentius Petri verfasste im selben Jahr ein lateinisches und ein schwedisches Manuskript zur Frage der verbotenen Verwandtschaftsgrade bei Hochzeiten.[161] Eine dritte Schrift des Erzbischofes wurde 1572 gedruckt: *Om förbudhen skylskap och swågerskap* (*Von verbotenen Verwandtschaften und Schwägerschaften*).[162]

Auf Befehl König Johans III. überarbeitete Laurentius Petri den Kirchenordnungsvorschlag, in dem er reichere liturgische Formen und ein Vorwort integrierte. Die schwedische Kirchenordnung, *Then Swenska Kyrkeordningen*, wurde 1571 in der königlichen Druckerei verlegt und erhielt durch königlichen Befehl Gesetzesstatus.[163] Die Kirchenordnung wurde im August 1572 von einer Synode in Uppsala angenommen.[164] Die Protokolle dieser Synode sind in einer handschriftlichen Fassung erhalten.[165] Der König hatte in elf Punkten seine Wünsche den Geistlichen mitgeteilt: Zuerst solle der Erzbischof ein „Buch zu den Zeremonien und Bräuchen der schwedischen Kirche gegen die Kalvinisten schreiben.[166] Die Teilnehmer der Synode baten Laurentius Petri am 20. August, seine Schrift *Von kirchlichen Statuten und Zeremonien* (1566) drucken zu lassen. Diesem Wunsch wurde erst 21 Jahre später, nach dem Tod des Erzbischofes, in einem anderen Kontext nachgekommen.[167] Die Beschlüsse der Synode wurden dagegen zeitnah in Stockholm gedruckt.[168]

Der im Frühjahr 1572 nach Schweden gekommene katholische Kaplan von Königin Katharina Jagiellonica, Johannes Herbst, ließ umgehend romfreundliche Literatur verteilen.[169] Martinus Olai Gestricius, Bischof von Linköping,

---

159 Holmquist, Reformationstidevarvet, T. 1, 445ff. Holmquist, Reformationstidevarvet, T. 2, 19.

160 Holmquist, Reformationstidevarvet, T. 1, 22–23.

161 „De gradibus prohibitis" (1571), in: Kungliga Biblioteket, Rålamb, Fol. Nr. 46. Ders., „Morsysters Dåtter" (1571), in: Martinus Aschaneus, Collectio et connectio […] in commune usum reservata (1629), Kungliga Biblioteket, F.b.2, Bl. 125r–128r.

162 Collijn, Bibliografi, Bd. 2, 415-416.

163 Collijn, Bibliografi, Bd. 2, 393-396. Kjöllerström, Kyrkoordningen. Holmquist, Reformationstidevarvet, T. 1, 448–449.

164 Holmquist, Reformationstidevarvet, T. 1, 450.

165 „Acta Synodica in Concilio Ubsal. Anno 1572", Acta Synodica 1895, 21–28.

166 Nach Kjöllerström, Striden, 264.

167 „Acta Synodica in Concilio Ubsal. Anno 1572", Acta Synodica 1895, S. 23.

168 Collijn, Bibliografi, Bd. 2, 424.

169 Kjöllerström, Kräkla, 63. Garstein, Rome, Bd. 1, 65–66.

verfasste eine Wiederlegung dieser Literatur, die er dem König vorlegte, der sie dem Erzbischof zur Bewertung weiterleitete.[170]

Gesangbuch, Katechismus, Evangeliar und Passionsgeschichte erschienen erneut im Jahre 1572 und sind als Sammelband überliefert.[171]

Das dem Umfang nach zweitgrößte Werk von Laurentius Petri erschien Anfang 1573: *Öffuer Historien om wårs HERRAS Jesu Christi werdigha Pino och Dödh* (*Zur Geschichte des würdigen Leidens und Tod unseres Herren Jesus Christus*).[172] Nach einer Predigt zu den Ursachen der Passion Jesu mit einem Aufruf zu Buße und Besserung, die als die rechte Art Christi Passion zu gedenken präsentiert werden, bietet das Werk zwanzig Predigten, die der biblischen Geschichte vom letzten Abendmahl bis zur Grablegung Christi folgen (Fig. 2).

Das letzte Werk, das der Erzbischof im Druck herausgeben konnte, war sein Hirtenbrief vom 24. April 1573, der dem Befehl des Königs, Gebetstage abzuhalten, Folge leistete.[173] Laurentius Petri ermahnte die Gläubigen, Gottes Güte zu beachten, die Undankbarkeit zu meiden und rief sowohl zur Danksagung als auch zur Buße auf. Der Brief schloss mit dem Wunsch „da pacem Domine in diebus nostris. Ein Wunsch nach Frieden der sich, für ihn selbst, nicht verwirklichte.

Der Erzbischof scheint der wachsenden Propaganda von Seiten von Johannes Herbst mit mehreren Schriften entgegnet zu sein, von denen nur eine bewahrt und posthum gedruckt wurde, die *Probatio Veri et Falsi Sacerdotii*.[174] Dieser Text wurde auf dem Sommerreichstag zu Stockholm vorgelesen und vom König wohlwollend aufgenommen.[175] Auf der Stiftsynode im Juni 1573 mahnte Laurentius Petri die Pfarrer zu einer gewissenhaften Ausübung des Amtes und einem fleißigen Lesen des Artikels der Rechtfertigung durch den Glauben.[176] Die letzte Schrift des Erzbischof war eine Schelte an den Hauptpfarrer von Sigtuna vom 24. August 1573; dieser hatte, gegen alle bestehenden Bestimmungen, ein Kind, das einer nomadisierenden Gruppe angehörte, getauft.[177]

---

170 Kjöllerström, Kräkla, 63.

171 Collijn, Bibliografi, Bd. 2, 412–415.

172 Collijn, Bibliografi, Bd. 2, 425–426.

173 Collijn, Bibliografi, Bd. 2, 424–425. Holmquist, Reformationstidevarvet, T. 1, 35.

174 In: Abraham Andreae Angermannus, Refutatio erroris Herbesti (Hamburg: Henricus Binderus, 1588). Siehe auch Collijn, Bibliografi, Bd. 3, 86–87.

175 Holmquist, Reformationstidevarvet, T. 2, 29 & 33. Kjöllerström, Kräkla, 66–67.

176 Holmquist, Reformationstidevarvet, T. 2, 34–35.

177 „Die Bartholomæi, Sigtuna Rectori" (1573), Kungliga Biblioteket, Rålamb, 903-905 und Kungliga Biblioteket, Engeström, Nr. 22, Bl. 67r–v.

Laurentius Petri verstarb am 26. Oktober 1573, 74 Jahre alt. Er hatte 42 Jahre das Bistum Uppsala geleitet.[178] Der Sitz des Erzbischofes blieb sieben Monate verwaist; die drei Nachfolger waren alle Schwiegersöhne von Laurentius Petri, der als ‚Laurentius Petri Nerici' (der latinisierten Form seiner Heimatprovinz Närke) oder als ‚Laurentius Petri der Ältere' in die Geschichte einging.[179]

Die posthumen Veröffentlichungen

In den Jahren 1587 und 1588 veröffentlichte Abraham Andreae Angermannus (1540–1607/08), ein Schwiegersohn und späterer Nachfolger von Laurentius Petri, in Wittenberg und Hamburg drei Werke des vierzehn Jahre zuvor verstorbenen Erzbischofes.

Laurentius Petris Werk *Om then förwandling som medh Messonne skedde* (*Die Verwandlung die mit der Messe geschehen ist*) wurde laut Abraham Andreae Angermannus 1542 verfasst.[180] Dies Werk ist eine eingehende Behandlung der Liturgiegeschichte in vier Dialogen zwischen Petrus, dem Alter-Ego des Laurentius Petri, und eines gewissen Simon, der die lateinische Messe verteidigt. Die Dialogform wurde von Laurentius Petri mehrmals gebraucht. Im ersten Dialog wird der Ablauf des Kanons der Messe auf ihre Notwendigkeit für die Konsekration beleuchtet. Im zweiten und längsten Dialog wird für die wahre Teilhabe der Gemeinde am Sakrament durch die Volkssprache argumentiert. Der Entzug des Kelches für die Laien wird im dritten Dialog als Ungerechtigkeit gebrandmarkt. Im vierten Dialog wird das Messopfer behandelt.

Es ist bemerkenswert, dass das Werk *Om kyrkio stadgar och caeremonier* (*Von Kirchen Statuten und Zeremonien*) lange nur in seiner auf 1566 zu datierenden Manuskriptform bekannt und verbreitet war.[181] *Von Kirchen Statuten und Zeremonien* war ursprünglich als ein Traktat geschrieben worden, das die Auseinandersetzungen mit den Kalvinisten kommentiert; es fand aber auch in der Debatte mit den Vertretern der römischen Kirche Verwendung und wurde schliesslich 1587 in Wittenberg gedruckt.[182] Die mit Herzog Christopher von

178 Dewailly, Petri.

179 Åsbrink/Westman, Ärkebiskopar, 222. Laurentius Petri Gothus (Erzbischof 1574–1579) und Andreas Laurentius Björnram (Ersbischof 1583–1591) waren nacheinander mit Margareta Petri verheiratet, Abraham Andreæ Angermannus (1593–1599) war verheiratet mit Magdalena Petri.

180 Collijn, Bibliografi, Bd. 3, 65–66. Holmquist, Reformationstidevarvet, T. 1, 294. Eckerdal, Förbättring, 95.

181 Linköping Stiftsbiblioteket, T 131, Bl. 149r–195r.

182 Collijn, Bibliografi, Bd. 3, 63–64.

Mecklenburg (1537–1592) verheiratete Prinzessin Elizabeth Vasa (1549–1597) besaß eine Kopie dieser zwei posthumen schwedischsprachigen Drucke von Laurentius Petri.[183]

Das dritte Werk, die *Probatio Veri et Falsi Sacerdotii*, ist das einzige Werk aus Laurentius Petris Feder, das im sechzehnten Jahrhundert in lateinischer Sprache im Druck veröffentlicht wurde. Die lateinische Sprache war der theologischen Auseinandersetzung über das Amtsverständnis mit den zum Teil ausländischen Geistlichen geschuldet und machte Laurentius Petris Argumentation somit leichter kommuizierbar. Die *Probatio* greift zum Teil auf ein Schreiben Martin Luthers aus dem Jahr 1523 zurück.[184] Mit dieser Auseinandersetzung war die theologische Debatte auch in Schweden im Zeitalter der Konfessionalisierung angekommen. Da wir kein Originalmanuskript dieser Schrift mehr kennen, hat ein Teil der Forschung eine Verschärfung des Tones durch den Herausgeber für möglich gehalten.[185]

Nachwort

Laurentius Petri war nicht wie u. a. Martin Luther Professor an einer Universität, sondern leitete über eine Dauer von mehr als vierzig Jahren ein geografisch großes, wenn auch dünn besiedeltes Bistum. Die Rolle des Erzbischofes von Uppsala veränderte sich durch die Reformation. Der Erzbischof war nun nicht mehr ein spätmittelalterlicher Kirchenfürst, sondern ein geistlicher Leiter. Die schwedische Kirche konnte zu einem nicht geringen Grad dank Laurentius Petri ihre episkopale Kirchenstruktur behalten. Das Werk des Erzbischofes war vor allem das eines zähen Verfassers der Kirchenordnung und eines Vermittlers, der der Reformation im schwedischen Kontext eine Heimat gab. Der Buchdruck war zu Zeiten des Laurentius Petri ein noch neues Medium in Schweden, das aber nun eine sichere Verbreitung ermöglichte.[186] Der Buchdruck wurde allerdings vornehmlich für Bibel- und Liturgieausgaben genutzt. Das Werk von Laurentius Petri wurde zu einem nicht geringen Teil mittels Handschriften verbreitet und konnte somit seine Wirkung entfalten. Die Schriften von Erzbischof Laurentius Petri sollten wie die seines Bruders Olaus Petri durch eine

183 Czaika, Elisabet Vasa, 91–92.

184 Luther, „De instituendis ministris ecclesiae ad senatum Pragensem Bohemiae“ (1523), in: Luther, Gesamtausgabe Weimar, Bd. 12, 169–196, zitiert nach Ahlberg, Nattvardsuppfattning, 284–285.

185 Brodd, Biskopsämbetet, Anm. 5.

186 So Laurentius Petri im Vorwort der Kirchenordnung von 1571, in Färnström, Kyrko-ordning, 16.

Herausgabe zugänglich gemacht werden. Ein Wunsch der seit 1593 auf seine vollständige Erfüllung wartet. Laurentius Petris Schriften sind Zeugnisse ihrer Zeit, sie können uns ein differenzierteres Bild einer bewegten und zum Teil auch stürmischen Vergangenheit geben. Das Bild vom Schiff auf der wilden See, dass Laurentius Petri als für die Kirche angemessenes Bild betrachtete, kann uns zu einer dynamischen Betrachtung dessen, was wir „Reformation" nennen, ermutigen.

Jason Lavery

Mikael Agricola and Finland's Vernacular Reformation

The best-known figure of Finland's Reformation is Mikael Agricola (1510–1557). Agricola created the literary basis of the Finnish language by translating the Word of God into Finnish. Agricola's achievements helped him to win promotion in 1554 to the post of bishop of Turku. After his death in 1557, he became known as the "Father of the Finnish language".[187]

The extant literature concerning Agricola's writings largely focuses on linguistic and theological questions. This article will examine the favorable conditions that allowed Agricola to produce normative ecclesiastical literature in Finnish while others could not. Among these conditions were access to a printing press, his vision for Finnish as a comprehensive written language and not just an ecclesiastical language, the availability of qualified assistants, and the availability of sources from the Lutheran reformation for him to draw on.

Vernacularization and the Swedish Kingdom's Reformation

In the decades between the arrival of Lutheran reform in the Swedish kingdom in the 1520s and the adoption of the Augsburg Confession by the Uppsala Assembly in 1593 as the foundational creed of the Swedish kingdom's church, a variety of groups with different but largely coexisting approaches to reform existed in the Swedish kingdom. Despite this fragmented theological environment, consensus prevailed among religious and temporal authorities in vernacularizing the Mass and Scripture. Vernacularization was the common ground of reform of the church's teachings and practices. The consensus concerning use of the vernacular bridged the church's doctrinal and liturgical divisions for decades. Long before the Swedish kingdom's church became irrevocably Lutheran in the 1590s, it had become irrevocably vernacular.

The process of putting the Word of God into the vernacular had a significant impact on the kingdom's two most spoken languages. Swedish had a pre-Reformation medieval literary tradition which did not extend much into

187 This article addresses a question that is examined in greater detail in Lavery, *Reforming Finland.*

the spiritual realm. Finnish, the language of around eighty percent of the inhabitants of the Diocese of Turku, also known as Finland, for its part has no surviving pre-Reformation literary tradition at all. As a literary language Finnish is understood to have started in the Reformation era.

Mikael Olofsson Agricola

Mikael Agricola was born in Torsby, a village in the parish of Pernå (Pernaja in Finnish) in the region of Uusimaa (Nyland) on Finland's south central coast. The exact year of Agricola's birth is unknown, but by tracking backwards from later milestones in his life historians estimate his birth sometime in the years 1507–1510. Little is known about Agricola's parents. The name of his mother is unknown. His father, Olof, was a peasant (as his son's adopted surname suggests) who died sometime in the early 1540s, leaving behind his wife, son Mikael, and three daughters.[188] One of the few scholarly debates concerning Agricola has centered over whether he spoke Finnish or Swedish as his first language. Evidence in favor of Swedish is that he grew up in Torsby, a Swedish-speaking village, but a village likely with some Finnish speakers within it and certainly majority Finnish-speaking villages nearby. In books that he bought Agricola wrote marginal comments in Swedish and not Finnish. Evidence in favor of Finnish is Agricola's obvious fluent command of Finnish, a command so masterful that he could create a literary language. In the 19th and into the 20th century scholars, informed by the growth of nationalism based on the Finnish language, largely believed that Agricola's first language had to be Finnish because of Agricola's fluency and the assumption that no Swedish speaker would care enough to put the Word of God into Finnish. This debate over the last couple of decades has settled into the conclusion that no definitive proof exists for either position. The most recent contributions to this discussion have come from Agricola's biographer, Simo Heininen, and linguist Kaisa Häkkinen. Both have argued that the question of Agricola's language is secondary to his achievements. Even if Agricola's first language were Swedish (and they both suggest it likely was), it would put him in at the beginning of a long tradition of Swedish speakers who worked to develop Finnish as a literary language.[189]

Agricola attended his first school in Finland's second largest city, Vyborg (Viipuri). His success in reaching this school stemmed from both his intellectual

188 Juusten, Suomen piispainkronikka, 59.

189 Czaika, Minnet, 15–25. Häkkinen, Mikael Agricolan, 84–102. Häkkinen, Spreading, 32–33. Heininen, Nuori, 95–96. Heininen, Mikael Agricola, 26. Ikola, Agricolan, 25–68.

talents and his father's sufficient financial means. In 1528 young Agricola moved to Turku with his teacher, Johannes Erasmusson, to serve in the administration of the new bishop of Turku, Martinus Skytte. After Erasmusson died in 1529, Agricola took his position as the bishop's chancellor.[190] In the fall of 1536, Agricola left for studies in Wittenberg. There he started his work to translate the New Testament in Finnish. In the spring of 1539 Agricola completed his studies and returned to Turku to take the position of headmaster of the Cathedral School in Turku, the diocese's flagship school.[191]

Often Agricola is referred to as "Finland's reformer". Agricola's activities do not correspond to commonly understood definitions of a reformer in sixteenth-century Europe. Reformer generally implies a heroic, transformative leader in the vanguard of breaking down the old order, such as Martin Luther (1483–1546), Jean Calvin (1509–1564), or even Olaus Petri (1493–1552). Few clues illuminate Agricola's specific involvement in advancing Lutheran reform in the Swedish kingdom for the first decade of his activity as a clergyman. By the time Agricola returned to Finland in 1539, change was well underway. Agricola's work in putting the Word of God into Finnish occurred at a time when others were engaged in the same work. The term reformer generally connotes someone who engaged in detailed theological argument. No evidence exists to suggest that Agricola produced any entirely original theological writings. His known written works are translations of religious works and compilations of extant materials for a Finnish-speaking audience. The only sources that shed some light on Agricola's thought consist of the introductions and marginal comments in his published works, which consist of about two percent of the 2,500 pages of Agricola's combined works. Even here, Agricola's views of Christian teaching are very general and practical rather than specific and speculative.[192] Agricola's reputation as a reformer lies in his ability to actually publish his translations of sacred texts into Finnish and hold various high ecclesiastical offices from the end of the 1520s until his death in 1557.

Early Attempts to Put the Word of God into Finnish

During the reign of King Gustav (1523–1560), most of the reforming energy in the Swedish kingdom's church lay in putting as much of Scripture, liturgy, and prayer into the vernacular as possible. In 1530 the Stockholm City Council

190 Juusten, Suomen piispainkronikka, 59. Heininen, Mikael Agricola, 25.

191 Heininen/Heikkilä, Kirkkohistoria, 69. Arwidsson, Handlingar, 153–156 & 161–163.

192 Holma, Schwenkfeldiläisten, 45–46.

decided to hold Mass regularly in Swedish. In the following year, Olaus Petri published a new Lutheran-influenced Swedish Mass.[193] In 1536, the church council of Uppsala decreed the use of Swedish in the Mass where possible. Olaus Petri's handbook, first published in 1529, was decreed for use in the performance of sacraments and rituals.[194] According to the sixteenth-century clergyman and chronicler Paulus Juusten (1516–1575) already in 1534 the first Mass in Swedish was performed in Turku Cathedral by the sexton Laurentius Canuti, although likely parts of the Mass or forms of a low Mass had been performed in Swedish even earlier.[195]

These measures taken to advance the use of Swedish did not exclude or hinder the development of Finnish as a liturgical language. In 1533 Stockholm's Finnish speakers started regular services in their own language. At first, Finnish speakers probably attended Mass in Swedish and or Latin at the city church, and then went to listen to a Finnish sermon at the Dominican convent's church.[196] The establishment of a Finnish congregation in Stockholm suggests the strength of the overall movement to increase the use the vernacular in religious services in the Swedish kingdom. Unlike the Swedish- or German-speaking community in Stockholm, the Finnish-speaking community had no known preexisting organization for religious activity in Finnish. The overwhelming majority of Finnish speakers in Stockholm at the time was probably so fluent in Swedish that it could have easily remained invisible within the Swedish-speaking congregation of the Stockholm City Church. To create a Finnish congregation, Finnish speakers had to overcome both the discomfort of no Finnish-language ecclesiastical infrastructure and the comfort likely that they likely felt in the Swedish-speaking community.

Inside the Diocese of Turku during the 1530s attempts were made to put the liturgy and scripture into Finnish. Four surviving manuscripts preceded the publication of Agricola's own work in the 1540s. One of the manuscripts is a very fragmentary translation of the Gospels, the other three are translations of the Mass with Olaus Petri's Mass as the probable basis of translation. The most complete and comprehensive of these is the Westh Codex. This codex is named after one of its owners, Matthias Westh, (d. 1549). Westh is believed to be the first preacher for the Finnish congregation in Stockholm in 1533, later moving on to become a chaplain and school headmaster in the Finnish city of Rauma.

---

193 Pahlmblad, Mässa, 239–241. Schalin, Studier, 132–133.

194 Pirinen: 1956, 79

195 Leinberg, Postilla, 268. Pirinen, Turunen, 82

196 Knuutila, Tukholman, 100–101. Pihlajamaa, Mathias West, 71–92. Pihlajamaa, Raamatunlauseet, 93–116.

Westh was one of the owners of the codex, and it is believed that he was one of the authors if not the only author of it.[197]

Agricola and Publishing

Why was Agricola able to surpass these efforts to put the Word of God into Finnish, efforts that preceded his own work by years? One obvious reason is that Agricola succeeded in getting his works into print. This was not particularly easy, since in Agricola's time there was only one publishing house in the Swedish kingdom—that run by Amund Laurentsson (d. 1575?) in Stockholm. Laurentsson only published books permitted by the king. Moreover, publishing was not a widespread activity in the Swedish kingdom. Over the course of the 16th century, some six hundred books were published in the Swedish kingdom. In German-speaking Europe, some 110,000 works were published. The population of German-speaking Europe was about ten times that of Sweden, but it produced over 183 times as many books, so the difference cannot be explained in terms of demography.[198]

Agricola was never able to find a reliable income source for his translation work. Nothing in the sources suggests that King Gustav ever gave Agricola any large grants for Agricola's translation work save for some small reimbursements from the royal treasury.[199] Agricola's manuscripts became ready for print in the 1540s, the same decade in which Gustav moved strongly to take the diocese's property, thus depriving Agricola of possible revenue streams. Scholars have long presumed that Agricola received financial support from people within Finland in the form of testaments and charitable contributions, such as from the nobleman Erik Fleming. Considering Agricola's wide and close connections to elites, it is plausible that he received some donations, but no direct evidence supports the assumptions of charitable generosity.[200]

In order to get his books published. Agricola had to convince Amund Laurentsson of the profitability of his books, even after he had published several of them with the publisher. Agricola emphasized his scarcity of resources in a letter to Amund Laurentsson dated 1 April 1551 in which he asks Laurentsson to publish his psalter by acting "as the glory of God demands and the teaching and cultivation of the poor and crude common people of Finland require". Agricola then launched an extended explanation of the widespread food shortages facing

197 Häkkinen, Westhin, 43–92. Knuutila, Tukholman, 79–113.

198 Collijn, Bibliografi. VD16.

199 Tarkiainen/Tarkiainen, Mikael Agricola, 305–306.

200 Heininen, Mikael Agricola, 360. Lahtinen, Mikael Agricola, 24–35.

his diocese at that moment. In Turku there was "no grain for sale". In pleading poverty Agricola was making a case to Amund Laurentsson to publish the book without subsidies.[201] Agricola's psalter was published in 1551.

In 1551, Agricola revealed his concern about the possible end to his publishing run in his translation of parts of the Old Testament entitled *Weisut ia Ennustoxet Mosesen Laista ia Prophetista Wloshaetut* (Hymns and prophecies from the books of Moses and the prophets). The book is a translation of parts of the Pentateuch as well as the historical and prophetic books of the Old Testament. It has parts of the books of Isaiah, Jeremiah, Ezekiel, and Daniel. The Book of Lamentations and the first nine of the twelve Minor Prophets are translated in their entirety. Agricola's inspiration for this digested version of the Old Testament came from Johannes Bugenhagen, who had a similar digest in his psalter.[202] In the introduction of Hymns and Prophecies Agricola reveals his motivation for publishing this work. He concluded that he likely would not be able to translate the entire Bible, and this work would have to suffice. He states in the introduction that "If we Finns do not get the entire Bible printed, because we are so poor, we will not fall into unbelief. Rather, I am taking from the Bible the best part of the hymns in the names of the holy prophets. In the same way a bee seeks nectar and honey from an herb, this book follows the psalter as a roaring lion [follows his prey]".[203]

In the next year Agricola published his last work *Ne Prophetat* (The Prophets) in 1552. This work was a translation of the books of Haggai, Zechariah, and Malachi. These books were originally supposed to be published in Hymns and Prophecies, but poor travel conditions prevented them from reaching Stockholm before Hymns and Prophecies went to press.[204] Agricola revealed the importance of the profit motive in the introduction of this his last work. In the introduction of *Ne Prophetat*, Agricola states forebodingly and prophetically that "Much more would come from the Bible, if these [his previous works] would be bought and used".[205] This statement can be read as an epitaph to Agricola's literary career. The beginning and end of Agricola's publishing run to a great extent stemmed from business decisions by his publisher.

In the final analysis, Agricola succeeded in getting his works into print, because Amund Laurentsson calculated that they would be profitable. During the 1540s Agricola likely was Laurentsson's most important author. Many of

---

201 Arwidsson, Handlingar, 318–330. Tarkiainen/Tarkiainen, Mikael Agricola, 321–323.
202 Heininen, Mikael Agricola, 306–308.
203 Agricola, Mikael Agricolan teokset, vol. 3, 438.
204 Heininen, Mikael Agricola, 303.
205 Agricola, Mikael Agricolan teokset, vol. 3, 719.

the important religious works in Swedish, such as the Bible, were already published before 1543, and so Laurentsson likely was looking for new publishing opportunities when Agricola offered his works. This raises the question whether Agricola would have gotten his works published if he had completed them in the 1530s, when Laurentsson publishing books in Swedish for a much larger market.

Finnish as Both a Temporal and Ecclesiatical Language

Agricola was able to make a sustained impact on both the Reformation and the Finnish language by understanding the need to establish Finnish as comprehensive a written language as possible in order for it to survive as an ecclesiastical language. It was not enough to just to translate the Mass as had been done by those associated with the Westh Codex. Often Agricola is compared to Olaus Petri, the driving force in putting the Word of God into Swedish. The two men introduced the vernacular into the church from two fundamentally different points of departure. Swedish already had a long written literary tradition. Swedish was a language of written communication. There was some tradition of writing and translating sacred texts as well, such as the monk Jöns Budde's work in the 15th century.[206] Putting the Word of God formally into Swedish expanded the scope of an already existing literary language. Putting the Word of God into Swedish made sense, since all other aspects of life were expressed in written Swedish. For his part, Agricola was introducing a new written language. For Finnish to succeed and survive as a language of religious activity, it had to be made relevant to other parts of human activity.

Even though only a small percentage of the population was literate, Agricola understood that the written language would be read to the illiterate, and thus it must be recognizable to the masses. Agricola based his written Finnish mostly on the dialect spoken around Turku, where most of the population lived. His understanding that he was creating a new written language is exemplified by his first publication, a spelling primer (*Abckiria*) for Finnish in 1543, which also served as a catechism (Fig. 3). Agricola's primer opens with the command, "Learn now, young and old, who have a pure heart, God's commands and mind, which you can express in the Finnish language. The law troubles the soul, but Christ comforts it again. Read good child this introductory lesson without

206 Lamberg, Jöns Budde.

hindrance. Remember these lessons always, and Jesus will always grant His mercy".[207]

Like many aspects of Finland's reformation, the quality of existing primary sources concerning Agricola's work is not ideal. No complete copy of the spelling primer has survived. In fact, it was long believed that no copies of it survived until 1851, when the first eight pages of the primer were discovered in the university library in Uppsala inside the cover of another book. In 1904, two fragments from the first and fourth pages were found in the Chamber Archives (now in the National Archives) in Stockholm. The final four pages were found in 1966 in the diocesan library in Västerås. Studies of the documents over the generations have produced a consensus concerning the dating of the primer. The first printing of the primer is believed to have occurred in 1543 and is in any case considered Agricola's first printed book. A second and third printing of the primer occurred in 1551 and 1559 respectively.[208]

The primer starts with an analysis of the alphabet. Agricola divides letters into four categories: vowels, diphthongs (with pronunciation guide), consonants, and so-called "foreign" letters, three of which actually are very Finnish letters—ö, ä, and y—and ij, which is understood as the common double-i in modern Finnish. Agricola's determination of various Finnish letters as foreign and vice versa (he listed several foreign consonants, such as b and z, as Finnish) suggests that Agricola was heavily dependent on foreign models in creating this part of the primer.[209] The rest of the primer consists of material that belonged to most catechisms of the time: the Ten Commandments, the Apostles' Creed, the Our Father, and the Hail Mary. It offers explanations of baptism, confession, and the Eucharist, as well as prayers for meals, the morning, and bedtime. It concludes with a spelling of numbers in Finnish one through twenty and then the tens until one hundred, then one thousand.[210] Several direct quotations from the Bible would appear again in Agricola's publication of the full New Testament. Most of the catechistic material for this work was borrowed from catechisms written by Luther, Philipp Melanchthon (1497–1560), and Andreas Osiander (1496–1552). Agricola's borrowing was not verbatim and he provided many of his own innovations. In the Apostolic Creed he referred to the church as "Christian" rather than "Catholic" in the way of the German catechisms. He put in his primer prayers for the ringing of bells, a medieval tradition not recognized in any of the German Lutheran catechisms.[211]

---

207 Häkkinen, Abckiria, 1.
208 Heininen, Mikael Agricola, 164–165.
209 Häkkinen, Abckiria, 62–92.
210 Häkkinen, Abckiria, 1–24.
211 Heininen, Abckirian.

Agricola further demonstrated his eclectic approach to creating sacred texts in Finnish in his prayer book (*Rucouskirja*) of 1544 (Fig. 4). This book, with 678 prayers and 887 pages, is unique among prayer books of its time in both its size and breadth of sources used. Of all of the prayers in the book, the largest amount, 220, came from the medieval *Missale Aboense* (1488). The prayer book of the Schwenckfeld movement, *Bekantnus der Sünden*, provided forty-six prayers for Agricola's book, making it the second largest source of prayers. Luther's followers condemned this movement as heretical even before Agricola went to Wittenberg to study in the 1530s. Agricola translated thirty-eight prayers from Erasmus's prayer book of 1535, yet another example of Agricola's willingness to go beyond only safe Lutheran sources. Despite his eclectic approach, Agricola signaled that he indeed was a Lutheran reformer. The prayers tied to saints' days had all references to their intercessory agency and merit eliminated from them.[212] For Agricola, the importance of the prayer book lay in the believers' ability to communicate with God in Finnish. Agricola emphasized to the clergy the importance of using the vernacular in prayer by stating *"Kylle se cwle Somen kielen, ioca ymerdä Caikein mielen"*. Literally this has been understood in English as "He [God] who hears the Finnish language call understands the mind of all". In other words, God hears and understands Finnish prayers.[213]

Like the spelling primer, the prayer book has both sacred and profane elements. The book opens with an almanac-style calendar common in medieval prayer books. It lists saints' days and marks the periods of fasts. The presence of fasts and the plethora of saints' days suggest that Agricola was not that interested in reforming these parts of the medieval church, at least at that moment. Similarly, in the spirit of medieval holism, the religious calendar addresses more profane activities, above all, agriculture. The calendar describes what agricultural activities are performed in which months. It lists various herbs and how they should be consumed. This calendar should be taken with great caution as a guide to agriculture and food culture in sixteenth-century Finland. Agricola refers to many imported herbs not widely available. He writes about the cultivation of grapes, something not possible in sixteenth-century Finland. Agricola borrowed from extant calendars, some of them produced in more southern parts of Europe.[214]

In 1548 Agricola completed his best-known work, a Finnish edition of the New Testament. It embodies the characteristics of Agricola's previous works in method and content. In the introduction, Agricola reveals that he used

---

212 Holma, Schwenkfeldiläisten, 39 & 191–200.

213 Agricola, Mikael Agricolan teokset, vol. 1, 91. Laitinen/Schoolfield, Beginnings, 34.

214 Terttu Lempiäinen, Agricola, 48–83.

sources in Greek, Latin, German, and Swedish for his translation. He included in the introduction of the New Testament useful information about Finland. He discusses Finland's history and political geography by describing the spread of Christianity to Finland by St. Eric and St. Henry in the 12th century. Agricola does not frame the expansion of the Swedish Crown across the Gulf of Bothnia as some kind of unwelcome conquest, but rather as a necessity to Christianize the country. Agricola goes on to list the various regions or historical provinces of Finland: Finland Proper, Satakunta, Häme, Karelia, Uusimaa, Raseborg, and Ostrobothnia.[215] This introductory, non-scriptural material makes an argument for the wider relevance of Finnish as a written language for a people with a past and space of its own.

Agricola's Assistants

Agricola intended to use the published the New Testament as a basis for publishing the entire Bible in Finnish. Even though Agricola ultimately lacked the necessary money and time to reach his goal, he succeeded in publishing parts of the Old Testament. In 1551 he published a psalter in which Agricola asks the reader to "pray for those who translated these [psalms] into Finnish".[216] This statement raises the question of possible contributors to Agricola's works. In his chronicle Paulus Juusten tells his version of his own role in the making of the psalter:

"At this time, he [Agricola] published a psalter in Finnish. It was, however, entirely translated in the Turku school under the rectorship of Paulus Juusten. He had directed pupils to translate the Psalms to improve their style, just as one remembered blessed Doctor Luther doing so. He [Juusten] listened to and corrected their Finnish translations during the hours when pupils' assignments were usually accepted and corrected, often after dinner in his room. But it is not important in whose name it [the Psalms] are published, for it was translated so it could be of great benefit to the Finnish people.[217]

Agricola's biographer and leading expert on Agricola for decades, Simo Heininen, has categorically rejected the idea that the students at the Cathedral School could have helped him at all, despite Juusten's statement. Heininen argues that students would not have had the language skills to translate the Psalms. Several factors would suggest that student help was possible and even useful to Agricola.

215 Agricola, Mikael Agricolan teokset, vol. 2, 15–19.
216 Agricola, Mikael Agricolan teokset, vol. 3, 214.
217 Juusten, Suomen piispainkronikka, 59–60.

One factor was that Agricola did not just spend his days translating, but he had other tasks as well ranging from running the Cathedral School until 1548, to cataloging the church's property for King Gustav Vasa, and to providing assistance to the aging Bishop Martin Skytte who died in 1550. Agricola then was acting bishop until Gustav Vasa appointed him bishop of Turku in 1554. It is no slight to Agricola's achievement to suggest that a human being with all of these tasks did not avail himself of help. He clearly was the overwhelming driving force in putting the Word of God into Finnish. Students could have provided useful sounding boards for how psalms were rendered in Finnish. Researchers in today's world often receive assistance from students that is not always perfect. It does not mean that such help is useless. Moreover, even Heininen recognizes that other clergymen likely associated with the school likely helped with translation work.[218]

Agricola's works

1543 *Abckiria* (spelling primer)
1544 *Rucouskiria Bibliasta* (prayer book)
1548 *Se Wsi Testamenti* (The New Testament)
1549 *Käsikirja Castesta ia muista Cristikunnan Menoista* (handbook)
1549 *Messu* (The Mass)
1549 *Se meiden herran Jesusen Christusen Pina* (Christ's passion)
1551 *Dauidin psalttari* (psalter)
1551 *Weisut ja Ennustoxet Moosesen Laista ja Prophetista Uloshaetut* (Hymns and prophecies from the books of Moses and the prophets)
1552 *Ne prophetat* (the books of Haggai, Zechariah, and Malachi)

Borrowing from Existing Works

Agricola benefitted from the existence of a broad array of Lutheran and other bodies of literature which he could translate for a Finnish audience. He did not translate works verbatim. An example of this is his Mass in Finnish that he published in 1549. Olaus Petri's Swedish Mass was the main source of inspiration for Agricola's liturgy. Petri's Mass in turn was based on Martin Luther's German Mass of 1526.

218 The most recent version of Heininen's position is printed in his examination of Agricola as a translator of the Psalms; Heininen, *Mikael Agricola psalmien suomentajana*, 386-388

Agricola's Mass deviates from Petri's and Luther's Masses in that it has no music. In a wider context of European Protestantism, Agricola distinguishes himself by his relative indifference to music. Some of this indifference might have been driven by the high cost of printing music. Even if he could easily publish music, no evidence suggests that Agricola had any significant training or interest in music. The musicologist Erkki Tuppurainen points out that the overall atmosphere for liturgical music in Agricola's time was not very positive. In their search for suitable covers for their account books, royal bailiffs raided music libraries in the kingdom's monasteries for heavy parchment. In some cases, manuscripts of liturgical music just disappeared. Monastic choirs and choristers similarly disappeared from many parishes.[219] In this environment Agricola might not have seen much of a future for music in the liturgy.

Jyrki Knuutila in his study of liturgical standardization in Finland has uncovered other distinct aspects of Agricola's Mass. It and other sixteenth-century Finnish Masses retained more aspects of the medieval liturgy of the Turku diocese. The Finnish Masses maintained the pastor's response to the reading of the Gospel "Glory be to you dear Lord" as well as the maintenance of processional prayers. In Agricola's Mass a call to communion follows the confession of sins. This call was adapted from the call to communion in Luther's German Mass and has no equivalent in Finnish- or Swedish-language masses of the time. Agricola's Mass and other sixteenth-century Finnish Masses used only Finnish. Swedish masses offered at several junctures the option of using Swedish or Latin. Finnish masses did not offer the option to use Swedish, Latin, or any other language.[220]

In 1549 Agricola published *Käsikiria Castesta ia muista Cristikunnan Menoista* (A handbook about baptism and other rituals of Christendom). For this work Agricola borrowed heavily from similar works by Olaus Petri, Martin Luther, and Caspar Huberinus (1500–1553).[221] The book is his only one that offers glimpses into Agricola's views on the debates at the time concerning the sacraments. In respect to baptism, he argues strongly for the baptism of children. A newborn child is "possessed by the devil" who can then through baptism become "a child of God". He echoes Luther's argument that baptism is a gift of grace by God and thus does not need to be earned by age or professions of faith.[222] This argument for infant baptism is lifted loosely from Luther's *Taufbüchlein* from 1526. Such an argument does not exist in Olaus Petri's handbook of 1548 which otherwise serves as the primary basis for Agricola's

219 Tuppurainen, Westhin, 29–42.
220 Knuutila, Liturgisen, 9–40.
221 Häkkinen, Käsikirja, 7–12.
222 Häkkinen, Käsikirja, 3.

handbook. This is again another example of how Agricola did not tie himself to one Lutheran thinker but rather availed himself of many available writings.[223] Agricola's argument for infant baptism was probably not directed against any Anabaptist movement in Finland or the Swedish kingdom—there is no evidence of one. Rather, he was arguing for infant baptism to people who did not practice it and or were uncertain about the practice in the new religious order.

Agricola accepted marriage as both a temporal tradition and divine act. He called marriage a "human decree, for which we spiritual and ecclesiastical servants have nothing to decree or impose".[224] Agricola then mentioned that marriage is "a divine decree confirmed in the Old and New Testament". Like the other reformers of the Swedish kingdom's church of his time Agricola maintained the sacramental nature of the marriage ceremony.[225] He roundly condemned priestly celibacy. Marriage according to Agricola was "bound by the Word and promise of God and not invented or started by humans, unlike the wicked celibacy of monks and nuns".[226] Marriage should be open to all, regardless of vocation. Agricola criticized the "mockery" with which marriage ceremonies were treated.[227] Agricola's writing on marriage was one of few written in the Swedish kingdom during Gustav Vasa's era. The strong temporal traditions of marriage in the Swedish kingdom meant that relatively few actually had their marriage ceremony performed in a church. This probably helped take the kingdom's reformers' focus off marriage, unlike in Central Europe, where the sacramentality of marriage was a significant topic of discussion to Central European reformers.[228] The reform of marriage by Agricola and others was in the final analysis modest. They wanted to eliminate celibacy as a means of reducing sin. Agricola obviously understood that he was not going to eliminate medieval forms of temporal marriage, rather, he wanted the church to play a greater role in the marriage process as a means of improving morals.

The last part of Agricola's handbook gives advice concerning death and dying. In fact, over half of the handbook addresses these questions. Agricola gives detailed instructions on what kind of prayers the pastor should say with the dying person: prayers for forgiveness, professions of faith, and then the sharing of the Eucharist. Anointing of the sick is not included in these instructions.

223 Pentti Lempiäinen, Kastekäytäntö, 86.
224 Häkkinen, Käsikirja, 15.
225 Knuutila, Avioliitto, 255–279.
226 Häkkinen, Käsikirja, 15.
227 Häkkinen, Käsikirja, 15.
228 Korpiola, Marriage, 131–169.

Agricola gives a worldlier bit of advice in that pastors should tell the dying to have a completed will.[229]

As in the case of marriage, funerals often did not include the church in the medieval Swedish kingdom. Neither Agricola nor Olaus Petri sought to change well-known ways of burial, rather they wanted to include the church more into these events. Agricola is considered more traditional in terms of reforming medieval Christian burial ceremonies in that he was more open to prayers for the dead. Lutheran reformers in Germany emphatically opposed prayers for the dead in funerals. Funerals and their prayers were meant for the living. A funeral reminded the living of their mortality and the final judgment of God that all would have to face. Olaus Petri shared German Lutherans' rejection of prayers for the dead. Agricola maintained an opportunity for congregations to pray for the dead. One can agree with Olavi Rimpiläinen in his study of burial practices that Agricola's funeral service was for both the living and the dead.[230]

Mikael Agricola succeeded where many fell short in putting the Word of God into Finnish by applying to his work a vision of Finnish as a comprehensive written language. He also exploited his access to a printing press. He benefitted from the free labor of students and colleagues at the Turku school. He drew from a wide body of works written by other reformers. Agricola's major significance lies not only in that he put the Word of God into Finnish, but that he did so with visibility and durability. He created Finnish as both a written and printed language. Over seventy percent of the words used by Agricola are still used in Finnish. Much of the rest is understandable to a reader of modern Finnish, especially if the reader can decipher Agricola's neologisms derived from Swedish.[231] Agricola was a realistic and pragmatic reformer. He understood the serious limitations under which he worked. The people first needed the basic texts of Christianity in their language. He had to submit to the laws of the market to get any of God's Law published in the vernacular. In this environment getting as much of Scripture and the Mass out into the vernacular as possible was the only realistic and effective course of action. Agricola pursued this course with a great deal of success.

229 Häkkinen, Käsikirja, 29–30.
230 Rimpiläinen, Läntisen, 147.
231 Rapola, Mikael Agricola, 138.

Otfried Czaika

Ein weites und weitgehend unbekanntes Feld

Schwedische Gesangbücher und Lieddrucke des 16. Jahrhunderts

Was wir von schwedischen Kirchenliedern und Gesangbüchern aus dem 16. Jahrhundert wissen

Der schwedische Reichsbibliothekar und Buchhistoriker Isak Collijn (1875–1949) publizierte in den 1920-er und 1930-er Jahren die schwedische Nationalbibliographie, die Werke seit Beginn des schwedischen Buchdrucks bis zum Jahr 1600 verzeichnet.[232] In den Folgejahren veröffentlichte Collijn zudem eine Bibliographie zum 17. Jahrhundert, die allerdings weder dieselbe Beschreibungstiefe besitzt wie die Bibliographie bis zum Jahr 1600 noch denselben Anspruch auf Vollständigkeit hatte.[233] Bis zum heutigen Tag sind Collijns Bibliographien – in Ermangelung neuerer Darstellungen – das Standardwerk, dass über die Geschichte des frühen Buchdrucks im schwedischen Reich Auskunft gibt.

Diese Bibliographien sind gleichzeitig das wichtigste Hilfsmittel nicht nur für Buchwissenschaftler, sondern auch für Hymnologen. Bis etwa zur Mitte des vergangenen Jahrhunderts arbeiteten schwedische Buchhistoriker und Hymnologen eng miteinander zusammen. Auch in den vergangenen gut fünfzig Jahren war die hymnologische Arbeit durchaus ergiebig und hat sich aktiv mit dem seit dem 16. Jahrhundert gewachsenen Erbe des schwedischen Kirchenlieds befasst. Die wissenschaftliche Beschäftigung mit der Geschichte des schwedischen Kirchenlieds seit dem 16. Jahrhundert wurde dabei u. a. auch staatlicherseits gefordert und gefördert, da die evangelisch-lutherische Kirche bis zum Ende des 20. Jahrhunderts eine Staatskirche war.[234] So befasste sich etwa in den 1970er und 1980er Jahren eine staatliche Kommission mit der Revision des schwedischen Gesangbuchs. Die in diesem Zusammenhang pu-

232 Collijn, Bibliografi.

233 Collijn, Bibliografi 1600-talet. Ephemeres Schrifttum, wie z. B. Gelegenheitsgedichte, Personenschriften oder Leichenpredigten, wurde cum grano salis vollständig in die Bibliographie bis zum Jahre 1600 aufgenommen, in der Bibliographie zum 17. Jahrhundert allerdings nur sporadisch aufgenommen.

234 Berntson/Nilsson/Wejryd, Kyrka.

blizierten Rapporte sind nicht nur sehr forschungsnah, sondern produzierten auch durchaus forschungsrelevante Resultate.[235]

Collijns Bibliographie gibt – die zwei Varianten bzw. Neuauflagen des Gesangbuchs aus dem Jahr 1536 (*Swenske songer*) eingerechnet – bibliographische Angaben zu insgesamt zwanzig im 16. Jahrhundert gedruckten Gesangbüchern. Knapp die Hälfte (9) der Gesangbücher, die übrigens während des gesamten 16. Jahrhunderts ohne musikalische Notation gedruckt wurden, konnte Collijn allerdings entweder nur sekundär erschließen oder waren ihm nur fragmentarisch bekannt.[236]

In den 1960-er Jahren wurde auf Island zudem ein bisher unbekanntes schwedisches Gesangbuch aus dem Jahr 1562 entdeckt.[237] In den vergangenen Jahren konnte ich zudem zwei Exemplare des Gesangbuchs aus dem Jahre 1582 ausfindig machen, wovon eines sich in der Roggebibliothek in Strängnäs befindet und eins in der Albertina zu Leipzig.[238] Das von Collijn verzeichnete Fragment dieses Gesangbuches enthielt nur das Titelblatt und Teile des Kalendariums, gab also nicht über den Inhalt dieses Werkes Auskunft.[239] Damit sind uns heute insgesamt 21 gedruckte schwedische Gesangbücher aus dem 16. Jahrhundert bekannt, von denen dreizehn praktisch vollständig erhalten sind, der Rest als Fragment bekannt ist oder nur sekundär belegt werden kann.

Neben den Werken, die eindeutig als „Gesangbuch" zu identifizieren sind – also *Swenske songer* aus dem Jahr 1536 sowie dessen (mögliche) Vorläufer und alle Werke, die den Titel *Then Swenska Psalmeboken* (*Das schwedische Gesangbuch*) tragen, existiert eine größere Anzahl kleinerer Drucke, die eines oder mehrere Kirchenlieder bzw. geistliche Lieder beinhalten. Zu diesen Lieddrucken zählen etwa die polemischen *Gesänge vom Antichrist* (*Några Wijsor om Antichristum*, publiziert [1530] und [1536]),[240] *Einige Geistliche Gesänge* (*Någhra andeliga wijsor*, 1572)[241] oder auch *Eine Weise von der Eitelkeit dieser Welt* (*Een Wijsa om thenna Werldennes fåfengeligheet*, 1583).[242]

Die bibliographische Sicherung der im Druck erschienenen schwedischen Gesangbücher und Lieddrucke hat sodann selbstverständlich die Basis dafür

235 SOU 1975:2, Psalmer. SOU 1975:3, Psalmer. SOU 1975:4, Psalmer. SOU 1981:49, Psalmboken. SOU 1981:50, Psalmboken. SOU 1985:17, Psalmboken. SOU 1985:18, Psalmboken. SOU 1985:19, Psalmboken.

236 Malmgren/Kroon, Reformationsskrifter.

237 Czaika, Psalmeboken, 22–24 bietet einen Überblick über die heute bekannten schwedischen und finnischen Gesangbuchdrucke des 16. Jahrhunderts.

238 Czaika, Psalmeboken. Czaika, Episode II.

239 Collijn, Bibliografi, Bd. 2, 514.

240 Czaika, Antichristum.

241 Collijn, Bibliografi, Bd. 2, 406.

242 Collijn, Bibliografi, Bd. 3, 7.

geschaffen, dass der hymnologischen Forschung ein Textkorpus zur Verfügung stand, mit dem gearbeitet werden konnte. Während der Textbestand des ersten vollständig erhaltenen Gesangbuchs aus dem Jahre 1536 (*Swenske songer*) gut vierzig Kirchenlieder umfasste, war er bis zum Ende des 16. Jahrhunderts auf über 120 angeschwollen. Im Jahre 1695 erschien dann das erste „offizielle", d. h. vom König approbierte, Gesangbuch, das insgesamt 413 Kirchenlieder umfasste.[243] Hymnologen wie Emil Liedgren[244] oder in den vergangenen Jahrzehnten auch Per-Olof Nisser[245] haben mit dieser Quellengrundlage gearbeitet und u. a. die Erstveröffentlichung von Kirchenliedern, den Erscheinungstakt sowie die Frage der verwendeten Melodien o.ä. diskutiert. Die buchhistorische Forschung, insbesondere Collijns bibliographische Arbeit, dienten dabei als Hilfswissenschaft der Hymnologie, aber auch anderer historisch arbeitender Disziplinen wie z. B. der Sprach- und Literaturwissenschaft.

Collijns bibliographische Arbeit bildet also – um mit Aleida Assmann zu sprechen[246] – nicht nur den Kanon für die Buchgeschichte, sondern insbesondere auch für die Hymnologie. Dass es – wiederum im Anschluss an Assmann – auch ein Archiv gibt, aus dem bisher nicht Bekanntes an die Oberfläche des historischen Erinnerns gespült werden kann, wurde bereits durch den Hinweis auf das in den 1960-er Jahren auf Island gefundene Gesangbuch aus dem Jahre 1562 oder die kürzlich entdeckten Exemplare des Gesangbuchs von 1582 angesprochen. Das Spannungsverhältnis zwischen Kanon und Archiv ist jedoch weitaus intrikater als es die in den etwa letzten fünfzig Jahren gemachten Funde bisher nicht bekannter Gesangbücher zunächst nahezulegen scheinen.

Was wir von schwedischen Kirchenliedern und Gesangbüchern aus dem 16. Jahrhundert nicht wissen

Die buchgeschichtliche Forschung hat sich in den vergangenen Jahren vermehrt der Frage nach den „verlorenen Büchern" (engl. *lost books*) zugewendet, also jenen Ausgaben, die entweder in physischer Form verloren gegangen sind, aber wenigstens sekundär erschlossen werden können oder aber noch nicht einmal sekundär erschlossen werden können.[247] Als Ergebnis avancierter mathematischer Berechnungen, die Format, Auflagengröße, Textsorte, Sprache,

243 Psalmboken 1695.

244 Liedgren, Psalm.

245 Nisser, Samband.

246 Assmann, Aleida, Canon. Siehe hierzu auch Aleida und Jan Assmanns Studien, u. a.: Assmann, Aleida, Geschichte; Assmann, Jan, Gedächtnis; Assmann, Jan/Müller, Ursprung.

247 Sie hierzu die verschiedenen Beiträge in: Bruni/Pettegree, *Lost books*.

Überlieferungsgrad etc. mit einbeziehen, kann festgehalten werden, dass von den in der Frühen Neuzeit angefertigten Auflagen weniger als 50% durch ein oder mehrere erhaltene Exemplare zu belegen sind.[248] Die Diskussion über die verlorenen Bücher kann übrigens mit Aleida Assmanns Theorie zu Kanon und Archiv parallelisiert werden. Assmann geht nämlich davon aus, dass es nicht nur einerseits Objekte, Texte etc. gibt, die das kanonische historische Narrativ konstituieren, sondern dass es andererseits auch ein Archiv gibt, aus dem Artefakte an die Oberfläche des Erinnerns kommen können und denen die Potenz innewohnt, die kanonische Erzählung zu modifizieren. Neben Kanon und Archiv existiert aber als dritter Aspekt das Vergessen, das aktiv (etwa Zerstörung durch *damnatio memoriae*) oder passiv (z. B. Zerstörung durch natürliche Prozesse, den „Zahn der Zeit") sein kann. *Lost books*, vergessene Bücher, gehören also dieser dritten Kategorie an, dem was nicht überliefert, wirklich in Vergessenheit geraten ist, also dem worüber sich nur mehr oder minder qualifizierte Spekulationen anstellen lassen. Bibliographien hingegen konstituieren die kanonische Meistererzählung: Das, was vorfindlich ist, erinnert werden kann und soll, wird – oftmals wie im Falle von Collijns Bibliographie – in eine nationale Erinnerungskultur, in diesem Fall „das Schwedische", implementiert.

Mit Hinblick auf die Buchgeschichte bilden das Archiv alle diejenigen Werke, die zwar bis in unsere Zeit überliefert sind, aber nicht ihren Weg in die kanonische Erzählung gefunden haben, weil sie beispielsweise bewusst als „nichtkanonisch" bewertet wurden,[249] oder aber, weil sie bisher nicht aufgefunden worden sind. Die bereits erwähnten schwedischen Gesangbuchausgaben aus den Jahren 1562 und 1582 gehörten also bis zu ihrer Auffindung dem Archiv an. Allerdings kann möglicherweise sogar behauptet werden, dass diese Werke bisher dennoch nicht der kanonischen Erzählung der Buchgeschichte angehören, da sie noch nicht Eingang in eine Bibliographie gefunden haben. In einem gewissen Sinne befinden sie sich in einem Vakuum zwischen Kanon und Archiv.

---

248 Proot, Survival. Eisermann, Lost Incunabula. Undorf, Lost Books. Green/McIntyre, Editions. Pettegree, Legion. Siehe hierzu auch u. a.: Proot/Egge, Editions.

249 Dies ist etwa der Fall mit der Leichenpredigt auf Elisabet Vasa (1549–1597), die 1598 in der deutschen Kirche zu Stockholm gehalten wurde und in Rostock im selben Jahr verlegt wurde; da das „Objekt" der Leichenpredigt, die Verstorbene eine schwedische Prinzessin war, hätte die Predigt sinnvollerweise in Collijns Bibliographie Eingang finden müssen, wurde von ihm aber nicht aufgenommen. Der Grund dafür ist wahrscheinlich in dem Umstand zu suchen, dass die Leichenpredigt auf Deutsch in der deutschen Gemeinde gehalten sowie in Rostock gedruckt wurde und es sich um eine weibliche Verstorbene handelt; hätte es sich um einen Sohn und nicht eine Tochter Gustav Vasas gehandelt, so ist zu vermuten, dass eine in Stockholm gehaltene Leichenpredigt aufgenommen worden wäre. Czaika, Elisabet Vasa.

In der Buchgeschichte entsprechen also die bekannten (in einem Katalog oder einer Bibliographie verzeichneten oder sonst vom historisch Diskurs benutzten) Bücher dem Kanon; die de facto existierenden, aber nicht verwendeten und/oder unbekannten Werke sind ein Teil des Archivs. Die verlorenen Bücher fallen schließlich unter die Kategorie des Vergessens.

Das Archiv – von Island bis Sachsen

Collijns Bibliographie ist wie jede Bibliographie eine Beschreibung eines Ist-Zustandes zum Zeitpunkt der Abfassung. Dass durch den Prozess der sukzessiven Neuerschließung alter Drucke bis dato unbekannte Werke zu Tage gefördert werden können, war Collijn wohl bewusst. Seine Biographie, die Werke bis zum Jahr 1600 verzeichnet, schließt daher auch mit einem Appendix ab, der Drucke verzeichnet, die bei Veröffentlichung der ersten Teilbände seiner Bibliographie noch nicht bekannt waren. So findet sich im Anhang u. a. eine Variante bzw. Neuauflage der *Gesänge vom Antichrist* (*Några Wijsor om Antichristum*, [1536]), die in Finnland entdeckt wurde als der entsprechende Teil der Bibliographie bereits erschienen war.[250]

In den etwa achtzig Jahren seit Abschluss von Collijns Bibliographie sind daher selbstverständlich eine längere Reihe von Drucken aus dem 16. Jahrhundert, darunter u. a. Gelegenheitsschriften, entdeckt worden.[251] Neben dem Gesangbuch von 1562 wurden in den 1960er Jahren in der National- und Universitätsbibliothek zu Reykjavik auch ein bis dahin nicht bekannter Katechismus, ein Gebetbuch und ein Evangelienbuch aufgefunden, die alle drei im selben Jahr von Amund Laurentzon in Stockholm gedruckt wurden.[252]

In den vergangenen Jahren wurden zudem in rascher Abfolge eine ganze Reihe frühneuzeitlicher Gesangbuchdrucke oder ephemerer Schriften entdeckt, die geistliche Lieder enthalten. Im Jahre 2010 entdeckte ich in der Wrangelschen Sammlung, die wenige Jahre zuvor als Donation der Roggebibliothek in Strängnäs vermacht wurde, das bis dato einzige, nahezu vollständige Exemplar

---

250 Collijn, Bibliografi, Bd. 1, 369–370.

251 Gustaf Bernström entdeckte z. B. einige bis dahin unbekannte Gelegenheitsschriften aus dem späten 16. Jahrhundert. Bernström, Nyfunna. Es handelt sich dabei um folgende Werke: Praetorius/Ambernus/Nicolai/Ruta, Carmina Gratulatoria; Goclenius/Kirchner/Chesnecopherus, Carmina Gratulatoria. Die finnische Buchhistorikerin Terhi Kiiskinen entdeckte vor einigen Jahren eine handschriftliche Abschrift eines bisher nur sekundär bekannten Werkes, Erik Falks (1510–1569) Een Tröstbook för Haffuandhe Quinnor (Trostbuch für schwangere Frauen); Kiiskinen, Källor.

252 Malmgren/Kroon, Reformationsskrifter.

des schwedischen Gesangbuchs von 1582. Vor wenigen Jahren fand die finnische Hymnologin Suvi-Päivi Koski in der Staats- und Universitätsbibliothek zu Dresden eine bisher vollständig unbekannte finnischsprachige Ausgabe von Martin Luthers (1483–1546) Kleinem Katechismus sowie ein finnisches Gesangbuch (*Yxi Vähä Suomekielinen wirsikiria*).[253] Beide Drucke wurden 1607 in Rostock angefertigt. Das Gesangbuch[254] stellt eine bearbeitete Version von Jaakko Finnos (1540–1588) vermutlich im Jahr 1583 erstmals gedruckten Werkes dar. Für die Ausgabe von 1607 zeichnete Simon Johannis Carelius († 1610) verantwortlich, der nach seinen Studien in Rostock (Juli 1605 bis 1607) Rektor der Schule im finnischen Viborg wurde.[255] Carelius ist als Verfasser sonst nicht in Erscheinung getreten.

Nur wenige Monate, nachdem ich eine auf dem Exemplar der Roggebibliothek basierende Edition des schwedischen Gesangbuchs von 1582 veröffentlicht hatte, identifizierte ich in den Sammlungen der Albertina in Leipzig ein zweites – und zudem unversehrtes – Exemplar dieses Werkes. Die von mir im Mai 2017 vorgenommene Autopsie des Bandes förderte weitere bisher unbekannte schwedische Drucke aus den 1580er Jahren zu Tage: Das Leipziger Exemplar des Gesangbuchs von 1582 ist nämlich mit fünf weiteren Lieddrucken zusammengebunden, von denen bisher kein einziger bibliographisch belegt war.

Es handelt sich dabei um folgende Drucke:

1) Peder Dåleman, *Een skiön Wijse om Gudz Son (Eine schöne Weise von Gottes Sohn)*, Stockholm: Andreas Gutterwitz, 1584, 4 Blätter, Oktav. Von diesem Werk ist eine ältere Auflage, gedruckt bei Andreas Gutterwitz in Stockholm im Jahre 1583, in Collijns Bibliographie nachgewiesen.[256]
2) *Een wijsae, om thenne Werldennes fåfengeligheet (Eine Weise von der Eitelkeit dieser Welt)*, Stockholm: Andreas Gutterwitz, 1584, 4 Blätter, Oktav. Von diesem Werk ist ebenfalls eine ältere Auflage, gedruckt bei Andreas Gutterwitz in Stockholm im Jahre 1583, in Collijns Bibliographie nachgewiesen.[257]
3) *Troon (Glaubensbekenntnis* in schwedischer und lateinischer Sprache), Stockholm: Andreas Gutterwitz, 1584, 8 Blätter, Oktav, mit unbedruckten Notenlinien. Auch zu diesem Werk ist eine ältere Auflage, gedruckt bei Torbjörn Tidemansson in Stockholm im Jahre 1578, in Collijns Bibliographie nachgewiesen.[258]

---

253 Ennennäkemätön kirjalöytö Saksasta.

254 Finno/Carelius, Yxi Vähä.

255 Callmer, Rostock, 34.

256 Collijn, Bibliografi, Bd. 3, 9.

257 Collijn, Bibliografi, Bd. 3, 7.

258 Collijn, Bibliografi, Bd. 2, 484–486.

4) *Een Andeligh Wijse på nyt öffuerseet och förmeret (Eine neue geistliche Weise, aufs Neue bearbeitet und vermehrt)*, s.l., s.t., s.a. [Stockholm: Andreas Gutterwitz, um 1584], 4 Blätter, Oktav. Der vorliegende Druck beinhaltet drei geistliche Lieder. Von diesem Druckwerk waren bisher keine anderen Ausgaben bekannt.
5) *Een skön Andeligh Wijse at tröste sigh medh på sitt yterste (Eine schöne geistliche Weise um sich am Lebensende zu trösten)*, s.l., s.t., s.a. [Stockholm: Andreas Gutterwitz, um 1584], 4 Blätter, Oktav. Auch dieser Druck beinhaltet drei geistliche Lieder und von diesem Druckwerk waren bisher ebenfalls keine anderen Ausgaben bekannt.

Insbesondere *Een Andeligh Wijse* und *Een skön Andeligh Wijse* erweitern nicht nur unsere Kenntnis über die schwedische Buchgeschichte, sondern auch das, was wir über die Geschichte des schwedischen Kirchenlieds im 16. und 17. Jahrhundert wissen. Zwar weisen diese beiden Werke kein Druckjahr auf, da sie jedoch einem Sammelband angehören, der außer diesen Drucken vier weitere umfasst, die in den Jahren von 1582 bis 1584 in Stockholm angefertigt wurden, kann als *terminus ante quem* für diese Drucke sowie gegebenenfalls auch für die Anfertigung des Sammelbandes, mit recht hoher Sicherheit das Jahr 1585 angenommen werden.

Die beiden Drucke enthalten insgesamt fünf verschiedene Lieder, von denen eins in beiden Werken abgedruckt ist (*Een skön Wijse/ om Christi Födsel – Frögder idher alle/J thenna Christenheet [Ein schönes Lied von Christi Geburt – Freut Euch alle in der Christenheit]*.

Eins dieser Lieder (*Een Wijse om Menniskionnes fåwisko och galenskap… [Ein Lied vom Unverstand und Wahnsinn des Menschen]* (in: *Een Andeligh Wijse*, A III v–A IV v: *Een Wijse om Menniskionnes fåwisko och galenskap… [Ein Lied vom Unverstand und Wahnsinn des Menschen])* ist nur durch diesen Druck bekannt und ansonsten nicht belegt.

Ein zweites Lied, *Mit Hierta hwi gremme tu tigh (Mein Herz wie grämst Du Dich*, A IIv–A IVr in: *Een skön Andeligh Wijse)* wurde bereits 1572 in der Liedsammlung *Några Andliga Wijsor* gedruckt und stellt eine Bearbeitung von *Warum betrübst du dich, mein Herz* dar, einem Lied, das Hans Sachs zugeschrieben wurde.[259]

Zwei weitere Lieder sind seit der zweiten Hälfte der 1580er Jahre als Bestandteile der schwedischen Gesangbücher bekannt. Die in *Een skön Andeligh Wijse* (A Ir–A IIv) abgedruckte schwedische Version (*När min tijd och stund kommen At iagh skal hädan fare*) von Nikolaus Hermanns *Wenn mein Stündlein*

259 Suphan, Hans Sachs, 34. Das Lied ist nicht nachgewiesen in: Sachs, Generalregister.

vorhanden ist war bislang als Erstdruck im schwedischen Gesangbuch von 1586 nachgewiesen. *Een skön Wijse/ om Christi Födsel – Frögder idher alle/J thenna Christenheet (Ein schönes Lied von Christi Geburt – Freut Euch alle in der Christenheit*, in: *Een Andeligh Wijse,* A IIv–A IIIr sowie in *Een skön Andeligh Wijse,* A IVr–A IVv) war bisher zum ersten Mal im schwedischen Gesangbuch von 1589 belegt.

Jag wil idher quäde aff hiertens grund (*Ich will Euch singen von Herzens Grund,* in: *Een Andeligh Wijse,* A Ir–A IIv) gehörte Emil Liedgren zufolge erst seit den 1680ern zum Bestand des schwedischen Kirchenliedgutes.[260]

In diesem letzten Fall kann also mit Sicherheit davon ausgegangen werden, dass die im Leipziger Sammelband nachgewiesene Version eines schwedischen Kirchenlieds den Erstdruck darstellt – etwa ein Jahrhundert bevor das Lied bisher nachgewiesen wurde. Doch auch für die drei, erst in den Gesangbüchern von 1586 und 1589 nachgewiesenen, Werke stellen vermutlich die Varianten in den Lieddrucken aus dem Leipziger Sammelband den Erstdruck dar, da – wie oben dargestellt – die Drucklegung von *Een Andeligh Wijse* und *Een skön Andeligh Wijse* in der ersten Hälfte der 1580er Jahre zwar nicht gesichert, so doch sehr wahrscheinlich ist.

Doch auch die drei bisher nur in anderen Varianten bekannten Werke bereichern unser Wissen über die schwedische Druckgeschichte und die Geschichte des schwedischen Kirchenlieds ungemein: Sie stellen nämlich Folgeauflagen schon bereits früher erschienener Werke dar. Von keinem dieser Drucke war bisher bekannt, dass derartige Nachdrucke angefertigt wurden. Damit verändert sich das Bild des schwedischen Kirchenlieddruckes um 1580 markant. Insbesondere kann somit belegt werden, dass diese Werke vom Buchmarkt nachgefragt wurden, so dass für die Stockholmer Drucker Neuauflagen ein lohnendes Geschäft waren.

Die in Leipzig aufgefundenen schwedischen Drucke erweitern überdies die schwedische Nationalbibliographie des 16. Jahrhunderts um fünf neue Titel und somit um etwa 1%.[261] Nicht zuletzt unterstreichen die Leipziger Funde ein-

260 Liedgren, Psalm, 239.

261 Collijn weist etwa 640 „schwedische" Drucke für das 16. Jahrhundert nach; dabei sind allerdings auch eine größere Anzahl in niederdeutscher, hochdeutscher und lateinischer Sprache in Mitteleuropa gedruckter Ausgaben von den Offenbarungen der Heiligen Birgitta eingerechnet. Zumindest die niederdeutschen und hochdeutschen Ausgaben der Offenbarungen waren nicht für den schwedischen Markt bestimmt. Collijn nahm diese Drucke auf, da er den Anspruch hatte alle Drucke zu verzeichnen, die einen Verfasser haben, der „schwedisch" war, also in Schweden geboren wurde. – Selbstverständlich machen die in Leipzig aufgefundenen Werke nur mit Hinblick auf die Titel der schwedischen Nationalbibliographie etwa 1% aus; da es sich hier um nur wenige Blatt umfassende Werke handelt, ist der Anteil dieser Werke an Druckbögen, weitaus geringer als zu veranschlagen. Collijn, Bibliografi, Bd. 1, ix–xxxiv.

drücklich, dass dem Archiv die Potenz innewohnt, die kanonische Beschreibung der Buchgeschichte und der Hymnologie zu modifizieren und zu erweitern. Hiermit gewinnt schließlich auch die Frage nach den verlorenen Büchern an Aktualität.

Sammelbände als Repositorium schwedischer Kirchenlieder

Bis auf das Exemplar des Gesangbuches von 1582, das auch durch das Fragment der Königlichen Bibliothek zu Stockholm und das nahezu vollständige Exemplar der Roggebibliothek in Strängnäs bekannt ist, sind alle anderen Drucke des Leipziger Sammelbandes nur als Unikate überliefert. Dieser Umstand belegt die Bedeutung, die Sammelbänden bei der Überlieferung frühneuzeitlicher Drucke zukommt.

In der internationalen Debatte zur Buchgeschichte ist die immense Bedeutung, die Sammelbände bei der Tradierung frühneuzeitlicher Drucke haben, durchaus bekannt und anerkannt.[262] Im skandinavischen Gespräch ist das Faktum, dass Kolligate ein vergleichsweise stabiles Repositorium bilden, das die Überlieferung zahlreicher Werke sichert, wenn überhaupt, dann nur am Rande bemerkt worden. Insbesondere religiöse Gebrauchsliteratur wie Katechismen, Gesangbücher oder ephemere Lieddrucke sind der Nachwelt häufig nur deshalb bekannt, weil sie mit anderen Werken zusammengebunden waren. Ein Sammelband ist ein umfänglicheres Objekt als ein Einzelband oder vielleicht gar nur ein nichteingebundener, nur wenige Seiten umfassender Druck; ein teurer und gleichzeitig fester sowie das Werk schützender Einband, der mehrere Werke umfasste, war zudem preiswerter als mehrere Drucke einzeln einzubinden. Gleichzeitig besaß ein Sammelband einen höheren (Gebrauchs-)Wert. Sammelbände wurden also nicht nur in wirtschaftlicher Hinsicht als „wertvoller" erachtet, da sie mehrere Drucke beinhalteten. Gleichzeitig schützten sie die Werke besser vor den Unbillen der Umwelt und Zeit. Diesen Umständen ist es zu verdanken, dass Werke, die in einen Sammelband eingebunden wurden, einen höheren Tradierungsgrad als Einzelwerke aufweisen.

Von den zwanzig bekannten schwedischen Gesangbüchern des 16. Jahrhunderts können fünf nur sekundär erschlossen werden oder sind nur als wenige Seiten umfassende Fragmente bekannt.[263] Zu den nur sekundär erschließbaren

262 Proot, Survival.

263 Siehe hierzu und zu den folgenden Ausführungen die Liste der schwedischen Gesangbücher im Anhang dieses Artikels; dort finden sich auch jeweils die Hinweise auf Collijns Bibliographie; Angaben zu Sammelbänden und den haltenden Institutionen. Neben eigenen Studien am Exemplar haben mir freundlicherweise folgende Kollegen Angaben zu Sam-

Gesangbüchern zählen das vermutlich älteste Gesangbuch aus dem Jahre 1526 (auch auf 1528/29 datiert) sowie dessen im Jahre 1531 gedruckter Nachfolger.[264] Die drei in den vierziger Jahren des 16. Jahrhunderts veröffentlichten Gesangbücher (1542, 1543 und 1549) sind als Fragmente überliefert, die nur wenig Aufschlüsse über den Liedbestand dieser Werke geben.

Die Reste des Gesangbuches von 1549 und des bis vor wenigen Jahren einzigen bekannten Zeugens des Gesangbuches von 1582 wurden Einbänden jüngerer Werke entnommen, wo die Blätter als Verstärkungsmaterial dienten. In all jenen Fällen, in denen uns nur sekundäre Angaben über die schwedischen Gesangbücher des 16. Jahrhunderts vorliegen oder nur bruchstückhafte Fragmente überliefert sind, ist es selbstverständlich unmöglich, valide Aussagen über die Gestalt eines möglichen Ursprungsbandes zu tätigen: Was heute als Gesangbuchfragment bekannt ist, kann ein mit anderen Werken zusammengebundenes Kolligat repräsentieren, das später makuliert wurde. Ebenso ist es möglich, dass die Reste der Gesangbücher einem Einzelband entstammen oder aber die Seiten Ausschuss darstellten, der (möglicherweise relativ zeitnah) einer Weiterverwendung zugeführt wurde. Es ist auch nicht ausgeschlossen, dass es sich um Korrekturfahnen handelt und das Endprodukt verschollen ist, während die makulierten Korrekturvorlagen dem Buchbinder als Verstärkungsmaterial zugeführt wurden. Allerdings halte ich es für relativ unwahrscheinlich, dass schwedische Gesangbücher eine strengere redaktionelle Bearbeitung und Druckfahnenkorrektur durchliefen. Der hierfür notwendige wirtschaftliche Mehraufwand wäre kaum vertretbar gewesen. Generell wurde bei der Herstellung religiöser Gebrauchsliteratur weniger akribisch vorgegangen als etwa bei der Produktion wissenschaftlicher Quellenausgaben oder repräsentativer Prachtwerke. Die schwedischen Gesangbücher des 16. Jahrhunderts sind zwar keine typographischen Katastrophen, sie sind aber ebenso wenig Werke, auf die höchste Sorgfalt verwendet wurde.

Vierzehn, im 16. Jahrhundert gedruckte Gesangbuchauflagen, sind in zeitgenössischen Sammelbänden überliefert. Allerdings haben Sammelbände nicht zwangsläufig die Werke vor dem Zahn der Zeit geschützt. Die in Sammelbänden überlieferten Gesangbücher aus den Jahren 1572 und 1576 weisen umfassende

---

melbänden, die schwedische Gesangbücher des 16. Jahrhunderts beinhalten, vermittelt: Dr. Wolfgang Undorf (Königliche Bibliothek, Stockholm), Dr. Håkan Håkansson (Universitätsbibliothek Lund), Dr. Krister Östlund (Universitätsbibliothek Uppsala). Für die rasche und unkomplizierte Hilfe möchte ich an dieser Stelle meinen wärmsten Dank aussprechen!

264 Zur Überlieferungsgeschichte dieses Werkes und den Diskussionen, ob ein schwedisches Gesangbuch oder ein Lieddruck als Vorform des Gesangbuches bereits in den 1520er Jahren vorlag oder nicht: Ek, Psalmböcker. Fransén, Källorna. *Dietz, Salmebog*. Andersen, Salmebøger. Collijn, Bibliografi, Bd. 1, 339.

Blattverluste auf, so dass auch sie in gewissem Sinne den Fragmenten zugerechnet werden müssen.

Das erste vollständig erhaltene schwedische Gesangbuch aus dem Jahre 1536 (*Swenske songer*) liegt in drei leicht voneinander abweichenden Auflagen vor, von denen jede von je einem erhaltenen Exemplar repräsentiert wird. Von den in den Jahren 1567 (Stockholm), 1586 (Lübeck) und 1586 (Stockholm) sind je zwei Exemplare überliefert, wovon alle, mit Ausnahme des zweiten Exemplars des Stockholmer Gesangbuchdrucks von 1586, in Sammelbänden anzutreffen sind.

Das einzige schwedische Gesangbuch, das in mehr als zwei Exemplaren überliefert ist, ist das aus dem Jahre 1582, wobei ein Exemplar allerdings – wie bereits mehrfach aufgezeigt – nur ein Fragment ist. Die Gesangbücher aus den Jahren 1562, 1572, 1576, 1589 (Lübeck), 1589 (Stockholm), 1594 (Lübeck) und 1594 (Stockholm) sind alle in Sammelbänden überliefert und nur mit einem Exemplar erhalten.

Nur zwei Gesangbücher, Exemplar B des 1586 in Stockholm gedruckten und ein vermutlich ebenfalls in Stockholm gedrucktes aus dem Jahre 1594, sind als Einzelbände überliefert, wobei das letztere Exemplar wiederum nur fragmentarisch erhalten ist und sich daher kaum valide Aussagen über einen ursprünglichen Band machen lassen.

Die Exemplare des ersten, vollständig erhaltenen Gesangbuchs, *Swenske songer 1536*, werden durch zwei nahezu identische Sammelbände repräsentiert, wovon allerdings einer im 19. Jahrhundert geschlachtet wurde.[265] *Swenske songer* 1536 war in beiden Fällen mit einer Ausgabe von *Davids Psaltare* 1536 sowie mit *Någhra Wijsor om Antichristum* [1536] zusammengebunden. Der einzige Unterschied zwischen den beiden Sammelbänden war allerdings, dass das eine Kolligat zwei unterschiedliche Varianten von *Swenske songer* beinhaltete, während das andere keine solche Doppelung aufweist. Da *Swenske songer* im Vergleich zu *Davids Psaltare* ein relativ dünnes Werk ist, kann nicht ausgeschlossen werden, dass der Buchbinder versehentlich zwei Exemplare in denselben Sammelband aufnahm. Aus inhaltlichen Gesichtspunkten – es handelt sich um Varianten mit relativ wenigen typographischen Abweichungen – macht die Doppelung von *Swenske songer* keinen Sinn. Von dem im Jahre 1567 gedruckten Gesangbuch sind zwei Exemplare überliefert, wovon das eine u. a. mit *Davids Psaltare* zusammengebunden war, das andere mit Luthers *Kleinem Katechismus* und Gebetbuch, einem Perikopenbuch (*Evangelier och Epistlar*) sowie einer Leidensgeschichte Jesu (*Passio*).[266] Eine identische Kopplung, also

265 Klemming, Psalmboken, 104.
266 Dahlberg, Skrifter.

Gesangbuch, Katechismus, Perikopenbuch und Leidensgeschichte in einem Sammelband, findet sich auch bei dem Exemplar des Gesangbuchs von 1562 und im zweiten Sammelband, der auch ein Lübecker Exemplar des Gesangbuchs von 1586 (Exemplar B) umfasst, sowie bei folgenden Ausgaben: 1586 (Stockholm), 1589 (Lübeck), 1589 (Stockholm), 1589 (Lübeck) sowie bei beiden Ausgaben, die im Jahre 1594 erschienen (Lübeck und Stockholm). In der Literatur wurde daher immer wieder angenommen, dass das Zusammenbinden dieser vier kirchlichen Bücher ein nahezu standardisiertes Vorgehen belegt und ggf. auch Rückschlüsse auf einen kirchlich-liturgischen Gebrauch dieser Werke gezogen werden können. Dass diese vier Werke häufig zeitnah, d. h. im selben Jahr oder im Folgejahr gedruckt wurden, scheint auf den ersten Blick die Annahme eines nahezu industriellen Workflows und die kirchlich-liturgische Nutzung zu stützen.

Allerdings existieren genügend Belege, dass die schwedischen Gesangbücher des 16. Jahrhunderts eben nicht (nur) mit diesen Texten, sondern auch mit anderen zusammengebunden wurden. Neben *Swenske songer* 1536 gilt dies auch für die in den Jahren 1567 (Exemplar A), 1572, 1576 und 1582 gedruckten Gesangbücher sowie Exemplar A der Lübecker Ausgabe von 1586.

Interessant ist der Sammelband, der auch Exemplar A der Ausgabe von 1567 umfasst: Wie bei den überlieferten Exemplaren des Gesangbuches von 1536 ist auch hier *Davids Psaltare* miteingebunden. Zudem beinhaltet dieser Sammelband noch Olaus Petris im Jahr 1562 in Stockholm aufgelegte Predigt über Totschlag (*Predican emoot mandråp*).

Das Gesangbuch von 1572 ist mit drei ephemeren Lieddrucken zusammengebunden: *Någhra andeliga wijsor* (*Einige geistliche Lieder*), *Then Parapbolen om Samaritanen, Luce X.* (*Die Parabel vom Samariter, Luk. 10*) sowie *En wijsa om dryckenskap* (*Ein Lied von der Trunksucht*). Der Druck von *Någhra andeliga wijsor* gibt neben einigen bis daher nicht bekannten schwedischen Kirchenliedern auch die vier vermutlich 1536 zum ersten Mal gedruckten polemischen Lieder vom Antichrist (*Några wijsor om Antichristum*). Auch hier lässt sich ebenso wie beim Leipziger Exemplar des Gesangbuchs von 1582 die immense Bedeutung ablesen, die Sammelbänden als Repositorium ephemerer Lieddrucke zukommt: Wie die Drucke des Leipziger Sammelbandes so ist auch keiner der mit dem Gesangbuch von 1572 zusammengebundenen Drucke in einem weiteren Exemplar überliefert.

Der Sammelband, der auch das Gesangbuch von 1576 beinhaltet, umschließt neben dem ephemeren Lieddruck *Någhra nyttiga Andeliga wijsor* (*Einige nützliche geistliche Lieder*) auch einen Katechismus und ein Perikopenbuch (beide gedruckt in Stockholm, 1577) – aber keine Leidensgeschichte. Auch hier sind alle im Sammelband miteinander verbundenen Drucke in keinem weiteren Exemplar überliefert.

Die beiden in den vergangenen Jahren entdeckten Bände, die das Gesangbuch von 1582 beinhalten, sind mit ephemeren Lieddrucken zusammengebunden: das Exemplar der Roggebibliothek in Strängnäs mit *Een Wijsa om thenna Werldennes fåfengeligheet* (*Eine Weise von der Eitelkeit dieser Welt*), das Leipziger Exemplar mit den oben ausführlicher kommentierten fünf ephemeren Lieddrucken.

Exemplar A der Lübecker Ausgabe von *Then swenska psalmeboken 1586* ist schließlich mit einem Perikopenbuch und einer Leidensgeschichte (beide Lübeck, 1586) sowie einem gegenüber der Ausgabe von 1576 um ein Kirchenlied erweiterten Druck von *Några nyttigha andeligha Wijsor* zusammengebunden.

Bis in die 1580er Jahre existiert also eine relativ breite Flora an verschiedenen Sammelbänden. Die Kombination des schwedischen Gesangbuches mit Katechismus & Gebetbuch sowie Perikopenbuch und Leidensgeschichte taucht zum ersten Mal bei dem Sammelband aus Reykjavik auf, der diese vier Werke in den 1562 in Stockholm gedruckten Ausgaben umschließt. Davids Psaltare war nicht nur mit den Varianten von *Swenske songer 1536* zusammengebunden, sondern auch mit Exemplar A des Gesangbuchs von 1567. Neben den Sammelbänden, die alle vier Drucke, Gesangbuch, Katechismus & Gebetbuch, Perikopenbuch und Leidensgeschichte, kombinieren, trifft man aber auch auf Sammelbände, bei denen einer dieser Drucke fehlt; an Stelle des Vierten ist ggf. ein ephemerer Lieddruck mit in das Kolligat eingebunden. Schließlich, so gibt es auch – wie soeben aufgezeigt – eine Reihe an Sammelbänden, die eine Gesangbuchausgabe nicht mit Katechismus & Gebetbuch, Perikopenbuch und Leidensgeschichte, sondern mit einem oder mehreren ephemeren Lieddrucken verbinden.

Ein näherer Blick in die verschiedenen Sammelbände, die u. a. auch schwedische Gesangbücher des 16. Jahrhunderts umfassen, sowie ein Abgleich mit Collijns Bibliographie enthüllt folglich das beinahe erschreckende Faktum, dass die anderen dort mit eingebundenen Werke größtenteils ebenfalls nur als Unikate überliefert sind: Die in Stockholm 1567 gedruckten Ausgaben von Katechismus & Gebetbuch, Perikopenbuch und Leidensgeschichte sind nur einmal überliefert – in dem Sammelband, der auch Exemplar B des Gesangbuches von 1567 umfasst. Dasselbe gilt für die fünf Jahre zuvor (1562) ebenfalls in Stockholm aufgelegten Ausgaben dieser Drucke, die mit dem in Reykjavik aufbewahrten Exemplar des Gesangbuchs von 1562 zusammengebunden sind. Ebenso sind alle Drucke (seien es nun Katechismus & Gebetbuch, Perikopenbuch und Leidensgeschichte oder ephemere Lieddrucke), die in Sammelbänden mit den Gesangbüchern von 1572, 1576, 1582 (Exemplar A), Stockholm 1586, Stockholm 1589 und Stockholm 1594 verbunden sind, nur als Unikate tradiert worden. Interessanterweise sind die in Lübeck 1586, 1589 und 1594 gedruckten Ausgaben von Katechismus & Gebetbuch, Perikopenbuch und Leidensgeschichte auch außerhalb von Kolligaten, die das jeweilige Gesangbuch umfassen, überliefert. Ob dies schierer Zufall ist oder ggf. auf eine höhere Auflage dieser Werke und vielleicht auch bessere Vertriebskanäle bzw. Vermarktung schließen lässt, ist jedoch völlig unklar.

Exemplar B des Gesangbuches von 1582 umschließt auch *Een wijsae om thenne Werldennes fåfengeligheet*; ein weiteres Exemplar dieser Ausgabe ist belegt. Die Drucke, die mit Exemplar A des Gesangbuchs von 1567 einen Sammelband ausmachen (*Davids Psaltare* 1560; *Predican emoot mandråp* 1562), sind mehrfach überliefert.

Acht Sammelbände, die auch jeweils ein schwedisches Gesangbuch umfassen (1562, 1567 [Exemplar B], 1572, 1567, 1582 [Exemplar A], Stockholm 1586, Stockholm 1589 sowie Stockholm 1594), geben also insgesamt 30 nur einmal überlieferte Drucke, die der schwedischen Nationalbibliographie des 16. Jahrhunderts zugerechnet werden müssen. Das sind also fast 5% der Gesamtzahl schwedischer Drucke aus dem 16. Jahrhundert.[267]

Generell kann also festgestellt werden, dass ohne Überlieferung von Drucken in Sammelbänden nicht nur unsere Kenntnis des schwedischen Kirchenliedgutes des 16. Jahrhunderts, sondern insgesamt auch die Kenntnis schwedischer Drucke des 16. Jahrhundert noch weitaus fragmentarischer wäre als sie ohnehin schon ist.

Das Vergessen

Insbesondere der Umstand, dass die Drucke des Leipziger Sammelbandes nur als Unikate überliefert sind und zudem auch generell die Mehrzahl der schwedischen Gesangbücher des 16. Jahrhunderts nur als Unikate oder in kaum mehr als zwei Exemplaren erhalten sind, illustriert eindrücklich den generell sehr schlechten Überlieferungsgrad von Gesangbüchern und (ephemeren) Drucken, die geistliche Lieder beinhalten.

Diesbezüglich ist wieder ein Blick in die schwedische Nationalbibliographie instruktiv: Wie bereits angemerkt, sind zahlreiche Gesangbücher nur als Fragment bekannt; von den übrigen ist meistens nur ein Unikat erhalten, selten mehrere Exemplare.[268]

Diese extrem ungünstige Überlieferungslage lässt sich zumindest zum Teil dadurch erklären, dass Gesangbücher und andere Lieddrucke Gebrauchsliteratur darstellten. Diese Werke wurden oftmals von vielen Generationen gelesen und folglich zerlesen. Umfassende Revisionen, insbesondere Erweiterungen

267 Siehe hierzu insbesondere meine Anmerkungen in Fußnote 260.
268 Czaika, Psalmeboken, 22–24.

des Liedbestandes, machten zwar ältere Gesangbücher für die Mitwirkung bei Gottesdiensten weitgehend unbrauchbar, sie konnten allerdings für private Andacht und Erbauung weitergenutzt werden. Neben dem Umstand, dass viele Gesangbücher über Generationen hinweg praktisch aufgebraucht werden, so folgten viele auch ihren Besitzern mit ins Grab und fanden somit nicht in private oder öffentliche Bibliotheken Eingang. Dass Gesangbücher in der lutherischen Konfessionskultur als Grabbeigaben genutzt wurden, lässt sich nicht nur in Zentraleuropa, sondern auch in weiten Teilen des europäischen Nordostens, im Baltikum und in Skandinavien nachweisen.[269]

Dieser schlechte Überlieferungsgrad schwedischer Gesangbücher und Lieddrucke des 16. Jahrhunderts aktualisiert jedoch die Frage nach den verlorenen Büchern. Aufgrund der hohen Anzahl nur als Fragment oder Unikate überlieferter Werke ist davon auszugehen, dass ein hoher Prozentsatz der Gesangbücher und Lieddrucke den verlorenen Büchern zuzurechnen ist. Vermutlich liegt der Überlieferungsgrad dieser Textsorten im schwedischen Reich bei deutlich unter 50%. Diese Einschätzung wird gerade auch dadurch verstärkt, dass – wie oben dargestellt – viele Gesangbücher nur in Sammelbänden tradiert worden sind.

Dass in den vergangenen Jahrzehnten nur selten Duplikate, meistens hingegen Unikate oder Fragmente bisher unbekannter Gesangbücher und Lieddrucke gefunden wurden, stützt diese These noch zusätzlich. Der Leipziger Sammelband – aber auch die auf Island, in Dresden oder Strängnäs entdeckten Werke – sprechen eine beredte Sprache: Vermutlich sind in der Zukunft noch weitere Funde nur einmalig erhaltener Gesangbücher und Lieddrucke zu erwarten. Gleichzeitig gilt aber auch, dass jeder Fund eines nur als Unikat überlieferten Werks den niedrigen Erhaltungsgrad dieser Textsorten unterstreicht und die Wahrscheinlichkeit erhöht, dass zahlreiche Auflagen bis in unsere Zeit nicht einmal mit einem einzigen erhaltenen Exemplar überlebt haben.

Der Leipziger Sammelband stellt also eine Deixis dar, die darauf verweist, wie wenig wir über die schwedische Druckgeschichte und zugleich die Geschichte des schwedischen Kirchenlieds in der frühen Neuzeit wirklich wissen. Die bis heute überlieferten Werke blieben oft nur durch glückliche Zufälle in Bibliotheken erhalten – und sind oftmals Teile von Sammlungen, die z.T. weit außerhalb der ehemaligen Grenzen des schwedischen Reiches liegen: auf Island, in Dresden oder in Leipzig.

All dies bedeutet schlussendlich, dass wir nur höchst unzureichend über die Geschichte des schwedischen Kirchenlieds und die Druckgeschichte von

269 Troels-Lund, Liv, 272. Meyer, Volksleben, 155. Wiegelmann, Konzepte, 161. Bonenberger, Überlieferungen, 185. Medick, Laichingen, 451. Köhle-Hezinger, Alltagskultur, 246. Tiililä, Rukoilevaisten kirjoja. Kõivupuu, Eestlase eluring, 191.

Gesangbüchern und Lieddrucken informiert sind. Als Historiker haben wir damit nur zwei Möglichkeiten, die jede für sich unbefriedigend ist: Wir können erstens darauf verweisen, dass unser Wissen über die schwedische Druckgeschichte und ebenso die Geschichte des schwedischen Kirchenlieds höchst fragmentarisch ist und ergo rein deskriptiv vorgehen und die offensichtlich vorhandenen Leerstellen im Material nicht füllen bzw. abwarten, ob weitere künftige Zufallsfunde nicht gewisse, wenn auch bei weitem nicht alle Leerstellen füllen können. Allerdings wird somit keine Approximation an die Geschichte des 16. Jahrhunderts erreicht, sondern nur der durch die Zufälle der Überlieferung gesteuerte heutige Ist-Zustand der Tradierung beschrieben. Zweitens so kann der Historiker, obwohl er ja in einer starken Tradition des „wie es eigentlich gewesen"[270] steht und seit dem Humanismus seinen Quellen (*ad fontes!*) verpflichtet sein sollte, versuchen, sich spekulativ der Geschichte der frühen Neuzeit anzunähern. Eine solche historische Approximation ist selbstverständlich unbefriedigend, aber vermutlich die einzige Möglichkeit gewisse, vorsichtige Aussagen zur Geschichte des schwedischen Buchdrucks und Kirchenlieds im 16. Jahrhundert zu treffen.

Es gibt jedoch zwei Variablen, die auf die Darstellung massiven Einfluss haben: Zum einen wissen wir nicht, wie hoch der Prozentsatz der verlorenen Bücher ist. Allerdings denke ich, dass es durchaus mit Hinblick auf die neueste Forschung realistisch ist, den Anteil der verlorenen Gesangbücher auf ca. 50% anzusetzen. Dies kann übrigens aufgrund der oben dargestellten Gründe – generell niedriger Überlieferungsgrad, Gebrauchsliteratur, Benutzung von Gesangbüchern als Grabbeigabe – durchaus viel zu niedrig angesetzt sein.

Sodann kennen wir freilich auch nicht die Auflagenhöhe schwedischer Gesangbücher. Der Buchhistoriker Erik Eriksson ist vor einigen Jahrzehnten davon ausgegangen, dass die Auflage eine schwedischen Gesangbuches in der frühen Neuzeit etwa zweitausend Exemplare umfasste.[271] Dies ist u. a. mit Hinblick auf die neuere Forschung durchaus wahrscheinlich, die davon ausgeht, dass Auflagenhöhen von unter eintausend Exemplaren wirtschaftlich kaum tragbar waren – sofern es sich nicht um repräsentative Prachtwerke handelte, die vereinzelt gar nur in weniger als hundert erschienen. Aus schwedischen Zollakten der 1540-er Jahre, die den Import von Papier zum Druck von Gesang- und Gebetbüchern verzeichnen, lässt sich ableiten, dass die Auflage des nur fragmentarisch erhaltenen Gesangbuches von 1543 vermutlich bei 1500 oder mehr Exemplaren lag.[272]

---

270 Ranke, Verwandschaft, 285. Siehe hierzu auch: Repgen, Rankes Diktum.

271 Eriksson, 1600-talstryck. Eriksson, Psalmbokshistorien.

272 Stockholms tullböcker 18/8 1543 und 26/10 1543, Riksarkivet, Tullböcker, 51309/292:1).

Mit diesen Variablen lässt sich nun die Anzahl der im 16. Jahrhundert gedruckten schwedischen Gesangbücher zumindest in einer gewissen Spanne berechnen. Geht man davon aus, dass wir mit den zwanzig Gesangbüchern alle Auflagen kennen und die Auflagenstärke im Durchschnitt nicht größer als eintausend Exemplare war, wurden in schwedischer Sprache (das finnischsprachige Gesangbuch des Jaakko Finno von 1583 ist hier nicht eingerechnet)[273] insgesamt 20.000 Exemplare gedruckt. Stellen die zwanzig überlieferten Auflagen allerdings nur 50% aller tatsächlich gedruckten Ausgaben dar und lag die Durchschnittsauflage bei zweitausend Exemplaren so erhalten wir am anderen Ende der Spanne 80.000 Exemplare. Auch diese Ziffer kann noch zu niedrig gegriffen sein, sollten weitaus mehr als 50% der Gesangbuchauflagen nicht bis heute tradiert worden sein und/oder die Auflagenstärken deutlich über zweitausend Exemplaren gelegen haben.

Selbst die vermutlich viel zu niedrig angesetzte Anzahl von 20.000 gedruckten Exemplaren der verschiedenen Varianten des schwedischen Gesangbuchs belegt, dass es sich hier um einen absoluten Bestseller des 16. Jahrhunderts handelt. Das schwedische Reich hatte im 16. Jahrhundert maximal eine Bevölkerung von einer Million Einwohner, davon etwa 750.000 im schwedischen Mutterland, 250.000 im finnischen Reichsteil. Die Städte waren im europäischen Vergleich sehr klein, Stockholm hatte etwa fünftausend Einwohner verteilt auf einige hundert Haushalte. Die mittelschwedische Stadt Karlstad beispielsweise, von Herzog Karl, einem Sohn Gustav Vasas, 1584 gegründet, zählte im Jahre 1616, also über drei Jahrzehnte nach ihrer Gründung, erst 35 Höfe mit insgesamt etwa zweihundert Einwohnern.[274] Im europäischen Vergleich – z. B. zu Italien, Frankreich oder dem Heiligen Römischen Reich – war der Urbanisierungsgrad des schwedischen Reiches also sehr gering.[275] Doch nicht nur das Stadtbürgertum, sondern auch der Adel machten nur einen kleinen Teil der Bevölkerung aus. Selbst wenn schon während des 16. Jahrhunderts ein gewisser Teil der gedruckten Gesangbücher zerlesen oder sonst unbrauchbar geworden sein sollte, so decken die gedruckten Exemplare – seien es nun etwa 20.000, 80.000 oder mehr – weit mehr als nur den Bedarf der einzelnen Kirchspiele ab.

Die Anzahl der vom schwedischen Gesangbuch im 16. Jahrhundert hergestellten Exemplare dürfte also derart hoch gewesen sein, dass sie den Bedarf kirchlicher oder weltlicher Eliten und auch den des Stadtbürgertums weit übertraf. Die Konsumenten der schwedischen Gesangbücher müssen also auch auf dem flachen Land unter der eher bäuerlichen Bevölkerung des schwedischen

---

273 Collijn, Bibliografi, Bd. 3, 5–6.
274 Linder/Thor, Trä, 34.
275 Czaika, Metropolen.

Reiches zu suchen sein. Dies wirft allerdings völlig neue Fragen auf, die hier nicht beantwortet, sondern nur präsentiert werden können: Wie war es um die Lesefähigkeit der schwedischen Bevölkerung im 16. Jahrhundert bestellt? War sie tatsächlich so gering, nur wenige Prozent, vielleicht 1–3%, wie häufig von der Forschung angenommen wird? War die Reformation wirklich der langsame, nur schleppende Prozess als der sie in den vergangenen Jahrzehnten von der Forschung präsentiert wird? Sprechen nicht die zigtausend im schwedischen Reich zirkulierenden Exemplare des schwedischen Gesangbuchs (von ephemeren Lieddrucken ganz zu schweigen!) nicht eine völlig andere Sprache? Offensichtlich gehörten das schwedische Gesangbuch – so wie auch weniger umfangreiche Lieddrucke – zu den absoluten Bestsellern im 16. Jahrhundert. Zudem zielen Gesangbücher und Lieddrucke nicht in erster Linie auf die stille Erbauung des Individuums in den heimischen vier Wänden ab, sondern involvieren durch den Aspekt des (halb-)öffentlichen Gesangsvortrages immer eine größere Gruppe an Zuhörern oder gar Mitwirkenden. Nicht zuletzt hat der musikalische Vortrag auch mnemotechnische Vorteile: Die Melodie erleichtert das Erinnern der Worte. Auch hierdurch wird wiederum die Frage aktualisiert, inwieweit das schwedische Reich im 16. Jahrhundert nicht relativ rasch vom evangelischen Kirchenlied erobert wurde und die verschiedenen Gesellschaftsschichten entsprechend von der *vera doctrina lutherana* durchdrungen wurden.

Dass das schwedische Gesangbuch im 16. Jahrhundert ein Kassenschlager war, belegen übrigens auch die drei in Lübeck in den 1580er und 1590er Jahren angefertigten Nachdrucke.[276] Deutsche Buchdrucker hatten offensichtlich erkannt, dass das Gesangbuch in Schweden ein höchst nachgefragtes Werk war und die Stockholmer Offizin nicht genügend Neudrucke bzw. Exemplare herzustellen vermochte. Es mag anachronistisch sein, die Lübecker Nachdrucke des Gesangbuches als „Raubdrucke" darzustellen, die Existenz dieser Neuauflagen belegt jedoch, dass der Markt nur unzureichend gesättigt war und die Lübecker Drucker hier durch Neuauflagen Verdienstmöglichkeiten sahen. Dies legt auch den Schluss nahe, dass es sich nicht um kleine Auflagen von nur einigen hundert Exemplaren, sondern eher um auflagenstarke Neuausgaben von mehreren tausend Exemplaren handelte, die entsprechend Profit abwerfen sollten.

Auch wenn wir niemals Sicherheit über die tatsächliche Menge an Auflagen des schwedischen Gesangbuches im 16. Jahrhundert gewinnen werden und auch die Auflagenhöhe sich nur punktuell rekonstruieren oder nur durch mehr

---

276 Collijn, Bibliografi, Bd. 3, 37–38 (1586) [VD16 S 10329]. Collijn, Bibliografi, Bd. 3, 91–93 (1589). Collijn, Bibliografi, Bd. 3, 187 (1594).

oder minder qualifizierte Rechenoperationen abschätzen lässt, so belegen die Funde der vergangenen Jahre ebenso wie die neueste buchhistorische Forschung über die verlorenen Bücher eindrücklich, dass das Forschungsfeld weitaus grösser und spannender ist als es die kanonische bzw. normative Meistererzählung der schwedischen Nationalbibliographie zunächst nahezulegen scheint. Neben den Büchern, die seit dem Erscheinen von Collijns Bibliographie entdeckt wurden, gibt es nicht nur die Bücher, die noch im Archiv schlummern und ihrer Entdeckung harren, sondern auch diejenigen Ausgaben, die für immer bis auf das letzte Exemplar verschwunden sind und an die nicht einmal mehr sekundäre Angaben o.ä. erinnern.

Der Leipziger Sammelband belegt eindrücklich jedoch noch etwas Anderes: Die unter dem Titel *Then Swenska Psalmeboken* publizierten Werke sind das Ergebnis eines Prozesses. Die Erweiterungen der Textbasis, die Aufnahme neuer Kirchenlieder, involviert nicht nur eine handschriftliche, kontrafaktische Rezeption mitteleuropäischer Vorlagen und die Neuabfassung von Kirchenliedern in schwedischer Sprache,[277] sondern stützt sich zudem auf weniger umfangreiche Lieddrucke, die in den Vorjahren herausgegeben worden waren. Dies belegen etwa die seit 1530 mehrmals gedruckten *Några Wijsor om Antichristum*, von denen ein Lied (*O Rom går thet nu så med tich (O Rom, geht es jetzt so mit Dir?)*[278] in den Textbestand des schwedischen Gesangbuches Eingang findet. Dies belegen aber auch weitere in den 1570er Jahren erschienene Lieddrucke und auch die beiden nur als Unikate im Leipziger Sammelband überlieferten Lieddrucke: Da diese aller Wahrscheinlichkeit nach in der ersten Hälfte der 1580er Jahre gedruckt wurden, konnten die Kompilatoren späterer Gesangbuchausgaben auf diese Werke zurückgreifen und Texte daraus in eine Neuausgabe aufnehmen. Auch hier lassen sich gegebenenfalls Rückschlüsse auf den Buchmarkt im 16. Jahrhundert schließen: Der Verkaufserfolg weniger umfangreicher Lieddrucke konnte den Grund dafür legen, neuabgefasste oder neubearbeitete Kirchenlieder in eine Folgeauflage von *Then Swenska Psalmeboken* aufzunehmen. Auch die schwedischen Gesangbücher sind also kein kano-

---

277 Das in der Königlichen Bibliothek zu Stockholm erhaltene Exemplar von *Några Wijsor om Antichristum* umfasst auch handschriftliche Aufzeichnungen, darunter Vorformen bzw. konkurrierende Versionen zu Kirchenliedern, die auch in den gedruckten Gesangbüchern Aufnahme fanden; Czaika, Antichristum.

278 *O Rom går thet nu så med tich* wurde neu abgedruckt in: Någhra nyttiga Andeliga wijsor (Stockholm: Tidemansson, 1576). Das einzige erhaltene Exemplar dieses Druckes ist mit dem seinerseits nur als Unikat überlieferten Gesangbuch von 1576 zusammengebunden (Then swenska psalmeboken 1576, Stockholm: Tidemansson, 1576). Collijn, Bibliografi, Bd. 2, 449–454. Collijn, Torbjörn Tidemansson, 5. Dieses Kirchenlied fand auch Aufnahme in das Gesangbuch von 1695 und wurde in finnischer Sprache auch im finnischen Gesangbuch aus dem Jahre 1701 abgedruckt. Siehe hierzu: Cleve, Finländsk psalm, 61.

nisches Dokument an sich, sondern involvieren Texte, die in ältere Lieddrucken bereits veröffentlicht waren, und illustrieren somit die Prozesshaftigkeit der Kanonbildung.

Anhang: Die Überlieferung schwedischer Gesangbücher des 16. Jahrhunderts

1) **[1526 oder 1528/1529]**
[Svenska visor eller sånger], *[Stockholm: Kungliga tryckeriet, 8:o]*.
Ursprünglicher Band nicht zu erschließen. Nur sekundär erschlossen; Existenz umstritten. Collijn, Bibliografi, Bd. 1, 339.

2) **[1531]**
[Svenska sånger eller visor], *[Stockholm: Kungliga tryckeriet]*.
Nur sekundär erschlossen.
Collijn, Bibliografi, Bd. 2, 19–20.

3) **1536**
Swenske [s]onger eller wisor nw på nytt prentade, förökade, och under en annan skick än tilförenna utsatte, Stockholm: Kungliga tryckeriet, 8:o.
Ursprünglich Sammelband mit *Davids Psaltare* (Stockholm, 1536), *Några Wijsor om Antichristum* [Stockholm, 1536] und *Swenske Songer* (Nr. 4).
Sammelband im 19. Jhd. aufgelöst.
Kungliga biblioteket, Stockholm.
Collijn, Bibliografi, Bd. 2, 38–40.

4) **1536**
Swenske songer eller wisor nw på nytt prentade, förökade, och under en annan skick än tilförenna utsatte, Stockholm: Kungliga tryckeriet, 8:o. [Auflage mit von Nr. 3 und 5 abweichendem Satz].
Ursprünglich Sammelband mit *Davids Psaltare* (Stockholm, 1536), *Några Wijsor om Antichristum* [Stockholm, 1536] und *Swenske Songer* (Nr. 3); Sammelband im 19. Jhd. aufgelöst.
Kungliga biblioteket, Stockholm.
Collijn, Bibliografi, Bd. 2, 40.

5) **1536**
Swenske songer eller wisor nw på nytt prentade, förökade, och under en annan skick än tilförenna utsatte, Stockholm: Kungliga tryckeriet, 8:o. [Auflage mit von Nr. 3 und 4 abweichendem Satz].
Sammelband mit *Davids Psaltare* (Stockholm, 1536), *Några Wijsor om Antichristum* [Stockholm, 1536].
Im Besitz der Kirchengemeinde von Tövsala (Taivassalo), Finnland.
Collijn, Bibliografi, Bd. 1, 368.

6) **[1542]**
[Then swenska psalmeboken], [Lübeck, Georg Richolff], 8:o.
Ursprünglicher Band nicht zu erschließen. Fragment.
Kungliga biblioteket, Stockholm (Fragment von Bogen B–D).
Collijn, Bibliografi, Bd. 2, 109–114.

7) **1543**
[Then swenska psalmeboken], Stockholm: Amund Laurentzson, 12:o.
Ursprünglicher Band nicht zu erschließen. Fragment.
Kungliga biblioteket, Stockholm (Fragment von Bogen F).
Collijn, Bibliografi, Bd. 2, 124–128.

8) **1549**
Then Swenska Psalmeboken förbätrat och medh flere Songer förmerat och Kalendarium, Stockholm: [Amund Laurentzson], 12:o.
Ursprünglicher Band nicht zu erschließen. *Exemplar A* und *Exemplar B*: Fragmente.
Kungliga biblioteket, Stockholm (*Exemplar A*: 16 Blatt); Uppsala Universitetsbibliotek (*Exemplar B*: Bogen 1).
Collijn, Bibliografi, Bd. 2, 166–168.

9) **1562**
Then Swenska Psalmeboken förbätrat och medh flere Songer förmerat och Kalendarium, Stockholm: Amund Laurentzson, 8:o.
Sammelband zusammen mit Katechismus, Gebetbuch Perikopenbuch sowie einer fragmentarischen Leidensgeschichte (alle Stockholm, 1562).
Landsbókasafn (National- und Universitätsbibliothek), Reykjavik.
Nicht in Collijns Bibliographie nachgewiesen.
Malmgren, Reformationsskrifter [Faksimile].

10) **1567**
Then Swenska Psalmeboken förbätrat och medh flere Songer förmerat och Kalendarium, Stockholm: Amund Laurentzson, 8:o.
Exemplar A: Sammelband zusammen mit *Davids Psaltare* (Stockholm, 1560) sowie Olaus Petris *Predican emoot mandråp* (Stockholm, 1562). *Exemplar B*: Sammelband zusammen mit Katechismus & Gebetuch, Perikopenbuch und Leidensgeschichte (alle Stockholm, 1567).
Schloss Maltesholm (*Exemplar A*); Suomen Kansalliskirijasto (Finnische Nationalbibliothek, Helsinki) (*Exemplar B* mit relativ umfassendem Blattverlust).
Collijn, Bibliografi, Bd. 2, 343–345.
Klemming, 1883 [Faksimile].

11) **1572**
[Then swenska psalmeboken], Stockholm: Amund Laurentzson, 8:o.
Sammelband zusammen mit *Een ny wijsa huru menniskian sigh beklagha och*

åter trösta må sowie *Then parabolen om samaritanen* und *Någhra andeliga wijsor* sowie *En wijsa om dryckenskap, och thet onda som ther medh fölier* (alle [Stockholm, 1572]).
Uppsala universitetsbibliotek (Blatt 1–18, 23–24, 65, 90, 113, 131, 134–135 fehlen). Collijn, Bibliografi, Bd. 2, 404–405.
Klemming, 1884 [Faksimile].

12) **1576**
[Then swenska psalmeboken], Stockholm: Torbiörn Tidhemanson, 8:o.
Sammelband zusammen mit *Någhra nyttiga andeliga wijsor* (Stockholm, 1576), Katechismus und Perikopenbuch (beide Stockholm, 1577).
Kungliga biblioteket, Stockholm (Blatt 1–34 fehlt).
Collijn, Bibliografi, Bd. 2, 449–451.

13) **1582**
Then Swenska Psalmeboken förbätrat och medh flere Songer förmerat och Kalendarium, Stockholm: Anders Torstenson, 8:o.
Exemplar A: Sammelband mit: *Een skiön Wijse om Gudz Son* sowie *Een wijsae om thenne Werldennes fåfengeligheet* und *Troon* (alle Stockholm, 1584) sowie *Een Andeligh Wijse* und *Een skön Andeligh Wijse* (beide Stockholm um 1584). *Exemplar B*: Sammelband mit *Een wijsae om thenne Werldennes fåfengeligheet* (Stockholm, 1583). *Exemplar C*: Fragment, ursprünglicher Band nicht zu erschließen.
Universitätsbibliothek Leipzig (*Exemplar A*). Roggebibliothek Strängnäs (*Exemplar B*: zwei Blatt fehlen sowie geringere Schäden am Anfang des Werkes). Kungliga biblioteket, Stockholm (*Exemplar C*: Fragment: Titelblatt und Teile des Kalendariums). Collijn, Bibliografi, Bd. 2, 514.
Czaika, Psalmeboken [Edition].

14) **1586**
Then swenska psalmboken förbätrat och medh flere Songer förmerat, Lübeck: Johann Balhorn, 8:o.
Exemplar A: Sammelband zusammen mit *Några nyttigha andeligha Wijsor*, Perikopenbuch und Leidensgeschichte (alle Lübeck, 1586). *Exemplar B*: Sammelband zusammen mit Katechismus & Gebetbuch, Perikopenbuch, *Någhra nyttigha andeligha wijsor* sowie Leidensgeschichte (alle [Lübeck, 1586]).
Kungliga biblioteket, Stockholm (*Exemplar A*: Blatt 1–39 fehlt). Uppsala Universitetsbibliotek (*Exemplar B*: Blatt 2–17 sowie Blatt 81 & 82 fehlt).
Collijn, Bibliografi, Bd. 3, 37–38 [VD16 S 10329].

15) **1586**
Then swenska psalmboken förbätrat och medh flere Songer förmerat och Kalendarium, Stockholm: Andreas Gutterwitz, 8:o.
Exemplar A: Sammelband zusammen mit Perikopenbuch (Stockholm, 1585)

sowie Katechismus & Gebetbuch und Leidensgeschichte (beide Stockholm, 1586). *Exemplar B*: Kein Sammelband.
Kungliga biblioteket, Stockholm (*Exemplar A* und *Exemplar B*).
Collijn, Bibliografi, Bd. 3, 43–44.

16) **1589**
Then swenska psalmboken på nytt öffuersedd, förbättrat och medh flere Songer förmerat och Kalendarium, Lübeck: Asverus Kröger, 8:o.
Sammelband zusammen mit Katechismus & Gebetbuch und Leidensgeschichte (Lübeck, 1588) sowie Perikopenbuch (Lübeck, 1589).
Linköpings Stiftsbibliotek.
Collijn, Bibliografi, Bd. 3, 91–93.

17) **1589**
[Then swenska psalmboken], Stockholm: Andreas Gutterwitz, 8:o.
Sammelband zusammen mit Katechismus und Gebetbuch, Perikopenbuch und Leidensgeschichte (alle Stockholm, 1590).
Åbo Akademis Bibliotek (Turku) (*Exemplar A*: Blatt 1–71, 145–146, 151–155, 157–158, 185 und 192 fehlen).
Universitätsbibliothek Rostock (*Exemplar B*: 16-seitiges Fragment).
Collijn, Bibliografi, Bd. 3, 319–321.

18) **1594**
Then swenska psalmboken, Stockholm: Andreas Gutterwitz, 8:o.
Sammelband zusammen mit Katechismus & Gebetbuch sowie Perikopenbuch (beide Stockholm, 1593) sowie Leidensgeschichte (Stockholm, 1594).
Kungliga biblioteket, Stockholm.
Collijn, Bibliografi, Bd. 3, 182–185.

19) **1594**
Then swenska psalmboken. Lübeck: Asverus Kröger, 8:o.
Sammelband zusammen mit Katechismus & Gebetbuch sowie Perikopenbuch sowie Leidensgeschichte (alle Lübeck, 1594).
Kungliga biblioteket, Stockholm.
Collijn, Bibliografi, Bd. 3, 187.

20) **[1594?]**
Then swenska psalmboken, [?].
Kein Sammelband.
Kungliga biblioteket, Roggebiblioteket, Strängnäs (Blatt 1–18, 33, 161, 169 und 176 fehlen).
Collijn, Bibliografi, Bd. 3, 188–189

Kajsa Weber

Buch und Konfessionskonflikt

Übersetzung, Kompilation und Paratext in Petrus Johannis Gothus' *Sköna och märkliga skriftens sentenser* (1597)

Nach dem Tod Königs Johanns III. (1537–1592) im November 1592 begann ein erbitterter Kampf um die politische und konfessionelle Zukunft des schwedischen Reiches. Der Konflikt um den Thron Schwedens zwischen dem neuen katholischen König Sigismund (1566–1632) und dem lutherischen Herzog Karl (1550–1611) führte schließlich 1598 zum Krieg und zum Sieg Karls, der 1604 als Karl IX. gekrönt wurde. Der Konflikt wird in der Forschungsliteratur als eine Auseinandersetzung zwischen dem neuen König Sigismund, Herzog Karl, dem Reichsrat, den Ständen und der Geistlichkeit beschrieben. Die Arenen, in denen diese Auseinandersetzung ausgetragen wurde, sind die Reichstage oder reichstagsähnliche Versammlungen.[279]

Der folgende Beitrag versteht sich als medienhistorische Studie und widmet sich in diesem Sinne beispielhaft dem Buchmarkt: konkret, dem von Petrus Johannis Gothus (1536–1616) im Juni 1597 – also inmitten des Konfessionskonflikts[280] – herausgegebenen Buch *Sköna och märkliga skriftens sententier* (Fig. 5).[281] Dabei gilt es besonders herauszuarbeiten, wie Gothus die Möglichkeiten des Übersetzens, des Kompilierens und des Paratexts nutzte, um im Konfessionskonflikt Stellung zu nehmen und sein Publikum zu beeinflussen. Dadurch soll ein Versuch unternommen werden, den Zusammenhang zwischen Buch und Konfessionskonflikt in Schweden in den 1590 Jahren zu beschreiben. Mehrere frühere Studien haben dem Zusammenhang zwischen Buchdruck und Konfessionalisierung ihre Aufmerksamkeit geschenkt,[282] dennoch sind medi-

---

279 Montgomery, Värjostånd. Montgomery, Cura religiones.

280 Der Begriff Konfessionskonflikt wird hier im Anknüpfung an Schilling, Konfessionskonflikt, und Lotz-Heumann, Die doppelte Konfessionalisierung, verwendet.

281 Vollständiger Originaltitel: Skööna och merkeliga scrifftennes sententier, förclarade aff salig d. Martino Luthero, och aff androm höglärdom, medh tröstrijkom ordom. Vthtålkade aff Petro Iohannis Gotho Norcopensi. Im Beitrag wird die abgekürzte und modernisierte Form *Sköna och märkliga skriftens sententier* (kurz „Skööna") benutzt. Bibliographische Daten Collijn, Bibliografi, Bd. 3, 256–257.

282 Unter anderem Schnurr, Kölner Kriegs 1582–1590. Kaufmann, Herrgotts Kanzlei. Hasse, Zensur.

enhistorische Studien zum Konfessionskonflikt am Ende des 16. Jahrhunderts nicht in demselben Masse im Fokus der Forschung gewesen wie das Thema Buch und Reformation.[283] Die Studie versteht sich daher auch als Beitrag zu einer wachsenden Forschungsrichtung.[284]

Petrus Johannis Gothus' *Sköna och märkliga skriftens sentenser*

Im Juni 1597 gab der schwedische Übersetzer, Verleger und Autor Petrus Johannis Gothus das Buch *Sköna och märkliga skriftens sentenser* in Rostock heraus.[285] Petrus Johannis Gothus war 1536 in Norrköping geboren, studierte während der zweiten Hälfte der 1560er Jahre in Rostock und fing danach an, bis zu seinem Tod 1616, als Übersetzer, Autor und Verleger zu arbeiten. Während einer langen Zeit scheint er in Stockholm und Rostock tätig zu sein, aber ab 1596 zog er dauerhaft nach Rostock.[286] In der früheren Forschung wird Gothus' Rolle als Übersetzer und Vermittler von lutherischer Theologie betont.[287] Zum allergrößten Teil waren es Übersetzungen deutscher theologischer Literatur ins Schwedische, besonders hervorzuheben ist seine Übersetzung der *Confessio Augustana* ins Schwedische im Jahr 1581 im Zusammenhang mit der Hochzeit der schwedischen Prinzessin Elisabeth Vasa (1549–1597) mit Christoph zu Mecklenburg (1537–1592). Die Übersetzung sollte das eindeutige lutherische Profil der Prinzessin bezeugen.[288]

Sköna och märkliga skriftens sentenser war eine Kompilation und ist als lutherische Erbauungsliteratur zu bewerten. Die Texte darin geben dem Leser Ratschläge, wie ein christliches Leben zu führen sei. Das Buch setzt sich aus vier Haupttexten, einem Vorwort, einer Dedikation und einem Portraitmedaillon Martin Luthers zusammen.

---

283 Ich verzichte hier auf ausführliche Hinweise, und genüge mich mit Kaufmann/Mittler, Reformation und Buch.

284 Wichtige Ausgangspunkte für eine Forschung um Konfessionalisierung und Buchdruck/-Literatur in der zweiten Hälfte des 16. Jahrhundert findet sich in Lotz-Heumann/Pohlig, Confessionalization.

285 Gothus, Skööna. Collijn, Bibliografi, Bd. 3, 256–257.

286 Czaika, Gothus. Schück, Gothus.

287 Allgemein zu Übersetzungen in Schweden während des 17. Jahrhunderts: Hansson, Översättningslitteratur. Zu Gothus Übersetzungen: Collijn, Bibliografi, Bd. 3, 256f. Ingebrand, Predikan, 259. Holmquist, Reformationstidevarvet, T. 2., 208. Lindroth, Lärdomshistoria 1989, 264, bezeichnet dagegen Gothus Übersetzungen als „rekatholisierend". Schück, Historia, Bd. 1, 96–102.

288 Czaika, Elisabet Vasa, 21–28.

Das Vorwort beginnt mit einer Ermahnung, Gottes Wort zu lieben; dann wird Martin Luther (1483–1546) als Beispiel eines Christen, der das Gottes Wort auch in Zeiten von Gefahr liebt, hervorgehoben. Darauf folgen fünf Ermahnungen, wie ein christliches Leben geführt werden soll. Es endet mit der Überzeugung Gothus', dass der Glaube eine Gabe Gottes ist, durch den der Mensch gerechtfertigt wird. Das sei Luthers Text zu entnehmen. Diese Gewissheit will Gothus mit seinem Werk seinen Landsleuten vermitteln. Dies wäre bereits eine ausreichende Beschreibung des Inhalts des Vorwortes, wenn da nicht zusätzlich die beiden Bibelzitate wären, die Gothus im Vorwort einander gegenübergestellt hat: das dem Apostel Petrus zugeschriebene Wort, wonach man Gott fürchten und den weltlichen Herrscher ehren soll, und das des Evangelisten Matthäus, wonach man Gott mehr fürchten soll, weil Gott über die Ewigkeit richtet: "Fürchtet Gott und ehret den König, sagt der heilige Petrus, 1. Petrusbrief 1. Fürchtet die nicht (sagt unser Herr Christus) die den Körper töten und doch keine Macht haben, die Seele zu töten, sondern fürchtet mehr den der Seele und Körper in der Hölle verderben kann, Matthäus 10.“[289]

Die beiden Zitate im Zusammenhang gelesen sind wörtlich gesehen dahingehend zu deuten, dass man Gott fürchten soll, aber nicht den König, da der König nur den Leib töten kann, Gott aber die Seele retten kann. Wie die Analyse zeigen wird, nutzt Gothus in dem Zitat die biblische Geschichte, um seine eigene Gegenwart zu verstehen. Er versucht seinen Lesern etwas über das Verhältnis zwischen König und Untertanen zu vermitteln, aber was? Worum ging es Gothus in *Sköna och märkliga skriftens sententier*?

Bevor die Suche nach einer Antwort beginnen kann, soll erst kurz etwas zu Leser und Auflagen gesagt werden, bevor dann Übersetzung, Kompilation und Paratext als Analysewerkzeuge, mit deren Hilfe wir die Bedeutung eines frühneuzeitlichen Textes besser verstehen lernen, vorgestellt werden. Wie groß die Auflage von Gothus' Buch wirklich war, kann nicht exakt ermittelt werden. Für das Gebiet des Heiligen Römischen Reiches hat man errechnet, dass eine kleine Auflage in den 1590er Jahren im Durchschnitt die Produktion von 450 Exemplaren eines Buches bedeutete; zwischen 1550 und 1600 lag der Schnitt für ganz Europa (mit Ausnahme von Italien) bei 600.[290] Es ist nicht unwahrscheinlich, dass auch die für den Absatz hauptsächlich in Schweden durchgeführte Auflage von Gothus' *Sköna och märkliga skriftens sententier* bei zwischen 400 bis 600

289 Gothus, Skööna, A4^{v}. Schwedisches Zitat: „Fruchten GUDS och ären Konungen säger then helige Petrus 1. Per. 1 Fruchten icke them (säger wår HERRE CHRistus) som dräpa Kroppen och haffua doch inga macht til at dräpa Siälena Vthan fruchten meera honom som kan förderffua Siäl och krop i Heluete Matth. 10.“

290 Neddermeyer, Schriftlichkeit, 127–133, 390–395.

Drucken lag.[291] Dass Auflagen, insbesonders von Gesangbüchern, wesentlich grösser sein konnten, hat neuerdings Otfried Czaika nachgewiesen.[292]

Im Unterschied zu vielen anderen, auf Schwedisch publizierenden Autoren wie zum Beispiel Olaus Petri am Anfang des Jahrhunderts, hatte Gothus keine anderen Einkünfte – das heißt, er verdiente sein Geld seit den 1590er Jahren bis zu seinem Tod ausschließlich als Verleger, Übersetzer oder Autor. Da er damit nicht ohne Erfolg war, muss davon ausgegangen werden, dass er Bücher produzierte, für die er einen Absatzmarkt sah und auch fand. Er war gezwungen, das zu übersetzen, was er auch verkaufen konnte. Gleichzeitig können wir davon ausgehen, dass er über die Jahre Kenntnisse über den schwedischen Buchmarkt gewonnen hatte und dass seine Bücher deswegen eben nicht nur für ein paar ausgebildete Theologen gedacht waren, sondern ein breiteres Publikum fanden. Viele seiner Bücher enthielten Widmungen an Bürger,[293] so auch *Sköna och märkliga skriftens sententier*. Auch wenn diese Widmungen alleine nicht ausreichen, um nähere Beziehungen zwischen Gothus und diesen Personen zu rekonstruieren,[294] geben sie doch Hinweise auf Personen, die in Gothus Augen in Schweden Interesse an seiner Produktion haben konnten.

Übersetzung, Kompilation und Paratext in der frühen Neuzeit

In neueren literaturwissenschaftlichen Studien ist deutlich herausgearbeitet worden wie Übersetzung, Kompilation und Paratext eine große Bedeutung für Sinnkonstruktionen in frühneuzeitlichen Büchern zukommen. Kompilationsliteratur war während der gesamten frühen Neuzeit eine gängige Literaturgattung. Durch Kompilationen, manchmal nur aus Teilen eines Textes bestehend, wurden alte Texte immer wieder neu verwendet und in neue Zusammenhänge eingefügt.[295]

Frühneuzeitliches Übersetzen hat in den letzten zehn Jahren ein verstärktes wissenschaftliches Interesse gefunden.[296] Die Praxis des Übersetzens in der frühen Neuzeit unterscheidet sich sehr von dem modernen Verständnis des

291 Diese stimmt auch mit den Angaben Hansson, Översättningslitteratur, 220–225, überein.

292 Czaika, Wijsor.

293 Vgl. Schück, Gothus.

294 Vogel, Kulturtransfer, 40.

295 Heß, Florilegien. Blair, Too Much.

296 Siehe unter anderem Barker/Hosington, Crossroads. Belle/Hosington, Translation. Chartier, Hand, 98–119. Toepfer/Kipf/Robert, Antikenübersetzung. Einen Überblick im Zusammenhang mit dem Begriff „Wissenszirkulation" bietet Brilkman, Circulation.

Übersetzens. Bedeutet heute Übersetzen die Repräsentation des Ursprungstextes in der Zielsprache, waren frühe neuzeitliche Translationen mehr als bloße Kopien des Ursprungstexts in eine andere Sprache. Vielmehr waren Übersetzungen eine komplexe Konstruktion von Bedeutung, in der sich Übertragung, Interpretation und Kompilation mischten, und die Übersetzer die Ausgangstexte „reduzierten und erweiterten". Sie „aktualisierten und dramatisierten oder transponierten ihre Prätexte in andere Stilregister und Gattungskontexte, um sie den Erfordernissen des Anlasses und den Erwartungen ihrer Adressaten anzupassen".[297] Da der frühneuzeitliche Übersetzer seine Arbeit selten als Kopieren oder Übertragung verstand, sondern viel mehr als Bearbeitung einer Textvorlage, bietet die Übersetzung eine hervorragende kulturhistorische Quelle, um Bedeutungsverschiebungen, Kulturtransfer und Sinnkonstruktionen zu hinterfragen.

Paratexte wie zum Beispiel Titel, Untertitel, Register und Widmungen boten frühneuzeitlichen Autoren die Möglichkeit, ihre Texte „neu zu perspektivieren, sie in dieser Form zu edieren und auf diese Weise zu instrumentalisieren".[298] Ein besonders wichtiger Paratext in der frühen Neuzeit war die Vorrede, die die Funktion der Erläuterung und Präsentation des Werkes, implizit auch der werbenden Ankündigung und der Legitimation[299] übernahm. Kaum ein Werk der frühen Neuzeit wurde ohne Vorrede gedruckt. Frühneuzeitliche Vorworte erfüllten mehrere Funktionen, unter anderem boten sie dem Autor eine Möglichkeit, sich selbst zu dem übersetzten Werk zu äußern. Oft wurde das Vorwort benutzt, um den Text in einen politischen und religiösen Zusammenhang zu stellen, zum Beispiel propagandistisch in konfessionellen Auseinandersetzungen zu nutzen.[300]

Aufgrund der Möglichkeiten des Übersetzens, Kompilierens und des Einsatzes von Paratexten genügt eine Analyse des Textinhalts der *Sköna och märkliga skriftens sententier* allein nicht. Vielmehr muss hier nach Gothus' Ursprungstexten, ihren Entstehungskontexten gefragt werden, um zu erkennen, was Gothus mit den einzelnen Texten gemacht hat und wie er sie zusammengefügt und ihnen einen neuen Sinn gegeben hat. Es geht im Folgenden darum, die Praktiken Gothus', also „seine Hand" zu erkennen, um daraus Rückschlüsse auf die Bedeutung des Werkes für den Konfessionskonflikt in den 1590er Jahren zu ziehen. Dieser Artikel ist ein Beitrag zur Erweiterung unserer Kentnisse

---

297 Toepfer/Kipf/Robert, Antikenübersetzung, 13.

298 Von Ammon/Vögel, Einleitung, XIII, und die Beiträge in diesem Band. Zum Paratext in Übersetzungsliteratur: Belle/Hosington, Thresholds of Translation. Der Begriff „Paratext" wurde von Genette entwickelt; Genette, Paratexte.

299 Vogel, Kulturtransfer.

300 Schwitzgebel, Vorrede, 5.

über *Sköna öch märkliga skriftens sententier*, da das Buch im Moment in der Forschung lediglich als ein Beispiel für ein Trostbuch und Erbauungsliteratur beschrieben worden ist.[301] *Sköna och märkliga skriftens sententier* bietet aber viel mehr, als die bisherige Forschung bekanntgemacht hat. Welcher Kontext entstand, als die verschiedenen, von Gothus benutzten Texte zusammengeführt wurden? Welche Aussagen präsentierte das neu entstandene Buch und welche Rolle spielten diese Aussagen in dem Kontext, in dem es herausgegeben wurde? Wie nutzt Gothus den Paratext, um seine Aussagen zu schärfen?

Um diese Frage zu beantworten, werden im ersten Schritt Gothus' Übersetzungspraktiken analysiert, um seine Quellen zu identifizieren; in einem zweiten Schritt wird dann seine Arbeit mit den Quellen erkennbar, abschließend werden in einem dritten Schritt die Paratexte, also Gothus' Kontextualisierung seiner Übersetzung, analysiert. Zunächst muss aber noch kurz die politische und konfessionelle Situation in Schweden 1597 geschildert werden. Anhand dieser Kenntnisse können verschiedene Aspekte des Werkes in ihren Aussagen analysiert werden.

Konfessionskonflikt in Schweden

Das letzte Jahrzehnt des 16. Jahrhunderts im Schwedischen Reich war von einem Konfessionskonflikt geprägt.[302] König Johann III. hatte während seiner Regierungszeit versucht, in der konfessionellen Landschaft zu navigieren, ohne sich letztendlich festzulegen. Als er im November 1592 starb, war die Interimsfrage ungeklärt und das Schlachtfeld offen für andere Akteure, die Konfession Schwedens nach ihren Vorstellungen festzulegen. In diesem Prozess waren Politik und Konfession aufs Engste miteinander verbunden. Johanns Thronfolger, der katholisch erzogene Sohn Sigismund befand sich, als sein Vater starb, in Polen – wo er seit 1587 König war – und wurde zur Krönung nach Schweden gerufen. Sigismunds Großvater, Gustav Eriksson Vasa (1496–1560), hatte seinen Söhnen Herzogtümer zugesprochen. Einer dieser Söhne, Herzog Karl, Johanns Bruder und Sigmunds Onkel, hatte schon während Johanns Regierungszeit Oppositionspolitik gegen den König getrieben. Da Sigismund rechtmäßiger

301 Estborn, Bönböcker, 213.

302 Die folgende Darstellung beruht auf Montgomery, Värjostånd. Montgomery, Cura religiones. Strömberg-Back, Lagen. Holmquist, Reformationstidevarvet, T. 2. Berntson/Nilsson/Wejryd, Kyrka. Die Forschung macht sich das Konfessionsparadigm nur in begrenztem Maße zu Nutze. Es fehlt an neuen Untersuchungen, die den Zusammenhang zwischen politischem Kampf, konfessionellem Konflikt und dem europäischen Konfessionalisierungsprozess in den Fokus stellen. Eine Ausnahme ist Schmidt, Professoren im Norden.

Thronfolger war, blieb Karl nur die Möglichkeit, Sigismunds Fähigkeit als Hüter der „wahren Religion" im Land infrage zu stellen, um selbst eine eigenständige Politik führen zu können. Der Konflikt zwischen Sigismund und Karl um den schwedischen Thron entwickelte sich daher in der folgenden Zeit zu einem Konfessionskonflikt. Schon bevor Sigismund nach Schweden kam, versammelten sich die Stände im Frühling 1593 in Uppsala, zur sogenannten „Uppsala möte". Im Beschluss wurde die *Confessio Augustana* als Bekenntnisschrift der schwedischen Kirche angenommen. Herzog Karl kam in der weiteren Auseinandersetzung mit Sigismund, in der dessen Fähigkeit als Beschützer des wahren Glaubens von Karl immer wieder infrage gestellt wurde, regelmäßig auf die Entscheidung der Stände zurück und zog daraus die Legitimation für seine Verteidigung der wahren Lehre.

Vor der Krönung in Februar 1594 wurden gegenseitig Eide abgelegt, wobei Sigismund versprach, dass seine Untertanen bei der *Confessio Augustana* bleiben sollten. Karl versprach dem König zu huldigen, vorausgesetzt auch hier, dass er und sein Herzogtum bei der wahren Lehre bleiben konnten. Dies war entscheidend, da die legitime Macht Sigismunds von seiner Fähigkeit abhing, die lutherische Konfession zu wahren. Dadurch bestand die Möglichkeit, dass sich Karl von seinem Eid gegenüber den König freisprechen konnte. Nach der Krönung verließ Sigismund Schweden und reiste nach Polen, zuvor hatte er aber Karl verboten, Reichstage einzuberufen.

Karl sah sich als Hüter des wahren Glaubens und nutzte dies, um Sigismunds Macht weiter infrage zu stellen. Er trieb den Konflikt weiter an und nutzte die ihm gegebenen Machtmittel, um die Position der Katholiken weiter zu schwächen; das Kloster in Vadstena wurde auf Karls Beschluss im Jahre 1595 geschlossen, der königstreue Hochadlige Arvid Stenbock wurde der Untreue gegenüber den Beschlüssen von Uppsala beschuldigt, und der neugewählte Erzbischof Abraham Andreae Angermannus (1540–1607) wurde mit einer Visitation bevormundet. Karl seinerseits wurde verstärkt beschuldigt, den Konflikt um die Konfession voranzutreiben, nur um den Gegensatz mit dem König zu vertiefen. Die Stände und der Reichsrat, die Geistlichkeit und der Erzbischof waren gespalten, da sie einerseits verpflichtet waren, ihrem rechtmäßigen König zu huldigen, andererseits aber den Beschlüssen von Uppsala 1593 und (wie es scheint in unterschiedlichem Maße) dem Luthertum anhingen. Auf dem Reichstag in Arboga im Frühling 1597 – einem Reichstag, den Sigismund als illegal deklariert hatte, da nur er Reichstage einberufen durfte, und der deswegen besonders von Angehörigen des Hochadels spärlich besucht war – suchte Karl die Legitimierung zu erhalten, seinen Konflikt mit Sigismund erfolgreich voranzutreiben. Wie die politische und konfessionelle Zukunft Schwedens aussehen würde, war im Frühjahr und Sommer 1597, als *Sköna och märkliga skriftens sententier* erschien, keineswegs geklärt.

Übersetzungspraktiken und die Wittenberger Gesamtausgabe

Das Buch *Sköna och mäkliga skriftens sententier* setzt sich aus vier Texten zusammen. Dies sind *Utvalda sententier med vilka Martin Luther har tröstat sig,*[303] *Många sköna skriftens sententier*[304] an welches weitere kleine Textabschnitte angefügt sind wie zum Bespiel *En förtrogen förmaning Martin Luthers till Georg II av Anhalt.*[305] Darauf folgt *Sententier som av andra höglärda män förklarade är*[306] und schließlich *De gamla heliga fäders kristliga tankar.*[307] Diesen sind verschiedene Paratexte zur Seite gestellt.[308]

Im Folgenden werden Gothus' Übersetzungspraktiken analysiert, um seine Quellen offenzulegen. Der zweite Text, der die Hauptmasse des Werkes ausmacht, *Många sköna skriftens sententier,* beinhaltet hauptsächlich Bibelsprüche, die mit einem Kommentar Luthers versehen waren. Es handelt sich um sehr kurze Kommentare, und nicht um Auslegungen. Der Text war nach Bibelbüchern gegliedert, so wurden Luther-Sprüche zu Mose, dem Buch der Psalmen, Jesaja, Matthäus, Lukas, Johannes, dem Römerbrief und dem ersten/zweiten Brief Petrus gesammelt.

Der Text gehört zu der Gattung der Lutherflorilegien,[309] das heißt, es ist ein Text, der Auszüge aus dessen Werken bietet.[310] Verschiedene Formen von Lutherflorilegien oder Kompilationsliteratur zu Luther waren in der frühen Neuzeit sehr häufig. Luthers Texte wurden nach der Reformation selten neu

303 Gothus, Sköna, C1^{r}–C8^{v}. Vollständiger Titel: I förstonne åre här infóörde några vthwalda Sententier vthaff then heliga Scrifft medh hwilka then salige Guds Mannen D. Martinus Lutherus haffuer hugswalat och trösstat sigh vthi sina swåra och stoora anfechtningar/ androm til Exempel förestälte/ vthi lijka fall och anfechtning.

304 Ibid., D1^{r}–R2^{v}. Vollständiger Titel: Många sköna Scrifftennes Sententier/ aff hwilka hwar Christrogen Menniskia kan haffua godan Lärdom/ Tröst och styrkia i theña Werldennes margfalleliga twång/ förklarade aff (Salig i HERRANDM) Doctore MARTINO LVTHERO, medh tröstijkom Ordom.

305 Ibid., R2^{v}–R5^{r}. Vollständiger Titel: En trogen Förmaning til sanna Boot och Christeliga Böön then Salig D. MARTINVS LVTHER haffuer hafft vthi Förstens GEORGII aff Anhalt etc. och andra lärda Mäns närwarelse.

306 Ibid., R7^{r}–Z2^{v}. Vollständiger Titel: Fölia nu the Sententier som aff androm höghlärdom Män förclarade äre.

307 Ibid. Z3^{r}–Z8^{r}. Vollständiger Titel: The gamle helige Fäders och kyrkionnes Läares sköna och Chrlisteliga tanckar huru hwar Christrogen bör bära sitt Korss medh tålamod som GUDZ honom påläggia tädes indragne och förclarade aff D. Martino Luthero.

308 Es handelt sich um eine Dedikation an Johan Bagge, Jakob Bagge och Märta Eriksdotter, Ibid., A2^{r}, ein Vorwort unterzeichnet von Petrus Johannis Gothus A2^{r}–B8^{r} und ein Portraitmedaillon Martin Luthers, mit dem Text "Verbum domini manet in aeternvm", B8^{v}.

309 Koch, Lutherflorilegien.

310 Heß, Florilegien.

aufgelegt, umso häufiger aber Lutherflorilegien. Sie sollten für einen angemessenen Preis die Werke Luthers auch für einfache Pfarrer zugänglich machen; sie dienten der Verteidigung von Luthers Werk und sollten Luthers Theologie weiter verbreiten.[311] Es ist also wahrscheinlich, dass Gothus diese Sprüche nicht selbst zusammengetragen, sondern eine andere Sammlung übersetzt hat. Wie diese Untersuchung zeigen kann, hat Gothus seine Spruchsammlung einer Gesamtausgabe entnommen. Die Gesamtausgaben Luthers des 16. Jahrhunderts waren neben den Florilegien oft besonders wichtig, um Luthers Werke zu sammeln, ordnen, bewahren und zu verbreiten.[312]

Schon 1539, also noch zu Luthers Lebzeiten, begann man in Wittenberg mit diesem Unternehmen. Die sogenannte Wittenberger Gesamtausgabe, die das Material nach Themen ordnet, wurde zwischen 1539 und 1559 in neunzehn Bänden herausgegeben, zwölf Bände in deutscher und sieben in lateinischer Sprache.[313] Die Wittenberger Gesamtausgabe wurde scharf kritisiert, da die Redakteure auch Texte anderer Theologen eingearbeitet und Änderungen in Luthertexten vorgenommen hatten. Eine alternative Gesamtausgabe, die das Material zeitlich ordnete, wurde deswegen zwischen 1554 und 1558 in Jena herausgegeben; sie umfasste schließlich acht deutsche und vier lateinische Bände.[314] Diese Aufteilung entspricht auch den Hauptfronten in der innerlutherischen Auseinandersetzung um Luthers Erbe.[315]

Beide Gesamtausgaben verzeichnen sogenannte Bibel- und Bucheinzeichnungen Luthers, also Notizen Luthers in Bibelbüchern seiner Freunde. Diese wurden im Herbst 1557 in Band 9 der Wittenberger Gesamtausgabe (Deutsche Reihe) publiziert[316] und erschienen im Herbst 1558 in Band 8 der Jenaer Gesamtausgabe (Deutsche Reihe).[317] Ein genauer Vergleich der beiden Texte zeigt gewisse Unterschiede.[318] Fünfzehn Notizen sind nur in der Jenaer Gesamtausgabe zu finden. Es handelt sich um die Notizen mit den Nummern 30, 33, 39, 67, 89, 117, 159, 162, 251[a], 255, 279, 280, sowie noch drei weitere Texte: Luthers

311 Koch, Lutherflorilegien, 105.

312 WA, Bd. 60, 465–543.

313 Die Wittenberger Ausgabe (1539–1559) in WA, Bd. 60, 464–495.

314 Die Jenaer Ausgabe (1554–1558) in WA, Bd. 60, 495–543.

315 Michel, Kanonisierung, 110–236. Kolb, Luther, 141–150.

316 Luther, Gesamtausgabe Wittenberg, Bd. 9, 480[a]–535[b]. Die Bibelsprüche tragen den Titel „Vieler schöner Sprüche aus göttlicher Schrifft auslegung Darus lere und trost zu nehmen welche der Ehrwirdige herr D. Martinus Luther seliger vielen in ire Biblien geschrieben. Dergleichen Sprüche von andern Herrn ausgelegt sind auch mit eingemengt“.

317 Luther, Gesamtausgabe Jena, Bd. 8, 341[a]–380[b]. Die Bibelsprüche „Ausslegung vieler schöner tröstlicher Sprüche aus heiliger Schrifft von D. M. L. etliche seinen guten Herrn und freunden in die Biblien geschrieben“, Luther, Gesamtausgabe Jena, Bd. 8, 341[a]–380[b].

318 WA, Bd. 48, XXII–XXIV und Anhang II, 233–237.

Reimspruch vom Hausregiment, und zwei irrtümlich Luther zugeschriebene Auslegungen.[319] Ein Notiz, Nummer 222, ist nur in der Wittenberger Gesamtausgabe zu finden.[320]

Anhand dieser Merkmale lässt sich ein Vergleich mit Petrus Johannis Gothus' Text durchführen. Dabei zeigt sich, dass *Många sköna skriftens sententier* sehr eng der Wittenberger Gesamtausgabe folgt. Notiz 222, die nur in der Wittenberger Gesamtausgabe publiziert ist, ist ebenfalls in *Många sköna skriftens sententier* zu finden.[321] Von den 15 Notizen, die in der Jenaer Gesamtausgabe verzeichnet sind und in der Wittenberger Gesamtausgabe fehlen, ist bis auf eine keine in Gothus' Werk wiedergegeben! Es handelt sich dabei um Luthers Reimspruch vom Hausregiment, den Gothus auf Deutsch wiedergibt.[322]

Noch ein Beispiel dafür, in welchem Ausmaß Gothus von der Wittenberger Ausgabe beeinflusst wurde, kann hier angeführt werden: In der Wittenberger Gesamtausgabe Bd. 9 ist ein Reim Luthers an Peter Barberer mit einem kurzen erläuternden Text zu finden.[323] Derselbe Reim mit Einleitung ist auch bei Gothus (auf Deutsch) zu finden.[324] In der Wittenberger Ausgabe wie bei Gothus wird Barberer namentlich genannt, in der Jenaer Gesamtausgabe dagegen nicht.[325]

Anhand dieser Erkenntnis lässt sich vermuten, dass Gothus eine Übersetzung aus der Wittenberger Gesamtausgabe unternommen hat. Die Wiedergabe des Hausspruchs zeugt aber auch davon, dass Gothus die Jenaer Gesamtausgabe mitbenutzt hatte, wenn auch nicht als Grundlage für die ganze Übersetzung. Noch eine weitere Beobachtung bestätigt, dass Gothus mit beiden Gesamtausgaben gearbeitet hatte. Der größte Unterschied zwischen den beiden Gesamtausgaben ist der Umgang mit den überlieferten Notizen anderer Theologen. In der Wittenberger Ausgabe sind diese mit verzeichnet, und zwar zusammen mit Luthers Notizen, in der Jenaer Ausgabe fehlen sie gänzlich. Der Umgang mit Luthers Notizen in der Wittenberger Gesamtausgabe wurde kritisiert, da Luthers herausragende Rolle für die Reformation verwischt würde, wenn seine Notizen zusammen mit anderen Theologen publiziert würden. Die Jenaer Ausgabe versuchte dies zu korrigieren. Gothus hat für sein Werk eine mittlere Position

---

319 Ibid. S. XXIII, 233–237.

320 Ibid. S. XXII.

321 Gothus, Sköōna, N4^r–N5^r. Vgl. Luther Gesamtausgabe Wittenberg, Bd. 9, 518^b. WA, Bd. 48, 170.

322 Gothus, Sköōna, R5^r–R6^r. WA, Bd. 48, 233–235; zum Vergleich die Stelle in der Jenaer Gesamtausgabe: Luther, Gesamtausgabe Jena, Bd. 8, 380^a.

323 Luther, Gesamtausgabe Wittenberg, Bd. 9, 514^b–515^b.

324 Gothus, Sköōna, M3^r–M5^r.

325 Luther, Gesamtausgabe Jena, Bd. 8, 365^b–366^b.

gewählt und schuf damit einen neuen Text. Der vierte Text in Gothus' Werk, *Sententer som av andra höglärda män förklarade är*, ist nämlich eine Sammlung von Notizen Wittenberger Theologen, wie Phillip Melanchthon (1497–1560), Justus Jonas (1493–1555), Caspar Creuziger (Cruziger, 1504–1548), Georg Major (1502–1574), Johannes Bugenhagen (1485–1558) und Nicolas Amsdorf (1483–1565). Ein Vergleich der Notizen mit den Notizen anderer Theologen in der Wittenberger Ausgabe ergibt, dass Gothus die Notizen in derselben Reihenfolge wie in der Wittenberger Ausgabe gedruckt hat, aber diese nicht wie in seiner Vorlage zusammen mit denen von Luther wiedergegeben. Als er mit der Übersetzung aus Band 9 arbeitete, hatte er also auch Zugang zu Band 8 der Jenaer Gesamtausgabe und sich von ihr inspirieren lassen, Luthers Notizen in der Weise deutlicher hervorzuheben, dass die Notizen anderer Theologen nicht zusammen mit denen Luthers gedruckt wurden, sondern als eigener Text.

Gothus wollte offensichtlich nicht die Notizen anderer Theologen weglassen, aber gleichzeitig war es ihm wichtig, die besondere Leistung Luthers hervorzuheben. In seiner Einleitung schrieb er: „die Reden und Schriften des seligen Mannes Gottes hatten eine besondere Gnade und Kraft"[326] und weiter „alle Sentenzen der heiligen Schrift, die uns Doktor Martin Luther erklärt hat, stehen für sich am Anfang, gefolgt von den Sentenzen anderer hochgelehrter Männer (die zu Zeiten Luthers lebten) aus der heiligen Schrift eingeführt und erklärt".[327] Gothus wollte also vermeiden, Luthers Leistung durch Vermischung mit Texten anderer Theologen in ihrer Bedeutung zu relativieren.

Dass Gothus die Gesamtausgabe als Quelle für den Haupttext gewählt hat, ist nicht unwichtig. Auch die anderen Texte des Werkes erweisen sich als Übersetzungen aus Band 9 der Wittenberger Gesamtausgabe, was vorher in der Forschung nicht bekannt gewesen ist.[328] Aus der Wittenberger Gesamtausgabe stammt auch *En förtrogen förmaning Martin Luthers till Georg II av Anhalt*.[329] Der Text folgt in der Gesamtausgabe, wie in Gothus' Kompilation, dem gleichen Text, nämlich *Många sköna skriftens sententier*. Der Text ist im Zusammenhang mit der Ordination von Fürst Georg von Anhalt zum Bischof von Merseburg im August 1545 entstanden. Die Ordination wurde von Luther durchgeführt.[330]

---

326 Gothus, Skööna, B7^{r}. Schwedisches Zitat: "then salige Gudz Mannen haffuer hafft ena besynnerliga nådh och krafft medh sitt taal och Scriffter".

327 Gothus, Skööna, B7^{v}. Schwedisches Zitat: "alla thens helga Scriffts sententier som oss Doctore MARTINO LVTHERO förklarade äre särledes i förstonne för sig aleena och så sedan serdelis the Sententier som aff androm höglärdom Män (som på then tijdh med Luthero leffde) aff Schrifftenne inföörde och förclarade warde".

328 Vgl. Estborn, Bönböcker, 213. Collijn, Bibliografi, Bd. 3, 256–257.

329 Luther, Gesamtausgabe Wittenberg, Bd. 9, 534^{b}–535^{a}.

330 WA, Bd. 48, 228–230.

Der fünfte Text, *De gamla heliga fäders kristliga tankar*, ist auch in der Wittenberger Gesamtausgabe Band 9 zu finden.[331]

Auch der erste Text in Gothus' Kompilation, nämlich *Utvalda sententier med vilka Martin Luther har tröstat sig* stammt aus Band 9 der Wittenberger Gesamtausgabe. Frühere Forscher, wie Sigfrid Estborn und später Isak Collijn, haben bemerkt, dass dieser Text in Gothus' Kompilation die Übersetzung einer von dem lutherischen Theologen und ehemaligen Wittenberger Professor für Hebräisch, Matthias Flacius (1520–1575)[332] durchgeführten Bearbeitung von Luthers Trostsprüchen mit dem Titel *Etliche tröstliche Vermanungen*[333] aus dem Jahr 1550[334] ist.[335] Das Buch beinhaltet „Trostmaximen mit Angaben einschlägiger Bibelstellen, die Luther für eigene Zwecke während seines Coburg-Aufenthaltes zusammengestellt hatte"[336] und entstand im Zusammenhang mit dem Widerstand gegen das Augsburger Interim. Trotz des kaiserlichen Publikationsverbots entwickelte sich Magdeburg in den Jahren um die Jahrhundertmitte zu einem Zentrum des lutherischen Widerstands gegen das Interim. Mehrere hunderte Publikationen gegen das Interim wurden in der kurzen Zeit zwischen 1548 und 1552 in Magdeburg gedruckt und über das Reich verteilt.[337] Flacius' *Etliche tröstliche Vermanungen* waren ein Teil dieser publizistischen Aktivitäten. Es ist aber unklar, ob Luther der Autor war[338] oder ob Flacius selbst die Textstellen zusammengetragen hat.[339]

Ursprünglich war Luthers Text zur Zeit des Reichstags 1530 in Augsburg entstanden, wo über die religiöse Auseinandersetzung im Reich verhandelt wurde. Die Protestanten kämpften um die Anerkennung als legitime Religionsgemeinschaft, während sich der Kaiser einer solchen Anerkennung widersetzte.[340] Martin Luther war nicht anwesend, sondern befand sich in Coburg. Luther schrieb in dieser Zeit Briefe an seine Freunde, die am Reichstag anwesend waren[341] – vor allem an Melanchthon, dessen *Confessio Augustana* auf dem Reichstag verlesen wurde. In 22 Thesen beschrieb er, „dass der Gläubige im Falle einer Verfolgung oder Verleumdung von Seiten seiner Gegner nicht bange

331 Luther, Gesamtausgabe Wittenberg, Bd. 9, 439[a]–439[b]
332 Über Flacius: Ilić, Flacius. Pohlig, Flacius. Olson, Flacius.
333 Flacius, Vermahnungen.
334 Hausleiter, Flacius, 164.
335 Estborn, Bönböcker, 213. Collijn, Bibliografi, Bd. 3, 257.
336 Kaufmann, Herrgotts Kanzlei, 375.
337 Kaufmann, Herrgotts Kanzlei, 493–554.
338 Hausleiter, Flacius.
339 WA, Bd. 30/II., 698.
340 Kaufmann, Reformation, 570–594.
341 WA, Bd. 30/II, 697–408.

sein solle, denn gerade darin zeigt sich, dass er auf dem richtigen Weg sei, denn, wer offen und rechtgläubig für das Wort Gottes eintrete, der werde, wie schon die Heilige Schrift zeigt, von seinen Gegnern zwangsläufig verfolgt."[342] Luther wollte die Seinen in einer bedrohlichen Situation unterstützen.

Flacius' Text aus dem Jahr 1550 wurde schon früh nach dem Erstdruck in die Gesamtausgaben aufgenommen, da sie als en orginaler Luthertext galt – und zwar in der Wittenberger Gesamtausgabe Band 9,[343] in dem Gothus die Vorlagen für diesen und andere Texte gefunden hatte.

Die Vermutung Estborns und Collijns ist insofern richtig gewesen, dass Gothus einen Text benutzt hatte, bei dessen Entstehung Flacius eine ausschlaggebende Rolle gespielt hatte. Gothus hatte aber mit allergrößter Wahrscheinlichkeit nicht die Veröffentlichung aus dem Jahr 1550, sondern die Gesamtausgaben als Vorlage gehabt. Das zeigt die Analyse der anderen Texte im Werk. Dieser Befund ist nicht nur deswegen interessant, weil sie neues Licht auf Gothus' Werk von 1597 wirft, sondern weil sie zu der Vermutung führt, dass auch andere auf Schwedisch herausgegebene Luther-Kompilationen eine ähnliche kompliziertere Entstehungsgeschichte haben könnten als bisher vermutet. Estborn und Collijn bauten ihre Analysen auf den damals vorhandenen bibliografischen Informationen auf. Die Digitalisierung früher neuzeitlicher Buchbestände in Europa hat dazu geführt, dass heute ganz andere bibliografische Werkzeuge zur Verfügung stehen, um Transferleistungen auf dem frühneuzeitlichen Buchmarkt zu untersuchen. Zusammen mit ähnlichen Befunden anderer Forscher lässt dies vermuten, dass die Rezeption des europäischen religiösen und wissenschaftlichen Wissens im frühneuzeitlichen Schweden größer und vielfältiger war als allgemein angenommen.[344] Anhand der hier präsentierten Ergebnisse und den neuen Möglichkeiten wird klar, dass eine Überarbeitung der schwedischen Nationalbibliographie zum 16. Jahrhundert neue Erkenntnisse bringen würde.[345]

Zusammenfassend kann festgestellt werden, dass alle Texte des Werkes Übersetzungen aus der Wittenberger Gesamtausgabe Band 9 stammten. Dies machte Gothus aber in seiner Veröffentlichung nicht deutlich.

---

342 Flacius, *Etliche tröstliche Vermahnungen in das heilige Wort betreffenden Sachen*, in: Controversia et Confessio Digital. Herausgegeben von Irene Dingel. <http://www.controversia-et-confessio.de/id/fb12821f-3eb1-4663-9740-bb6d12a267fd> (Zugriff am 08.03.2019).

343 Luther, Gesamtausgabe Wittenberg, Bd. 9, 395^{b}–398^{a}.

344 Undorf, Gutenberg. Czaika, Sveno Jacobi.

345 Zur Notwendigkeit einer Überarbeitung der schwedischen Nationalbibliografie zum 16. Jahrhundert siehe Czaika, Psalmeboken, Abschnitt 2.

Übersetzungspraktiken und das Thema der Bedrohung der Lutheraner

Gothus' Arbeit mit der Wittenberger Gesamtausgabe als Hauptquelle für seine Übersetzungen fördern zu Tage, wie wichtig die Gesamtausgabe für die Verbreitung von Luthers Texten in der zweiten Hälfte des 16. Jahrhunderts war. Dabei ist es wichtig zu erkennen, dass beide Gesamtausgaben, aus denen sich Gothus hier bedient, keineswegs akademische Randprodukte der lutherischen Theologie waren, sondern im Zentrum der Auseinandersetzung um Luthers Erbe standen. Es war darüber hinaus natürlich auch eine gewaltige wissenschaftliche Leistung, Luthers Texte zu sammeln, zu edieren und herauszugeben.[346] Gothus hat sich der vornehmsten Quelle zu Luther in seiner Zeit bedient und er hat die Gesamtausgaben so genutzt, wie sie gedacht waren, nämlich als sichere Quelle für autorisierte Texte des Reformators.

Gothus' Übersetzungsarbeit ist an sich sehr genau, er bleibt dem Originaltext treu und benutzt nicht der Praktiken des „erzählendes Übersetzens".[347] Diese Herangehensweise hat vermutlich mit der Autorität der Quelle zu tun, da es Gothus' Ziel war, Luthers Wort möglichst unverändert zu übertragen und auf Schwedisch erklingen zu lassen. Trotzdem ist seine Arbeit als eine Veränderung seiner Vorlagen zu sehen. Da es eben die Gesamtausgabe war, die seine Hauptquelle war – und nicht Luthers eigene Texte – lässt sich darüber auch mehr herausfinden über Gothus' Arbeitsweise und Motiv. Studiert man Band 9 der Wittenberger Ausgabe wird deutlich, dass hier der zentrale Text der frühen Reformation abgedruckt wurde. Die Wittenberger Gesamtausgabe wurde dafür scharf kritisiert, nicht alle Werke Luthers gedruckt zu haben; der neunte Band sollte diese Beschwerden entkräften, indem das bislang noch ungedruckte Material aus den Bänden 1 bis 5 der Jenaer Ausgabe publiziert wurde.[348] Schon auf dem Titelblatt wurde dem Leser klar, dass Band 9 zentrale Texte der frühen Reformation beinhaltete; hier finden sich zum Beispiel die 95 Thesen und der Brief an Albrecht von Mainz vom Oktober 1517, Luthers Bericht von der Leipziger Disputation und die Briefe, die im Zusammenhang mit dem Reichstag in Worms 1521 entstanden.[349] Insgesamt beinhaltet der neunte Band eine Fülle von Texten zur frühen Reformation, vor allem Briefe und Vorreden Luthers, zusammen mit zentralen publizierten Texten. Verglichen mit den anderen Titelblättern der beiden Gesamtausgaben verdeutlicht das Titelblatt von Band 9 der Wittenberger Ausgabe wie kein anderes die zentrale Bedeutung Luthers für die Reformation. Das muss Gothus interessiert haben!

---

346 Michel, Kanonisierung.

347 Toepfer, Übersetzungswerk, 55.

348 WA, Bd. 60, 483.

349 Luther, Gesamtausgabe Wittenberg, Bd. 9. WA, Bd. 60, 483.

Es sind Luthers Auseinandersetzungen mit dem Papst, die Gothus anzogen und zu denen er in seinem Buch einen Bezug herstellen wollte.

Hier wird denn auch Gothus' Arbeit mit seiner Quelle deutlich; Er versuchte einen Zusammenhang zwischen dem seiner Meinung nach heldenhaften Kampf Luthers gegen den Papst in den 1520er Jahren und die Bedrohung der Lutheraner in seiner Gegenwart im schwedischen Reich Ende des 16. Jahrhunderts zu konstruieren. Die Auswahl der Texte aus der Wittenberger Gesamtausgabe sollte diesem Zweck dienen.

Das Thema der Bedrohung war ein Kernelement der lutherischen Konfessionskultur der zweiten Hälfte des 16. Jahrhundert. Der konfessionalisierte Katholizismus war durch die Stabilisierung und Erneuerung seit dem Trienter Konzil am Ende des 16. Jahrhundert auf dem Vormarsch. Länder wie Schweden, die für die katholische Kirche verloren gegangen waren, sollten wiedererobert werden. Netzwerke, in denen unter anderem Jesuiten und fürstliche Beichtväter wichtig waren, wurden tätig, um die Rekatholisierung voranzutreiben.[350] Sowohl der Vormarsch der Katholiken als auch die Siege für die Reformierten führten während des letztes Jahrzehnts des 16. Jahrhunderts zu einer Situation, in der die Wahrnehmung vorherrschte, in einer Zeit der Entscheidung im konfessionellen Kampf zwischen diesen drei Konfessionen zu leben.[351] Das Luthertum sticht aber hervor, weil es besonders tief von Vorstellungen der Bedrohung und Apokalypse in den Jahren vor der Jahrhundertwende geprägt war.[352]

Die Bedrohung wurde zum Hauptthema des Werkes. Luthers Text aus dem Jahr 1530 fand Eingang in Gothus' Werk unter dem Titel *Utvalda sententier med vilka Martin Luther har tröstat sig* und war die perfekte Illustration des Handelns eines Christens in einer Bedrohungssituation. Gothus' Übersetzung machte dem Leser gleich zu Anfang klar, worum es ihm ging: Wenn Beschwerden, Betrübnisse und Verfolgungen des Wortes Gottes wegen eintreffen, soll der Gläubige freimütig sein und sich trösten und seine Angelegenheiten Gottes gnädigem, barmherzigem Willen unterwerfen.[353]

Gothus hatte dementsprechend einen Text für die schwedische Publikation ausgesucht, der die Bedrohungs- und Krisensituation der Lutheraner themati-

---

350 Nelson, Jesuit legend. Bireley, Catholicism. Grundlegendes zur katholischen Konfessionalisierung bei Reinhard/Schilling, Konfessionalisierung.

351 Schilling, Konfessionalisierung, 108–112, 394–411.

352 Leppin, Antichrist. Pohlig, Gelehrsamkeit. Kaufmann, Konfession. Kaufmann, 1600. Barnes, Himmel.

353 Gothus, Skööna, C1^{r}. Schwedisches Zitat: „beswäringar bedröffuelser och förförlielser förefalla för GUDS Ord skul" und „frimodige och tröste och sättiom saakena vthi GUDS nådiga barmhertige wilia".

sierte. Das am Anfang dieses Beitrages vorgestellte Zitat aus dem Vorwort, in dem das Verhältnis zwischen König und Untertanen angesprochen wird, muss im Zusammenhang mit dem Thema des Buches gelesen werden; es geht Gothus um die Bedrohung der Lutheraner, insbesondere wenn die Konfession des Königs nicht mit der der Untertanen übereinstimmt – wie im Fall Schwedens im Jahr 1597. Dieses wird auch im Vorwort von Gothus betont. wo Martin Luther als Beispiel eines Mannes vorgestellt wird, der in Zeiten von Gefahr nicht an Gottes Wort gezweifelt, sondern fest daran geglaubt hat. Luther „ist freimutig durch allerlei Gefahren, die ihm in den mannigfaltigen Zwängen dieser Welt begegnet sind, gewandert".[354] Dieser Abschnitt am Anfang des Vorworts setzt den Ton für das ganze Buch – es geht um die Bedrohung der Gläubigen und darum, wie man sich in Zeiten der Gefahr verhalten soll.

Paratexte und Luthers Autorität

Gothus' Übersetzungspraktiken haben gezeigt, wie er Textteile aus der Wittenberger Gesamtausgabe gewählt hatte, die Trost spendeten in bedrohliche Situationen. Eine Analyse der Paratexte im *Sköna och märkliga skriftens sententier* kann diese Kenntnis noch vertiefen und eine Antwort auf die Frage geben, was Gothus seinen Lesern über das Verhältnis zwischen König und Untertanen mitteilen wollte.

Zu den Paratexten im Werk gehören die Dedikation, das Vorwort und das bereits erwähnte Portraitmedaillon. Das Vorwort – wie üblich in frühneuzeitlichen Büchern – wirbt für das Werk, präsentiert die Absichten des Autors und versucht den Nutzen des Werks für den Leser hervorzuheben. Besonders fällt die Betonung auf der Autorität Luthers auf. In Gothus' Werk wird er als Lehrer und als Mann mit besonderen Gaben präsentiert. So schreibt Gothus unter anderem, „man sieht deutlich, welches große Licht der selige apostolische Lehrer Luther aus Gottes heiligem Wort gehabt hat."[355] Luther wird explizit auch dadurch als Vorbild hervorgehoben, dass „der selige Mann, Gottes Doktor Martin Luther" auf Gottes Wort als sein „Schatz, Schild, Waffen und Degen" vertraut habe und „freimutig" Gefahren entgegnet ist.[356] Luthers Autorität und Gabe wird von Gothus außer Frage gestellt. Nach seinem Tod 1546 kam dem

354 Ibid., A3^{r}. Schwedisches Zitat: „frimodeliga wandrat genom allahanda farligheeter som henom i thenna Werldennes margfalleliga twång äre komne i möte".

355 Ibid., B6^{v}. Schwedisches Zitat: "man clarliga seer hwilkit stoort Liws then salige Apostoliske Läraren Lutherus haffuer hafft vthi Guds helige Orde". Vgl auch Ibid, B7^{r}.

356 Ibid., A3^{r}. Schwedische Zitate: „then salige GUds Mannen Doctor MARTINVS LVTHERVS" und „Skatt Sköld wapn wäria".

Reformator Luther fast die Position eines Propheten des Luthertums zu. Im Laufe des 16. Jahrhunderts schwand seine Bedeutung, aber er blieb Lehrer der Lutheraner zumindest während der gesamten Frühen Neuzeit.[357]

Insgesamt erscheint Luthers Name acht Mal im Vorwort, vier Mal in Antiqua, vier Mal in Fraktur gesetzt, wodurch er visuell besonders betont wird.[358] Auf dem Titelblatt leuchtet Luthers Name in Rot. Wie oft von Buchwissenschaftlern betont, ist ein Buch nicht nur Träger von Information in Form von Text, sondern auch das Layout des Buches stellt einen Informationsträger für den Leser dar.[359]

Auch eine bildliche Darstellung Luthers findet sich in dem Werk. In einem Medaillon wird Luther mit Doktormantel darstellt.[360] Dieses Bildnis Luthers ist eines der am häufigsten reproduzierten Bilder des Reformators im 16. Jahrhundert und geht auf ein Bild Lucas Cranachs d. J. aus dem Jahr 1546 zurück.[361] Dieses Portraitmedaillon mit seiner Darstellung Luthers wurde schon vorher für den schwedischen Markt produziert und in dem Katechismus 1586 in Lübeck gedruckt. Auch in dem 1588 ebenfalls in Lübeck gedruckten Katechismus finden sich solche Darstellungen.[362]

Der Name und das Bildnis Luthers sind Merkmale des Werkes und senden besondere Signale an den Leser. Die starke Betonung von Luther ist als identitätsstiftendes Merkmal zu bewerten. Luthers Gabe wird als positiv bewertet, seine Person als Beispiel für ein christliches Leben hervorgehoben. Aber noch viel mehr ist er die Leitfigur, hinter dessen Name sich die Lutheraner versammeln. Die Person Luthers als identitätsstiftendes Merkmal ist ein häufig vorkommendes Thema in der lutherischen Buchproduktion der zweiten Hälfte des 16. Jahrhunderts und ist als Bestandteil der lutherischen Konfessionskultur zu werten.[363]

Neben seinen Bemühungen, Luthers Autorität zu betonen, fällt bei Gothus' Arbeit auch das Bestreben auf, Luthers Texte dem Volk näher zu bringen. Durch die Paratexte wird *Sköna och märkliga skriftens sententier* dem Leser als ein Ausschnitt aus Luthers Textproduktion präsentiert. Durch die Lektüre sollte der Leser einen Zugang zum Denken des Reformators gewinnen. Dies wird nicht nur im Vorwort deutlich, in dem der Nutzen der Übersetzung betont

---

357 Kolb, Luther. Kolb, Umgestaltung.

358 Gothus, Skööna, A3^{r}, B3^{r}, B4^{r} (zwei Mal), B6^{v} (zwei Mal), B7^{v} (zwei Mal).

359 Beispiele: Zedelmaier, Vergilius. Pettegree, Brand. Mar, Page.

360 Gothus, Skööna, B8^{v}.

361 Schilling, Lebensstationen, 160–163, Abbildung 87.

362 Collijn, Bibliografi, Bd. 3, 42, 82–84

363 Kaufmann, Konfession, 19–20, 67–111. Kaufmann, Herrgotts Kanzlei. Kolb, Luther. Pohlig, Gelehrsamkeit.

wird,[364] sondern auch in seiner Auswahl. Geht man zurück zur Wittenberger Gesamtausgabe Band 9, fällt auf, dass die Texte, die Gothus für sein Werk ausgewählt hat, kurze Sprüche oder Erklärungen zu Bibelstellen liefern. Es handelt sich nicht um lange Auslegungen, sondern um komprimierte Aussagen. In dem neunten Band gibt es nur zwei Texte, die in ihrer (auch typographischen) Form den von Gothus gewählten Vorlagen ähneln, indem diese – rein optisch – kurze Erläuterungen sind.[365] Gothus hat also Textvorlagen gewählt, die leicht zugänglich zentrale lutherische Gedanken transportieren. Die Textteile können alle einzeln gelesen werden und somit auch einen eher ungewohnten Leser ansprechen. Es ist zu vermuten, dass Gothus somit ein Publikum anspricht, das lutherische Theologie rezipieren will. Gothus hat vor allem ein Produkt produzieren wollen, das einen Absatzmarkt hatte.

Noch ein Beleg für die besondere Art und Weise, mit der Gothus sein Projekt der Verbreitung lutherischer Theologie betrieb, findet sich im Vorwort, in dem Gothus besonders die Bedeutung von Luthers Vorwort zum Römerbrief betont, in dem Luther herausarbeitet, dass der Mensch allein durch die Gnade Gottes das Heil erlangt.[366] Gothus hat nicht nur auf Luthers Vorwort verwiesen, sondern dieses teilweise – genauer gesagt den Teil, in dem Luther beschreibt, was Glaube ist – selbst (frei) übersetzt und in sein eigenes Vorwort integriert.[367] Gothus hat also einen absolut zentralen Text der lutherischen Theologie ausgewählt, den Kernbereich des Texts übersetzt und in einer leicht zugänglichen Art und Weise präsentiert.

Dass Gothus sich mit seinem Werk an Laien wandte, wird auch im Zusammenhang mit der Übersetzung von Luthers Römerbrief klar. Gothus schreibt, „ein solcher, lebendiger, wirksamer und seligmachender Glaube ist nur bei ganz wenigen Menschen auf der Erde in diesen Zeiten zu finden gewesen".[368] Ein Stück weiter im Vorwort heißt es dann, dass er „wünscht von Herzen, dass eben dieses Leben und diese gute Lehre meinen geliebten Landsleuten durch diese Übersetzungen etwas mehr bekannt gemacht werden möge, dass sie mit

364 Dass dies war gängige Praxis unter Übersetzern war, macht Hansson, Översättningslitteratur, 73, deutlich.

365 Es handelt sich um kürzere Stichpunkte zu Thema Synagoga (398[a]) und Klosterleben (399[b]). Diese sind nicht von Gothus aufgenommen worden.

366 Vgl. WA, Bd. 7, 1–28.

367 Gothus, Skööna, B3[r]–B4[r].

368 Ibid. B4[v]. Schwedisches Zitat: "een sådan leffuande werkande salighgörande Troo hoos ganska få Menniskior på iordenne i thenna tijdh".

mehr Ernst gesucht und ihr nachgeeifert würde".[369] Gothus will also Luthers Einsichten im schwedischen Reich verbreiten.

Zusammenfassend hat die Analyse der Paratexte gezeigt, wie Gothus Luthers Autorität betont und Luther als identitätsstiftendes Merkmal einsetzt. Die Paratexte machen auch deutlich, dass die Zielgruppe der Kompilation nicht ausgebildete Theologen war, sondern wie auch üblich im Zusammenhang mit der zeitgenössischen Erbauungsliteratur, gläubige Lutheraner, die in ihrem Glauben gestärkt werden sollten.

Gothus und der Konfessionskonflikt

Am Ende dieser Untersuchung ist es angebracht, wieder zurück zur Frage zu kommen, was Gothus seinen Lesern über das Verhältnis zwischen König und Untertan mitteilen wollte. Die Analyse der Übersetzungsarbeit hat gezeigt, dass es Gothus um die Bedrohung der Lutheraner ging, und die Analyse der Paratexte zeigt, dass er Luthers Autorität besonders aus dem Grunde hervorhebt, um den Reformator als identitätsstiftende Bezugsfigur herauszuarbeiten. Das Bibelzitat im Vorwort, dass man Gott fürchten soll, aber nicht den König, da der König nur den Leib töten kann, Gott aber die Seele retten kann, muss daher im Zusammenhang mit dem Thema des mutigen Bekenntnisses in einer Bedrohungssituation und im Zusammenhang mit dem im schwedischen Reich bestehenden Konflikt zwischen Katholiken und Lutheranern verstanden werden. *Sköna och märkliga skriftens sententier* kann als ein Ausdruck der Wahrnehmung verstanden werden, dass die Auseinandersetzung um Schwedens Thron zwischen König Sigismund und Herzog Karl für den Fortbestand des wahren Glaubens im schwedischen Reich entscheidend war. Petrus Johannis Gothus' Übersetzung und Kompilation bezeugen einen sehr bewussten Umgang mit einem Stoff des deutschen Luthertums und belegen zudem die klare Absicht, die lutherische Seite im Konfessionskonflikt stärken. Der Hinweis im Vorwort, wonach der König nicht zu fürchten sei, weil er nur den Leib töten könne, ist als deutlicher Hinweis an das Publikum zu verstehen, dass König Sigismund nicht aus Furcht vor körperlichen Strafen zu folgen sei. Stattdessen mahnt Gothus – wie Luther in dem in *Sköna och märkliga skriftens sententier* übersetzten Text aus dem Jahr 1530 – die Gläubigen, sich nicht unterdrücken zu lassen, sondern für den wahren Glauben einzustehen. Diese Zeilen im Vorwort

369 Ibid. B6^{v}–B7^{r}. Schwedisches Zitat: "önskar aff hiertat att samma Liws och goda Lära måtte minom älskeligom Landzmän genom thena vthtålkningena något kunogare warda och medh meera alwar söökt och effterfolgd".

waren im Schweden des Jahres 1597 politischer Sprengstoff, da sie den Aufruhr gegen den König legitimierten. Das war Gothus' Botschaft.

Dies ist ein wichtiger Schlusssatz, da in der bisherigen Forschungsliteratur Petrus Johannis Gothus als Teilnehmer an dem Konflikt genannt, ihm aber keine Bedeutung darin zugeschrieben wird. Montgomery, die ausführlich den Konflikt analysiert hat, konzentriert sich ausschließlich auf das Spiel zwischen Herzog, König und den Ständen.[370] Holmquist nennt Gothus einen Verfechter des Luthertums.[371] Aber keiner der beiden geht darauf ein, wie Buch und Konfessionskonflikt einander beeinflusst haben. Wie die Untersuchung gezeigt hat, macht Gothus deutliche Aussagen in dem Werk, die Bezug auf die Auseinandersetzungen zwischen Karl und Sigismund nehmen. Er – und seine Leser – können daher sehr wohl als Mit-Akteure im Konfessionskonflikt und der Buchmarkt als eine Arena für die Austragung eines politischen und konfessionellen Konflikts gesehen werden.

Sköna och märkliga skriftens sententier ist in diesem Beitrag beispielhaft für die Rolle des Buchmarktes im Konfessionskonflikt beschrieben worden. Es gibt Hinweise auf eine viel größere publizistische Aktivität im Zusammenhang mit dem Konflikt zwischen König Sigismund und Herzog Karl als bisher angenommen. Petrus Johannis Gothus war nicht alleine als Publizist für die lutherische Seite in dem Konflikt in Schweden aktiv; zum Beispiel gab Vitus Börner im selben Jahr eine Leichenpredigt über die schon erwähnte schwedische Prinzessin Elisabeth Vasa heraus, in welcher der bewaffnete Widerstand gegen unrechtmäßige Fürsten als rechtmäßig beschrieben wurde.[372] Erst eine größere Untersuchung der Buchproduktion kann die Rolle des Buchmarktes im Konfessionskonflikt in schwedischen Reich enthüllen. Buch und Konfessionalisering scheint weiterhin ein vielversprechendes Forschungsfeld zu sein.

370 Montgomery, Värjostånd, 22.
371 Holmquist, Reformationstidevarvet, T. 2, 208.
372 Czaika, Elisabet Vasa, 28.

Elena Dahlberg

The Library as a Site of Early Modern Ideology

Two 17th-Century Latin Poems on Uppsala University Library[373]

What shapes book collections and libraries? What changes them? To answer these questions, we should look at the institutional context of the librarians' work.[374] This approach also applies to the early modern university library. The construction of the early modern university library was tightly bound to the state-building programmes of the fledgling nation states: regarded as part of the *apparatus status*, this institution was then enlisted in the service of the state and through its collections mirrored the state's policies and ideologies. The creation of Uppsala University Library is an example *par excellence* of this phenomenon. At a time when Sweden was growing into a military state of impressive might and when it was under threat from the forces of the Counter-Reformation, its king Gustav II Adolf (1594–1632) made several generous donations to Uppsala University and its library. In addition, he also created new professional chairs at the university. Furthermore, the king managed to increase the university library's collections with thousands of valuable books and manuscripts that his army had confiscated from Jesuit libraries on the continent. All this, viz. the newly established chairs as well as the newly acquired collections of books, served his political and cultural agenda. Gustav II Adolf's clever investments in the fields of culture and education are constantly praised and justified by his loyal Lutheran writers, including poets. This article will discuss two Neo-Latin poems that through their descriptions of Uppsala University Library and its collections serve the purpose of promoting Gustav II Adolf's ideological project. In addition, it will seek to explain why the authors had chosen the medium of Latin verse to convey such ideas.

---

373 I am most grateful to Keith Sidwell and Hans Helander for their valuable comments on my translations of the Latin texts discussed in this article. I am also thankful to Sofia Guthrie for her criticism on an earlier draft of this text. My special thanks to Josef Eskhult who brought to my attention Jonas Columbus's *Victoria Brunsbergensis*, a poem that constitutes the topic of the latter part of this article. In addition, I would like to extend a special thanks to The Calgary Institute for the Humanities at the University of Calgary for providing the perfect environment for writing.

374 See Goeing/Grafton/Michel, Knowledge, and Crawford, Library, both of which volumes contain several insightful texts about the library's various institutional milieus through time.

A state under construction: Gustav II Adolf's administrative reforms and education politics

As Michael Roberts has shown, the growth of Sweden into an empire was a gradual process. Adhering to the so-called old school of historians, Roberts contends that it was Sweden's worry for its safety that prompted its development into a military state and thereafter its emergence as an empire with a sophisticated administrative system. Both the military campaigns and the various domestic reforms carried out by Gustav II Adolf and his Lord High Chancellor Axel Oxenstierna (1583–1654) formed part of a deliberate plan, a plan that would guarantee their country's security and prosperity.[375] The most impressive part of this project was without doubt the creation of the amazingly efficient system of *Collegia*, the High Boards that even today constitute the basis of Sweden's state agencies. It is telling that Peter the Great of Russia was later inspired to organize his machinery of government in the same way.[376]

The new form of government demanded a new sort of civil servant. Gustav II Adolf could not rely on the old practice of importing administrators from abroad. The officials to operate his new *apparatus status* had to obtain their training at home. Here the role of the university was crucial. As the Uppsalian Academy had been suffering from financial difficulties for decades, it became one of Gustav II Adolf's primary concerns to help this university to recover and to redevelop.[377] As its clever patron, Gustav II Adolf saw to it that the university would have new professional chairs to teach the prospective officials and a new curriculum to be taught to these young men. He also gave the university several generous donations: in 1624, the king presented it with 317 manors from the Vasa family's own estates, which from then on would be held free from all taxation. Finally, yet importantly, he endowed the university library with thousands of valuable books and manuscripts that he had confiscated from Jesuit libraries during the Thirty Years' War. The university library was an impoverished institution, whose collection up to that point had consisted of scholastic literature taken over from the Franciscan monastery in Stockholm, and the new acquisitions were more than welcome to furnish it.[378] As Uppsala University Library's former chief librarian Ulf Göranson has pointed out, the incorporation of this new material into the library's collection was also an ideological enterprise, as the recently acquired items had a symbolic value: their former owners were the Jesuits, whose main task was to spread the ideas of the

375 Roberts, Experience, 2. Roberts, Gustavus Adolphus, chap. 1.

376 Roberts, Gustavus Adolphus, 80.

377 Annerstedt, Historia, chap. 5.

378 Annerstedt, Historia, 264.

Counter-Reformation in this part of Europe. By confiscating their literature, Gustav II Adolf deprived them of their main weapon to fight the Reformed church.[379]

In the eyes of the modern observer, these 17th-century lootings are difficult to justify, but this was the normal state of affairs in the early modern viewer's opinion. In his authoritative handbook on international law *De iure belli ac pacis* (1625), Hugo Grotius afforded justification for these kinds of spoils.[380] It is no wonder, then, that Gustav II Adolf's appropriation of the enemy's libraries meets with the approval of his Lutheran writers, who praise it in the same way that they praise all other achievements of their ruler. This article will discuss two such 17th-century poems that through their descriptions of Uppsala University Library's early years promote Gustav II Adolf's political and cultural programme. The contribution will also argue that Latin verse was then regarded as one of the most powerful instruments for conveying ideological messages of this kind.

Laurentius Fornelius's *Gustavus Sago-Togatus* (1631)

The Uppsala scholar Laurentius Fornelius (1606–1673) must be counted among the most prolific writers active during Sweden's period of greatness. Fornelius's *oeuvre* consists of academic dissertations, an extensive manual on poetics, and poetry in Latin and Greek.[381] Fornelius was close to Gustav II Adolf. After his university studies in the Netherlands, he joined Gustav II Adolf in his camp at Nürnberg in Germany. He stayed with the king until his death in 1632.[382] He

379 Göransson, Kulturarvsbyten, 74.

380 Göransson, Kulturarvsbyten, 74–76.

381 Fornelius's literary achievements are still awaiting full study. The most comprehensive account of his life and works is Lénström/Gegerfelt, Fornelius. See also Helander, Literature, who discusses Fornelius's Latin poems as manifestations of the most characteristic ideas of Swedish Neo-Latin literature of the period. Quotes from and references to Fornelius's poetry can be tracked through the *Index* in Helander, Literature.

382 In his self-epitaph, Fornelius mentions that he saw the wounds on Gustav II Adolf's body, which suggests that he was with the king during the battle of Lützen:

Gothia me genuit, Batavi fecere Magistrum,
Upsalia excepit. Porticus haec sepelit.
Me melius nemo GUSTAVI vulnera regis
Vidit, id in saxo hoc, Lector, habeto novum.

("Gothia gave birth to me; the Dutch made me a master. Uppsala received me. This portico buried me. Nobody saw King Gustav's wounds better than I did. O reader, accept the news on this stone".)

The epitaph contains two clear allusions to Virgil. First, Fornelius reuses the initial words of the Roman poet's epitaph: "Mantua me genuit, Calabri rapuere, tenet nunc Parthenope"

was appointed professor of poetry in Uppsala in 1635. One year later, he became a professor of theology at the same university. Between the years 1640–46, he was the university's rector.

In 1631, a year before the dramatic death of Gustav II Adolf, Fornelius published his epyllion *Gustavus Sago-Togatus (Gustavus armed and gowned)*.[383] As the title indicates, the poem celebrates Gustav II Adolf's deeds in war and peace (see Fig. 6). Composed in hexameter, it is 772 lines long. The print also contains congratulatory poems to Fornelius.

The poem itself can be divided into three natural parts. In the initial verses, Fornelius describes the glorious past of the Swedish nation and offers an account of the Swedish Reformation. The second part is devoted to Gustav II Adolf's military exploits. The final part of the poem provides a fascinating picture of Gustav II Adolf's new state apparatus. It is here that the poet acknowledges the king's donations to Uppsala University and admires the University Library's riches.

The very opening of the poem reveals the source of Fornelius's inspiration, vv. 1 f.:

> Te GUSTAVE cano Princeps Auguste, Gothorum
> Svecorumque simul, geminae Rex inclyte gentis.[384]

The poet reuses the first words of the opening line of the *Aeneid*: "Arma virumque cano, […]" ("Arms and the man I sing, […]").[385] Imitation of the first verse of the *Aeneid* is the usual way of both Neo-Latin and vernacular writers of epic works to announce their model and to introduce their subject. Thus, the English poet Abraham Cowley (1618–1667) signals the grandiose ambitions of his *Davideis*, an epos on the life of the Biblical King David, by starting it in the following way: "I sing the man who Judah's sceptre bore/ In that right hand which held the crook before."[386]

("Mantua gave birth to me; the Calabrians took me, now Naples holds me".). In addition, Fornelius's first hexameter line brings to mind Verg. *Ecl.* 9, 32 f.: [...] *et me fecere poetam/ Pierides;* […] ("Me, too, the Pierian Muses made a poet".).

383 Epyllion is a narrative poem of a smaller size than an epic poem. Its usual metre is hexameter.

384 The spelling of all the Neo-Latin texts cited in this article has been slightly modernised: in as far as all abbreviations have been expanded; the ligatures Æ, æ, Œ and œ have been rendered as *Ae*, *ae*, *Oe* and *oe*; *J* and *j* have been substituted with *I* and *i*. Italics and capitalised words have been kept. The punctuation has been adjusted to modern punctuation rules. – "I sing of you, o Gustav, venerable Prince, renowned King of the twin races of Goths and Swedes at one and the same time". All translations of the Neo-Latin texts quoted in this article are my own.

385 All translations of the *Aeneid* are from Fairclough, Aeneid.

386 The passage is analysed in Hardie, Hero, 142 f.

Fornelius alludes to Virgil again when describing Gustav II Adolf's looks, vv. 562 f.:

> Os humerosque Deo similis GUSTAVUS, ut ante
> Diximus, aspectu divinos spirat honores.[387]

This is how Trojan Aeneas is described in the *Aeneid* 1, 588 f., a passage where he meets Dido for the first time: "restitit Aeneas claraque in luce refulsit,/ os umerosque deo similis; [...]" ("Aeneas stood forth, gleaming in the clear light, godlike in face and shoulders").

It is obvious that Fornelius reuses the *Aeneid* for a reason. By appropriating Virgil's epic and the image of Aeneas, he portrays Sweden as a new empire and Gustav II Adolf as its energetic leader. Some two hundred verses earlier, the Swedish poet actually offers a modified version of the biblical concept of the Four Empires of history, namely the Assyrian, the Medo-Persian, the Greek, and the Roman, by seeing Sweden as the last great monarchy in this chain.[388] There is no doubt that Fornelius wants to perform as a *vates*, a new Virgil who predicts a bright future for his country.[389]

The most remarkable part of the poem is Fornelius's description of Sweden's new state system. This part of the poem is entitled *Regni Sueciae quinque collegia* (The five High Boards of the Realm of Sweden). There, the poet admires the wise government of Sweden with its recently introduced system of High Boards,

387 "As we said before, Gustav is godlike in face and shoulders. With his appearance he radiates divine dignity".

388 *Gustavus Sago-Togatus*, vv. 204–209:
Te stupet imperii quadruplicis ortus et auctus,
Regnatique orbis mirantur iure Monarchae.
Sacra quid Assyriae faciant moderamina terrae,
[...]
[...] ut sese GUSTAVO laudibus aequent?
("The beginning and development of the four-fold empire is amazed at you. The Monarchs of the world, which they govern with royal authority, wonder justly. What can the consecrated rudder of the Assyrian realm possibly do? [...] How can they possibly, as far as glory is concerned, compare themselves with Gustav?)
For further analysis of this part of Fornelius's poem, see Helander, Literature, 417.

389 The *Aeneid* came to exercise an immense influence on many a poet of the Humanist Era: Virgil's epos offered stylistic and thematic models for the presentation of heroes from both secular environments and the world of the Christian Church. Petrarch's *Africa* was one of the first among these early modern epics inspired by Virgil's epos. On the *Aeneid*'s paramount importance for Renaissance writers, see Kallendorf, Virgil, and Gwynne, Epic. On Aeneas as the archetype of the epic hero, see Hardie, Aeneid.

Collegia. The very first board to be celebrated is the *Collegium Iustitiae*, vv. 589–599:

> Haec inter Regni Suecici collegia, primum
> IVSTITIAE occurit, quod triplex ordo deinceps
> Pulchre distinguit, Medius, Supremus et Imus.
> Ex quibus ordinibus plebeii Legiferi imum
> Civium habent, Suecici iuris legumque periti.
> Custodes legum, quos sangvis honestat avorum,
> Nobiliore satu, quibus et provincia quaeque
> Gaudet, habent medium, consultae gloria famae.
> Illustres comites, quorum praelustrius exit
> Splendor, delecti proceres, clarique Barones,
> Magnificique viri sedem obtinuere supremam.[390]

The other high Boards of the Realm celebrated by Fornelius are the *Collegium Martiale* (vv. 630–662), the *Collegium Ammiralitatis* (vv. 663–671), the *Collegium Cancellariae* (vv. 672–680), and the *Collegium Camerae* (vv. 681–689). Fornelius owes his thorough descriptions of these colleges to Johannes Simonius's (1566–1627) *Oratio de auctoriate regia* (1626). Simonius was a Professor Skytteanus, whose task was to train future government officials and diplomats and to promote the king's new ideas and reforms in his own writings.[391] Simonius's *oratio* is thus in line with his pedagogical and political mission.

It is obvious that Fornelius in his verses relies on Simonius, in whose text we also find the names of those who represented the High Board of Justice:

> Primum est IVSTITIAE, cuius tres sunt ordines, supremus, medius et infimus. Ex quibus hunc obtinent Legiferi civitatum, plebeii quidem, sed honesti et iuris Svetici periti; istum Provinciarum Nomophylaces, viri praecipiae nobilitatis et dignitatis; supremum vero illustrissimi, Illustres et Generosi Viri, Dominus MAGNVS, Comes de Wisingsburg, Senator et Regni Archidapifer, Dominus ABRAHAMVS, Comes de Wisingsburg, Iudex provincialis Westmanniorum et Dalkarliorum; Dominus PHILIPPVS SCHEDING in Arnöö, Dominus GABRIEL OXENSTERNA Liber de Kimetho, omnes et singuli Regni

390 "Among these Boards of the Swedish Realm, the first that we meet is the Collegium of Justice, which in turn is beautifully divided into threefold ranks: the Middle, the Highest, and the Lowest. Of these ranks, the common citizens with law-giving mandates, who are familiar with the Swedish legal system and its laws, occupy the lowest one. The guardians of the laws, graced by their ancestors' blood, of a nobler stock, and whom every province can boast of, occupy the middle one, a renowned body of glorious legal knowledge. Illustrious counts, whose splendour manifests itself with even greater grandeur, carefully chosen noblemen, and renowned Barons along with eminent lords have secured the supreme seat".

391 On the establishment of the Skyttean Chair, see Lewin, Skytte, and Ingemarsdotter, Ramism, 241–246. About Simonius, see Lewin, 31–35.

Senatores: quibus additus est primaria nobilitate Vicepraeses Dn. IACOBVS IACOBI, vir generosus et amplissimus.[392]

When explaining to the reader that the Swedish kingdom has so much to be proud of, Simonius says that its religious zeal and laws are among its assets. Moreover, he emphasises the role that the educational state institutions play in maintaining and furthering the religious ardour in the kingdom's people. And the university, *Academia*, is one of these institutions. In the same section Simonius reveals his Lutheran view on the question of the Eucharist and argues that it is the view that the University and other state schools have to follow:

Exigis, quae anima sunt Rerumpubl[icarum], Relligionem et leges? Utrumque hic per DEi gratiam vernat, viret, floret. Viget hic ius aequabile: legibus omnia diiudicantur. *Doctrina* vero, quae in Ecclesiis et scholis florentissimi huius Regni a clarissimis et admodum reverendis, praestantissimis et doctissimis viris, Archiepiscopo, Episcopis, Doctoribus, Professoribus, verbique divini praeconibus certatim publice proponitur, est eadem, quam Prophetae et Apostoli tradiderunt, quam ipse CHRIstus Dominus ad nos e sinu aeterni Patris attulit, tum Sacramenta iuxta institutionem Christi pie distribuuntur et administrantur. Huic suae Ecclesiae assidet et semper adest Servator noster, et dat gratiam, ne Evangelium suum sit ociosum, sed cordibus, ceu tribus satis fermenti massa, mixtum, fructum ferat uberrimum. Ipse recreat convivas suo verbo, veroque suo corpore et sangvine corroborat; ipse docet mentes piorum easque confirmat, ne a veritate aberrent, sicut et ipse precatur: santifica eos, Pater, in veritate tua! Sermo tuus est veritas. Haec est doctrina, quam huius Regni Ecclesiae, Academia, templa, et scholae constanter profitentur.[393]

---

392 Simonius, Oratio, unnumbered. "The first one [i.e. the first Board] is that of Justice, whose ranks are three in number: the top one, the middle one, and the lowest one. Of these, the latter is possessed by citizens with legislative mandates, commoners, yet honourable people and experts in Swedish law. Guardians of the laws from the provinces, men of exceptional nobility and merit, represent the second one. The highest one is represented, indeed, by the most illustrious, men of renown and noble birth, Lord Magnus [Magnus Brahe (1564–1633)], Count of Visingsborg, Royal Councillor and Seneschal of the Realm [Swedish: Riksdrots], Lord Abraham [Abraham Brahe (1569–1630)], Count of Visingsborg, Judge of the Provinces of Västmanland and Dalarna, Lord Philip Scheiding [Philip von Scheiding (1578–1646)] in Arnö, Lord Gabriel Oxenstierna [Gabriel Gustafsson Oxenstierna (1587–1640)], Baron of Kimito, all and each a Royal Councillor. To them is added, for his distinguished noble origin, Lord Jacob Jacobi [Jacob Jacobsson Snakenborg (?–1627)], Vice Protector, a man of good birth and very highly renowned."

393 "Are you examining religion and laws that represent the state's soul? Both of them flourish, display vigour and bloom here by the grace of God. The just right thrives here: everything is adjudicated under laws. Indeed, the doctrine that is zealously put forth publicly in the churches and schools of this finest kingdom by men of utmost fame and the greatest esteem, the most excellent and learned – the Archbishop, the Bishops, the Teachers, the Professors, and the heralds of the divine word – is the same doctrine that the prophets and apostles handed over, the doctrine that Lord Christ himself brought to us from the bosom of the eternal Father. In these conditions, the Sacraments together with Christ's teachings are spread

Even though Simonius's point about the university's responsibility in spreading this ideal is very clear, the author does not offer any detailed picture of the university itself. Here, Fornelius seizes the opportunity to show off as a good narrator himself: as a skilful versifier, he integrates a description of Uppsala University into his poetic account of the Swedish state (see Fig. 7). He thus manages to present it and its library as part of the country's *apparatus status*. His starts with an encomium to Gustav II Adolf, vv. 690–693:

> Nunc cantanda venit facilis Clementia Regis.
> Nunc celebranda nimis tua Munificentia Princeps,
> Non celebranda satis, neque sit mirabile, nostros
> Namque modos spacio natura coërcuit arcto.[394]

Clementia explicitly refers to the King's engagement in the development of the university. After acknowledging it, Fornelius stresses that it is especially praiseworthy due to the fact that "nostros [...] modos [...] natura coërcuit" ("nature has restricted our bounds"). This line can be interpreted in two different ways. The poet may refer to the tough climate of the country that is situated in the cold North. Another reading suggests that Fornelius uses "nostros [...] modos" to refer to his own skills as a versifier, as *modi* is the usual Latin term to denote metres in poetry.[395] Then, the phrase should be seen as the poet's humble *recusatio*, which implies that the poet is aware of the obvious discrepancy between the grandiose enterprises of his king and his own insufficient talent.

Besides his monetary donations, Gustav II Adolf also saw to it that the university received a new building. Its construction was finished in 1623.[396] When

---

and managed in a pious way. Our Saviour guards this Church of his and he is always present in it. And he provides his grace so that his Gospel is not idle, but brings the richest fruit to hearts by mixing it in, in the same way as the leavened dough of the commoners offers a sufficient amount of the Eucharist. He himself revives the Last Supper with his word, as well as he reinforces it with his true body and blood. He himself teaches the minds of the pious men and strengthens them so that they do not stray from the truth, which also he himself prays for. Sanctify them, o Father, in your truth. Your speech is the truth. That is the doctrine that our kingdom's churches, its university, cathedrals and schools uniformly avow".

394 "Now it is time to sing of the King's gracious benignness. Now, o Prince, it is time to celebrate exceedingly your generosity, which cannot be celebrated sufficiently. Nor should it be wondered at, as nature has restricted our bounds to a confined space". Cf. Ovid, Tristia 2, 53 f.: "invida me spatio natura coercuit arto,/ ingenio vires exiguasque dedit". ("As for me – grunding nature has confined me within a narrow space, granting me but meagre powers". Transl. A. L. Wheeler in Ovid, Tristia). In Ovid's case, the phrase refers to the poet's choice of genre and metre.

395 Cf. Horace, Ep. 1, 3, 13.

396 Annerstedt, Historia, 264.

Fornelius wrote his poem, the magnificent Gustavianum was already in place.[397] The new university building was very close to the Cathedral, which with its impressive size dominated Uppsala's skyline. To describe the latter edifice, the poet applies the *topos* of the greatness of Antiquity that is now surpassed, vv. 694–698:

Nescis Aonii praeclara palatia tecti,
Principis ad nutum patriis extructa sub oris?
Aspice, magnificis surgunt penetralibus aedes
Urbis ad australem Salanae hic utpote tractum,
Vasta structurae quae mole minantur Olympo.[398]

Fornelius elaborates on the topic. Despite Uppsala's disadvantageous climate, its Academy is greater than the famous Academy of ancient Athens, vv. 699–701:

Regia Suecorum hic Academia, qualis Athenis
Graecorum haud fuerit, quamvis obscura tenebris
Ante sub Arctois, vix nota priore sub aevo.[399]

Next to follow are the verses on the university library. Fornelius apologizes for his inability to do his topic justice and picks thus up his *recusatio* from the lines above. He mentions that the University has now new subjects in its curriculum and that the library, too, has received generous gifts from Gustav II Adolf, sect. *Bibliotheca Academiae Upsaliensis*, vv. 747–749:

Nec te praeteream, numeris licet hisce profanis,
Bibliotheca novis studiis sacrata Salanis,
Sumptibus immensis augusti Regis adaucta.[400]

---

397 The tower of the Gustavianum that is today the building's famous mark was added to the construction by Olof Rudbeck in 1662. See Annerstedt, Historia, 264.

398 "Do not you know that through the King's will remarkable palaces, the dwellings of the Muses have been erected on our shores? Behold how Uppsala's temple with its magnificent interior rises here towards the South, which with the monumental size of its structure threatens Olympus".

399 "Here lies the Royal Academia of the Swedes, such as did not exist in the Athens of the Greeks, although previously hidden in Northern darkness and hardly known in earlier ages". Cf. the description of Wittenberg as proposed in Weinrich, Aerarium Poeticum: "Qua sub Arctois latuit obscura tenebris, vicinoque, polo vix nota priore sub aevo"; Weinrich Aerarium poëticum, s.v. Witteberga Saxonia, p. 820. Weinrich's commonplace-book was re-printed many times, which proves its popularity among early modern poets.

400 "And I will not forget to mention you, o Library, although I celebrate you with my unlearned verses, You who are consecrated to the new studies conducted in Uppsala, You who are made greater through the rich donations of the venerable King". S. v. *Bibliotheca* in Weinrich, Aerarium Poeticum "Sumptibus immensis adaucta"; Weinrich, Aerarium Poëticum, 20.

Fornelius mentions the state, *status*, as one of the main beneficiaries of what the library has to offer, and the political, or perhaps rather confessional, context of the poem becomes now apparent:

> Te monumenta nimis Scriptorum docta celebrant,
> Quae statui nostro, quae relligionis, et arae
> Legibus et Christi sano famulantur in usu.[401]

"The sound way" is the Lutheran way, which for Fornelius was the only true one. Even though the university's new curriculum had become less theologically oriented, it still had to conform to the strict religious doctrine of the country. Here the poet's verses are in line with the message propagated in Johannes Simonius's *Oratio de auctoritate regia* that openly condemns Catholicism. In one of the initial passages of his speech, Simonius explains that piety is the most important characteristic of the ruler, a jewel to decorate the royal authority's diadem, as it will guarantee the country its firm foundations and growth. By asking rhetorical questions and referring to ancient authorities in the field, he convincingly defends his opinion. The argument reaches its *culmen*, when the orator contends that the adherence to Luther is the only way to achieve such a goal, as Luther's teachings help us keep our Christian faith free from papist superstitions:

> Princeps autem huius Diadematis unio et carbunculus est Pietas, ex qua Respubl[icae] et incrementum accipit et firmamentum maximum. Quod ita esse cur dubitemus nos, cum de eo nec Maecenas nec Seneca dubitarint? Ille enim apud Dionem diserte affirmat, nihil magnum facere eum, qui Deum et relligionem contemnat; hic vero aperte negat, posse quemquam supra fortunam emergere, nisi a Deo fuerit adiutus. Et profecto, quid ad comparandam inter mortales eminentiam, quid ad colligendam hominum benevolentiam, aut ad honorem consequendum deesse poterit ei Principi, qui Domino Iehovae servit? Qui, ut ingrediatur Dominus, portas regni sui altissime extollit? Quid Ecclesias et Scholas nutrit? Qui, ut Iehovae sacra faciat, cum populo in unum convenit? Nimirum, ut tota Aminadabi domus felix fuit propter Arcae praesentiam; ita Deus regnis et Politiis bene facit, illis, quae unam veram et sinceram relligionem, non quam quisque sibi pro arbitrio suo fingit, sed quae collatis sententiis cum ipsa scriptura examussim congruit,

---

401 "The learned achievements of the Authors make you exceedingly famous. They serve our State. They [the books] serve the laws of our religion and the laws of Christ's church in the sound way". S. v. *Bibliotheca* in Weinrich, Aerarium Poeticum "Quam monumenta nimis Scriptorum docta celebrant, quae statui cuivis, quae Relligionis et arae legibus et Christi sano famulantur in usu"; Weinrich, Aerarium Poëticum, 20. There is no doubt that Fornelius borrowed these expressions from Weinrich's book.

qualem eam esse profitemur, cuius vox in amplissimis his regnis ubique sonat et auditur, quam ab organo Dei Luthero, per quem a pontificiis superstitionibus perpurgata est, denominare non erubescimus. His, inquam, Politiis benefacit Deus, quae unam veram et sinceram relligionem fovent atque amplectuntur: quae, dum verae Ecclesiae hospitia manent, non dissipantur nec delentur; sed stant erectae, omnibusque bonis affluentes.[402]

Jonas Columbus's *Victoria Brunsbergensis* (1627/28?)

In 1626, the Swedish troops ravaging Prussia managed to get hold of the rich libraries of the Jesuit College in Braunsberg.[403] Among their texts, the 2,300 confiscated items included Bibles, writings of ancient authors, grammar books and early modern educational treatises.[404] There were also purely Catholic texts. All of these books and manuscripts immediately were incorporated into Uppsala University Library' collections. The Swedish scholar Jonas Columbus (1586–1663) praises this Swedish trophy in his short poem *Victoria Brunsbergensis (The Victory of Braunsberg)*. The poem is extant only in manuscript form,

402 "However, the main pearl of this diadem and its gemstone is Piety, from which the state receives its growth and most solid foundations. Why would we doubt that this is so, when neither Maecenas nor Seneca doubted it? In fact, the former affirms eloquently in Dio that no one who disrespects God and religion achieves anything great. The latter denies, indeed openly, that anyone can rise up over his destiny unless not assisted by God. And certainly, what could be lacking for the Prince who serves the Lord, if he (the Prince) wants to acquire a high position among human beings and earn the benevolence of his people and attain glory and honour? Who raises his kingdom's gates very high so that the Lord can enter them? Who rears the Churches and schools? Who comes together as one with his people in order to observe God's sacred rites? There is no doubt that Amminadab's entire family was prosperous because of the Ark's close presence. God thus favours kingdoms and states that cherish and embrace the true and pure religion, not the one that anyone invents according to his own fancy, but the one that through its collected propositions agrees perfectly well with the Scripture itself. And we proudly declare that exactly of this kind is the religion, whose voice resounds and is heard throughout these very spacious kingdoms, a voice that we do not feel ashamed to name after God's instrument Luther, through whom it [i.e. religion] is kept clean from pontifical [i.e. Catholic] superstitions. God gives his favour, I answer, to those states that cherish and embrace the only true and pure religion. As long as they remain the abode of the true Church, they [i.e. the states] are neither torn asunder nor extinguished, but stand upright and abounding in everything good". Simonius, Oratio, B2 f.

403 The fullest account of Gustav II Adolf's literary booty from Prussia is Walde, Krigsbyten, 53–106. Walde also gives valuable information on the original provenance of the Prussian material.

404 For the number of the books taken in Braunsberg, see Trypućko, Braniewo, 21. For their contents, see Hagström Molin, Krigsbytets biografi, 128 f.

in one autograph and one apograph.[405] At the time of its composition, Columbus was a professor of poetry and music at Uppsala, and like Fornelius, he was a loyal servant of his king.[406] Columbus's poem openly condemns the contents of the confiscated books, which means that the poet had a certain knowledge at least of their titles. The cataloguing of the books and manuscripts brought from Prussia took place in Stockholm between the months of the autumn of 1626 and February 1627.[407] The books were delivered to Uppsala in June 1627, but had to be kept in a storehouse until the library building was finished.[408] The edifice must have been completed in the second half of 1627.[409] The fact that the poet describes the library's physical appearance proves that he penned his verses on the victory of Braunsberg when the Jesuit books had been moved into the new building.[410] It is thus plausible to assume that Columbus wrote his poem sometime around 1627–28.

The opening verses address the town of Braunsberg, vv. 1–3:[411]

Ista libellorum multo Brunsberga suppellex
Tempore parta tibi, nuper quam miles ademit
cautibus eductus nostris, ubi sit, fortasse requiris.[412]

For the poet, the main achievement of the Swedish victory at Braunsberg is the Swedish army's booty, the books. *Libelli* has a negative ring, though: its

405 The autograph is preserved in Linköpings Stiftsbibliotek as part of Samuel Älf's Collection, vol. W 28. The apograph is kept in Uppsala Universitetsbibliotek, vol. R 383.

406 For Columbus's biography and literary activities, see Ekholm, Columbus. See also Lundström, Jonas Columbus. Jonas Columbus as a poet was for a long time overshadowed by his famous sons Johannes and Samuel Columbus. Several Neo-Latin scholars are now rehabilitating his poetic achievements: Anders Piltz at Lund University has edited Columbus's self-biographical elegies (Piltz, Johannes Columbus), whilst Mattias Lundberg at Uppsala University is preparing a study on Columbus as a music theorist. In addition, I am analysing his martial poems within a project on Latin poetry in the service of the Swedish state-building programme.

407 The cataloguing also concerned the books confiscated by Gustav II Adolf in Prussian Frauensburg. See Hagström Molin, Krigsbytets biografi, 124 f.

408 For the time of the delivery of the books to Uppsala, see Walde, Krigsbyten, 92. On their storage in Uppsala, see Hagström Molin, Krigsbytets biografi, 130.

409 Cf. Annerstedt, Historia, 265; Hagström Molin, Krigsbytets biografi, 130.

410 The library building came to host the old and new collections until 1691. Cf. Hagström Molin, Krigsbytets biografi, 135. On the order of the books in the first Uppsala University Library building, see Sjökvist, Ordning and Sjökvist, Order.

411 The text of the poem edited here follows Columbus's autograph. The punctuation has been adjusted to modern punctuation rules.

412 "O Braunsberg, perhaps, you are wondering where that collection of booklets is, a collection that was acquired over a long time and that the soldier, brought forth from our rocky shores, has now taken from you?" Metrically, the line is not a proper hexameter line.

diminutive suffix aims to render the objects' unimportance as if they were something without value. Columbus's word choice must be seen as an expression of the Lutheran writer's attitude to the Catholic contents of the Braunsberg collection. The reference to the long time over which the books were acquired by the Jesuit library proves that the Swedes knew about the provenance of many of them, as they also had confiscated the library's catalogues.[413]

"*Cautibus* [...] *nostris*" ("our rocks") refers to Sweden's rocky and barren nature. In Latin literature, *cautes* often denotes rough areas with an unpleasant climate. When Dido curses Aeneas for his heartlessness, she calls inhospitable Caucasus's "flinty rocks" for his true home, *Aen.* 4, 365–367:

> [...] nec tibi diva parens, generis nec Dardanus auctor,
> perfide, sed duris genuit te cautibus horrens
> Caucasus, Hyrcanaeque admorunt ubera tigres.[414]

Columbus continues to direct his words to the town of Braunsberg, to which he narrates Uppsala's early history, vv. 4–9:

> Desine, quod quaeris paucis, adverte, docebo.
> Svecigenum in patria praeclari nominis Urbs est,
> Ubbone, ut perhibent, ante Abrae tempora, quarto
> Rege Salam ad fluvium spacio fundata patenti,
> Dis superis multisque sacris augustus ut esset
> In Regno locus et dilecta sedes Monarchis.[415]

The poet mentions the mythological king Ubbe, a forgery that has its roots in Johannes Magnus's *Historia de omnibus Gothorum Sveonumque regibus* (1554). According to Johannes's fanciful historiography, Ubbe was the fourth king of the Swedish Goths and Uppsala's founder. Uppsala's meaning is thereof "Ubbes Sal" (Sw. "Ubbe's hall"; see Fig. 8).[416] Johannes states that Ubbe was a son of Magog, one of Noah's grandsons. The forgery was used to create an impressive genealogy

---

413 Walde, Krigsbyten, 92. Hagström Molin, Krigsbytets biografi, 128.

414 "False one, no goddess was your mother, nor was Dardanus founder of your line, but rugged Caucasus on his flinty rocks begot you, and Hyrcanian tigresses suckled you".

415 "Stop doing this. Listen, I will explain in a few words what you are seeking to learn. In the fatherland of the Swedish peoples, there is a city with a famous name, founded as they say, before Abraham's time by Ubbe, the fourth king, on the plain that stretches by the Sala River so that it might become a place in our realm venerable because of gods above and their many shrines, and a home chosen by the Monarchs".

416 Magnus: 1554, lib. I, cap. VI.

of the Swedish kings, which in turn would enhance Sweden's reputation as a country with long and glorious history.[417]

After providing the etymological background of the name of Uppsala, the poet continues his account of the city's early days: it is a place where the pagan ancestors of the Swedes used to worship their gods and it is here that the Royal coronations would take place. Some decades later, Olof Rudbeck would describe the pagan rites on the shores of Uppsala River in his *Atlantica*.[418]

Columbus acknowledges the royal gifts and admires the building that is the library's new home, vv. 10–14:

> Propterea semper Regali munere felix
> Extitit, at nostro hoc omni felicior aevo,
> Hic ubi nubiferas alte est educta sub auras
> Ingentis precii libros quae continet aedes,
> Et duplex ample librorum conficitur grex.[419]

Here we have an explicit reference to the redoubled amount of the library's books. The author also describes the building with its two floors. According to the contemporary accounts, the librarians kept most of the library's Catholic literature, including the Jesuit collection from Braunsberg, separately on the first floor, whilst the upper floor housed the literature to be used for teaching at the university.[420] Columbus justifies this division, as he sees the monastic books as scabby, whilst the writings of the Lutheran writers are chaste for him, vv. 15–17:

> Dividuus paries omnes qui ponitur inter
> Foetibus a sanis scabiosa peculia nobis
> Plurima quae data sunt abs te Brunsberga repellit.[421]

---

417 Johannesson, Renaissance.

418 E.g. *Atlantica*, lib. III, cap. X, §2.

419 "For that reason, it has always stood out as fortunate because of the royal gifts, but is even more fortunate in this age of ours than in every other, in this place where a building stands raised up high towards the cloud-bearing skies, a building that contains books of great value! And the herd of books is now made double".

420 Sjökvist, Ordning. Sjökvist, Order. Cf. Hagström Molin, Krigsbytets biografi, 139.

421 "A dividing wall that is put between all the books repels from [our] healthy offspring the scabby monastic trash, so numerous, that was given to us by you, o Braunsberg".

In classical Latin, *peculia* is a juridical term denoting a wife's property. In Medieval Latin, it denotes a monk's belongings.[422] As the term has its origins in the word *pecus* ("cattle"), the etymology offers a suitable metaphor: the poet invites us to compare the Catholic objects to animals suffering from scabies. Moreover, the line about the dividing wall evokes the image of a fence that helps keep the infected cattle apart from the uninfected one in order not to transfer the vermin. When Columbus in the previous passage chooses the phrasing *librorum grex*, "the herd of books", he picks this phrasing on purpose: he prepares the reader for several animal metaphors.

In the next lines, Columbus returns to the *topos* of the tough northern climate in order to emphasise the learned endeavours of the Swedes. To create a rhetorical effect in the description of the books that have increased in quantity, Columbus uses an alliteration with the repeating *ac-* in the phrase *accervit acervus*, words that he puts in the mouth of the amazed visitor to the library, vv. 18–20:

> Stat tamen illa nivis boreae secura vel imbris,
> Et quoties aliquis veniens novus advena spectat,
> Ah quantus, clamat, librorum accrevit acervus![423]

The closing lines uncover the poet's ideological agenda, vv. 21–24:

> Nunc hos nunc alios delibant ordine flores,
> Dulce mel et sanum comedunt, aconita sed horrent,
> Utile quodcunque in nostros convertimus usus.[424]

The bee metaphor appears already in Classical literature. By using the image of this industrious creature, the authors explored human nature in general and described various activities of human beings in particular.[425] Many of

---

422 Niermeyervan de Kieft, Lexicon, s.v. *peculium*.

423 "For all that, it stands unbothered either by northern snow or by storm. And every time some new visitor comes here and looks at it, he exclaims: 'O, what a heap of books has accumulated here'!"

424 "As those winged honey-making creatures flying over meadows taste now these flowers, then others, one after another, and eat sweet and healthy honey, but avoid poisonous plants, we turn everything that is useful to our purposes".

425 Hollingsworth, Poetics, offers an attempt to trace the history of this insect metaphor in Western literature from Homer to our days, focusing primarily on the most famous works of the West-European literary canon. Carlson: 2015 investigates several different apicultural metaphors as applied in the writings of ancient Greek and Roman authors, and thus provides a good background to their earliest uses in Classical literature.

these ancient texts are political in nature and employ the image of the bee as the symbol of an aspiring empire. Thus, Aeneas's and Achates's viewing of Carthage from a hill and their observation of the human activity in the city offer a visionary picture of an empire in the making, *Aen.* 1, 419–436 (line 427 missing):

Iamque ascendebant collem, qui plurimus urbi
imminet, adversasque adspectat desuper arces.
Miratur molem Aeneas, magalia quondam,
miratur portas strepitumque et strata viarum.
Instant ardentes Tyrii pars ducere muros,
molirique arcem et manibus subvolvere saxa,
pars optare locum tecto et concludere sulco.
[…]
hic portus alii effodiunt; hic alta theatris
fundamenta locant alii, immanisque columnas
rupibus excidunt, scaenis decora alta futuris.
Qualis apes aestate nova per florea rura
exercet sub sole labor, cum gentis adultos
educunt fetus, aut cum liquentia mella
stipant et dulci distendunt nectare cellas,
aut onera accipiunt venientum, aut agmine facto
ignavum fucos pecus a praesepibus arcent:
fervet opus, redolentque thymo fragrantia mella.[426]

The production of honey and its consumption are recurring tropes in both ancient and Neo-Latin texts. One of the most popular applications of these tropes is to the intellectual endeavours of human beings. In Classical literature, we find Horace, *Carm.* 4,2,27 ff., using this metaphor to describe his work as a poet. Seneca, *Epist.* 84,3 f., and later Macrobius, *Saturnalia*, *Praef.* 5, want us to imitate the bees in their ability to transform what they have collected into something new.[427] Early modern writers employ the simile to illustrate the work

426 "And now they were climbing the hill that looms large over the city and looks down on the confronting towers. Aeneas marvels at the massive buildings, mere huts once; marvels at the gates, the din and paved high-roads. Eagerly the Tyrians press on, some to build walls, to rear the citadel, and roll up stones by hand: some to choose the site for a dwelling and enclose it with a furrow. Here some are digging harbours, here others lay the deep foundations of their theatre and hew out of the cliffs vast columns, fit adornments for the stage to be. Even as bees in early summer, amid flowery fields, ply their task in sunshine, when they lead forth the full-grown young of their race, or pack the fluid honey and strain their cells to bursting with sweet nectar, or receive the burdens of incomers, or in martial array drive from their folds the drones, a lazy herd; all aglow is the work and the fragrant honey is sweet with thyme".

427 See Helander, Metaphors.

of scholars and scientists. In *The new organon* (1620), Francis Bacon contends that scientists must conduct themselves like bees and not in the fashion of ants or spiders: ants are just empirical in their gathering of what they find in order to build a pile, whilst spiders are only able to spin threads out of their bodies, i.e. they only apply theory. Bacon's point is that the bee offers the perfect way of handling the material it has collected: being both experimental and rational, it converts it into something different and useful:

> Qui tractaverunt scientias aut empirici aut dogmatici fuerunt. Empirici, formicae more, congerunt tantum, et utuntur: rationales, aranearum more, telas ex se conficiunt: apis vero ratio media est, quae materiam ex floribus horti et agri elicit; sed tamen eam propria facultate vertit et digerit.[428]

The bee-honey metaphor gained an incredible popularity at the time when a confessional divide between Catholicism and the various branches of Protestantism was taking shape. Among other literary genres, this popularity manifests itself in the genre of satire. One of the most spread of these satirical works was Marnix of Saint Aldegonde's *Den Byencorf der H. Roomische Kercke* (The Beehive of the Holy Roman Church), the first edition of which appeared in 1569.[429] In his allegorical work on the Catholic Church, the Calvinist author identifies the Catholics with the bees that produce polluted honey.[430] When Swedish Jonas Columbus is applying the bee-imaginary to his verses on the Swedish librarians' project, he is thus building on a long literary tradition.

Concluding remarks

As mentioned above, there were two clear purposes behind the Swedish authorities' decision to bring the Catholic books to Uppsala. First of all, the new items would enlarge the library's collections. In addition, the enemy was to lose what was his main weapon to fight the Reformed church, a weapon that consisted of texts full of important information and helpful guidance. The closing lines of Columbus's poem also suggest that Uppsala's Lutheran scholars saw one more

428 *Novum organum*, lib. I, cap. XCV. "Those who have treated of the sciences have been either empiricists or dogmatists. Empiricists, like ants, simply accumulate and use; Rationalists, like spiders, spin webs from themselves; the way of the bee is in between: it takes material from the flowers of the garden and the field; but it has the ability to convert and digest them". Bacon, Organon.

429 Its English version appeared in 1578.

430 See Beemon, Honey.

benefit of acquiring the blameful literature: it would enable them to acquaint themselves with its injurious content in a most thorough way and thus to make them fit for attacking the enemy's argument. The Swedish case is not unique. We find the same eagerness to acquire literature with "unsound" content in the example of English Thomas Bodley and his librarian Thomas James. When building up the Bodleian Library in Oxford, Protestant Bodley accepted gifts of items previously held by Catholic owners, bought books printed by Catholic publishers, and provided access to them to scholars from home and abroad.[431] And these "injurious" books were used in a very purposeful way: to further his Protestant cause, Bodley's right-hand man Thomas James made it into his task to study the new editions of the Latin patristics printed in Italy and France in order to prove that the Catholic printers intentionally had corrupted the original.[432] Both cases, Gustav II Adolf's Uppsalian project and Bodley's project in Oxford, demonstrate that the early modern university library was an ideologically charged site. Fornelius's and Columbus's religious devoutness also shows that the process of confessionalisation was still in full swing in Sweden in the early 1630s. This implies that we should see Columbus and Fornelius as some of the main actors behind this confessional politics, an enterprise that was tightly bound to the King's state-building project. As teachers and writers at the country's biggest educational institution, these two Swedes were fully committed to their state's ideological undertakings and helped it consolidate the confessional identity of its people. And they saw the library as a useful tool to exercise this type of social disciplining.

The last question to answer is why Columbus and Fornelius chose the Latin verse as their medium to convey their political and religious standpoints. There were at least three grounds of convenience for using it. First, we have to understand in what political circumstances the poets were working. Laurentius Fornelius and Jonas Columbus wrote their poems *Gustavus Sago-Togatus* and *Victoria Brunsbergensis* during the time of Sweden's formation as a nation state, with a view toward a long period of development for the Swedish superpower. The poets knew that writing poetry in the *lingua franca* would make it possible for them to communicate this message to their foreign reader.[433] Second, one

431 On Bodley's acquisition of books and manuscripts in Philip, Bodleian, 1–22. On Bodley's rules of admission in Philip, Bodleian, 19 f., and Jackson, Bodley, 258.

432 Philip, Bodleian, 15.

433 See Marc Laureys's studies on Neo-Latin literature as a political instrument, e.g. Laureys, Action, with its extensive bibliography. See also Enenkel/Laureys/Pieper, Discourses, that contains theoretical discussions on the subject. Many of the volumes of the *Renæssanceforum* also deal with the ideological and political uses of Neo-Latin poetry, e.g. Coroleu/Caruso/Laird, Latin, and Arlund Hass/Humble/Pade, Latin.

should not neglect the clear connection of Neo-Latin poetry with its ancient prototypes: Latin verse enabled the authors to portray a Sweden that would be associated with the greatness of Roman imperialism, a goal that they achieved through carefully chosen allusions to Virgil's *Aeneid*. Third, the writers knew that composing Latin poetry was the most natural way to advance professionally, as this form of literature had an immense political force in the realm of cultural patronage.[434] Indeed, both Fornelius and Columbus were successful in achieving their ultimate career goals.

434 Among the most recent studies on the role of literary patronage in the Renaissance period are de Beer, Poetics, and Gwynne, Patronage, both of which convincingly demonstrate how Neo-Latin poets composed panegyric poetry for princes and high-ranking clergymen, including popes, in order to advance in their career. See also de Beer, Patronage.

Martin Berntson

Religiöses Theater in Schweden

Komparative Perspektiven im Zeitalter der Konfessionalisierung

Theaterstücke hatten bereits vor der Reformation eine wichtige mediale Bedeutung in der westlichen *christianitas*. Während die Kirchenväter noch skeptisch gegenüber dem Theaterwesen ihrer Zeit gewesen waren, wurden religiöse Theaterstücke seit dem frühen Mittelalter immer häufiger verfasst und aufgeführt.

Die Geschichte des religiösen Dramas begann mit einem Dialog, der im Anschluss an den Evangelientext vom leeren Grab während des Gottesdienstes am Ostertag gehalten wurde. Mit diesem *Quem queritis* ("Wen sucht ihr?") genannten Drama begann eine sowohl innerhalb als auch außerhalb der Kirchenmauern anzutreffende Theatertradition.

Bis zum Ende des Mittelalters hatten sich verschiedene Formen von Mirakelspielen und Mysteriendramen fest etabliert und waren in der westlichen Kirche höchst populär geworden. Oftmals knüpften die Dramen direkt an biblische Themen an. Die Aufführungen konnten lange dauern, manchmal gar mehrere Tage. Zudem konnten die Dramen mit verhältnismäßig avancierter Bühnentechnik aufgeführt werden. Obwohl viele Dramen deutlich an die biblische Vorlage anschlossen, verhielten sie sich dennoch relativ frei gegenüber dem biblischen Text. Häufig wurden außerbiblische Dialoge, oftmals komischer Art, in den Text eingesprengt.[435]

Evangelische Theologen der Reformationszeit verfolgten keine einheitliche Linie gegnüber dem Theater als Ort medialer Vermittlung. Reformierte Theologen waren im Großen und Ganzen jeglicher Form von Theater negativ gegenüber eingestellt, unabhängig davon, ob es auf antiken oder biblischen Vorlagen gründete.

In der englischen Kirche sah man hingegen das Theater anfangs sehr positiv. Eine Reihe reformatorisch orientierter Theaterstücke wurde daher im Laufe des 16. Jahrhunderts aufgeführt. Seit Beginn des 17. Jahrhunderts wurden die anglikanischen Theologen durch die Rezeption puritanischer Ideen dem Theater gegenüber jedoch kritischer. In jener Zeit können wir in England eine Säkulariserung des Theaters beobachten: Während das weltliche Theaterwesen aufblühte, wurde das religiöse Drama in den Hintergrund gedrängt.

---

435 Muir, Drama.

In lutherischen Ländern herrschte jedoch eine ganz andere Attitüde; hier wurde das Theater als Vermittler geistlicher Lehre umso mehr geschätzt. Sowohl Martin Luther (1483–1546) als auch Philipp Melanchthon (1497–1560) hatten sich positiv über das Theater geäußert. Luther sah im Theater eine hervorragende Möglichkeit, Wissen über die biblischen Bücher zu vermitteln und war insgesamt auch dem antiken, also heidnischen Theater, insbesondere Terenz und Aesop gegenüber positiv eingestellt. Nicht nur in den lutherischen Territorien des Heiligen Römischen Reiches, sondern auch in den nordischen Ländern blühte das Schultheater während des 16.und 17. Jahrhunderts auf.[436]

Diese lutherische Theaterkultur hat ihre Entsprechung in der katholischen Kirche, in welcher ebenfalls die Theatertraditionen des Mittelalters weiterentwickelt wurde, allerdings vom Jesuitenorden. In Jesuitenschulen wurden Theaterstücke ein nahezu obligatorischer Teil des Unterrichts. Das Jesuitendrama erfuhr seine höchste Blüte etwa gleichzeitig mit dem lutherischen Schultheater. In beiden Konfessionen formierte sich allerdings zu Beginn des 18. Jahrhunderts Widerstand gegen das Theater als Vermittler religiöser Inhalte.

Dieser Artikel schließt an Ute Lotz-Heumann und Matthias Pohlig an, die frühneuzeitliche Schuldramen als „konfessionalisierte Literatur" bezeichnen. Ihnen zufolge war der Konfessionalisierungsprozess ein Teil der frühneuzeitlichen Umbildung der Gesellschaftsstruktur und beeinflusste das Bildungswesen dermaßen, dass viele literarische Werke bewusst Polemik gegen das konfessionell Andere und bzw. oder eine von konfessionellen Idealvorstellungen geprägte Moraldidaktik beinhalteten.

Lotz-Heumann und Pohlig stellen weiterhin fest, dass die Dramen, die am Hof oder von fahrenden Theatergesellschaften gespielt wurden, nicht in besonderem Masse vom Konfessionalisierungsprozess beeinflusst waren, das lutherische Schultheater und die Jesuitendramen hingegen schon, auch wenn es diesbezüglich unterschiedliche konfessionelle Ausprägungen gab.

Während die Jesuiten zahlreiche szenische Spezialeffekte verwendeten und inhaltlich die persönliche Verantwortung des Individuums für seine Erlösung betonten, zeichnete sich das lutherische Schuldrama, das gewöhnlich in der jeweiligen Volkssprache abgefasst wurde, nicht durch die direkte Verwendung von Spezialeffekten, sondern durch großen Wortreichtum und Argumentationskraft aus.

Das Jesuitendrama stützte sich zudem auf durchaus andere institutionelle Voraussetzungen als die lutherischen Schuldramen im Schweden der Frühneuzeit. Letztere wurden gerne unter freiem Himmel, z. B. auf Märkten vorgetragen;

436 Johannesson, Skoldramat, 83.

Jesuitendramen wurden hingegen auf festen Szenen unter Dach an den verschiedenen Jesuitenkollegien gegeben.[437] Den gängigen Regeln zu Folge sollten die Jesuitendramen jährlich aufgeführt werden und immer moralische Lehren vermitteln. Die Theaterstücke sollten ausnahmslos auf Latein gegeben werden, weibliche Rollenfiguren durften nicht vorkommen und ebenso wenig durften die Stücke die weltliche Liebe behandeln.[438]

In der Praxis konnte es allerdings geschehen, dass einzelne Szenen oder auch im Ausnahmefall ganze Dramen in der Volkssprache aufgeführt wurden. Während der Aufführungen konnte das des Lesens kundige Publikum der Handlung gewöhnlich durch die sogenannten *periochi* folgen. Diese waren eine Art Programmblatt, die die Handlung zusammenfassten und zudem heute oft die einzig erhaltenen Quellen zum Jesuitendrama darstellen. Gleichzeitig stand – wie Lotz-Heumann und Pohlig aufgezeigt haben – das gesprochene Wort nur selten im Fokus der Aufführungen. Die Jesuitendramen haben hingegen viel mit der Oper als späterer Kunstgattung zu tun, da hier alle Sinne und Gefühle angesprochen werden sollten und nicht nur der Intellekt und die Vernunft.[439]

Der Inhalt der Theaterstücke – von denen tausende Originalwerke aufgeführt wurden – konnte stark variieren, meist aber wurde erwartet, dass die Handlung zur moralischen Erziehung der Schüler und des Publikums beitragen sollte.[440]

Ziel war es, die Bedeutung eines frommen und tugendhaften Lebens zu unterstreichen und das Publikum dazu zu inspirieren. Jesuitendramen konnten z. B. Freundschaft, den Sinn des Leidens oder das rechtfertige Leben thematisieren. Die Handlung inkludierte eine wiederkehrende Warnung für das unbeständige weltliche Glück, die vergängliche Suche nach weltlichem Erfolg und die Bedeutung der Wachsamkeit allen gegenüber, die den Menschen in dieser Welt verführen wollten. Zur Verdeutlichung dieser Botschaft wurden die Helden des Dramas am Ende häufig mit Erlösung und himmlischer Seligkeit belohnt, während die bösen Akteure mit ewiger Verdammnis in der Hölle bestraft wurden.

Das Schultheater, das sowohl Schüler als auch häufig die Bevölkerung ganzer Städte als Publikum involvierte, wurde hingegen ein Instrument, das soziale und konfessionelle Zusammengehörigkeit beförderte. Ein wiederkehrendes Thema war im deutschen Sprachraum die Bedeutung von Gottes Gnade. Dies markiert einen deutlichen Unterschied zum Jesuitendrama, das die Bedeutung der Rechtfertigung aus guten Werken unterstrich.[441]

---

437 Schnitzler, Theatre, 284.

438 Misrahi, Theatre 239 & 241. Schnitzler, Theatre, 284–285. Oldani/Yanitelli, Theatre, 19.

439 Misrahi, Theatre, 239, 241 & 244. Schnitzler, Theatre, 284–285. Oldani/Yanitelli, Theatre, 19.

440 Misrahi, Theatre, 241 & 245. Oldani/Yanitelli, Theatre, 19.

441 Lotz-Heumann/Pohlig, Confessionalization, 44–45. Zum deutschen Schuldrama siehe: Metz, Drama.

Lotz-Heumann und Pohlig halten zudem fest, dass die konfessionalisierten Strukturen des Schultheaters nicht in erster Linien ihren Ausdruck in Polemik gegen Katholiken, sondern vornehmlich in der an die eigene Gruppe gerichteten Moraldidaktik fanden. Das Hauptinteresse richtete sich also weniger auf dogmatische Fragen *in strictu sensu* sondern vielmehr auf moralische Diskurse.[442]

Die Quellen

Genaue Berechnungen, wie viele konfessionelle Theaterstücke als Textzeugen aus dem schwedischen Reich bis heute überliefert wurden, sind kaum möglich, da allein schon eine solche Kategorisierung der Werke anachronistisch ist. Es kann jedoch festgehalten werden, dass eine grosse Anzahl Theaterstücke aus dem 16. und 17. Jahrhundert bewahrt sind, wovon die meisten vom Konfessionalisierungsprozess im Allgemeinen und einer lutherischen Konfessionskultur im Besonderen geprägt sind.

Zeitweilig ist dieser Einfluss markant, manchmal jedoch auch kaum feststellbar. Ein Problem, dass durch unsere heutigen Kategorisierungen aufgeworfen wird, ist u. a., dass in der Frühen Neuzeit Dramen mit biblischen Motiven neben Dramen klassischer Verfasser aufgeführt wurden. Unter den schwedischen Dramen des 17. Jahrhunderts existiert auch eine Reihe "rein" historischer Theaterstücke, die meist eine götizistische Tendenz aufweisen. Jegliche Auswahl von Dramen, die dazu beitragen kann, die Vermittlung eines konfessionellen Erbes zu illustrieren, wirft methodische Probleme auf.

Auch wenn es nicht möglich ist, während der Frühen Neuzeit eine klare Grenze zwischen "religiöser" und "weltlicher" Literatur zu ziehen, so wird der Fokus in diesem Artikel auf Dramen gerichtet, die ausdrücklich an die Bibel anknüpfen oder aber kirchengeschichtliche Themen verhandeln wie zum Beispiel den Prozess der Christianisierung oder die Reformation. Auch Dramen, die auf zeitgenössische politische Diskurse Bezug nehmen und z. B. die Ausrichtung der Religionspolitik nicht-lutherischen Mächten gegenüber beleuchten, werden hier beachtet. Damit ergibt sich eine Gesamtzahl von 22 bis heute erhaltenen Dramen mit dem soeben beschriebenen Inhalt aus den Jahren 1550 bis 1700.[443]

Von den Dramen, die biblische Motive verwenden, rekurrieren sieben auf das Alte Testament (Schöpfungsgeschichte, Gespräch im himmlischen Hof-

---

442 Lotz-Heumann/Pohlig, Confessionalization, 45. Zur moralischen Thematik der Schuldramen: Peil, Schuldramen.

443 Zum Jahr 1700 als Endpunkt und die Gründe für das Verschwinden des schwedischen Schultheaters siehe: Berntson, Bibeldramat.

staat, Joseph, Rebecka, David und Esther),[444] acht auf das Neue Testament (Weihnachtsevangelium, Die Weisen aus dem Morgenland, Jesus im Tempel, Belial, Judas, Der verlorene Sohn, Die Apostelgeschichte, Simon der Magier)[445] sowie zwei auf die Apokryphen des Alten Testaments (Tobit und Judith).[446] Schlägt man die apokryphen Bücher des Alten Testaments der Gruppe alttestamentarischer Dramen zu, so existiert also praktisch ein völliges Gleichgewicht zwischen alttestamentlichen und neutestamentlichen Texten, die als Vorlage für Dramen mit biblischen Motiven dienten.

Die zweite Gruppe – fünf Dramen mit kirchenhistorischen und zeitgenössischen politischen Motiven – ist in Sonderheit an die schwedische Geschichte gekoppelt (Christianisierung, Olaf Schoßkönig, König Gustav Vasa (1496–1560), Dreißigjähriger Krieg).[447]

Von etwa fünfzehn dieser Dramen wurden zeitgenössische Drucke angefertigt, die meisten jedoch nur in einer Auflage. Allerdings existieren vier Ausnahmen von dieser Regel. Zu diesen Ausnahmen gehört erstens das älteste schwedische Schuldrama, die vom schwedischen Reformator verfasste *Tobie Comedia*, die während der Frühen Neuzeit in insgesamt sieben Auflagen erschien. Fünf Ausgaben dieses Werkes wurden unter dem Originaltitel in Stockholm gedruckt (1550, 1556, 1561, 1592 und 1650) eine in Rostock (1609). Eine Stockholmer Ausgabe von 1621 erschien unter dem Titel *Tobiæ historia*. Thomas Petri Gevaliensis' (gest. 1605) *Josephi historia* kam in vier Ausgaben heraus, 1601 und 1609 unter dem Originaltitel sowie in Kalmar 1631 und in Stockholm 1642 unter dem Titel *Then sköne Josephi historia* (Fig. 9). Derselbe Verfasser gab auch *Konungh Dawidhz Historia* heraus, die in Stockholm in zwei Auflagen 1604 und 1650 gedruckt wurde (Fig. 10). Andreas Johannis Prytz' (1590–1655)

---

444 De creatione mwndi, (1590?). [Thomas Gevaliensis], Iosephi Historia, 1601. [Thomas Gevaliensis], Konungh Dawidhz Historia, 1604. Josephus Svenonis Chærberus, Itt gudeligit samtaal, 1642. Rebecca, 1674. [Petrus Carstenius], Thet himmelska consistorium, tilhoopa kallat, 1674. Esther, 1693.

445 Belial de Inferno (1590?). Jesus lärer i templet (1590?). Jacob Rondeletius, Judas Redivivus, 1614. [Hans Olofsson], Een lijten Andeligh Tragoedia, Om the tree wijsa Män, 1635. [Samuel Brask], Filius prodigus, 1645. [Samuel Brask], Acta et martyria apostolorum, 1648. [Petrus Laurbecchius], Simon magus, 1652. [Ericus Kolmodin], Genesis ætherea, Eller Jesu Christi födelse, 1659.

446 Olaus Petri, Tobie Comedia, 1550. Holoferni och Juditz historja opå Rijm (1590?).

447 [Johannes Messenius], Christmannus [Huru christendomen först kom i Sweriet] (o.J.). Andreas Johannis Prytz, Olof Skottkonung, 1620. [Andreas Johannis Prytz], En Lustigh Comoedia om…konung Gustaf den Första, 1622. [Arnold Johannes Messenius], Een Comaedia, uti hwilken hela konung Gustafz den I:s Regemente…, 1642. [Samuel Brask], Mars Germanicus Victus. Ther är Comaedia Om thet wälendade Tydske kriget, 1649.

Theaterstück *En Lustigh Comoedia om […] konung Gustaf den Första* erschien in zwei Auflagen, zuerst in Uppsala 1622 und sodann in Stockholm 1649.

Interessanterweise erschienen die Erstauflagen aller Werke, die Folgeauflagen erfuhren, vor 1622. Später erschienene Dramen sind durchgängig nur in einer Auflage gedruckt worden.[448]

Zum Inhalt der Theaterstücke

Eine Analyse des Inhalts der erhaltenen Theaterstücke aus dem Untersuchungszeitraum belegt, dass sämtliche Dramen erziehende Ziele verfolgten. Die Erziehung erfolgte dabei häufig auf zwei verschiedenen Ebenen.

Erstens sollte die Schuljugend, die die Dramen aufführte, dazu angehalten werden, gute und wohlgeartete Personen innerhalb der Funktionseliten des Reiches zu werden; dies sollte dadurch erreicht werden, dass sie sich darin übten, tugendhaft zu leben, aber auch höfich zu reden und eine rhetorisch korrekte Sprache zu führen.[449] Zweitens so wurden – wie schon oben bemerkt – die Theatherstücke nicht selten vor größeren Volksansammlungen wie z. B. auf Märkten aufgeführt.

Ein häufig wiederkehrendes Thema ist die Verbindung der Tugend des Einzelnen mit Gottes Handeln in der Welt. Dies wird mit dem häufig benutzten Topos eines ganz und gar tugenhaften Akteurs illustriert, der allerdings im Laufe der Handlung verschiedensten Versuchungen ausgesetzt ist. Diejeningen, die fest den wahren Glauben bewahren und ehrenvoll handeln, werden am Schluss des Dramas belohnt.

Diese Struktur tritt u. a. sehr deutlich in dem ältesten erhaltenen schwedischen Schuldrama zu Tage, *Tobie Comedia*, das höchstwahrscheinlich von Olaus Petri verfasst wurde. Dieses Drama hält sich relativ treu an die biblische Vorlage. Der alte Tobit hält an Gottes Geboten fest, obwohl seine Umwelt ihn dazu ermahnt, pragmatisch zu sein und obwohl er zahlreichen persönlichen Schicksalsschlägen ausgesetzt ist.

Diese tugendhafte Einstellung wird auch von seinem Sohn Tobias geteilt, der durch seine Wertschätzung der Ehe seine Gattin Sara von dem Dämon befreien kann, der zuvor ihre früheren Ehemänner getötet hatte. Schon im Prolog des Dramas erfahren die Zuschauer, dass Tobit ein frommer Mann war, der vielen Schicksalsschlägen ausgesetzt war, der aber auch diesen gottgesandten Versuchungen widerstand. Tobit wusste, dass alles Böse, das ihm widerfuhr, seinen

448 Collijn, Bibliografi: 1600-talet, 708–710 & 725–726.

449 Johannesson, Skoldramat, 100.

Ursprung in der Sünde des Volkes hatte.[450] Die Moral, die diese Geschichte vermittelt ist daher: alle Menschen sollen Tobits Beispiel folgen und auf Gott vertrauen, der am Ende alles gut fügen wird.

In ähnlicher Weise treffen wir in Andreas Johannis Prytz' Drama über Gustav Vasa (1622) den immer wiederkehrenden Gedanken, dass der junge König – trotz der zahlreichen Widerstände auf die er trifft – sich die ganze Zeit darauf verlässt, dass Gott in seiner Gnade alles zum Besten fügen wird,[451] was gewöhnlich dann auch so geschieht. In diesem Drama geht es nicht darum, dass Gustav Vasa versucht wird, sondern vielmehr darum, dass er als Gottes Werkzeug ein Teil von Gottes Gnadenwerk am schwedischen Volk ist.

In *Josephi historia* (Josephs Geschichte) wird dargestellt wie Joseph, der auf zahlreiche Widerstände trifft, immer standhaft in seiner Frömmigkeit und seinem Gottesglauben ist; deshalb hat auch Joseph ein letztendlich glückliches Schicksal.[452]

Thomas Petri Gevaliensis schrieb einige Jahre nach *Josephi historia* das Drama *Konungh Dawidhz historia* (König Davids Geschichte, 1604). Hier führt er den Gedanken aus, dass es die Standhaftigkeit des Menschen gegenüber Versuchungen ist, die ihm Glück verschafft. Das Theaterstück über König David handelt davon, wie Gott jenen hilft, die ihm von ganzen Herzen dienen. Auch wenn Gott die Seinen viel in dieser gottlosen Welt leiden lässt, verschafft er ihnen schlußendlich Ehre und Herrlichkeit.[453] Obwohl König David während seiner Jugend und Regierungszeit zahlreiche Probleme lösen musste, gelang es ihm letztlich doch, seine Feinde zu überwinden. In der Einleitung des Dramas weist der Verfasser auf die Gemeinsamkeiten von Josef und David hin, zwei Gestalten also, die ähnlich wie Christus nach vielem Leiden am Ende dennoch erhöht wurden.[454]

Im selben Drama wird auch der Gedanke reformuliert, dass Kinder, die ihre Eltern nicht ehren, gestraft werden – so wie es mit Absalom der Fall war, der

---

450 Hesselman, Skrifter, Bd. 4, 400 & 430.

451 Andreas Johannis Prytz, En lustigh comoedia, Om then stormechtighe Sweriges, Göthes, Wendes konung etc. konung Gustaf then första, huru han til regementet i Swerige bleff vphögd, tå han konung Christiern Tyrann, af landet vthdriffuit hade, oc huru han genom Gudz nådh vprättade Swerige ifrån påfwens mörcker och willfarelse, och införde ewangelii reena liws thet påfwen länge bortröfwat hadhe (Upsala: Eskil Matzson, 1622), 5, 68–69.

452 Thomas Petri Gevaliensis, Konungh Dawidhz historia ifrån thet han bleff smordh til konung i Betlehem aff propheten Samuel, in til thes han kom igen til Jerusalem, sedhan Absalon dödher waar. Nylighen vthsatt på rijm. Lustigh att läsa (Stockholm: Anund Olufson, 1604), 3, 11, 30.

453 Petri Gevaliensis, Konungh Dawidhz historia [...], 2.

454 Petri Gevaliensis, Konungh Dawidhz historia [...], 2–3.

gegen seinen Vater David Aufruhr machte, schließlich aber mit seinem langen Haar an dem Ast einer Eiche hängen blieb.[455]

Auch im gegen Ende des 16. Jahrhundert verfassten Drama *Holoferni och Juditz historja på rijm* (Die Geschichte von Holofernes und Judith in Reimen) wird verdeutlicht, dass Gott die Hochmütigen straft, jenen aber hilft, die fest zu ihm stehen und auf ihn in guten wie in schlechten Zeiten vertrauen. Judiths Rede an das Volk in Baityoula verdeutlicht, dass Gott barmherzig zu allen ist, die auf ihn bauen, aber dass seine Strafe dazu dienen soll, Weisheit bei seinen Kindern hervorzurufen, so dass sie ihn auf die rechte Art und Weise fürchten mögen. Geschieht dies, wird er ihre Sünden vergeben und ihnen gegen ihre Feinde beistehen. Gottes Vorsehung wird hier mit dem Vertrauen und der Macht des Gebetes verbunden. Das hier inszenierte Hauptproblem ist also dies: dass das Volk Gottes nicht Busse leistet und sich bessert und auch kein Vertrauen auf Gottes Hilfe hat.[456]

Gleichzeitig existieren einzelne Beispiele dafür, dass das tugendhafte Handeln einzelner Personen eher auf die Seligkeit gerichtet ist. Sowohl in Johannes Messenius′ (1579/80–1636) die Christianisierung Schwedens behandelnden Drama *Christmannus* (ohne Jahresangabe) als auch in *Acta et martyria apostolorum* (1648) wird der Gedankengang ausgeführt, dass ein wahrer Diener des Glaubens in dieser Welt leiden muss, um sodann grosse Freude in der Ewigkeit genießen zu dürfen.

Am deutlichsten wird dies in *Acta et martyria apostolorum*. Bereits im Prolog wird ausgeführt, dass das Drama von Paulus und anderen Aposteln handelt, die das Wort Christi predigen und deshalb den Tod als Märtyrer erleiden. Dies wird als ein glückliches Ende dargestellt, da Christus mit großer Ehre seine Getreuen aufnehmen wird und sie ewige Freude genießen dürfen.[457] Auf eine für diese Theaterstücke ungewöhnliche Art und Weise erklärt Petrus im vierten Akt – nachdem einige Apostel hingerichtet wurden, – dass das irdische Leben nicht viel Wert ist, wenn man es mit dem ewigen Leben vergleicht, das er selbst ganz sicher erlangen wird.[458]

Die Verbindung des tugendhaften Handelns des Menschen mit Gottes Handeln in der Welt scheint auf den ersten Blick fremd für lutherisches Denken zu sein. Dies war es jedoch nicht für die dogmatischen Vorgaben der lutherischen Orthodoxie bzw. für die lutherische Theologie im Zeitalter der Konfessionen.

Bereits Martin Luther formulierte den Gedanken, dass Gott durch den Glauben etwas Neues im Menschen schafft, das sodann seinen Ausdruck in guten

455 Petri Gevaliensis, Konungh Dawidhz historia […], 50ff.
456 Sylwan, Holofernes, 40.
457 Brask, Acta 1878, 112.
458 Brask, Acta 1878, 181.

Werken findet. Das konkordistische Luthertum, das auch auf die schwedische Theologie im 17. Jahrhundert einwirkte, kennt sodann die Lehre vom *tertius usus legis*, dem dritten Gebrauch des Gesetzes, das auch für den Christen gilt. Auch dem Glaubenden dient das Gesetz also als Wegweiser und zur Instruktion. In der nachkonkordistischen Theologie werden folglich der Glaube und seine Früchte etwas stärker betont als in der frühen evangelischen Theologie.[459]

In der Gesellschaft der schwedischen Großmachtzeit wurden Misserfolge im Leben häufig als Versuchungen Gottes gewertet. Zudem existierte eine lebhafte Vorstellung davon, dass die Menschen für Unglücke und Katastrophen verantwortlich waren. Erfolg im Leben eines Menschen konnte als eine Folge des individuellen, menschlichen Handelns und als Ausdruck von Gottes Wohlwollen gewertet werden. Dies hängt auch teilweise mit dem Glauben an die Vorsehung Gottes zusammen, dem zu Folge Gott ständig das Weltgeschehen lenkt und durch seine Allmacht die Schöpfung aufrechterhält.[460]

Dem nachkonkordistischen Luthertum war der Gedanke nicht fremd, dass Gott in die Welt eingreift, um die Frommen vor Gefahren zu erretten oder vor den Verbrechen der Gottlosen zu schützen, so wie er es z. B. tat als er Noah vor der Sintflut, Lot aus Sodom und Joseph aus der Gefangenschaft errettete.[461] Die guten Werke, die der Mensch tut, sind letztendlich von Gott hervorgerufen und „schmücken den, der sie ausführt, mit Geschenken und besonderen Belohnungen".[462]

In der Perspektive des nachkonkordistischen Luthertums existierte also das Vertrauen darauf, dass der Mensch sein Wohlergehen in der irdischen Welt beeinflussen konnte, dass Gott den recht Glaubenden in diesem Leben mit Glück segnen konnte. Gleichzeitig gab es auch die Vorstellung, dass der wahre Glaubende verfolgt wird und in diesem, von Unrecht geprägten Leben, leiden muss.

Sofern ein tugendhafter und recht glaubender Mensch Erfolg hatte, wurde dies als Ausdruck dafür gesehen, dass er Gott auf seiner Seite hatte. Zwischen dem Handeln des Menschen und seinem Glück bzw. Unglück im irdischen Leben wurde also eine klare Verbindung konstruiert; tugendreiche Menschen werden durch das Leben versucht, ihre Standhaftigkeit mit Glück und Erfolg belohnt. Gleichzeitig gab es eine prinzipielle Offenheit für die Vorstellung von Gottes Vergeltung im diesseitigen Leben: Gott straft das, was böse ist und er

459 Hägglund, Mönster, 106–107. Hägglund, Arvet, 83 & 115.
460 Savin, Klädnader, 36.
461 Hägglund/Sjöberg, Hafenreffer, 60–63.
462 Hägglund/Sjöberg, Hafenreffer, 66–67.

tut dies so, dass es den Menschen dazu bringen kann, den rechten Weg zu erkennen.[463]

In den schwedischen Schuldramen der Frühen Neuzeit agieren aber auch Personen, die keine Vorbilder waren, sondern ganz im Gegenteil einen negativen Gegenentwurf zu den tugenhaften Hauptpersonen darstellen. Eine häufig auftretende Gestalt ist der Teufel, der in erster Linie kein negatives Gegenbild ist, sondern vielmehr alles Böse in der Welt verkörpert. Eben deshalb ist er auch ein guter Lehrer.

Gott selbst ist in den Dramen nur durch sein Handeln an den Menschen gegenwärtig; in den Fällen, in denen Gott selbst auf der Szene in Erscheinung tritt, ist er eine auffallend passive Gestalt. Der Teufel, seine Dämonen sowie die Engel Gottes bilden in den Theaterstücken hingegen die aktiven transzendetalen Wesen.[464]

Am deutlichsten tritt der Teufel als Lehrer im Drama *Judas Redivivus* (1614) in Erscheinung, wo er den Epilog übernimmt, der dem Publikum die Moral des Stückes erklärt. Das Theaterstück endet damit, dass der Teufel in der Gestalt Karicks dem Publikum darlegt, was geschehen wird, wenn man dem Beispiel des bösen Judas folgt: Höllenstrafen! Alle, die ihre Eltern missachten und alle, die nicht treu der Obrigkeit dienen, werden in der Hölle enden.

Dasselbe Schicksal erwartet die Kinder und jungen Menschen, die sich weigern, gezüchtigt zu werden und sich nicht zu moralischem Handeln erziehen lassen. Karick nutzt übrigens in diesem Zusammenhang auch die Gelegenheit alle aufzuzählen, die böse Diener lieben und Pfarrer hassen; diese alle werden letztlich beim Teufel landen. Das Drama endet mit folgenden Worten:

> In summa alla dem som synder göra
> Plägar jag gärna till helvetet föra
> Jag vill med er ej ha något långt tal,
> Vakta var och en sig för helvetets kval.
> Och eftersom det nu lider mot kväll
> Klappa med era händer och farväl.[465]

Die Tugenden, die vorbildliche Personen in den Dramen auszeichnet – und die den weniger vorbildlichen fehlen – sind oftmals an das soziale Verhalten gekoppelt. Hiermit werden also Themen aufgegriffen, die im konfessionellen

---

463 Savin, Klädnader, 39–40, 49–50, 79, 131 & 140.

464 Berntson, Lärare.

465 Rondeletius, Judas 1871, 108. (*In Summa: Alle die Sündigen werde ich gerne in die Hölle geleiten. Ich werde euch keine lange Rede halten, Hütet euch alle vor den Qualen der Hölle. Da es nun Abend wird: Applaudiert und nehmt Abschied.*)

Zeitalter auch z. B. in der Haustafel thematisiert wurden. Wie bereits oben bemerkt, ist moralisches Handeln häufig mit der Vorstellung der guten Ehe verbunden. Hierbei geht es nicht nur darum, wie wichtig es für einen Mann ist, eine gute und christliche Ehegattin zu wählen, sondern auch darum, insgesamt eine tugendhafte Einstellung zur Ehe als Solches zu haben. Hauptaufgabe des Ehestandes und des Sexualaktes ist es insbesondere, die Gesellschaft mit Nachwuchs zu versehen.

Im Drama *Tobie Comedia* (1550) treffen wir den tugendhaften Tobit und seinen mindestens ebenso tugendreichen Sohn Tobias. Als Letzterer mit seiner Ehefrau Sara zu Bett gehen will, deren frühere sieben Männer auf demselben Brautlager gestorben waren, wird die Einsicht vermittelt, dass die Ehe nur dann etwas Heiliges ist, wenn sie aus der rechten Einstellung heraus resultiert und wenn sie zum Zweck geführt wird, dass sich der Mensch fortpflanzt. Um demselben Schicksal wie Saras vorherige Ehemänner zu entgehen, sorgt Tobias dafür, dass er und seine Gattin zunächst drei Nächte lang Gott anrufen und um Schutz und Gnade bitten. Nachdem Tobias durch diese Gebete bezeugt hat, dass er nicht aus Unkeuschheit zur Ehe getrieben ist, sondern allein aus dem Grund, Kinder zu bekommen, die ihrerseits dazu erzogen werden sollen, Gott zu dienen, geht er erst in der vierten Nacht zu seiner Braut und zeugt Kinder – und überlebt.[466]

Wie wichtig es ist, die Ehe unter frommen Voraussetzungen einzugehen, zeigt sich auch in der Haupthandlung des Dramas *Rebecca* (1674). Die hier erzählte Geschichte wie Abraham seinen Sohn Isaak verheiratet, handelt von der Bedeutung, dass der Sohn eine fromme Frau aus der eigenen Heimat heiratet und nicht eine heidnische Frau aus der Lokalbevölkerung – gleichgültig wie hübsch letztere sein mag. Bereits in der ersten Szene des Dramas betont Abraham seinem Sohn gegenüber, dass es eine Grundvoraussetzung für die Bewahrung von Gottesfurcht und Gehorsam ist, dass er mit einer tugendreichen Frau zusammengegeben wird, die ihn nicht zu Abgötterei und moralisch zweifelhaften Sitten verführt. Selbstverständlich erweist sich Rebecka als die ideale Gattin, die praktisch alle Tugenden auf sich vereint und zudem auch hübsch ist.[467]

Teil des Ehestandes zu werden, handelt in dieser Hinsicht in erster Linie um Reproduktion. Waren die Kinder dann geboren, war es wichtig, diese richtig zu erziehen, d. h., dass sie nicht selbstverliebt bzw. „selbstherrlich" wurden. Das gesamte Theaterstück *Judas Redivivus* (1614), das einer der bemerkenswertesten

466 Hesselman, Skrifter, Bd. 4, 427.

467 Beronius, Rebecka, 329 & 367.

Beiträge zu diesem Genre darstellt, widmet sich explizit dieser wichtigen Gesellschaftsfrage. Die Moral dieses Dramas ist einfach: In ihrer Kindheit sind Kinder ordentlich zu züchtigen, um zu verhindern, dass sie während sie heranwachsen selbstverliebt und gemeinschaftsgefährdend werden.

Dieses moralische Motiv wird durch eine Erzählung von Judas exemplifiziert, die auf mittelalterlichen Legenden basiert. Zentrale Motive in diesem Drama wurden sowohl diesen Legenden der Geschichte von Moses als auch der von König Ödipus entlehnt. In Kürze so beinhaltet diese Legende, dass die biologischen Eltern von Judas ihn in einem Korb im Wasser aussetzen, der zur Insel Skariot getrieben wird. Dort wird er von einem Königspaar adoptiert, er selbst weiß jedoch nicht, dass er ein Adoptivkind ist. Nachdem er seinen jüngeren Bruder getötet hat, begibt er sich nach Jerusalem, wo er ohne Absicht auch seinen biologischen Vater tötet und sich mit seine Mutter verheiratet. Als er dessen gewahr wird, was er getan hat, schließt er sich in der Legende (nicht jedoch im Theaterstück) Jesus und seinen Jüngern an; die darauffolgende Handlung folgt den Texten der Evangelien.

Insgesamt folgt das Theaterstück der Grundstruktur der Legende, allerdings mit einem wesentlichen Unterschied: Judas trifft weder Jesus noch die Jünger, sondern tut Dienst bei Pontius Pilatus in Jerusalem. Anstatt bei den Jüngern Buße zu tun, geht er in ein Kloster in Jerusalem, verrät schließlich die Mönche und sorgt dafür, dass das Kloster geschlossen wird. Ergriffen von der Einsicht in sein sündiges Handeln begeht Judas – in Anlehnung an die Texte der Evangelien – Selbstmord.

Die Morallehre dieses Stücks ist Folgende: Die Adoptiveltern von Judas, insbesondere sein Vater, erzogen ihn viel zu weich. Obwohl er schon in seiner Kindheit boshafte Ansätze Bedienten und Schulkameraden gegenüber aufwies, wurde er von seinem Vater nur verwöhnt, anstatt dass dieser ihn ordentlich züchtigte und ihn damit zu einem besseren Menschen machte. Judas war also nicht zwangsläufig dazu prädestiniert, Böses zu tun – er hätte als Kind nur mehr Prügel benötigt. Interessanterweise repräsentieren in diesem Drama durchgängig die Frauen die harte – und dem Verfasser zu Folge richtige – Einstellung in der Erziehung der Kinder. Sowohl Judas´ biologischer Vater als auch sein Ziehvater werden hingegen negativ gezeichnet, als allzu weiche Personen.

Die Betonung des tugendhaften Handels für verschiedene Beziehungen in der Gesellschaft interagiert auf vielfache Art und Weise mit dem Prozess der Konfessionalisierung. Anderes passt allerdings weniger gut in das Bild des nachkonkordistischen Luthertums oder in die Schablone der „lutherischen Orthodoxie“: die Vorstellung von der Inspiration der Bibel. In verschiedenen Überblicksdarstellungen zur Lehre und dem Gebrauch der Bibel während der schwedischen Großmachtzeit wird die Lehre von der Verbalinspiration hervorgehoben, die zudem eine Abgrenzung gegenüber der Verwendung von nichtbiblischem Material zur Interpretation der Bibel implizieren sollte.[468]

Im Drama wird die Bibel gerne als normativer Kompass für die Jugend herangezogen. Im Theaterstück *Filius prodigus* (1645) darf der verlorene Sohn auf seinem Weg aus dem Heimatland beispielsweise eine Bibel mit sich tragen, der er zu folgen ermahnt wird und nach der er sein Leben ausrichten soll.[469] Ein deutlicher Ausdruck für seinen Abfall ist allerdings, dass er seine Bibel einem böse gesonnenen Jesuiten gibt, der der Meinung ist, dass der gemeine Mann dies Buch nicht lesen soll. Zu diesem Zeitpunkt hat der verlorene Sohn bereits alles durch Spiel und schlechte Sitten verloren. Die Weggabe der Bibel – und das Versprechen in ein Jesuitenkolleg einzutreten – ist das Letzte, das geschieht bevor er schlussendlich dazu gezwungen wird, eine Anstellung als Schweinehirt anzunehmen.[470] Allerdings gibt es in diesem Drama keinerlei Belege für eine Vorstellung von der Verbalinspiration. Im Gegenteil ist es überraschend wie frei die Verfasser des Stückes sich zu den biblischen Vorlagen stellten.

In der Dichtung und im Drama des Barock war es nicht ungewöhnlich, dass Gestalten aus der griechisch-römischen Mythologie einen Platz einnahmen, obwohl die Werke christlichen Motiven verpflichtet waren.[471] In Samuel Petri Brasks (1613–1668) Drama *Mars Germanicus Victus* (1649) wird der Dreißigjährige Krieg dramatisch gestaltet (Fig. 11). Allerdings trägt nicht das Papsttum die Hauptschuld am Krieg, sondern die mystische Gestalt der Rachegöttin Erynnis sowie die Götter Mars und Pluto. Im Drama werden zudem die historischen Gestalten Gustav II. Adolf und Christina zu den mythologischen Figuren Hercules und Diva Sepentrionalis umgewandelt, die ihrerseits mit den Personifizierungen geographischer Orte – Germania und Europa – interagieren.[472]

Auf eine ähnliche Art und Weise werden in anderen Theaterstücken die personifizierten Tugenden verwendet, um den biblischen Inhalt zu bereichern. Im Drama *Thet Himmelska Consistorium* (Das himmlische Konsistorium, 1674) spielt die Handlung am himmlischen Hofstaat wo Gott und die Engel beschließen, wie sie sich gegenüber dem Menschen verhalten sollen, der kürzlich den Sündenfall begangen hat. Die verschiedenen Engel nehmen wie in einer Gerichtsverhandlung rechts und links von Gottvater Platz. Linker Hand sitzen

468 Ingebrand, Bibeltolkningen, 169, 173–178. Brilioth, Predikan, 121. Burgess, Interpretation, 105. Hagen, Scripture.

469 Samuel P. Brask, Filius prodigus, seu imperitus peregrinans. Thet är een comoedia om then förlorade sonen, eller een oförfaren wandringzman [...] Och hållen i Linköpingz pedersmässo marknadh XXIX Junij 1645 (Linköping: Christopher Günther, 1645), 13.

470 Brask, Filius prodigus, seu imperitus peregrinans, 64–65.

471 Platen, Bländverk, 58.

472 Brask, Mars 1878, 227.

die „weicheren" Eigenschaften Gottes, der Friede, die Einigkeit, die Freundlichkeit, die Gnade, die Milde, der Langmut und der Sachtmut sowie die Güte. Rechts sitzen die „härteren" Eigenschaften, die Rechtfertigkeit, die Strenge, die Beständigkeit, die Heiligkeit und die Wahrheit.

Im Gerichtssaal tritt auch der Verteidiger des Elends des Menschengeschlechts auf sowie selbstverständlich der als Ankläger agierende Lucifer. Die Handlung des Dramas ist davon geprägt, dass die verschiedenen Eigenschaften Gottes für oder gegen eine harte Strafe des Menschen plädieren. Gott selbst äußert sich erst gegen Ende des Dramas. Er zeigt sich deutlich von der Rede des Elends für den Menschen bewegt und begnadigt – zu Lucifers großem Verdruss – den Menschen. Dieses Drama soll interessanterweise eine Reihe Zwischenakte gehabt haben, in denen als Balett Cupido, Bacchus, Venus und andere mythologische Gestalten auftraten.[473]

In ähnlicher Form treffen wir in Josephus Svenonis Chærberus (gest. 1651) *Itt gudeligit samtaal* (Ein göttliches Gespräch, 1642) den himmlischen Saal, diesmal aber mit den Akteuren Rechtfertigkeit, Wahrheit, Frieden und Barmherzigkeit.[474] Diesem Drama liegt übrigens die Legende von den vier Töchtern zu Grunde, die ihren Ursprung in einer jüdischen Midrash aus dem 5. Jahrhundert hat und während des 12. Jahrhunderts von Hugo von Sankt Viktor und Bernhard von Clairvaux weiterentwickelt wurde. In Sonderheit Bernhards Interpretation wurde für ein weit verbreitetes Drama genutzt. Chærberus unterstreicht deutlich, dass der Text auf ein Gedicht "des heiligen Kirchenlehrers" Bernhard von Clairvaux zurückgeht.[475]

Wie man sieht, war es nicht immer von Bedeutung, eine klare Trennungslinie zwischen biblischem Material und anderen Erzählungen zu ziehen. Bei den Theaterstücken, die neutestamentliche Motive verarbeiten, finden sich mehrere Beispiele dafür, dass die Verfasser nicht sehr daran interessiert waren, die Grenze zwischen dem eigentlichen Bibeltext und jüngerem Legendenstoff zu betonen.

Das Drama *Simon Magus* (1652) handelt von Simon dem Magier, von dem das achte Kapitel der Apostelgeschichte berichtet. Der Inhalt des Theaterstücks ist allerdings in erster Linie der apokryphen Legende von Simons bösen Taten in Rom entlehnt, die erst relativ spät nach der biblischen Erzählung verfasst wurde und in einer frühen Variante in den in der zweiten Hälfte des zweiten Jahrhunderts niedergeschriebenen Petrusakten überliefert ist.

---

473 Komedi (Inhaltswiedergabe von Petrus Carstenius, "I Jesu nampn! Amen. Thet himmelska consistorium, tilhoopa kallat").

474 Chærberus, Samtaal 1876, 210.

475 Hansellis Vorwort in Vitterhetsarbeten, 203–204.

Auf dieselbe Art und Weise vermengt auch Samuel Petri Brasks umfangreiches Drama *Acta et martyria apostolorum* (1648) das biblische Material der Apostelgeschichte mit jüngerem Legendenstoff. Das Drama eröffnet zwar mit der Mission des Paulus und anderer Apostel und schließt damit direkt an die Apostelgeschichte an. Ohne dies zu markieren, werden sodann aber spätere Legenden verarbeitet wie z. B. die Mission des Apostels Andreas in Skythien, die des Apostels Thomas in Mesopotamien oder das Martyrium des Mattias in Äthiopien.[476]

Wie bereits erwähnt, wird das Drama *Judas Redivivus* (1614) vollständig aus mittelalterlichem Legendenstoff gespeist; ein neutestamentlicher Kern existiert in der Figur des verräterischen Judas, die größtenteils aus der mittelalterlichen Legendenbildung von der Jugend und dem Leben des Judas berichtet. Die bekannteste Version dieser Geschichte findet sich in der von Jacobus de Voragine († 1298) zusammengestellten *Legenda aurea,* in welcher die Judas-Figur sowohl an die Gestalt des Moses als auch die des König Ödipus angelehnt erscheint.[477]

Als ein letztes Beispiel kann hier auf das im letzten Jahrzehnt des 16. Jahrhunderts entstandene Drama *Belial ex inferno* verwiesen werden. Dieses Drama handelt von dem Rechtsprozess gegen Jesus, der vom Dämon Belial initiiert wurde.[478] Das Drama baut auf einer Legende auf, die beispielsweise in dem im Jahr 1483 gedruckten und von Jacobus de Teramo (1349–1417) verfassten Buch *Cy commence le Procès de Belial à l'encontre de Jhésus* (deutsch etwa "Hier beginnt Belials Prozess gegen Jesus“) überliefert ist.

In den hier vorgestellten Dramen war es also nicht besonders wichtig, dass die Verfasser dem Bibeltext strikt folgten. Wie ihre mittelalterlichen Vorläufer so verhielten sie sich tatsächlich sehr frei zu dem Bibelstoff und gestalteten ihn ähnlich frei wie Motive aus der antiken Mythologie. Inspiriert von sowohl mittelalterlichen Traditionen wie der vom Humanismus hoch geschätzten antiken Dichtung, konnten die Verfasser auf relativ spielerische Art und Weise mit dem Bibeltext umgehen.

Für die Verfasser der Dramen war es – im Unterschied zu unserer Zeit, die sich auf der anderen Seite der Aufklärung befindet – nicht von Bedeutung, zu einer dunklen Vorzeit vorzustoßen und herauszufinden wie die Dinge sich wirklich verhielten. Zudem sollte daran erinnert werden, dass in der Zeit vor der Aufklärung die Distanz zwischen Bibeltext und seinem Leser weitaus geringer war. Zwar waren die Dramenverfasser sich dessen bewusst, dass sie in einer

476 Brask, Acta 1878, 147–177, 182–188.

477 Rondeletius, Judas 1614.

478 Belial 1864, 25–27.

anderen Zeit als der biblischen lebten, sie sahen aber keine Notwendigkeit dafür, eine Distanz zum Bibeltext herzustellen.

Vielmehr müssen diese Texte als ein Ausdruck dafür verstanden werden, eine Moraltradition und Dogmatik auszudrücken, die mit vielfältigen Mitteln letztendlich nicht nur die Schuljugend, sondern auch alle anderen bilden sollte. Die vermutlich gut bekannten biblischen Erzählungen wurden zur Vermittlung moralischen Wissens benutzt. Dies setzte allerdings voraus, dass die Zuschauer bzw. die Leser abstrakt denken konnten, also hinter die Fassade der reinen Dramenhandlung blicken konnten und im Stande waren, das zu vermittelnde grundlegende Wissen zu dechiffrieren. Eine derartige Verwendung des Bibelstoffes ist freilich kein Alleinstellungsmerkmal für das konfessionelle Luthertum, sondern erinnert deutlich an das Schultheater des Mittelalters und das zeitgenössische Jesuitendrama.

Einer der bedeutenderen Momente der lutherischen Konfessionskultur ist der antikatholische Impetus. In einigen Stücken wurden Katholiken als Negativbilder eingebaut; diese Figuren haben aber nur selten einen besonderen Stellenwert. Im Drama *Filius Prodigus* täuscht ein böser Jesuit die Hauptperson, aber das Ziel ist hier nicht in erster Linie ein negatives Bild von Katholiken zu vermitteln, sondern vornehmlich auf den gefallenen Zustand des verlorenen Sohnes hinzuweisen.[479] In gleicher Art und Weise gibt es Negativbilder vom Papst und den Jesuiten in *Mars Germanicus*. Aber – wie bereits aufgezeigt – so ist es nicht das Hauptanliegen, die Katholiken als Verursacher des „Teutschen Krieges" anzuklagen. Stattdessen wird der Krieg als ein nach homerischem Modell gestaltetes Spiel heidnischer Gottheiten dargestellt.

Fazit

Die frühneuzeitlichen schwedischen Schuldramen passen relativ gut zu Lotz-Heumanns und Pohligs Beschreibung deutscher Schultheaterstücke als „konfessionelle Literatur". Ähnlich wie ihre deutschen Entsprechungen waren die Dramen deutlich an einer verbalen Argumentation in der Volkssprache orientiert und unterschieden sich damit in gewissen Sinne von dem eher an den menschlichen Sinnen orientierten Theater der Jesuiten. Allerdings muss beachtet werden, dass unser Wissen von der für – zumindest für die schwedischen – Dramen verwendeten Szenographie, den Requisiten und der Musik durchaus fragmentarisch ist. Wie auch Lotz-Heumann und Pohlig feststellen, so

479 Brask, Filius, 13.

bestand das konfessionelle Moment nicht vornehmlich in konfessioneller Polemik oder der Aktualisierung von Dogmen, sondern im moralischen Duktus der Theaterstücke.

Diesbezüglich existiert eine Reihe von Schnittstellen zum Jesuitentheater, das ebenfalls häufig die Aufgabe hatte, Schauspieler wie Publikum zu bilden und somit zu einem frommen und tugendreichen Leben zu ermahnen. Die generellen Unterschiede zum Jesuitendrama sind daran zu erkennen, welche Moralfragen die Stücke inszenierten. In den schwedischen Theaterstücken werden z. B. regelmäßig Fragen der Eheanbahnung, Liebe und Kindererziehung diskutiert. Dies war im Jesuitentheater so nicht der Fall, das – so es den Regeln folgte – weder romantische Liebe, noch Frauenrollen umfassen sollte.

Sodann scheinen die schwedischen Theaterstücke eine deutliche innerweltliche Ausrichtung zu besitzen: Tugenreiches Handeln wird bereits in diesem Leben belohnt, während das Jesuitentheater im Anschluss an die mittelalterliche Jenseitsfürsorge, die u. a. auch Exempelpredigten prägte, anschloss und oftmals auf außerweltliche Belohnungen verwies. Diese Unterschiede sind doch alles andere als verwunderlich. Belohnung für tugendreiches Handeln in dieser Welt ist kein Topos, der im Widerstreit zur lutherischen Theologie steht. Demgegenüber wäre es im Rahmen einer lutherischen Konfessionskultur durchaus kompliziert die Idee zu vermitteln, dass tugendreiches Handeln zum ewigen Leben führen könnte.

Was lehrt uns ein Studium der frühneuzeitlichen schwedischen Theaterstücke mit Hinblick auf die Theologie des konfessionellen Zeitalters in Schweden? Meines Erachtens nuancieren diese Theaterstücke unsere noch immer recht stereotypen Auffassungen des konfessionellen Zeitalters, die darauf abheben, dass es nur um mechanisches Pauken eines rein lutherisch-dogmatisch geprägten Wissens ging, das zudem seinen Ausgangspunkt in einer buchstabengetreuen Bibellektüre hatte.

Zu aller erst ist es ein bedeutungsvolles Faktum, dass Dramen als Instrument des Lernens fungierten. Eine wichtige Vermittlungsfunktion hatten im Konfessionalisierungsprozess selbstverständlich die Predigt und das Memorieren katechetischer Kenntnisse; die Bedeutung estetischer Wirkmittel wie Kirchengesang, Kunst und Theater wird demhingegen häufig vergessen. Die Betonung des tugendhaften christlichen Lebens, die wir in einer Reihe von Dramen antreffen, die Bedeutung der Bemühungen, Gott durch unsere Handlungen zu erreichen und zu bewegen deuten darauf hin, welche wichtige Rolle der aktiven christlichen Lebensführung in der lutherischen Theologie des konfessionellen Zeitalters zukam. Dies wiederspricht übrigens nicht der Vorstellung, dass der Mensch im Prozess der Rechtfertigung Gott gegenüber völlig passiv ist. Weiterhin ist bemerkenswert, wie frei sich die Dramen dem Bibelstoff gegenüber verhalten: Wie oben ausgeführt, wurde es als völlig unproblematisch angesehen, dass die Autoren z. B. neue Intrigen in ein biblisches Drama einfügten oder dass sie biblische Texte mit Legendenstoff vereinten. Mit Hinblick auf das gängige Bild einer am Alten Testament und dem Gesetz orientierten „lutherischen Orthodoxie" ist es diesbezüglich auch bedeutsam darauf zu verweisen, wie fließend die Grenzen zwischen Altem und Neuen Testament sein konnten.

Zu guter Letzt ist es interessant, die oftmals burlesken und grobkörnigen humoristischen Züge vieler Dramen zu betrachten. Gerade diese sollten das oftmals von der „lutherischen Orthodoxie" vermittelte Bild als eine dunkle, langweilige und trostlose Zeit nuancieren können. Die burlesken Züge, auch in Kombination mit der deutlichen innerweltlichen Orientierung der Theaterstücke, machen vermutlich die wichtigste Akzentverschiebung zu sowohl der spätmittelalterlichen als auch der pietistischen Frömmigkeit aus, bei welcher der Fokus deutlicher auf außerweltliche Dinge gerichtet erscheint, gerne auch in Kombination mit einer nachdrücklichen Weltverachtung. Der spirituelle Sitz im Leben der Theaterstücke ist vielmehr eine Wertschätzung des Lebens im Hier und Jetzt: der Glaubende wird dazu aufgefordert ein guter Mitmensch zu sein, seine Berufung zu schätzen und zu leben. Dies schließt allerdings nicht aus, dass er auch lachen, gut essen und trinken und die „wunderbaren Umstände", die ein Theaterstück ausmachen, genießen sollte.

Aus dem Schwedischen von Otfried Czaika

Tuija Laine

Mystics, Separatists and Ordinary Lutheran Readers and Writers

Book Culture and Reading Among the Finnish Commoners from the 17th to the 19th Centuries

Introduction

In this article, I shall examine the reading and writing of common people from the 17th to the 19th centuries in Finland. Three different stages can be seen in the development of reading and reading habits in the premodern time, which I shall present here. Among the common people, there were both ordinary Lutheran believers and Pietists, as well as separatists, who were interested, for example, in mystical texts. My aim is to show that even commoners considered reading and religious texts to be important and that they understood them in different ways, depending on their education and social context.

The meaning of the term "literacy" is different in Finnish from in English. In Finland, writing was not seen as very important; in fact, on the contrary, it was even regarded as a potentially harmful luxury for common people who did not need it. Reading was seen as very important, however, because everybody's right and duty was to study the basic knowledge of Christianity. For that reason, literacy came to mean reading, not writing. In my article, I use "literacy" in this Finnish sense of the word.

The first stage of literacy until the first decades of the 18th century – from reading by heart towards reading from the book step by step

For a long time, the Church and the upper classes in an ambition to civilize the common people as a group, not individual subjects, primarily addressed book culture for the commoners. In the early modern period, book culture belonged mostly to learned men, and from the 18th century onwards more and more for the bourgeoisie as well. With the Reformation, the literacy of peasants was underlined, and from the 16th century, there were even books printed in vernacular languages, because Luther promoted the idea of everybody's duty to read the word of God by themselves. In Finland, then the eastern part of the

Swedish realm, this led in the 1540s and 1550s to the translation into Finnish of the most basic religious books by the reformer Mikael Agricola (1510–1557): a primer (1543), a book of prayers (1544) and the New Testament (1548), as well as some parts of the Old Testament (1551–1552). Agricola's *Abckiria* was the first Finnish primer, but it still aimed at the clergy in order to help them use basic religious texts in Finnish in the same textual and oral form as in their Swedish or Latin teaching and preaching. Hardly any peasants owned the book.[480]

The first remarkable literacy campaign took place in the Swedish realm in the last decades of the 17th century. The Bishop of Turku Johannes Gezelius the Elder (1615–1690) oversaw this campaign in Finland. Even before Gezelius, however, there had been bishops who were interested in the education of the commoners. For example, the Bishop of Turku Ericus Erici Sorolainen (1546–1625) published a small catechism, as well as a larger version, and a collection of sermons in two parts, all in Finnish. Gezelius' ambitions were much more extensive. He was very goal-oriented in developing the education of country folk, schoolchildren and the clergy. Gezelius wrote and published on his own printing press many basic religious books: a catechism, a hymnal and the Bible, as well as a lot of schoolbooks and sermon aids for the clergy. His catechism, published in 1666 in both Finnish and Swedish, ran into over 60 Finnish editions until the first years of the 19th century (*Ett rätt barna-klenodium*, Fig. 12). It was the most used catechism in Finland during the 17th century and the first half of the 18th century, and many elderly people were allowed to use it even after that, because they knew its formulation. Gezelius also wrote and published many instructions on teaching the catechism, organization of the school system, and education of the common people.[481]

Bishop Gezelius also published on his printing press for the first time forms for church examination registers. Before that, priests had only handwritten registers to use. The Swedish and Finnish system of keeping church examination registers of all persons who could read their catechisms provides us with extensive sources for the research of literacy in Finland from the end of the 17th to the first decades of the 20th century. The teaching of literacy and the catechism was primarily the task of parents, not the school, and the ability to write was not considered as necessary for the peasantry as in many other countries. The most important reason for learning to read was that it opened the door to knowledge of the Scriptures and Christianity. The task of the priesthood was not to teach

---

480 Heininen, Mikael Agricola, 156–157.

481 Tuija Laine, Johannes Gezelius, 382 & 398–399. Esko Laine/Tuija Laine, Kirkollinen, 274. More about Finnish 17th-century religious education in Tuija Laine, *Finnish primary religious books from the sixteenth*, *Aapisen*, and *Finnish primary religious books from the seventeenth*.

but to examine literacy and the knowledge of Christianity gained through the catechism; according to the Swedish Church law of 1686, only a literate person could attend the Holy Eucharist, marry or become a godparent.[482]

In the early decades of the 17th century, Ericus Erici's catechism was used, but after the publication of Gezelius' catechism, it came to be regularly employed in church examinations. Written from a pedagogical point of view, Gezelius' catechism consisted of four parts: a primer, the catechism itself, an examination of questions of Christian doctrine, and a collection of Bible verses. The first part was the easiest. When it had been mastered, the pupil was ready to continue to the next, more demanding section. Children who learned quickly taught the others. For the sake of the unity of the realm, the Swedish King Charles XI. ordered the catechism (1689) by Archbishop Olaus Svebilius (1624–1700) to be used for learning Christianity and in Church examinations. However, Bishop Daniel Juslenius only translated it into Finnish in 1745, and therefore it cannot be considered as having been in common use before that.[483]

During Gezelius' period in the Swedish realm, there was an emphasis on reading comprehension. Reading by heart often caused misunderstandings of read texts when readers could not remember memorized sentences in the right way. That is why Gezelius underlined reading from the book. It helped understanding and it made it possible to concentrate more on the content of the text read. Gezelius also encouraged people to acquire and read more good books than the catechism in order to improve their literacy skills as well as their knowledge of the Christian faith. As examples of these, he mentioned hymnals, prayer books, Johann Gerhard's *Pyhät tutkistelemuxet* (Meditationes sacrae) and Nicolaus Hunnius' *Epitome Credendorum*. Despite Gezelius exhortations and active work in publishing basic religious books, there were few books in the homes of peasants during his time.[484] Literacy among the common people was still weak, and the meaning and advantages of literacy were not yet very clear for them. The situation became better only in the last half of the 18th century. Gezelius' active work in the education of the common people had laid a good foundation for its development throughout the 18th century.

James Blakeley has pointed out that the major part of the rural population in early modern Europe was unaware of theological differences between the emerging confessions. Although pastors had been preaching in the parishes for decades, early ignorance maintained.[485] This held true also in the eastern

---

482 Johansson, Alfabetiseringen, 6. Johansson, Literacy, 28–30, 39–40.

483 Tuija Laine, Johannes Gezelius, 381–399, 382 & 398–399. Esko Laine/Tuija Laine, Kirkollinen, 274.

484 Gezelius, Methodus informandi 1683, A4r. Commonitiones (1673) 1791, 302–303.

485 Blakeley, Confronting, 101–117.

part of the Swedish realm. The efforts of Gezelius and his predecessors in their educational work were aimed only at reading ability. His entire enterprise was motivated by the theological or pious purposes of the Reformation. As far as known, Gezelius did not have neither conscious political passions nor any other purposes to strive. As a man of a *via media,* he avoided extremisms of all kind in his life time, both in theology and in social or political issues. The Lutheran Catechisms, however, consisted of not only the Ten Commandments, the Apostle's Creed, Our Lord, sacraments and prayers but also of instructions, a Table of duties, how the commoners were expected to behave themselves in various occasions. Gezelius himself, as well as his predecessor Ericus Erici had done before, left the Table of duties out of his version of the Catechism, not because of political reasons but because he wanted to reserve the capacity of uneducated commoners for reading the main articles of Lutheran Faith.

The catechism written by Gezelius was, however, not the only one of its kind in Sweden. Most of the Catechism authorized in the Swedish Realm contained the Table of duties and the Bible citations, which determined in detail the duties of husbands and wives, servants and children and required both discipline and industriousness, self-termination and ability to subordinate oneself. Not only the sporadic commandments but also the entire mentality of the latter chapters of the typical Lutheran catechisms reflected the spirit of confessionalism: authority, discipline and unwillingness to compromise. They expressed the limits of the allowed and the prohibited. They indicated the right faith but also what was regarded unacceptable and foreign to the Lutheran way of life. Reading the Catechism simply opened the gates for the political influence of the common people. By learning how to read, the peasants in Finland were exposed to the political intensions of the Crown in a way that was never seen before. By forcing the peasantry to attend church weekly and read their catechisms by heart, the temporal power could, in the long run, achieve its goals: the political and confessional unity. From the perspective of the King and government, the political indoctrination in a spirit of confessionalism and the Gospel, the religious message of justification and of grace alone in Catechism were the two sides of a coin.

The second stage – emergence of literacy and books, even for children

During the 18th century, both literacy and the supply of books in Finnish increased. Although the king had ordered the official catechisms to be used in church and in examinations during the Swedish Era, many other catechisms, often representing different religious persuasions, sects or revivalist movements, were also published and used in parishes and private devotions during the last decades of the 18th century.[486] These catechisms are not necessarily identified in the communion books, but we can obtain information on them and their use from estate inventory deeds, as well as minutes kept during visitations executed by deans and bishops.

Teaching Christianity to children became important in Finland during the 18th century for several reasons. By then, a large number of parents were already able to read and thus were in a better position to teach their children. Furthermore, when the Church no longer needed to worry about adults' knowledge of Christianity, it could concentrate its efforts on children. However, not all children in the 17th and 18th centuries had the possibility of going to school. Many schools were located in towns and cities, and they were often intended for middle- and upper-class children. In some countries (e.g. Denmark and Russia), there were also peasant schools; nevertheless, peasant children were mostly taught at home, usually by their mothers. Giving children a basic education in reading and Christianity was common practice in many countries, and children had the possibility of continuing their education later at school. In Sweden, church law ordered parents to teach their children to read and learn their catechism. Only if parents were incapable of doing that were they allowed to receive help from the Church. For everybody in the Swedish realm, reading skills and knowing the catechism were preconditions for attending the Eucharist and getting married.[487]

In general, the 18th century is characterized by the rise of children's literature. In the Swedish realm, this trend was first seen in catechisms. Four different catechisms were published in Finnish for teaching Christianity to children. The German Pietist Johann Jakob Rambach (1693–1735) wrote one of them, while the three others were composed by Swedish vicars and bishops, Daniel Godenius (1702–1768), Olof Gråberg (1716–1767) and Johan Möller (1738–1805) and translated from Swedish. Daniel Godenius' and Olof Gråberg's catechisms were planned to be used together, because Godenius only included the basics, while Gråberg went further with his teaching. Godenius' catechism, which was targeted at very small children, was based on mothers teaching children to memorize sentences by heart. Based on the number of published editions, Godenius and Gråberg were more popular in Sweden than in Finland, whereas John Möller's catechism was widely used in Finland, especially in the 19th century. In fact, Möller wrote three different versions for different levels, of which only the intermediate text was translated into Finnish.[488]

---

486 Tuija Laine, Uskonnollisen. Tuija Laine, Aapisen, 98.

487 Laasonen, Johannes Gezelius, 269–272. Eklof, Schools, 19–49. Heywood, Growing up, 132. Appel, Printed in Books, 71. Appel/Fink-Jensen, Introduction, 6–8.

488 Tuija Laine, Aapisen, 98–113.

Auction catalogues and estate inventory deeds show that these catechisms, even those of Godenius and Gråberg, were read in different parts of Finland. Unfortunately, the sources cannot tell us about the children who owned them, only about the adults, but it is certain that they were purchased either when their current owners themselves were still children or for their own children. In addition, some of the owners were teachers who used catechisms at work. It is interesting to see that these catechisms for children are mentioned in the sources so often (16 matches together), even though they were not official textbooks on Christianity at that time. The official catechism, written by Bishop Olaus Svebilius in 1689, is mentioned 52 times. In church examinations, which were conducted by priests and sometimes even bishops, it was primarily adults' reading skills and knowledge of Christianity that was investigated; however, children were also questioned. Children's skills were recorded in so-called "children's books", handwritten books with information on the child's name, date of birth and his/her reading skills.[489]

At the turn of the 18th century, for the Lutheran orthodoxy Christianity meant not only the Lutheran doctrine, but also a Christian life. For those attending Eucharist for the first time, inner devotion, understanding of reading, and applying Christianity in one's life were underlined even before the advent of Pietism. Pietism, on the other hand, emphasized the meaning of personal piety and faith.[490]

Already in the Catholic time, knowledge of some Christian texts was required of the attendees of the Eucharist. During the time of Bishop Gezelius the Younger (1647–1718), in the last decade of the 17th and the beginning of the 18th century, attendees were examined several times. From the 1720s onwards, there were discussions in the diocese of Turku/Åbo on how to improve the understanding of the Eucharist – people often regarded the Eucharist as not much more than an external act and did not see it as a tool for personal transformation. All these discussions laid the basis for the formation of a confirmation school.[491]

One of the first places where attendees of their first Eucharist were taught more profoundly was Ilmajoki in Finnish Ostrobothnia. In 1735, teenagers were taught one week, with the ambition of following up with an even longer teaching period in spring. Those who could read and had learned their Christianity were taken together to the first Eucharist as a group. This system was called confirmation school, and it became common practice from 1740 in the diocese of Turku. The idea of the confirmation school was to strengthen knowledge of

---

489 Tala, Kirkon, 17–18. HENRIK: Daniel Godenius, Olof Gråberg.

490 Taipale, Rippikoulun, 145 & 230.

491 Kilström 1958, 80–81. Taipale, Rippikoulun, 155–156.

Christianity among the common people and to teach them that the Eucharist was not a formality (*opus operatum*). Because it was essential in confirmation school to know Christian doctrine, the publication of catechisms for teenagers was introduced in order to provide them with resources.[492]

Although it was important to learn to read from a book, memorizing by heart was seen as equally important. When children were very young, their mothers taught them prayers, songs and extracts from the Bible to be learned by heart. This was the first step towards reading, at least in England, France, Scandinavia and the English colonies in America. Even blind teachers could use this method. Often the teaching of children at home was the task of grandparents, who had time to teach children because they no longer had the strength to perform harder work, and their sight may already have been weakened. In Finland, many people – at least at first – learned their catechism by heart, so that they could answer the questions the priests asked them in catechism examinations. However, because repeating texts mechanically can prevent real understanding of the subject matter, it was deemed not only necessary to learn to read, but also to understand what had been read. Bishop Gezelius had underlined this already in the last half of the 17th century. When reading from a book became common practice among almost all parishioners, the Church started to stress reading by heart. Now those who learned texts by heart could check forgotten parts in the book, while the threat of misunderstanding and erroneous memorization was minimized as well. It was also possible to learn longer texts, if necessary, because no teacher was needed. This method had some advantages, people could meditate on Christian texts while working, and the poor no longer had the need to buy books. Remembering texts by heart allowed people to have a library with them in their heads wherever they went.[493]

In the Lutheran Church, there was also a long tradition of having meetings at parishioner's houses, reading devotional books, singing psalms and praying. These meetings were called "home devotions". The ideal was to hold home devotions regularly, but in fact, they were not very common, even though priests from time to time reminded parishioners to have them. Improving literacy, as well as having home devotions, required new books. The supply of religious books for common people was much larger in the 18th century, especially during its last decades, compared to earlier periods. It became common to have one's own hymnal in the church, and there could be several hymnals in the same house, as men and women had separate places in the church and both needed

492 Taipale, Rippikoulun, 156–157, 173–175 & 178–182. Laasonen, Historia, 329–331.

493 Laasonen, Johannes Gezelius, 262–263. Haynes, Bookshelf, 28. Jajdelska, Silent Reading, 130–132. Heywood, Growing Up, 132.

their own hymnals. Especially in Western Finland, where literary skills were greater than in the eastern part of the country, owning devotional literature was quite common, even in peasant families in the latter half of the 18th century. Thus, it is not surprising that a number of religious sects and groups with a special interest in reading were born in the western parts of Finland. In the last section of my article, I shall concentrate on them and new ideas of reading among the peasantry.

The third stage – new reading habits and new readers from the last decades of the 18th century

Although reading at first was not very popular among peasants, over the course of time, even they appreciated the new possibilities that it offered. At least some of them did. Already at the turn of the 17th century, Pietism spread from Germany through the Baltic region to Northern Europe. It required a personal attitude to religion, conversion and self-knowledge (*nosce te ipsum*). At the same time, devotional literature written by English puritans was being read in the Swedish realm. Both Pietism and Puritanism encouraged people to read for themselves. For these movements it was important that people had common meetings where they could read together and discuss religious questions. The new meetings differed from traditional "home devotions", because they gathered together people from different families. These meetings, which had their roots in the German *collegia pietatis* tradition, were called conventicles in Sweden. Conventicles were illegal from 1726 onwards. We do not know if the Pietists were interested in reading more than other people. The fact that we have more sources, which give us information about their reading habits, may be simply because they were often accused in court of holding heretical views.[494]

I shall here introduce some examples of the Finnish common people and peasants for whom reading not only meant a compulsory learning of the catechism by heart, but also had a more multi-faceted and deeper meaning. I shall concentrate on peasants in order to show that even in this group; we can find active and new kinds of reading, as well as extensive reading, rather than merely repeating old texts.

494 Hellekant, Uppbyggelselitteratur. Laasonen, Historia, 246–247 & 256. Esko Laine, Iltahetki Tukholmassa, 64–66. Wallmann, Pietismi, 124.

Separatist movements

From the point of view of the Church, it was necessary that people learned their catechism, but at the same time, it was very important that the books that people read were Lutheran or accepted by the Lutheran Church. In the case of Pietists, this did not always happen. Pietists read many Lutheran books, of course, but they also studied those written by members of different separatist movements. Some puritan and Pietistic books were purified by censors, removing chapters which emphasized Puritan or Pietistic ideas (for example, predestination or communities of real believers), but that did not always help. It was not possible to remove every anathema without in the process re-writing the very same books, and some books were so heretical that they did not make it past the censors. Because the censorship did not work so effectively, however, they were bought, copied and read among Pietists anyway.[495]

In the first decades of the 18th century, there were many religious awakenings in Finland. Some of them were ecstatic, and some did not accept the sacraments and order of the Lutheran Church. Usually these movements did not last very long; they were repressed by church authorities or they withered away. Nevertheless, these movements laid the ground for the Finnish revivalist movements of the 19th century.[496]

One of these groups was the movement of the Ericsson's brothers in Ostrobothnia in Western Finland, together with another separatist group there, which closely followed them. They looked down on Lutheran orthodoxy as a habit, rejected Christian baptism, waited for the end of the world and warned about the Eucharist of the Church, which could cause harm to those who ate it in an inappropriate way. They were also very critical towards the clergy, and they did not attend church services. These separatists justified their behaviour by saying that reading the Bible and the sermons of Martin Luther and Johann Arndt (1555–1621) at home gave them more consolation than listening to sermons of local priests in church. They said that they did not see any reason to attend services which caused them problems with their own conscience. They also read texts written by mystical spiritualists and radical Pietists, such as Jakob Böhme (1575–1624), John Pordage (1607–1681) and Gottfried Arnold (1666–1714).[497]

During interrogations in court, members of the movement were asked about the literature they had read. Most of them told that they had read the Bible

495 Nordstrandh, Litteratur.

496 Matthias Akiander mentions several religious movements from the 18th century; Akiander, Upplysningar.

497 Loimaranta, Erikssonien, 31–32, 34–36, 66, 288–289.

or just the New Testament; some, who probably could not read themselves or did not have their own copy of the Bible, had listened to Bible readings at illegal meetings. Although most of them owned and had read other books as well (e.g. popular books within Lutheran orthodoxy by authors such as Johann Gerhard and Johann Arndt, books by English authors (especially Arthur Dent (†1607) and books by mystical spiritualists such as Jakob Böhme and Thomas Bromley (1530–1587)), the Bible was most important, most read and most highly recommended by separatists.[498]

In 18th-century Finland, this was very exceptional, as we have seen. Very few peasants owned a Bible. The first Finnish Bible was printed in Stockholm in 1642, but in general it was owned only by parishes and some priests. In 1732, the second Finnish New Testament ever to be published after Mikael Agricola's first translation 1548 saw the light of day. In previous research, it has often been supposed that peasants acquired Scriptures only when the clergy sold or gave away their own Bibles and bought new ones. This cannot be the whole truth. Especially in Ostrobothnia (e.g. in Oulu, where there had also been some kind of separatist movement in the beginning of the 17th century), many peasants owned a Bible in 1661–1750. Because the third edition of the Bible was published only in 1758, it is unlikely that the clergy had given away their books before 1758. Peasants must have gotten their Bibles in the earlier phase as well.[499]

Separatists told the court that they had also read the New Testament only. Some of them could read Swedish or German, so it was possible that they read the whole Bible or the New Testament only in different languages. In many areas in Ostrobothnia, many inhabitants alongside Finnish spoke Swedish.[500]

It is clear that reading the Bible was crucial for Pietists, and especially for the before-mentioned separatist groups, because they wanted to interpret the Bible themselves and find support for their ideas. However, how did they use the Holy Scripture? In the view of the Pietists and separatists, the Bible was to be explained only to children, and parents were responsible for the education of their children. Children were taught because they could not interpret passages of the Bible by themselves. Adults were not taught, as the text of the Bible was held to be effective without teaching. The Holy Ghost taught everything necessary for the reader or the listener of the Bible. For this reason, from the perspective of separatists, listening to priests' sermons and teachings was harmful.[501]

---

498 Tuija Laine, Aapisen, 82–83.
499 Tuija Laine 2003, 30.
500 Tuija Laine, Aapisen, 84–85.
501 Tuija Laine, Aapisen, 85.

Other books read by separatists were hymnals, which were commonly used as devotional books, both in private devotions and home devotions, and books by Johann Gerhard (1582–1637), Johann Arndt (1555–1621), Arthur Dent and Thomas Bromley. Gerhard's and Arndt's books were very common among people in the 18th century, and so was on of Dent's, although a Lutheran section was added into his book by the translator because the book itself was regarded too "English" (i.e. too puritan). Dent's *Totisen käändymisen harjoitus* (A Plaine Man's Pathway to Heaven) also caused an ecstatic movement in Kalanti in Western Finland when a shepherd girl read it in the woods and became very scared, thinking she was going to burn in hell because of her sins (Fig. 13).[502]

One of the most interesting books read by the members of Ericsson's movement was Thomas Bromley's book, *The Way to the Sabbath of Rest.* Thomas Bromley was an English mystic who had been influenced by the German shoemaker and spiritualist Jacob Böhme. Bromley refused the Church as an institution, as well as the Bible as a normative book. Afterwards Bromley belonged to the Philadelphian movement led by Jane Leade. Bromley's book on resting on the Sabbath tells how the soul is progressing through regeneration and a deadening of the self towards heavenly and godly perfection and light. After having been rejected by the censors, this book was regarded illegal. Still, it was published in the Swedish realm. A Swedish edition had been published in 1740 without the printer's name, and already in 1756, the book was translated into Finnish in Ostrobothnia. The translator was a peasant, Matthias Sauso, from the village of Vähäkyrö. He was one of the so-called mystics of Ostrobothnia, who mostly translated forbidden literature and distributed it in manuscripts in the last decades of the 18th and the first decades of the 19th century.[503]

We do not know exactly how separatists read these books. Probably someone read aloud while others listened. Not all could read, and often these devotional books were not quite easy to read and understand either. Moreover, this reading was not very traditional. From these books, people took ideas that were not accepted by the Church. As studying these books then further strengthened these very ideas, they influenced thinking in a very deep way.

Intensive or extensive reading?

When Rolf Engelsing published his research on the German bourgeoisie and its reading habits (*Der Bürger als Leser*) in 1974, he introduced his theory

502 Österbladh, Laihian. Sulkunen, Liisa Eerikintytär.

503 Tuija Laine, Ylösherätys.

about intensive and extensive reading. Intensive reading was traditional; it was directed at religious texts, which were read repeatedly, many times. Those texts (e.g. devotional literature, catechisms and hymnals) did not consist of anything new, and the purpose of reading them was not to find new aspects or new information, but to strengthen old ideas. According to Engelsing, in the 18th century extensive reading emerged as readers searched new texts, including more profane texts, which were not religious. The purpose of those texts was to inform or amuse their readers. The new kind of reading was especially typical for the middle class. Printing presses produced many new books including emerging genres like fiction and travel writing, and all these found readers among estates of burgesses.[504]

There are many correct points in Engelsing's theory. The first books and booklets were religious, and without doubt, they were often read repeatedly. On the other hand, book production increased everywhere in Europe in the 18th century and the bourgeoisie found new literature genres. Some nearly lost their minds when so many books were suddenly available, many of which were also more emotionally touching than the old literature they were used to. However, is the theory of intensive and extensive reading, following each other in the last decades of the 18th century, too simple or too black-and-white an interpretation of reading? Is not reading, with all of its methods and habits, much more complicated? Do not different men, women and children have different motivations for their reading in different situations? For all of these reasons, many researchers have criticized Engelsing's theory, Robert Darnton among them. Engelsing researched only one social class and one area, and he drew very broad conclusions from his data. Perhaps he was not even trying to create an all-encompassing theory about changes in reading culture everywhere.[505]

The theory of intensive reading as regards old religious texts is very interesting, though, because it draws attention to the question of religious reading, its meaning and its different forms and habits. Overall, religious reading has been studied quite little. Often it has been left out of books, which deal with reading. Even in some studies of book history, there can be seen the same phrases about religious books or their reading that Engelsing emphasized: they were the first books that people read, they were read repeatedly, and afterwards people read other books when more profane books were available and literacy had improved.

---

504 Engelsing, Lesergeschichte.

505 Darnton, Lamourette, 165–166. Darnton, History of Reading, 148. Tunturi, Metodeista, 170–171.

The problem with these points is that they paint the picture that religious reading was suitable only for commoners, peasants or those whose literary skills were poorly developed. One might then think that scholars did not read religious literature, nor did noblemen. If in some cases they happened to do so, there rapidly follow explanations: these people also had much "better" and "more civilized" literature at their hands, or their odd reading habits were based on a specific sect or religious movement they belonged to. Thus, the reader of religious texts has often – but not always – been seen as stupid or unintelligent, rather than as a thinking person.

It has not always been understood clearly enough that, just as we have different profane texts, we also have different religious texts. Different texts have been read and used in different situations and by different people. There were many texts which were read repeatedly in masses or during private devotions, but not even all the devotional books or texts were read many times by the same men. Even religious texts might have been used for extensive reading, as readers may have tried to find more and more of such texts to read. What is quite sure is that reading them might evoke the same dangerous consequences as reading works of the new genre, fiction. Even reading repeatedly can have meaning for readers, as it does not necessarily mean repeating sentences without arriving at any new ideas. What is also clear is that the reading of the same old texts did not disappear when extensive reading became more common. Even today, there are people who repeatedly read the same texts – profane, religious or both – and this does not mean that they would not read new texts to get information or amuse themselves.[506]

Tuomas Ragvaldinpoika

One of the best-known poets among the common people was Tuomas Ragvaldinpoika (1724–1804) from Tyrvää in Western Finland. He was physically disabled and unable to work, which left him with a lot of time to concentrate on literary projects. He wrote many hymns and poetry for funerals and marriages, but also about his own difficult situation as a crippled man with a harelip.[507]

According to the church examination registers of Tyrvää, Tuomas Ragvaldinpoika was a good reader, and his writings reveal his knowledge of the New

506 Tuija Laine, Aapisen.

507 Tuomas Ragvaldinpoika [1763]. Raittila, Tuomas Ragvaldinpoika. Esko M. Laine, Tuomas Ragvaldinpoika.

Testament and catechism. He also worked as a children's tutor, teaching catechism. In 1761, he wished to publish new prints from some sermons from the 17th century, but because he was self-educated, the Chapter of Turku did not allow him to do so.[508]

It is evident that he was familiar with many basic religious books and was able to use them in his own literary work. The application that he wrote to the Chapter of Turku was written by imitating printed text. This may tell us about his respect towards printed books, but it also testifies to his being a self-educated man without any formal education. As a reader, he was an active person who did read not only for his own edification, but also for the good of other people.[509]

Kaisa Juhantytär

Another example of reading peasants is Kaisa Juhantytär (1782–1856), a housewife from Noormarkku in the Satakunta region of Western Finland. Kaisa could also write, and she penned many psalms. They have not been published, but were saved as a manuscript. All of these writings show that this woman knew her Bible very well, and she must have had a Bible that she read.[510]

The most interesting of her psalms, the first and longest in her collection, consists of 31 verses. In this psalm, Kaisa Juhantytär recounts the fortunes of the women mentioned in the Bible: 17 verses adress the women of the Old Testament, two treat the women of the apocryphal books, and 11 focus on the women of the New Testament. Women represent different social groups and different kinds of positions. There are prophets and queens, mothers and wives, martyrs and widows. Many of these women are very resourceful. For example, Abigail spoke with King David when Nabal had been very rude to David's men and David was going to attack him; after listening to Abigail, the king calmed down and decided not to do this.[511]

Kaisa Juhantytär sees the women of the Bible as active and devout people who did what God told them to do. Sometimes they did things, which were not reasonable from the "world's" point of view. That was the case, for example, when Mary used expensive oil to chrism Jesus' head. In the psalm, the writer underlines the equality of men and women in God's sight. According to Kaisa, many men would absolutely like to deny that women could have faith. In her view, this is not right, as all are equal and the grace of God has been given to

508 Esko Laine, Tuomas Ragvaldinpoika.
509 Tuija Laine, Aapisen, 170.
510 Makkonen, Kaisa Juhantyttären, 415–420.
511 Makkonen, Kaisa Juhantyttären, 423. Tiili, Kaisa Juhantytär, 97. Kuismin, Literacy, 11.

everybody. Each verse ends with the words: "Saan halleluja laula, waik maailma mitä pauha" – "I may sing hallelujah; the world can say nothing against it."[512]

These examples show that at the end of the 18th and the beginning of the 19th century, there were already quite modern forms of reading in Finland and, even among the peasants; there were those who not only read religious books but also used reading to develop their ideas and thinking. While at that time these people were still exceptions, their way of reading existed alongside the older types, and newer forms were being developed as well.

Conclusion

Already in the Middle Ages, the common people had to learn some Christian texts by heart. With the Reformation followed the demand for the production and publication of vernacular literature. In Finland, basic religious books were translated into Finnish by the Finnish reformer Mikael Agricola: a primer, the New Testament, a prayer book and some parts of the Old Testament books.

In the latter part of the 17th century, there was a broad literary campaign across the whole of the Swedish realm, to which Finland then belonged. Bishop Johannes Gezelius the Elder published basic religious books and textbooks, and he stressed reading from books. Common people learned to read during the 18th century, especially in Western Finland. When literacy improved among adults, more interest was concentrated on teaching children. Children's literature was published in many places in Europe, and in Finland, such publishing started with catechisms. By the last decades of the 18th century, children received several catechisms in Finnish.

Books and reading allowed the Lutheran doctrine to spread easier among the people, but it also facilitated new interpretations of the Bible. Pietists, separatists and mystics had their own illegal meetings and read books, some of which were not permitted for the common people in the 17th and 18th centuries. If somebody could not read by him or herself, he or she could at least listen to others reading aloud.

The 18th century saw the emergence of new reading habits. Books that are more secular were published, and increasing literacy made it easier for commoners to acquire books and other texts. Some self-educated people even started to use reading for the good of others by writing different texts themselves.

512 Makkonen, Kaisa Juhantytär, 418–421.

Esko Laine

Pietism as a Way to Modern Self in Early Modern Finland

A two-part legacy of German Pietism in Finland

Scholars of literature studies have already long paid attention to the change, which effected deeply on the construction of early modern societies, the genesis of modern self (modern subject). According to Finnish professor of Literature studies, Mikko Lehtonen, reformation, scientific revolution and enlightenment produced each from different directions a new kind of intellectual understanding in the early modern age. They created new concept of culture, social identity and modern self (subject). This new creation has since the beginning of 19th Century been dominant. One typical feature of it was man's separation from being a part of the nature. The new man identified himself with his intellect, to whom human feelings and his sensations were submitted. This led to the genesis of new Self, modern Subject, modern I.[513] Lehtonen does not mention Pietism as a factor in the process of developing of modern Self, but especially in Finland its Role was obvious.

Pietism was after the Reformation without any doubt the most significant phenomenon in Church History, also in Sweden and Finland. Nevertheless, it never led to neither cultural nor social breakthrough in all levels of society and culture like the Reformation did, although there were however cultural differences between the Nordic Countries. Unlike in Sweden and Finland, a kind of state-pietism became the predominant scheme of things in the Danish-Norwegian society in the 18th century. In addition, Haugeanism as a Pietistic popular movement managed to shake fundamental social and religious structures in Danish-Norwegian absolutist society within a few short years around 1800.[514]

In the North, pietism went literally ashore on the coastline in the eastern part of the Swedish Realm the same way it did in Denmark-Norway (including Greenland). It did so in the shape of literature, legally imported or smuggled, from Central Europe and Germany. To Finland, German pietism found its ways through the Baltic provinces and the Swedish mother country at the turn of 17th

513 Lehtonen, Kyklooppi, 17–18, 25 & 40–41.

514 Wallmann, Pietismus, 7. Wallmann, Beziehungen, 49. Gundersen, Haugean Revival, 160–161.

and 18th centuries.[515] The penalties for those who wrote, translated, performed, published or circulated forbidden religious texts ranged from exclusion from civil service professions to heavy fines.[516] The significance and achievements of pietism in the Swedish Realm cannot be diminished, but the question in what way pietism carried the legacy of Reformation and what was its own inheritance, are not easy issues to work out.

Pietists themselves emphasized the significance of deepening their religious lives, of practical Christianity and the praxis of personal piety in everyday life. The awakening and the demand of mending one's way were understood among Pietists as a natural continuation of the Reformation even though the final goal was set higher than that of the Reformation: profound renewal of the Church and ultimately changing the world entirely. This presumed a fundamental change of the self, a new concept of subject.[517]

The leading theologians in Turku at the turn of the 18th Century blamed Pietists for heterodoxy, but this did not stop them valuing their devotion and their deep personal practice of piety. Among Pietists, accusations of this kind boggled.[518] Even though they sometimes ruthlessly criticized the orthodox Lutheran understanding of priesthood, confession and sacramental praxis, most of them regarded themselves as still being Lutherans. Many adherents of Laurentius Ulstadius (1650–1732) in the flock of Finnish radical Pietists at the turn of the 18th century were young students from Turku Academy. Like in Denmark in the early 18th century, Pietism spread in Finland at first especially outside lecture halls where students could meet leading Pietists and study their writings[519].

One of these students, Olaus Ulhegius, questioned during an interrogation in front of the Academic Chapter in Turku the very ground of the Lutheran confession (*libros symbolicos*), while at the same time insulting several theological authorities (Martin Chemnitz, Nicolaus Hunnius) held in high regain by the Lutheran orthodoxy. However, he denied having criticized Luther itself or his doctrine such as he understood it. Corrected by the Chapter in many regards, he nevertheless admitted having neglected his Catechism reading and therefore not being fully aware of Lutheran doctrine in detail. In spite of that, he dared

---

515 Nordstrandh, Litteratur, 3–8 & 273–295. Tuija Laine, Kolportöörejä, 129. Gina Dahl, Religious Reading, 95. Kjærgaard, Genesis, 134–135 & 144.

516 Öhrberg, Threat, 116.

517 Brecht, Pietismus, 4. Brecht 1993b, 285, 288–289 & 291.

518 CAP VI, 361–362 & 542. Laasonen, Pietismus, 156–157.

519 Gina Dahl, Religious Reading, 95.

insist that the above-mentioned authorities, not he himself, interpreted Luther incorrectly.[520]

Ulhegius' elder kindred-spirit, Magister Petter (Petrus) Schäfer (1663–1729), the most radical fanatic among equals in Turku, denied being a Lutheran before the Chapter of the Academy in Turku in December 1689. The members of the Chapter were astonished why he addressed them, his interrogators, "Lutherans" in a derogatory tone of voice. Asked by the Chapter of his own religious identity he replied by describing himself not as a "Lutheran" but a "Christian".[521] Schäfer did however not break away from Luther in his so-called Confession, in which he summarized his beliefs in November 1689.[522] In front of bishop Gezelius, Schäfer quoted Luther, *Pestis eram vivus, moriens ero mors tua,* identifying himself with him and the bishop with the Pope. As the "carrier of truth" he, like Luther in Worms, could or would not withdraw his words and deny his accusations against the Academy and Ecclesiastical Chapter without betraying his ideals whatever the consequences might be. [523]

According to Thomas Kauffmann, the Pietists in Germany regarded Luther as an advocate for priesthood of all believers, a founder of small "autarkic" groups or communities and an interpreter of the Bible, i.e. a teacher. His example as such encouraged them to biblical interpretations of their own against the prevailing order based on Lutheran orthodoxy.[524] Philipp Jacob Spener's (1635–1705) original idea, as popularized in his Program *Pia desideria* 1675, was to make the Bible better known among lay people and to inspire commoners to read it autonomously (Fig. 14).[525] The Bible, however, became a weapon in the battle between pietism and orthodoxy. In the interrogations before the ecclesiastical chapter of Turku in the years 1689–1693, early Finnish Pietists realigned themselves with Luther also in their patterns of behavior. Like Luther at the Diet of Worms in 1521, they too invoked their conscience claiming themselves not to have offended Lutheran faith but on the contrary defended it from the pernicious influence of the new-Aristotelian school-metaphysics predominant at that time.[526]

---

520 CAP VI, 361–362. Trial of Olaus Ulhegius 23th August 1688.

521 CAP VI, 535. Trial of Petrus Schäfer 10th December 1689.

522 Uppsala Universitetsbibliotek, N. 47. Confession of Peter Schäfer 20.11.1689.

523 Riksarkivet, AE 118. II: 25. Eccleastical Chapter of Turku to Majesty 4.12.1703. Luther, Gesamtausgabe Weimar, Bd. 35. Schriften, Lieder. Lomakkeen yläreuna
Lomakkeen alareuna
Was fürchtst du, Feind Herodes, sehr. Laasonen, Pietismus, 157.

524 Kauffmann 2016, 722.

525 Wallmann, Pietismus, 47: "Das Wort Gottes reichlicher unter uns bringen".

526 CAP VI, 535–537. Trial of Petrus Schäfer 10th December 1689.

Pietism in the late 17th-century Finland was not a monolete phenomenon. It carried a two-part legacy of the Reformation. Among others, pietism shared with Lutheran orthodoxy the appreciation of late medieval and early modern spirituality. There were, for example, several references to the books of Johann Arndt (1555–1621), Thomas a Kempis (1380–1471) and Johannes Tauler (1300–1361) in Petter Schäfer's autobiographical conversion narrative, *Min Första Omwändelse*.[527] It shows that early modern Finnish pietists valued this kind of literature sharing their opinion of the nature of Christian spirituality and devotion with the Lutheran Orthodoxy, even though they interpreted and applied them differently.[528] In many regards, pietism efficiently promoted relaying the legacy of late medieval spirituality, which it had in common with Lutheran orthodoxy. The readings of late medieval devotional literature in the new form manifested in the works of Arndt spirituality opened the treasures of the Christian to those who were able to read without control or guidance from Clergy. A turn away from the old-fashion routine reading of catechism to independent reading of devotional books instead accelerated the genesis of modern subject in many regards. For some Pietists this was, however, not enough. Besides reading books written by Arndt and other reformers, they wanted for a more radical religious change. This duality in the concept of pietism has made the definitions of it controversial.

According to the prominent German Scholar, Professor Johannes Wallmann, difficulties in defining the concept of Pietism are caused mainly by the fact that the concept of Pietism itself actually includes two different and not coincident occurrences, which he calls "Pietism in wider and Pietism in narrower sense" (Pietismus in engem und in weiterem Sinn). The first of these, Pietism in a wider meaning, refers to a specific type of devotion without ranging over wider goals, such as changing the church and society. It aimed to renew the religious life, which had been corrupted, and to transfer the legacy of the Reformation to the coming generations in the shape of individual experiences through devotional literature. Pietism of this kind emerged at the turn of the 16th and 17th centuries. Its Roots in the Lutheran world go back to the then Superintendent of Braunschweig-Lüneburg, Johann Arndt.[529]

---

527 Riksarkivet, AE 124. Schäfer's autobiographical Conversion Narrative. Tuija Laine, Kolportöörejä, 127.

528 Riksarkivet, AE 124. Schäfer's spiritual Autobiography from his early years, Min Första Omwändelse. Laasonen, Johann Arndt, 115.

529 Wallmann, Pietismus, 10 & 15. Wallmann, Beziehungen, 49. Brecht, Pietismus, 9 criticizes Wallmann's idea according which the Arndt'ian movement (Arndt'sche Frömmigkeitsbewegung) would have been more literal as social.

For Pietism in a *narrower sense*, the renewal of spiritual practice alone was not enough. Philipp Jacob Spener and August Hermann Francke (1663–1727) required a deeper going change in every regard. In their thinking, "true Christianity" demanded more profound changes, first in the heart of a Sinner and then in the entire society. Francke taught that it was not possible to achieve these goals without awakening, i.e. rigorous conversion (*Busskampf*). "Spiritual improvement", such as more active church attendance was useless without a touch of Holy Spirit. Francke and his colleagues preached consequently a more fundamental change with strong impact on society and culture. The World and its vanities were to be denied entirely, as well.[530]

Pietism in a narrower sense brought with them deeper going demands for renewal of both the Church and the Society than the spirituality-orientated Pietistic movement of Johann Arndt. Senior preacher Philipp Jacob Spener from Frankfurt am Main was the first theologian in the Lutheran World who drew up a detailed programme, *Pia desideria,* how Pietistic change could and should be carried out. This was originally published as an introduction and attached to the Postil of Johann Arndt 1675, presenting for the first time both the goals and the methods of Pietism "in the narrower sense".[531]

According to Peter G. Wallace, the crucial issue that divided Lutheran Orthodoxy from Pietists was the penitential rite. Pietists found the prevailing practice of public absolution too formulaic to sustain inner conversion of the heart and they doubted that pastoral absolution conferred grace.[532] Pietists also felt that Lutheran Orthodoxy devoted too much energy in determining how the church might reform the world, which the Pietists argued could only be realized through the shared effort of clergy and laity. By arguing, that the unbound or inward power of the Holy Spirit was accessible to the believer without clergy. Pietists challenged the authority of the Lutheran orthodoxy and the state-church pattern based on it. According to Wallace, this emancipation was a crucial part of the continuing reformation in Pietism.[533]

Up to remote Scandinavia, both types of Pietism (Pietism in wider and in narrower sense) were known among Scholars but not among the ordinary people. Alarm bells rang in Turku, when without warnings, so-called Pietism appeared for the first time in the form of former teacher from North-Finland, Laurentius Ulstadius. In the August of the year 1688, he caused a Scandal in the

530 Schmidt, Wiedergeburt, 204–205. Wallmann, Beziehungen, 63–64. Brecht 1993c, 444–446. Schicketanz, Pietismus, 90–91.

531 Wallmann, Philipp Jakob Spener, 305–306. Wallmann, Pietismus, 45–50. On *Pia desideria* as social-program, see Schicketanz, Pietismus, 54–58.

532 Wallace 2002, 175–176. Heininen 2016, 100.

533 Wallace 2012, 175.

Cathedral of Turku by interrupting completely naked a sermon of a Priest called Gregorius Kulhovius in the middle of Evening Service. Loud and clear in the Turku Cathedral, Ulstadius proclaimed Lutheran doctrine was false because the Holy Spirit was not with the Lutheran pastors. [534] Before that incident these two types of pietism seems to have been seen separately in the eyes of Orthodoxy but the aggression of the conversion-orientated form of pietism, which was manifested clearly in the Ulstadius case, cast an incontestabel shadow on the moderate Arndt'ian pietism, too.

When the struggle between Lutheran Orthodoxy and Pietism in its *narrower sense* really started after Ulstadius' incident, the attitudes of Orthodoxy to Arndt and his writings changed to some regard. For example, in Uppsala 1703 a distinguished Theologian Martin Schütte attacked a newly published Swedish translation of Arndt's posthumous *Informatorium biblicum, das ist etzliche christliche Erinnerungs-Puncten*, a booklet consisting mostly of Bible citations supplemented by short dogmatic explanations. Schütte based his main arguments against that booklet on the criticism of Samuel Schelwig, a scholar then well-known from anti-Pietistic disputes in Danzig. Close reading of his criticism reveals, however, that the main target was not Arndt but Pietism in its narrower sense, which was said to change the original meanings of the booklet for its own purposes.[535]

The concept of Pietism originated in Germany in the 1670s. At that time, it referred only to the adherents of Spener or Francke who were taken to the Ecclesiastical Courts on the charge of religious "enthusiasm". The use of this concept was then limited to mockery. Like puritanism in England some decades before or methodism in the other half of 18th Century, pietism in Germany meant exaggeration of religious practices, emotions and talks, but with the exception that in Germany at that time not all enthusiasts but only those who could be connected to Spener or Francke were commonly mocked for their new religious convictions.[536]

In the Realm of Sweden the concept of Pietism, though not the phenomenon itself, was however unknown until the beginning of 18th century when the first anti-pietistic statutes were laid down.[537] Early Finnish and Swedish Pietists were therefore accused of a large variety of crimes in the Court of Academy, from offending the Authority of Clergy to heterodoxy in doctrine in general. In the

534 Kansanaho, Lauri Ulstadius, 115–118. Laasonen, Johannes Gezelius, 141. Heininen 2016, 100–101. Trial documents against Ulstadius have been published by Akiander, Upplysningar, Bd. 1, 6.

535 Nordstrandh, Litteratur, 136.

536 Wallmann, Pietismus, 8. Brecht, Pietismus, 4–5.

537 Pleijel, Pietismus, 46–49. Esko Laine 1997, 16–19.

eyes of the orthodox Lutheran clergy, Pietists were seen guilty beyond reasonable doubt but on the question on what crime. Opinions were divided, though, some of the leading opponents of early Finnish pietism conceived pietism as kind of a mental illness, others as heresy. Among those who went for mental illness, speculations ranged from melancholy to a kind of "spiritual dementia" (*dementia quidam spiritualis*). The Bishop of Turku, Johannes Gezelius the Younger (1647–1718), an Expert in this issue, however, refused to treat pietism as anything else than heterodoxy. He convinced the Ecclesiastical Chapter that the accused Pietists were adherents of a new hazardous heresy (*novitas*) which had to be stopped by the Authorities as soon as possible.[538]

The Privy Council of Sweden agreed with Gezelius. The first Swedish anti-Pietistic statute from 1702 depicted Pietism in its narrow sense as a fanaticism dangerous for society, against which the country needed to protect itself. The scandal in Turku probably cast a shadow over the statute. Rough measures like trials in both ecclesiastical and secular courts and immediate incarcerations of suspects were therefore regarded necessary. In a European context, Sweden and Finland were probably among the most hostile environments for the Pietism (in its narrow sense) until 1730 or 1766 the latest. That year, freedom of press was introduced for secular literature, and censorship regulated by laws and edicts (Censor librorum) was abolished.[539] Warnings of this kind were, however, not to be applied to Pietism in its wider sense, i.e. to the texts of Arndt. The reception of Arndt among Lutheran theologians seems to have been in all regards less contradictive and problematic in Finland and Sweden than in Germany.[540]

Pietistic Books in Finnish Translations and the first Finnish Pietistic Writers

Among those who could read Swedish or German, the writings of Johann Arndt were known in Finland long before the earliest translations into Finnish. Arndt's *Paradies Gärtlein* 1612 (in Finnish *Paratiisin yrttitarha*) was published for the first time in Swedish in the year 1646. Reprints followed each other frequently, the first as early as 1648. From the second half of the 17th century at least ten reprints are known.[541] Arndt's main work, *Vier Bücher von Wahrem Christenthum* (1605–1610), was translated and published in Swedish 1647–1648,

---

538 Uppsala Universitetsbibliotek, N. 53 Peter Schäfer to Majesty 11.11.1690; Laine 1997, 166–169. See also Riksarkivet, Concepts. Laasonen, Johannes Gezelius, 141. Öhrberg, Threat, 112–114.

539 Pleijel, Pietismus, 15, 34–36. Öhrberg, Threat, 115.

540 Schneider, Johann Arndt, 79–84.

541 Nordstrandh, Litteratur, 134. Tiililä, Rukoilevaisten kirjoja, 35.

his *Postill* some decades later, in 1703, entitled *Anderik förklaring öfwer alle evangeliske sön-högtijds- och aposteldagarstexter hela året igenom.* The Swedish translation of the Postil is based on a revised text by Spener. Printed copies of these translations found their readers. In Norrland, on the western coast of the Gulf of Bothnia, for example, *Paradies Gärtlein* together with *Vier Bücher von Wahrem Christenthum* were clearly the most favoured devotional books.[542]

Matti Repo has pointed out that Arndts' works were known in Reval already in 1617, at a time when Swedish armed forces, including with Finnish officers, were concentrated because of the war with Russia. The governor of Swedish Estonia, Gabriel Oxenstierna and his wife Anna Banér, were counted among the eager readers of Arndt. General Jacob De la Gardie was touched by Arndt as well. He also carried *Vier Bücher von Wahrem Christenthum* with him on the battlefields. Repo presumes, though without any convincing evidence, that also Finnish officers got in contact with Arndt's main works in the Baltic Countries. We know that especially the *Paradis Gärtlein* was highly appreciated by a great number of Finnish Clergymen, too. In the trials against Pietists prominent Lutheran Theologians such as the Bishop of Turku, Johannes Gezelius the Elder (1615–1690), actually encouraged the accused to read Arndt's' texts for consolation and devotion. Gezelius was not the only one who in Arndt's texts saw an antidote against pietism (in its narrower sense).[543] It is possible that even the common people in pews at Sunday services occasionally could hear citations of *Paradies Gärtlein*. In most cases, the church attendants especially among commoners had apparently no idea of the writer, Johann Arndt.[544]

The Finnish Estate Inventory Deeds from towns from early 17th Century to the end of the Swedish Era (1810) contain more than 600 references to the devotional books of Arndt in German or in Swedish translation.[545] In the database Henrik, there are 124 references to the works of Arndt recorded in the book auctions protocols from Finnish towns before 1809. People in the North of Finland (Tornio) and in Ostrobothnia (Pietarsaari, Kokkola) owned most of Arndt's books. According to Leif Erikson, Arndt's books seem to have been of relatively little value for Lars Levi Laestadius, the founder of Lestadianism (still the biggest revival in supporter rates in Scandinavia). This is peculiar, because the revival began in the river valley of Tornio. Probably this reflects cultural

---

542 Laasonen, Johann Arndt, 111. Tuija Laine, Aapisen, 72.

543 Salminen, Teologin, 26–27, 30 & 55. Repo, Johann Arndtin, 30–34. Tuija Laine, Aapisen, 72 & 87.

544 Repo, Johann Arndtin, 34.

545 On criticism of sources of The Finnish Estate Inventory Deeds from towns, see Laasonen, Johann Arndt, 112. For two references to the Latin version of *Vier Bücher von Wahrem Christenthum*, see Laasonen, Johann Arndt, 113

differences in reading cultures between towns (Tornio) and the surrounding countryside (river valley of Tornio).[546] Of all identified references to the books of Arndt in the Finnish Estate Inventory Deeds from towns, only 16% have been found in Helsinki. Most of Arndt's books ended up in private libraries in towns on the Finnish coast from north to south.[547] Most of the buyers seem to be men, officers, tradesmen, officials, civil and public servants, artisans but also teachers and clergymen.

Gina Dahl has studied religious reading among the Norwegian clergy between the years 1650–1800. According to her observations, also in Norway the books of Arndt were popular among the clergy. In the county of Jarlsberg however, between the years 1704–1738 Arndt's' books were only the fourth popular books. Comparing Dahl's figures with those in the Finnish Estate Inventory Deeds from about the same period, it seems that the popularity of Arndt was somewhat higher in Finland than in Norway. After the middle of 18th Century, the difference between these two Nordic regions became even more obvious due to a growing interest in historical issues among the clergy in Norway.[548]

Among buyers at Finnish book auctions, there were also some women. According to a law of 1734, women were not entitled to trade or do business on their own if their husbands were still alive. Yet, women's active presence at auctions was not exceptional. One of the female buyers at an auction in Turku 1776 was Catharina Margareta Pipping, wife of a judge at the Appeal Court in Turku, who bid an unknown amount of money for the *Paradijs lust-gård* in Swedish. Another example was the widow of tradesman Carl H. Etholen, Catharina Strandman, who a decade earlier purchased the same book in Swedish, as well. Private libraries of women from the nobility and the bourgeoisie in late 18th-century Finnish towns, such as the library of Margareta Sjöman at the time of her death in June 1798, usually included at least one book by Arndt.[549]

Most of the books of Arndt auctioned in Finnish towns in the 18th century were Swedish translations but there was also a market for German originals. Available information on book acquisition and ownership, it is clear that Arndt was the most popular Lutheran Writer of devotional literature in Finland during the Swedish Era, especially among the gentry. The Estate Inventory Deeds include also references to other writers close to Arndt and his spirituality.

The database *Kirjojen leviäminen Suomessa ennen vuotta 1850* (The spreading of books in Finland until 1850) reveals, however, that the golden age for spreading Arndt's books in Finland especially among the commoners was the

546 Erikson, Johann Arndt, 126–127.

547 Laasonen, Johann Arndt, 112–113.

548 Gina Dahl, Religious Reading, 100–101 & 109.

549 Tuija Laine, Kolportöörejä, 292–293. Ulväng/Murhem/Lilja, Auktionshandel, 106–107.

19th Century. Of the 152 references in the book lists of congregational libraries and of private book collections, more than 2/3 refer to ownership later than the year 1809. Obviously, the lack of Finnish translations delayed the spread of these books outside circles of literally educated people, i.e. the clergy and gentry.

Tarja-Liisa Luukkanen has recently studied the borrowing of the books from public Library in a small remote Finnish Community called Karstula on the second half of the 19th Century. Her study shows clearly the popularity of Arndt in the periphery at that time. According to Luukkanen, until the year 1888 Arndt's books came second right after Luther. Arndts' *Vier Bücher von Wahrem Christenthum* in Finnish translation were borrowed in Karstula 157 times. Most of the borrowers were men.[550]

Arndt's books played a special roll among the Pietists of the Finnish revival movements in 19th Century, too. The leaders of the Ostrobothnian Pietism published in their Newspaper *Tidningar i andeliga ämnen* advertisements where Arndt's books were presented as equal to Luther's works. Among the new-evangelicals, the reception of Arndt was however somewhat reserved. A pedlar of devotional books called Julin was warned when he was selling Arndt's books in Petolahti in Southern Ostrobothnia among Swedish-speaking evangelicals. According to some of that folks, the doctrine of Arndt was not seen in all regards coherent with Lutheranism. Yet in Satakunta, less than 100 miles further to the South, the local Pietists called the "supplicants", valued the works of Arndt just as much as the Pietists in Ostrobothnia. The so-called "jumpers", a movement that preceded that of the "supplicants" in Satakunta, gained essential influences from Arndt's mysticism, too.[551]

During the entire Swedish Age, only one title of Arndt was translated into Finnish, the *Paradies Gärtlein* (1612). It was published in 1732 entitled *Paratiisin yrttitarha*. This book, reprinted several times in the subsequent years (1764, 1775, and 1797) became very popular in Finland. Some Finnish scholars (such as Vasenius or Pipping) have assumed that a translation of this book might have come out already in the 1670s but not a single copy of such an edition has been recorded or preserved. The 1732 edition was translated by Samuel Wacklin, a Vicar from Osrtobothnia, one of the leading figures among Moravians in Finland. In 1731, the Ecclesiastical Chapter in Turku in whose hand the censorship

550 Luukkanen, Karstulassa, 196–200. In the 1860s, population of Karstula (including children and elderly) varied between 4700–5000 inhabitants.

551 Heino, Hyppyherätys, 121. Erikson, Johann Arndt, 123–125. According to Schneider, Johann Arndt, 74–75, the obvious contradiction between real Christianity (wahres Christentum) involving mysticism and the academically theology on the other hand can be seen in Arndt's first publication, *Theologia deutsch*.

over the manuscript was entrusted, criticized Wacklin's translation for "obvious mistakes" in several regards but decided to permit the printing anyway. Jacob Wilde who lay behind the translation by Wacklin however defended Wacklin's work with the argument that these so-called "obvious mistakes" actually were not errors at all, but could be reduced to simple differences between Finnish dialects.[552]

In a letter to the Swedish king, the Ecclesiastical Chapter asked for the prohibition by statute of the printing of Finnish books in Stockholm due to several mistakes and language errors in this particular translation. In his answer, the King reassured the Chapter that future printing of Finnish books in Stockholm should be possible only on the condition that the Chapter itself could supervise printing and control proofreading of manuscripts.[553]

The Great Nordic War (1700–1721) followed by the Russian occupation, known as the Great Wrath (1713–1721), greatly damaged the ecclesiastical life in Finland. The educational efforts of the Lutheran clergy drastically declined in many congregations. Afterwards, the country was in ruins. The vicar of Liperi in Northern Carelia, Georg Dannenberg, complained in a letter to the Ecclesiastical Chapter in Porvoo after the Great Wrath that the enemy had destroyed all books in the entire community. In addition, his colleague Henrik Winter, the vicar of Kitee, informed the Ecclesiastical Chapter that neither catechisms nor ABC-books were available for educational purposes in the congregation.[554]

After the clergy had escaped the arrival of Russian troops from their parishes to Stockholm, the parishioners had to cope without guidance and assistance in ecclesiastical matters including the practise of catechism. However, this regulation was not consistently followed in 1713 because of panic.[555] In such a chaotic situation, the main interest of the commoners was survival not reading, even though the Lutheran clergy never ceased to emphasize the significance of catechism reading for both the temporal and spiritual life. According to the law, it was permitted for a vicar to escape only in the case that there was at least one priest left in the parish.

The level of reading ability fell therefore fast in those gloomy years in many congregations especially in Eastern Finland where reading results already before the war were relatively lower than in the western part of the country. The Great

552 Tuija Laine, Kolportöörejä, 144.

553 Tiililä, Rukoilevaisten kirjoja, 35. Widén 1976, 288. Silfverhuth, Kirkon, 23. Tuija Laine, Kolportöörejä, 144.

554 Laasonen, Kansankulttuuri, 307. Laasonen, Johann Arndt, 112.

555 Rimpiläinen, Läntisen, 15–16, 19.

Wrath-catastrophe destroyed for the most part the achievements of the reformation on the local level, excluding those areas located mostly in Western Finland where the church administration and practices of ecclesiastical life could continue as normal as possible even under the reigning difficult circumstances. In those congregations where the reading ability went down dramatically during the Russian occupation (Marttila, Korppoo) the clergy could in 1721, after the peace treaty of Uusikaupunki quickly restore the order by assisting the secular authorities and forcing children, youth and young adults in assistance of secular authority to concentrate on the Catechism exercises again. In the eastern part of the country, the state of affairs was, however, different: the consequences of the occupation were still visible decades later. For example in Liperi, as late as in 1899 there were 103 families who did not possess even their copy of the New Testament.[556]

During the difficult years of the occupation many Finns who had suffered greatly under the Russian yoke adopted a critical stance towards their priests who had run to the capital in order to save their own skin. Many considered them traitors or at least cowards. The stance of commoners in many congregations after the Nordic War in the 1720–1730s toward the local clergy was therefore rather unfriendly if not openly hostile. In Northern Carelia, the Ecclesiastical Chapter tried to solve the lack of catechisms by sending free copies to the clergy for distributing them to the parishioners free of charge. Many poor peasants, however, refused them even then. In the 1740s, the clergy of Liperi still was struggling to distribute at least parts of the 300 copies of the Catechism that had been ordered from the Ecclesiastical Chapter from Porvoo by the vicar in order to re-boost the basic education in reading.[557]

Especially the clergy that had fled to Stockholm on its return had to overcome this kind of problems before being able to begin any improvements of the ecclesiastical life or reading exercises. By means of publishing devotional books like *Paratiisin yrttitarha* by Johann Arndt and *Totisen kääntymyksen harjoitus* (Plain man's pathway to Heaven) by the Englishman Arthur Dentdippel in 1732, the Clerical Estate and the Ecclesiastical Chapter in Turku tried to restore the spiritual life and confidence in the Church in Finnish congregations.[558] The *Paratiisin yrttitarha* (Paradies Gärtlein) was reprinted in Finland at least four times in 1764, 1775, 1819 and 1940.[559]

The earliest reference to a Finnish translation of *Paratiisin yrttitarha* can be found in a book auction record from 1766 when a copy was sold at an auction

556 Juva 1955, 134–143, 200. Laasonen, Pohjois-Karjalassa, 128.
557 Laasonen, Kansankulttuuri, 307–309. Vilkuna, Viha, 412–416.
558 Tuija Laine, Ylösherätys, 129.
559 Repo, Johann Arndt, 35.

in Oulu (in Northern Finland) by the tradesman Nathanael Hedman to another bourgeois from the same town. In 1785, bookbinder Petter Halling offered for sale in auction in the same town no less than six copies of this Finnish translation that he had bound himself. Both of them belonged to the gentry, but in 1836 also a poor but devout widow, called Nissilä-mor from Nakkila in Satakunta, had in her possession several devotional books, among them a copy of one of the three editions of Arndt's *Paratiisin yrttitarha*.[560]

Johann Arndt's mainwork, *Vier Bücher vom wahren Christentum* (1605–1610), was available in Finland in Swedish translation from the 1650s. Yet Finnish readers had to wait for a translation in Finnish for the use of common people until 1827 when one of the leaders of the Pietistic movement, Deacon Henrik Renqvist (1789–1866) finally finished his translation and had the first of the four books sent to the printing shop. For him, the *Vier Bücher vom wahren Christentum* was almost a Bible-like source of true Christianity. In his diary, Renqvist noted "From the books of Arndt I have learned faith fading in the hearts of those, who praye by fraudulent means. I also came to know that without a proper prayer faith would not grow. It will not survive in the souls of those, who do not praye."[561] The first volume of Renqvist's translation was reprinted in 1832 in Porvoo, 1834 in Turku, 1836 in Helsinki, 1849 in Hämeenlinna and 1887 in Helsinki. The fourth book came to the bookshops for the first time in 1847 and was followed by three editions until the year 1905.[562]

According to auction records, *Vier Bücher vom wahren Christentum* in Swedish translation seems to have been even more popular in Finland than the *Paradies Gärtlein*. There were, however, some exceptions. For example in the countryside in 19th-century Western Häme where the population was predominantly Finnish- speaking, the *Paratiisin yrttitarha* (Paradies Gärtlein) occupied 4th place on the list of favourite devotional books whereas we find the *Vier Bücher vom wahren Christentum* on the 14th place only.[563]

Memories of reading experience from 20th Century Ostrobothia, Carelia, Häme and Ingermanland tells us something about the popularity of Arndt's works in Finnish. For example, in Kurikka in Ostrobothnia, one informant tells of reading Arndt and the Bible as a family habit until the World War 2. In the database of Finnish reading experiences, there are other memories concerning reading Arndt's books from the time before 1939. For example, in Luopioinen

560 Akiander, Upplysningar, Bd. 2, 296. Suomalaisten lukukokemusten tietokanta (Nakkila).

561 Akiander, Upplysningar, Bd. 203. Suomalaisten lukukokemusten tietokanta (Ilomantsi).

562 Erikson, Johann Arndt, 122. Tuija Laine, Henrik Renqvistin, 206–209.

563 Ojanen, Kirkko, 78.

the informant's grandfather used to read Arndt's postil loud for his household on Sundays.[564]

In the introduction to his translation, Renqvist recites a list of names who had unsuccessfully tried to translate this book before. Among them the most significant was Bailiff Jacob Johan Malmberg from Kuopio (in Eastern Finland); he also translated both volumes of John Bunyan's *The pilgrim's progress* from German (Eines Christen Reise nach der seeligen Ewigkeit) to Finnish. The first volume was published in Turku in the year 1809, entitled *Yhden kristityn waellus autuahan ijankaikkisuteen*, the second in Oulu 1834 with the title *Christityn lesken ja lasten waellus ijankaikkisuuteen* (Fig. 15).

Renqvist also tells of his own role in the translation efforts of this book. Peter Väänänen, a bookseller from Kuopio commonly called "*Book-Peter*" (Kirja Pietari), in 1814 had asked him for a suitable person for translating Arndt's book from Swedish into Finnish and promised to pay 100 riksdaler when the translation of all four books would be finished. In spite of his efforts, Renqvist had not succeeded finding anyone for this work. Therefore, he felt compelled to execute it himself. However, during this work he realized that translating all four books would have cost at least 1000 riksdaler, if the translator had been a professional translator. This would obviously have raised the price of book so high that potential buyers would no longer afforded to purchase it. The only remaining option in this case was translating the book mainly by himself.

Renqvists' work, however, was interrupted for several years until he found the necessary time to finish it as prison chaplain in Svartholma castle in 1825. As the result of his hard exertion, the manuscript was ready in the year 1827. A bookbinder from Turku, Johan Dahlberg, bought the press sheets of Renqvist's translation, but before he could release it, his entire storage burned down in the Great Fire of Turku at the same year. Only the two first volumes survived the flames. Dahlberg would finally publish them a few years later in 1832 and 1835. Readers welcomed both volumes with great enthusiasm: almost 11 000 copies were sold in short time. However, for the third volume readers had to wait until 1843.[565]

The forth volume of Arndt's main work was translated under the supervision of Renqvist by his relative Gregorius Monell. The Ecclesiastical Chapter in Porvoo, however, permitted only the printing of parts of part four 1847: the first part of the manuscript was turned down because it was said to contain

---

564 Suomalaisten lukukokemusten tietokanta Kurikka, Taipalsaari, Luopioinen), "*Kotona luettiin Paratiisin yrttitarhaa, Raamattua ja käytettiin kunkin ajan virsikirjaa*" (At home we read Paratiisin yrttitarha, Bible and sang the Hymnal).

565 Tiililä, Rukoilevaisten kirjoja, 35–36, 74–75. Heino, Hyppyherätys, 89. Repo, Johann Arndt, 35. Erikson, Johann Arndt, 122.

ideas of a nature that the Chapter regarded misleading and outdated. In the introduction to that volume, Renqvist's ungrateful duty was to make the best of things by explaining that the controversial passages in the translations were contested among the scientists as well.[566] The same Gregorius Monell translated the last of Arndt's main works, his postil, into Finnish from Swedish in 1861.[567]

Spener, Francke and major Pietistic authorities in Finland

Pietistic literature (pietism in its narrower sense) arrived to Finland in the shape of works by Spener and Francke during the Nordic War in the early 18th century. Some titles had, however, already been smuggled into Sweden before the war. Contrary to the books of Arndt, the import of these texts was illegal. The confiscations on the coastline of Finland and Sweden show that most of the literature of this kind came from Germany or the Baltic provinces. Swedish church historian Ove Nordstrandh has pointed out that hard censorship could in some tense limit the possibilities of distributing these books and manuscripts in Finland, but not eliminate the import.[568]

In Sweden, newly converted Pietists began to translate Speners' book with great enthusiasm into Swedish as early as in the 1690s, but the Royal Censorship (Censor librorum) prevented the printing of the fruits of their efforts. Swedish officers and Pietistic orientated army chaplains translated books of Spener and Francke during the long years of captivity in Siberia during the Nordic War, but censorship in Sweden stopped effectively all their attempts of getting these translations printed on Swedish soil. Some of these people tried to publish the books of leading Pietists and Mystics' in the Baltic Provinces where the major part of Swedish armed forces were stationed in the Nordic War. In general, it was easier to succeed in this endeavour outside of the Swedish homeland borders than under the precise supervision of domestic censorship authorities.[569]

Before the second half of the 18th century, only two Swedish translations of Spener's works saw daylight. A few pages of Spener's postil *Der evangelische Glaubens-Trost* (1695) were attached to another book; one of his letters was published the same way.

During the so-called Era of Freedom (1721–1772) attitudes towards modest Pietism and Pietists such as Spener, however, took a turn in a more tolerating direction. Spener's writings were no longer offhand banned like before. On the

566 Silfverhuth, Kirkon, 192.

567 Tiililä, Rukoilevaisten kirjoja, 35–36, 74–75. Repo, Johann Arndt, 35.

568 Nordstrandh, Litteratur, 3–8.

569 Nordstrandh, Litteratur, 50–55, 64–68.

quiet, they found their way to public book markets in 1740s. Normally, not even the *Censor librorum* stepped in as he used to have done only a decade earlier. The breakthrough of Pietistic literature in large variety of genres took place, however, not until the "liberal" Gustavian Era (1772–1792), when Pietistic texts were openly advertised in the Newspapers.[570] The ban on Pietistic conventicles from the year 1726 officially remained in effect in Finland until the year 1869.

The reasons for criticism against the writings of Pietists changed between the tur of the century and the 1740s. In the second half of the 18th century, the enlightened gentry and bourgeoise in the towns regarded Pietistic literature anti-rational and therefore uninviting and old-fashioned. The element of heterodoxy in Pietistic writing did not annoy them any longer, at least not as much as it had done just a few decades before. Even though they did not appreciate Pietistic books, on the other hand they did not want to be denied their right to read them. Still, the predominantly enlightened theologians at Turku Academy established a difference between Spener's "better" and Francke's, not to mention radical Pietists "worse" writings.

In the year 1740, the heirs of the late merchant Ek sold two books belonging to his library on auctions. These books, Speners' catechism and his *Pia desideria,* were presumably the first legally auctioned works of Spener in Finland. Most of the copies of Speners books identified so far in Finland were auctioned later, in the 1770–1780s, a period which seems to have been kind of breakthrough for the sale of his writings in Finnish towns. The social background of buyers resemble that of buyers of the books of Johann Arndt with the exception that according to the database Henrik there were no women among them. The first Finnish translations of Speners' books, *Evangeliumin vapauden väärinkäytöksestä* and *Jumalan lasten autuudesta armon ja kunnian valtakunnassa*, were published not until much later, 1868–1869.[571]

In the Swedish Era, there were approximately 100 people are known by name to have had access to Spener's works. Most of them were clergymen, university professors, teachers or students. In the Finnish Estate Inventory Deeds from towns from the early 17th century to the end of the Swedish era (1810), so far 99 references to Spener's works have been identified. Karl Fredrik Mennander (1712–1786), bishop of Turku and a well-known bibliophile, had in his private library 32 of Spener's works, and another devout bibliophile, Johannes Forsskåhl (1691–1762), the vicar of Helsinki, owned 27 works of Spener.[572] The lack of

570 Nordstrandh, Litteratur, 266–269.

571 Tiililä, Rukoilevaisten kirjoja, 392–393. Esko Laine, Pietismi, 88–90.

572 Esko Laine, Pietismi, 90.

Finnish translations excluded, however, the commoners from this limited circle of readers.

The first Swedish translation of one of August Hermann Francke's books was published illegally 1703 in Västerås without the permission of the Royal censor. The translator, Jonas Salan, was a lecturer of History at the upper secondary school of Västerås, an honourable man with god reputation. Probably for this reason, his secret activities with smuggled literature annoyed the Swedish Authorities even more than usual. Ove Nordstrandh has supposed that it might have played a role even in the tightening of anti-Pietistic statutes in the early years of the 18th century.[573]

In the Finnish Estate Inventory Deeds, there are references to five books of Francke. Three of them being postils or minor collections of his sermons. This kind of literature seems to have been popular especially in Ostrobothnia. Not only wealthy tradesmen but also economically affluent women acquired them, especially at auctions. For example, Maria Enbom, the widow to a coppersmith in Northern Finland, purchased at an action in Tornio in the 1790s a sermon of Francke in Swedish translation, *Ett rättsinnigt wäsende i Jesu, /Ephes. 4, 21. /förestält uti menniskans fråga och andans swar*.

Selling the "antirationalistic" books by August Hermann Francke was legalized evidently later than that of the books of Philipp Jacob Spener for the reasons above mentioned. The first known auction in Finland where Francke's' books were available for the public took place in Turku in the year 1769. Carl Gustaf Loffman, a nobleman and military judge, sold Francke's sermons in Swedish translation to baron Carl Otto Yxkull. At that time, the Yxkull family belonged to the most high-ranking aristocracy in Sweden-Finland. While not uncommon among the Swedish-speaking aristocracy, until 1780 Francke's writings were, however, beyond the reach of only Finnish-speaking commoners.

The first Finnish translation of Francke's books, consisting of the first volume of the postil, was published in 1780 by the Society called *Pro fide et Christianismo*. The second volume came out the following year. The society *Pro fide et Christianismo* consisted of honourable and distinguished gentlemen from Sweden and Finland joined together for promoting christian literature in order to stop the spreading of the threatening secularism and free-thinking which they conceived as unfortunate side effects of the enlightenment.

The publication of Francke's Postil in Finnish proved a success in Ostrobothnia and Northern Finland, areas where Francke seems to have been rather unknown before, whereas in Häme or in other inland areas its reception was rather faint. For example in the Western Häme, it was ranked in the 19th century

573 Nordstrandh, Litteratur, 77–80.

only on 16th place on the list of most popular devotional books.[574] In Eastern Finland, the spreading of Francke's Postil was even more limited, probably because in general book ownership was more uncommon there. According to the Finnish Estate Inventory Deeds, many owners of that book had purchased it brand new or it was given to them as a present.[575]

Among the Pietists in Halle, at beginning of the 18th century Johann Jakob Rambach (1693–1735) seems to have been even more popular than his older colleague Francke. Rambach was known in Finland as a writer of passion-orientated devotional books. Taken all together, in the Finnish Estate Inventory Deeds there can be found references to 10 books written by Rambach. One of them was translated into Finnish, *Jumalan Auxi Huudosa*. The Frenckell printing house published it in 1764 – 16 years earlier than Francke's Postil saw the light of day. At the end of the 18th century, Francke's works, however, beat finally Rambach's devotional books in popularity.

Besides books of Spener, Francke and Rambach a large variety of more radical Pietistic German texts circulated in manuscript copies. For example, the well-known German "enthusiast" Johann Konrad Dippel (1673–1734), the so-called *Christianus Democritus*, sold his own writings secretly with help of straw men. Radical Pietists apparently seem to have been well informed about the Swedish censorship policy. Therefore, they were not even trying to find sympathy for their texts in the eyes of the authorities.[576] Instead, copies written by themselves or by kindred spirits were sold from hand to hand. Several sources show beyond all dispute that at least in Stockholm there existed a secret market for literature of this kind.

Pietistic manuscripts secretly circulating from hand to hand in Sweden-Finland in the early 18th century consisted normally of both translated citations from the works of continental Pietists and the texts of domestic writers. The most productive of these was a radical Pietistic Petter Schäfer, a fanatic person with a master degree from Turku Academy. Sincerely, Schäfer hated Lutheran orthodoxy personated by two bishops, Gezelius the Younger and Gezelius the Older. This fact did not however prevent him from referring to Luther when he was accused in the front of the ecclesiastical chapter in Turku in the 1690s. Beside Schäfer his young disciples, Jonas Tellman, the brothers Johan and Carl Tålpo and Samuel Kjellin (Kiellinus), worked hard on the same purpose. During the long years in incarceration and solitude in Turku Castle, Schäfer wrote letters, pamphlets, polemics, prophecies, confessions and lampoons almost on

574 Ojanen, Kirkko, 78.

575 Esko M. Laine, August Hermann Francken, 122.

576 Nordstrandh, Litteratur, 22, 266.

a daily basis. He also kept a secret diary in Finnish. Most of his writings he edited in order to send them to be printed, although that never happened. In spite of the efforts of the authorities to stopping him through isolation, Schäfer's activities continued also in Gävle, where he was moved on the eve of the Russian occupation of Turku in 1713.[577]

A typical example of a Pietistic manuscript from the early 18th century was a theological pamphlet called *Tanckar om Skrifft och afflösning* by Jonas Tellman. He gained the idea for this writing from Spener, on whose massive work *Theologische Bedencken* the pamphlet in outline was based. *Tanckar om Skrifft och afflösning* was, however, not a translation nor a summary of that book. In his pamphlet, Tellman both rewrites and commentates Spener freely in order to criticize the prevailing confessional praxis of the Lutheran orthodoxy. By allowing unconverted people to take part in communion, Lutheran orthodoxy defeated, according to Tellman, the need of repentance.

Tellman's work is a unique compilation, which describes perfectly the theological self-understanding of Finnish pietism and the targets of its criticism during the time of the Nordic War. *Tanckar om Skrifft och afflösning* is simultaneously polemical, pedagogical and meditative – a devotional text as well as an attempt to change the ecclesiastical life surrounding its author.[578]

Many of the students in the Academy of Turku, who were affected by Pietism during their studies, still were ordained during the Nordic War because of a striking lack of priests in the country during that period. Even those who were at first turned away by the ecclesiastical chapter for their openly Pietistic opinions, after some period of time usually managed gaining at least a permission (*venia concionandi*) to preach in private households. Especially Schäfer's young admirers preached at funerals, baptisms and at weddings. These sermons they send to be printed as soon as possible in the cover of smokescreen of the good name of those to whom these sermons were dedicated.[579] Once in the hands of the authorities, literature of this kind could then more easily pass censorship. Another reason was the high number of titles of this kind of sermons on the market that overstrained the resources of the censorship. The first Pietistic texts written by domestic writers belonged to this literary genre.

Minor pamphlets and Pietistic loaded sermons were however not the only Pietistic literary genres in early modern Finland. Besides these, the Postil of Johan Wegelius the Younger (1693–1764), called *Se Pyhä Evangeliumillinen Walkeus Taiwallisesa Opisa Ja Pyhäsä Elämäsä* (Stockholm, 1747–1749) played a

577 Nordstrandh, Litteratur, 179–181.

578 Uppsala Universitetsbibliotek, N. 1759. Jonas Tellman *Tanckar om Skrifft och Afflösning.*

579 Uppsala Universitetsbibliotek, N. 1995 r. Jonas Telbom En Prädikan hållen 14. Sept. A. 1712 uti Hans Excell. Grefwen Wredes Hofsal.

very important role in early Finnish pietism. It belongs to a group of devotional books which still were in use in Finland in the 20th Century.[580]

Wegelius' father, Johan Wegelius the Elder (d. 1725), vicar in Pudasjärvi and later in Tyrvää and a devoted Pietist in the 1690s, was an admirer of Spener. He also had some correspondence with him. It is also known that Johannes Wegelius the Elder translated Arndt's *Paradies Gärtlein* in the year 1703 into Finnish, although this work as far as we know was never printed. Johannes Wegelius the Younger inherited his father's zeal for Spener. That is why a Spenerian undertone became so evident in the Postil. Like Spener, Wegelius too stepped back from religious separatism. Erkki Kansanaho has called his theology "Pietistic orthodoxy" (*pietistinen ortodoksia*) by which he refers to Wegelius' efforts of maintaining a balance of some kind between moderate Spenerian pietism and Lutheran orthodoxy. As such, this concept however proved anachronistic already at his own time even though Wegelius was acquitted of the charge of heresy after being interrogated by the Ecclesiastical Chapter.[581]

Pietism and modern Self, Conclusion

Pietistic literature, which aroused simultaneously with Cartesian philosophy, notably shaped the modern subject. Especially the modern subject was reflected in Pietistic attitudes towards inward experiences of humans. The demand of conversion and how to live after conversion was essential in Pietism. Even though some kind of pattern for repentance can be seen in the writings of August Herman Francke, the process of conversion was, however, unique and individual. The narrow gate to pass, the *Anfechtung* caused by the sin and fall of humankind, was different for every one because everyone had to face his or her own sins and trespasses. Because of the individual character of Pietistic conversion, there were always people in different states of their spiritual development in the congregation. Depicting of conversion emphasized the subject at the expense of the community. The lack in Finnish Pietistic literature of polemics against heterodoxy in general and Lutheran orthodoxy in specific is striking.

Pietistic literature also effected the relation between sense and sensation, which according to Mikko Lehtonen was an essential part of the development of the modern subject.[582] Conversion itself and life after that in particular re-

580 Suomalaisten lukukokemusten tietokanta. Informant from Oulainen (North Ostrobothnia) remembers from her childhood two books, Bible and the Postil of Wegelius.

581 Kansanaho, Postillan, 9–10, 12, 109–112 & 217. Laasonen, Johannes Gezelius, 148–151.

582 Lehtonen, Kyklooppi, 18, 23 & 65.

quired constant observation and analysis of emotions in order to keep these in control. Perhaps not so much the role of intelligence as that of the conscience was strengthened in Pietistic poetry at the expense of emotions. An even more difficult task to analyze is the impact of Pietism on the concept of nature in early modern time. The Arndt'ian and radical Pietism both exploited metaphoric images of natural philosophy formed during the Renaissance. Especially the fourth volume of Arndt's *Vier Bücher von Wahrem Christenthum, liber Naturae,* is based on the very same concept that preceded the genesis of modern self.[583] Instead, Pietists made a strict distinction between inward and outward experiences. The final destination of the mystical way to divinity was the union with God, *unio mystica*. In order for the believer to progress further on this way, the mortification of all earthly desires was required: everything belonging to this, once vanishing world was to be deserted and denied. Through this, the gardens of vicarages transformed in texts of Pietists to the gardens of Paradise, *Paradisgärtlein*. The idea of nature as a metaphor of the fall of man, however, was to be found in the texts of Lutheran orthodoxy as well. In this regard then, Pietism as such was not closer to the modern I than the Lutheran orthodoxy.

583 Arvidsson, Naturlig teologi, 7–17.

Abbildungen

Jesus.

Thet Nyia Testamen-
tit på Swensko.

Fig. 1 *Thet Nyia Testamentit på Swensko*, Stockholm 1526.
Foto: Kungliga Biblioteket, Stockholm.

Öffuer Histo=
rien om wårs HER=
RAS Jesu Christi werdigha
pino och Dödh / någhra eenfalli
gha Sermoner eller Predi=
caner.

Lau. Op.

1572.

Fig. 2 Laurentius Petri *Öffuer Historien om wars HERRAS Jesu Christi werdigha pino och Dödh, någhra eenfalligha Sermoner elller Predicaner*, Stockholm 1573.
Foto: Kungliga Biblioteket, Stockholm.

Abckiria.

Michael Agricola
Chriſtiano Sa-
lutem.

Oppe nyt wanha/ia noori /
joilla ombi Sydhen toori.
Jumalan keſkyt / ia mielen/
iotca taidhat Somen kielen.
Laki / ſe Sielun hirmutta /
mutt Criſtus ſen tas lodhutta.
Lue ſijs hyue Lapſi teſte /
Alcu oppi ilman eſte.
Nijte muiſta Elemes aina /
nin Jeſus ſinun Armons laina

Fig. 3 Michael Agricola *Abckiria*, [Stockholm 1549.]
Foto: Kungliga Biblioteket, Stockholm.

Rucouſkir=
ia / Bibliaſta / ſe
on / molemiſta Teſtamen=
tiſta / Meſſuraamatuſta / ia
muuſta moneſta / iotca toyſe=
la polella Luetellan / coko=
onpoymettu Somen
Turuſſa.

M D XL IIII.

Fig. 4 Michael Agricola *Rucouskiria bibliasta*, Stockholm 1544.
Foto: Kungliga Biblioteket, Stockholm.

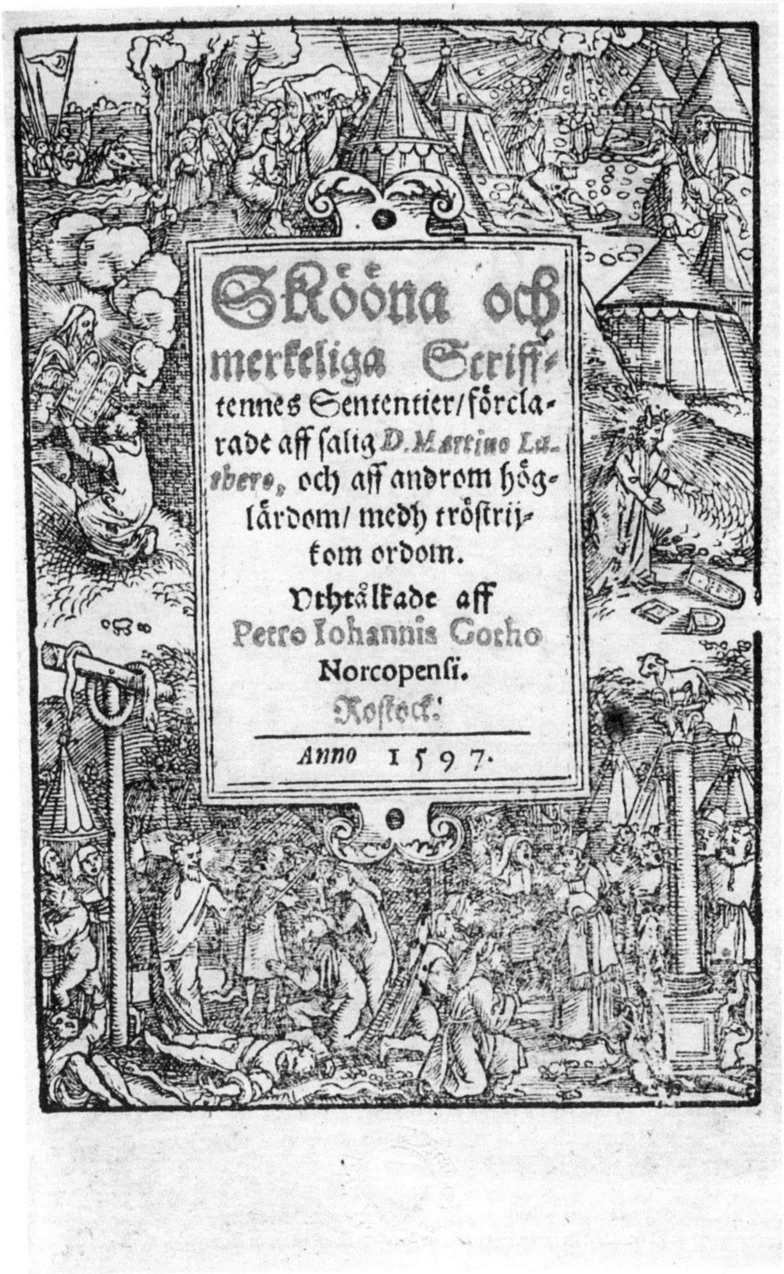

Fig. 5 [Martin Luther] *Skööna och merkeliga Scrifftennes Sententier … Vthtålkade aff Petro Iohannis Gotho*, Rostock 1597.
Foto: Kungliga Biblioteket, Stockholm.

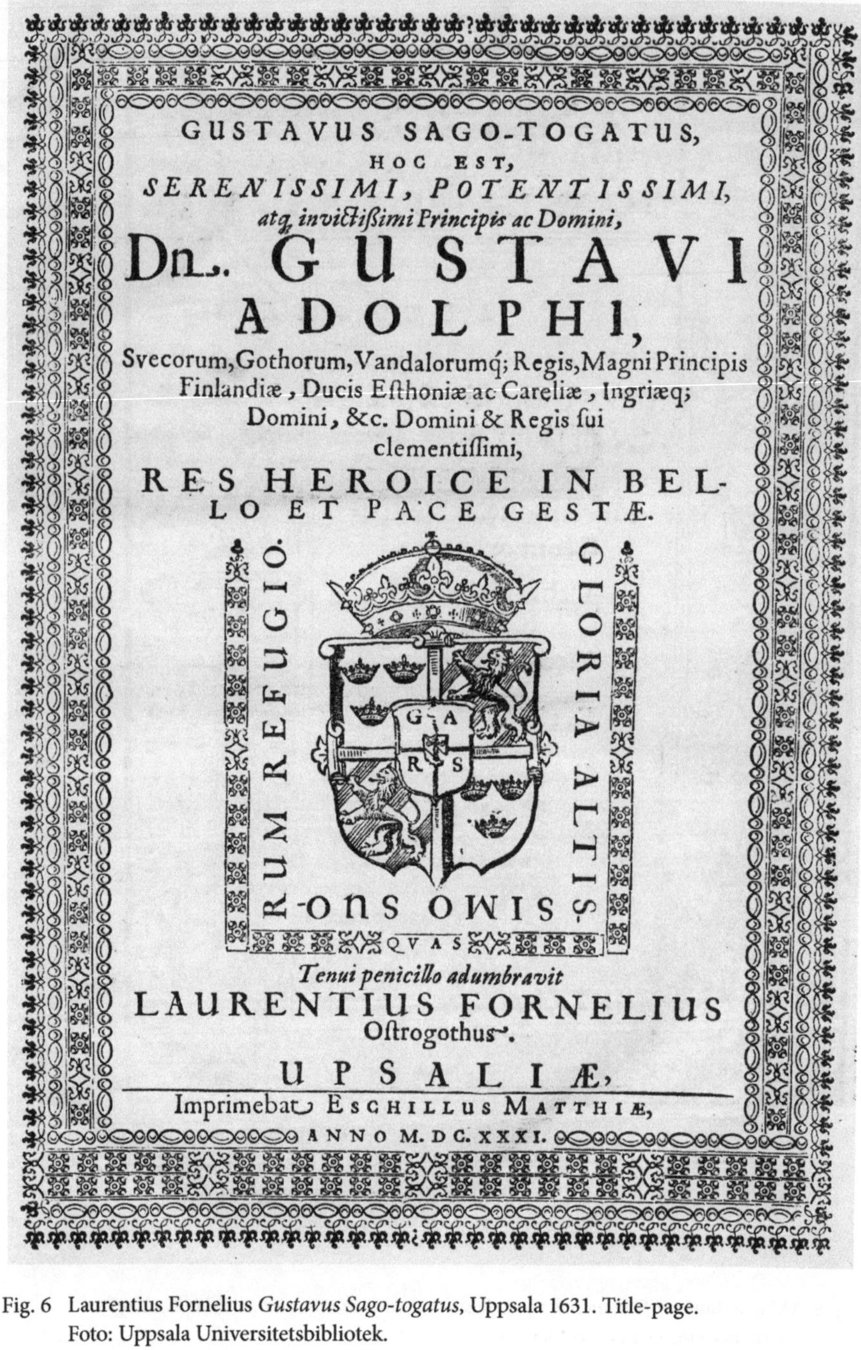

GUSTAVUS SAGO-TOGATUS,
HOC EST,
SERENISSIMI, POTENTISSIMI,
atq; invictissimi Principis ac Domini,
Dn. GUSTAVI
ADOLPHI,
Svecorum, Gothorum, Vandalorumq; Regis, Magni Principis
Finlandiæ, Ducis Esthoniæ ac Careliæ, Ingriæq;
Domini, &c. Domini & Regis sui
clementissimi,
RES HEROICE IN BEL-
LO ET PACE GESTÆ.

Tenui penicillo adumbravit
LAURENTIUS FORNELIUS
Ostrogothus.
UPSALIÆ,
Imprimebat ESCHILLUS MATTHIÆ,
ANNO M. DC. XXXI.

Fig. 6 Laurentius Fornelius *Gustavus Sago-togatus*, Uppsala 1631. Title-page.
Foto: Uppsala Universitetsbibliotek.

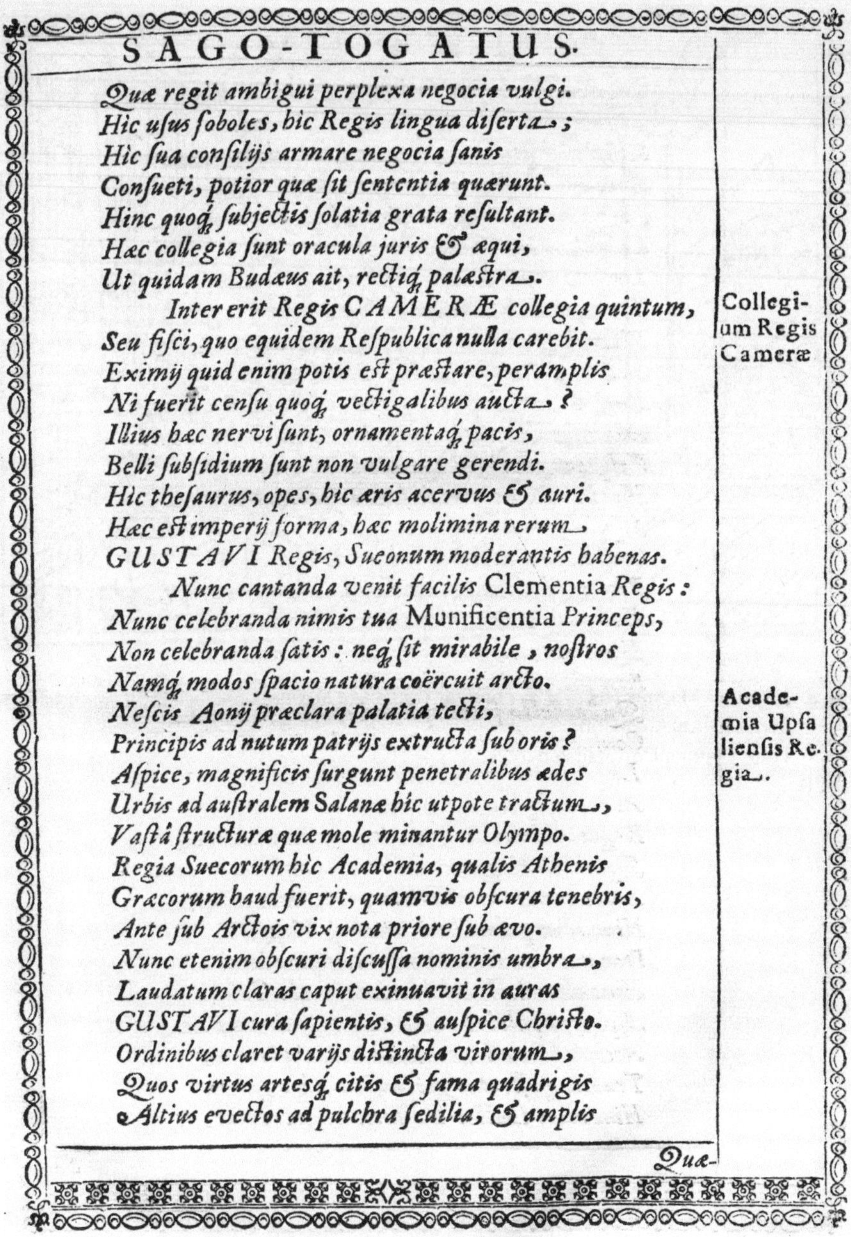

SAGO-TOGATUS.

Quæ regit ambigui perplexa negocia vulgi.
Hìc uſus ſoboles, hìc Regis lingua diſertæ;
Hìc ſua conſilijs armare negocia ſanis
Conſueti, potior quæ ſit ſententia quærunt.
Hinc quoq; ſubjectis ſolatia grata reſultant.
Hæc collegia ſunt oracula juris & æqui,
Ut quidam Budæus ait, rectiq; palæſtræ.
Intererit Regis CAMERÆ collegia quintum, Collegium Regis Cameræ
Seu fiſci, quo equidem Reſpublica nulla carebit.
Eximij quid enim potis eſt præſtare, peramplis
Ni fuerit cenſu quoq; vectigalibus auctæ?
Illius hæc nervi ſunt, ornamentaq; pacis,
Belli ſubſidium ſunt non vulgare gerendi.
Hìc theſaurus, opes, hìc æris acervus & auri.
Hæc eſt imperij forma, hæc molimina rerum
GUSTAVI Regis, Sueonum moderantis habenas.
Nunc cantanda venit facilis Clementia Regis:
Nunc celebranda nimis tua Munificentia Princeps,
Non celebranda ſatis: neq; ſit mirabile, noſtros
Namq; modos ſpacio natura coërcuit arcto.
Neſcis Aonij præclara palatia tecti, Academia Upſalienſis Regia.
Principis ad nutum patrijs extructa ſub oris?
Aſpice, magnificis ſurgunt penetralibus ædes
Urbis ad auſtralem Salanæ hìc utpote tractum,
Vaſtâ ſtructuræ quæ mole minantur Olympo.
Regia Suecorum hìc Academia, qualis Athenis
Græcorum haud fuerit, quamvis obſcura tenebris,
Ante ſub Arctois vix nota priore ſub ævo.
Nunc etenim obſcuri diſcuſſa nominis umbræ,
Laudatum claras caput exinuavit in auras
GUSTAVI cura ſapientis, & auſpice Chriſto.
Ordinibus claret varijs diſtincta virorum,
Quos virtus arteſq; citis & fama quadrigis
Altius evectos ad pulchra ſedilia, & amplis

Quæ-

Fig. 7 Laurentius Fornelius *Gustavus Sago-togatus*, Uppsala 1631. Section *Academia Upsaliensis Regia*.
Foto: Uppsala Universitetsbibliotek.

Fig. 8 Johannes Magnus *Historia de omnibus Gothorum Sveonumque regibus*, Rome 1554. The mythological king Ubbe.
Foto: Uppsala Universitsbibliotek.

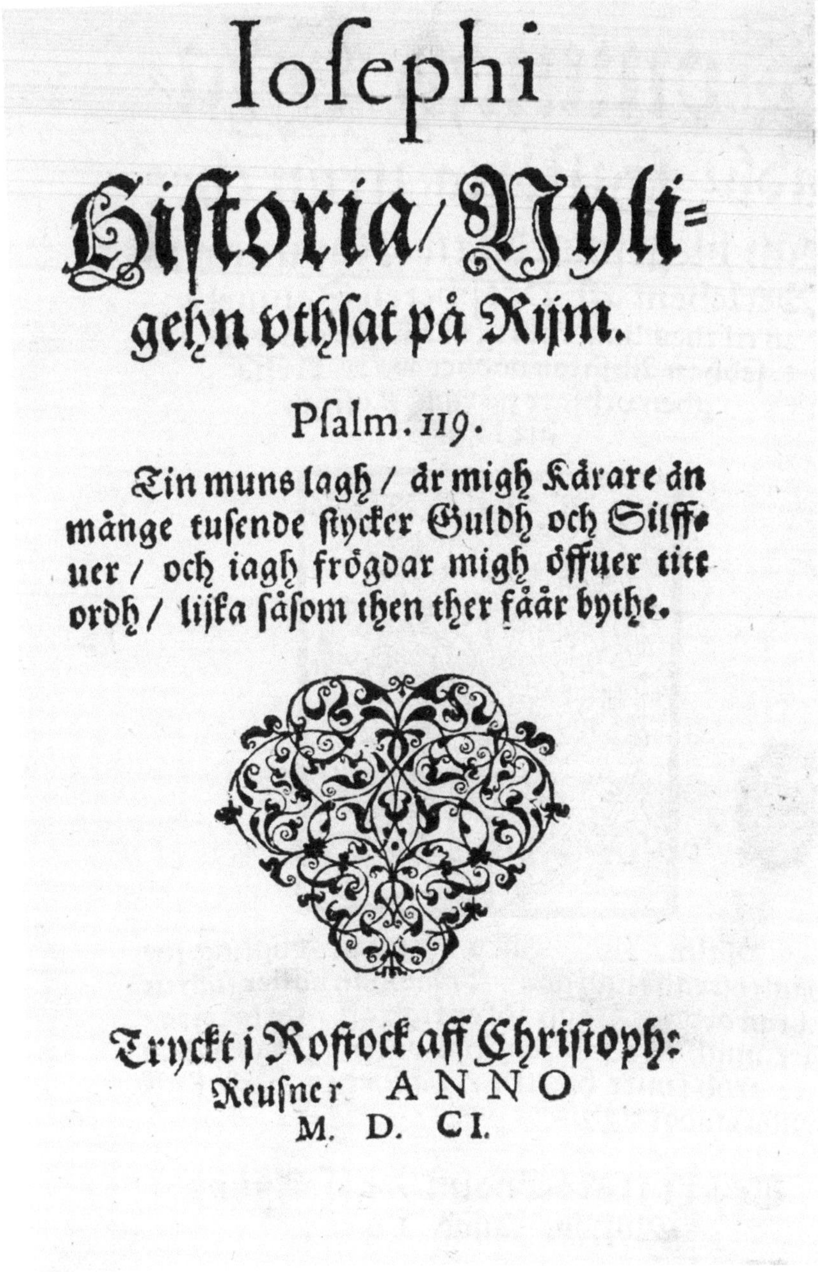

Ioſephi
Hiſtoria/ Nyli=
gehn vthſat på Rijm.

Pſalm. 119.

Tin muns lagh / är migh kärare än
månge tuſende ſtycker Guldh och Silff=
uer / och iagh frögdar migh öffuer titt
ordh / lijka ſåſom then ther fåår bythe.

Tryckt j Roſtock aff Chriſtoph:
Reuſner ANNO
M. D. CI.

Fig. 9 *Iosephi Historia, Nyligehn vthsat på rijm*, Rostock 1601.
Foto: Kungliga Biblioteket, Stockholm.

Konungh Da-
widhz Historia ifrån the-
han bleff smordh til Konungh j
Betlehem aff Propheten Samuel/
in til thes han kom igen til Jerusalem/
sedhan Absalon dödher waar/ Nyli-
ghen vthsatt på rijm. Lustigh
att låsa.

Psalm. 119. Huru skal een Yngling sin
wägh ostraffeligh gåå / Nåår han håller sigh in
l tijn ordh. Jagh söker tigh aff allo hiertta/
låt migh icke fela om tijn bodh. Jagh håller
titt ordh j mitt hiertta / på ther iagh icke skall
synda emoot tigh.

Tryckt j Stockholm / aff Anund
Olufsson. Anno 1604.

Fig. 10 *Konungh Dawidhz historia*, Stockholm 1604.
Foto: Kungliga Biblioteket, Stockholm.

MARS GERMANICUS
VICTUS.
Thet är
COMAEDIA
Om thet wälendade Tydske
Kriget.
Stält aff
SAMUELE P. BRASCK
Gymn. Lincop. Eloq. & Poës Lectore,
& P. in Egby & Rinna.
Och hållen i Linköping
den 29. Julij 1649.

Tryckt i Linköping hoos Christopher Günter/
Anno M. DC. L.

Fig. 11 Samel P. Brasck *Mars Germanicus victus*, Linköping 1650.
Foto: Kungliga Biblioteket, Stockholm.

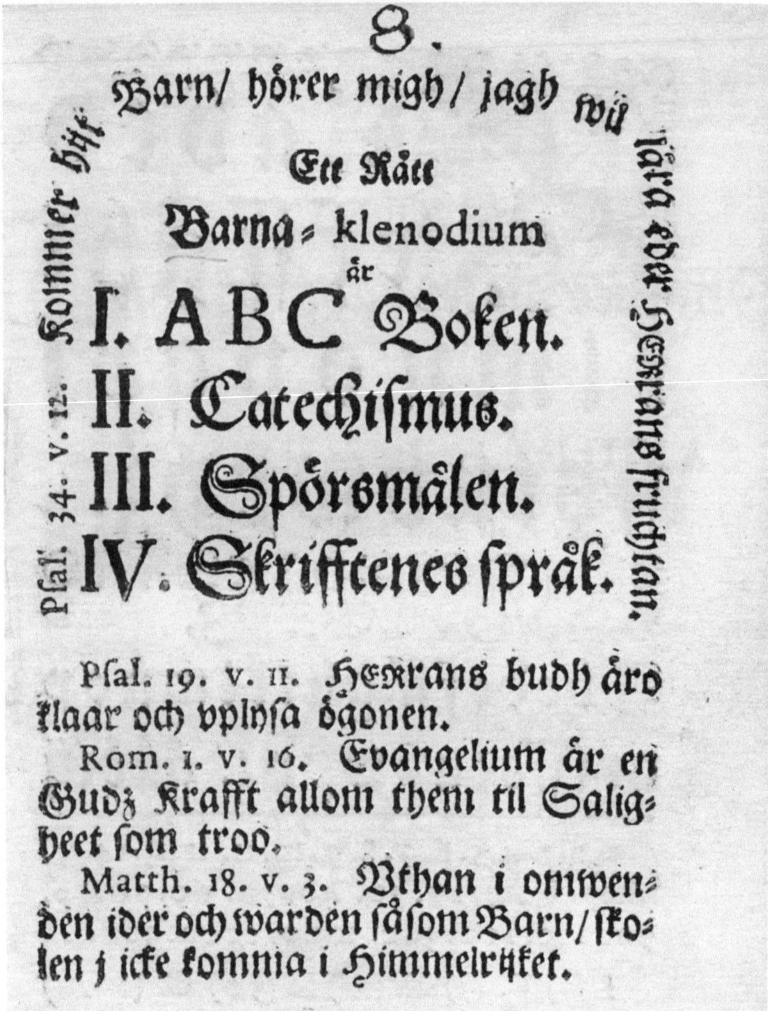
8.

Kommer hijt Barn/ hörer migh/ jagh wil lära eder HErrans fruchtan.

Psal. 34. v. 12.

Ett Rätt
Barna- klenodium
är
I. ABC Boken.
II. Catechismus.
III. Spörsmålen.
IV. Skrifftenes språk.

Psal. 19. v. 11. HErrans budh äro klaar och vplysa ögonen.
Rom. 1. v. 16. Evangelium är en Gudz krafft allom them til Salig- heet som troo.
Matth. 18. v. 3. Vthan i omwen- den ider och warden såsom Barn/ sko- len j icke komma i Himmelrijket.

Åbo/

Tryckt aff Petter Hanszon/ åhr
1666.

Fig. 12 [Johannes Gezelius d.Ä.] *Ett Rätt Barna-klenodium*, Åbo (Turkku) 1666. Foto: Kungliga Biblioteket, Stockholm.

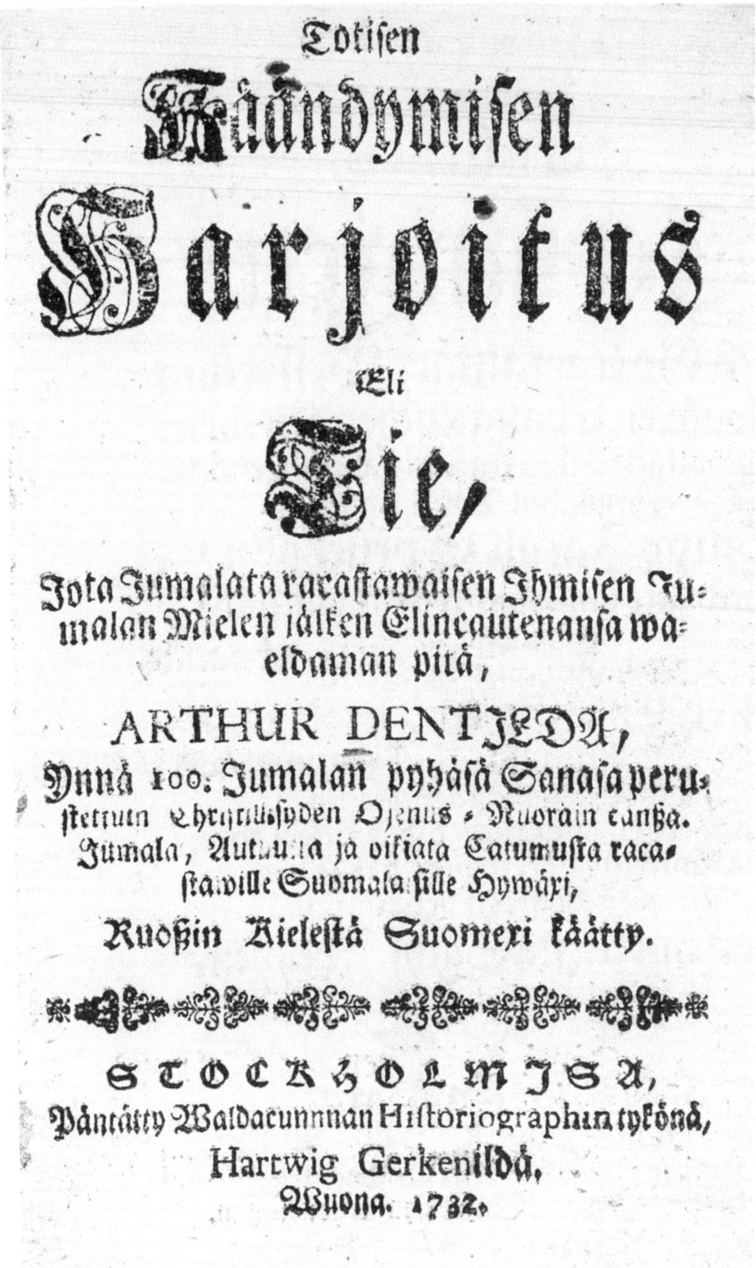
Totisen
Käändymisen
Harjoitus
Eli
Tie,
Jota Jumalata racastawaisen Ihmisen Ju-
malan Mielen jälken Elincautenansa wa-
eldaman pitä,
ARTHUR DENTILDA,
Ynnä 100. Jumalan pyhäsä Sanasa peru-
stettuin Christillisyden Ojennus Nuorain cansa.
Jumala, Autuutta ja oikiata Catumusta raca-
stawille Suomalaisille Hywäxi,
Ruoßin Kielestä Suomexi käätty.
STOCKHOLMISA,
Präntätty Waldacunnan Historiographin tykönä,
Hartwig Gerkenildä.
Wuona. 1732.

Fig. 13 Arthur Dent *Totisen käändymisen harjoitus*, Stockholm 1732.
Foto: Kungliga Biblioteket, Stockholm.

PIA DESIDERIA:
Oder
Hertzliches
Verlangen/
Nach Gottgefälliger Besserung
der wahren Evangelischen Kirchen/
sampt einigen dahin einfältig abzweckenden
Christlichen Vorschlägen/
Philipp Jacob Speners/ D.
Predigers und Senioris zu Franckfurt
am Mayn;
Sampt angehengten
Zweyer Christlichen Theologorum
darüber gestellten/und zu mehrer auferbau-
ung höchstdienlichen Bedencken.
Zu end werden angefügt die jenige Lehrer/
so die künfftige bekehrung der Juden in
ihren Schrifften behaupten.
Mit Churfürstl. Sächs. Freyheit.

Franckfurt am Mayn/
In verlegung Johann David Zunners.
Druckts Johann Dieterich Friedgen.
M DC LXXX.

Fig. 14 Philipp Jacob Spener *Pia desideria: Oder Hertzliches Verlangen*, Frankfurt am Main 1680.
Foto: Kungliga Biblioteket, Stockholm.

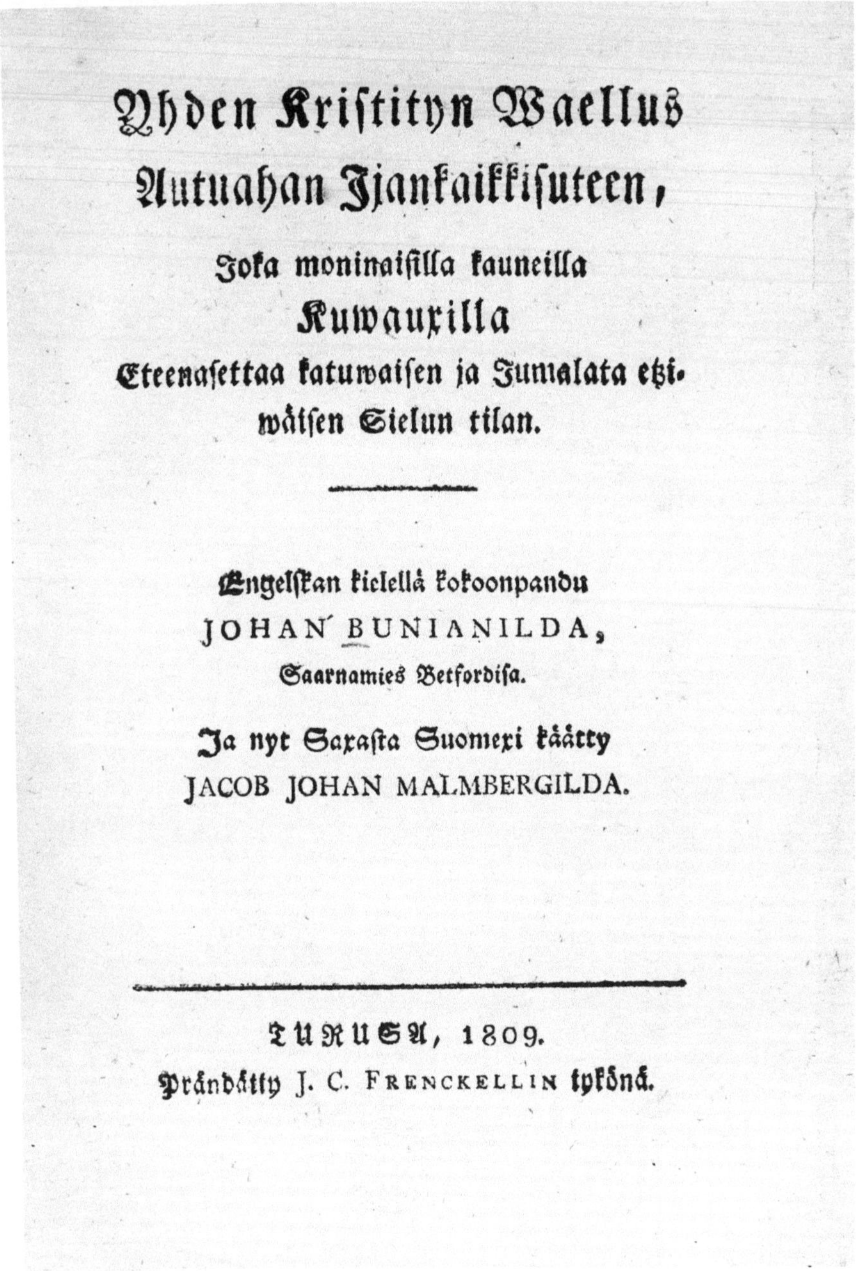

Yhden Kriſtityn Waellus
Autuahan Ijankaikkiſuteen,
Joka moninaiſilla kauneilla
Kuwauxilla
Eteenaſettaa katuwaiſen ja Jumalata etzi-
wäiſen Sielun tilan.

Engelſkan kielellä kokoonpandu
JOHAN BUNIANILDA,
Saarnamies Betfordiſa.

Ja nyt Saxaſta Suomexi käätty
JACOB JOHAN MALMBERGILDA.

TURUSA, 1809.
Prändätty J. C. FRENCKELLIN tykönä.

Fig. 15 John Bunyan *Yhden kristityn waellus autuahan ijankaikkisuteen*, Turku 1809. Foto: Kungliga Biblioteket, Stockholm.

Literaturverzeichnis

Ungedruckte Quellen & Online Quellen

Ennennäkemätön kirjalöytö Saksasta: 1600-luvun suomenkielinen katekismus ja virsikirja (http://yle.fi/uutiset/ennennakematon_kirjaloyto_saksasta_1600-luvun_suomenkielinen_katekismus_ja_virsikirja/8510483 [Datum der Internetabfrage: 28.02.2018]).

Henrik: Books and their owners in Finland up to 1809 (http://dbgw.finlit.fi/henrik/).

Kirjojen leviäminen Suomessa vuoteen 1850 (The spreading of books in Finland until 1850) (https://avaa.tdata.fi/web/kirjahistoria).

Kungliga Biblioteket, *Engeström* B. I.1.1.

—, *F.b.2.*

—, *Rålamb* Bd. 40.

Linköpings Stiftsbibliotek, Samuel *Älf*'s Collection, vol. W 28.

—, T 131.

Luther, Martin, *Luthers Werke im WWW*: Weimarer Ausgabe (http://luther.chadwyck.co.uk).

Messenius, Johannes, *Christmannus* [Huru christendomen först kom i Sweriet] (u.å.), Stockholm Kungliga Biblioteket, Codex Vp. 14.

SUECIA (https://suecia.kb.se)

Suomalaisten lukukokemusten tietokanta: tallennukset (https://elomake.helsinki.fi/raportti/red/?jarjesta=knt_312514 [Finnish reading experiences, RED]).

Uppsala Universitetsbibliotek, Rare Collections, vol. R 383.

—, N 1722.

—, N 1772.

VD16, Verzeichnis der im deutschen Sprachbereich erschienenen Drucke des 16. Jahrhunderts (http://www.bsb-muenchen.de/index.php?id=1681&type=0 [Datum der Internetabfrage: 01.11.2016]).

Gedruckte Quellen

Angermannus, Abraham Andreae, *Refutatio* erroris Herbesti (Hamburg: Henricus Binderus, 1588*Belial* de Inferno (1590er Jahre).

Brask, Samuel, *Acta* et martyria apostolorum, Linköping *1648*.

—, *Filius* prodigus, Linköping 1645.

—, *Mars* Germanicus Victus: Ther är Comaedia Om thet wälendade Tydske kriget, Linköping *1649*.

Carstenius, Petrus, Thet himmelska *consistorium*, tilhoopa kallat, Stockholm 1674.

Chærberus, Josephus Svenonis, Itt gudeligit *samtaal*, Västerås *1642*.

Commonitiones, Perbreves Commonitiones eller korta påminnelser, hvilka tilförene styckevis, efter som tilfälle hafver gifvits i Visitationerne, äro uti Församlingarna efterlemnade (1673); men nu på nytt Församlingarna, och i synnerhet Ven. Clero, i detta lofl. Stiftet til nytta och efterrättelse sammandragne och publicerade af Johanne Gezelio, S. S. Th. Doct. och Ep. Ab., in: O. Wallquist (Hg.), Ecclesiastique samlingar, T. 5 (4), Stockholm 1791.

Dåleman, Peder, Een skiön *Wijse* om Gudz Son, Stockholm 1584.

De creatione mwndi (1590er Jahre).

Esther, 1693.

Finno, Jaakko/Carelius, Simon Johannis, *Yxi Vähä* Suomenkielinen wirsikiria, Suomencocouxis Jumalata kijttä Suomenkielellä, tehty M. Jacobilda Suomalaiselda, ja muild Suomen papeilda. Cunnjalisten herrain Turun Pispan M. Erichin, ja Capitularesten tiedhost ja suosjost, H. Hemmingin Maschun kirckoherran vaevall ja culutuxell, ensins Präntätty Stocholmisa, Rostock 1607 (VD17 14:663252M).

Flacius, Matthias, Etliche tröstliche *vermanungen* in sache[n] das Heilige Gottliche Wort betreffend zu dieser betrübten zeit sehr nützlich vnd tröstlich zu lesen. D. Martinus Luther Anno M. D. XXX., Magdeburg 1550.

Friderich, Matthäus, Wider den *Sauffteuffel* (s.l., 1552) [VD16 F2767].

Gevaliensis, Thomas Petri, Konungh *Dawidhz* historia ifrån thet han bleff smordh til konung i Betlehem aff propheten Samuel, in til thes han kom igen til Jerusalem, sedhan Absalon dödher waar. Nylighen vthsatt på rijm. Lustigh att läsa, Stockholm 1604.

—, *Iosephi* Historia, Rostock 1601.

Gezelius, Johannes, d.Ä., *Methodus informandi* in Paedagogiis tam ruralibus quam urbicis. Nec non Scholis Trivialibus, Per Dioecesin Aboensem: Prius qvidem per partes exhibita: Jam verò Necessitate ita efflagitante, Et Ad desiderium multorum, Aboae 1683.

Goclenius, Rudolph/Kirchner, Hermann/Chesnecopherus, Nicolaus/et al., *Carmina Gratulatoria*, in novas honorum dignitates, Dn. *Johannis Schroderi* Nicopiensis Suecu, cm ei in illustrissima [...] Academia Marpurgenis summus in Philosophia gradus [...], Marburg 1599 [VD16 ZV 23354].

Gothus, Petrus Johannis, *Skööna* och merkeliga scrifftennes sententier, förclarade aff salig d. Martino Luthero, och aff androm höglärdom, medh tröstrijkom ordom, Rostock 1597.

Holoferni och Juditz historja opå Rijm (1590er Jahre).

Jesus lärer i templet (1590er Jahre).

Johannes Magnus, *Historia* de omnibus Gothorum Sveonumque regibus, Rome 1554.

Kolmodin, Ericus, *Genesis* ætherea Eller Jesu Christi födelse, Åbo (1659).

Laurbecchius, Petrus, *Simon* magus, Linköping 1652.

Luther, Martin, Der *Achte Teil* vnd letzte aller Bücher vnd Schrifften des thewren seligen Mans Gottes Doctoris Martini Lutheri vom XLII.Jar an bis auff seinen Christlichen Abschied aus diesem Leben vnd dasselbe Jar vollend hinaus bis auffs XLVII. geschrieben vnd im Druck ausgangen, Jena 1558.

—, Der *Neundte Teil* der Bücher des Ehrnwirdigen Herrn D.Martini Lutheri: darinnen die Propositiones vom Ablas wider Johan Tetzel begriffen welche der Vrsprung dieses gantzen handels vnd der herwiderbrachten reine Lere Christi gewesen sampt vielen Sendbrieuẽ an Bapst Keiser Fürstẽ vñ Bischoue vñ andern schrifften von dem 17. bis in das 33. jar Auch die Acta von der Religion auff den Reichstagen zu Worms Anno 1521. vnd zu Nürmberg Anno 1522. vnd zu Augsburg Anno 1530. sampt der Confession vñ Apologia zu solcher zeit Kei.Mai.vberantwort, Wittenberg 1557.

Messenius, Johannes, Een *Comaedia*, uti hwilken hela konung Gustafz den I:s Regemente, 1642.

Olaus Petri, *Tobie* Comedia, Stockholm 1550.

Olofsson, Hans, Een lijten Andeligh *Tragoedia*, Om the tree wijsa Män, Linköping 1635.

Praetorius, Laurentius/Ambernus, Jacobi/Nicolai, Petrus/Ruta, Peter, *Carmina Gratulatoria*, in honorem Ornatissimi & doctissimi Iuvenis Dn. *Laurentii Paulini* Gothi [...], Helmstedt 1592 [VD16 ZV 23353].

Prytz, Andreas Johannis, En lustigh *comoedia*, Om then stormechtighe Sweriges, Göthes, Wendes konung etc. konung *Gustaf* then första, huru han til regementet i Swerige bleff vphögd, tå han konung Christiern Tyrann, af landet vthdriffuit hade, oc huru han genom Gudz nådh vprättade Swerige ifrån påfwens mörcker och willfarelse, och införde ewangelii reena liws thet påfwen länge bortröfwat hadhe, Upsala 1622.

—, *Olof* Skottkonung, Uppsala 1620.

Psalmboken, Then swenska psalmboken. Med the stycker som ther til höra, och på föliande blad vpteknade finnas, uppå Kongl. Majtz. nådigste befalning [...] åhr M DC XCIII. Med flit öfwersedd, förbättrad, och förmehrad: och vngdomen til fromma, vti thenne beqwäme storlek åhr *1695*, Stockholm 1695.

Ragvaldinpoika, Tuomas, *Sen Wielä* wirhellisen Ilo-Weisu, Cosca hän Jumalan Siunauxen woimalla Ja Läkärin konstin awulla Parattin huulensa wirhestä. Caikille rackaille Risti weljille ja sisarille ylöskehoituxexi kijttämän Jumalata terwen ja hywin caunistetun ruumin edestä, [S.l.] 1763.

Rebecca, 1674.

Riksarkivet, AE 118.
—, *AE 124.*
—, Royal *concepts* 648, Privy Council to Majesty 14.7.1706.
—, *E 5702.*
—, *Kopiesamling* I Avskriftsamlingen Avd. II. Bd. 540.
—, Stockholms *tullböcker* 18/8 1543 & Stockholms tullböcker 26/10 1543, 51309/292:1.
RONDELETIUS, JACOB, *Judas* Redivivus, 1614.
RUDBECK, OLOF, *Atlantica* sive Manheim vera Japheti posterorum sedes ac patria, Uppsala 1679–1702.
SIMONIUS, JOHANNES, *Oratio* de auctoritate regia, et de Regni Svetici dignitate atque felicitate oratio ..., Uppsala 1626.
Troon (Glaubensbekenntnis in schwedischer und lateinischer Sprache), Stockholm 1584.
WEINRICH, MELCHIOR, *Aerarium Poëticum*, hos est, Phrases et nomina Poëtica, tam Propria, quam Appellativa, Poëtarum Latinorum, cum Veterum plerorumque omnium, tum Recentiorum quorundam, et praesertim Friderici Taubmanni, Seculi nostri Poëtae praestantissimi, Frankfurt am Main: Apud Thomam Matthiam Götzium, 1664.
WIJSAE, *Een wijsae*, om thenne Werldennes fåfengeligheet (Eine Weise von der Eitelkeit dieser Welt), Stockholm: Andreas Gutterwitz, 1584.
WIJSE, *Een Andeligh Wijse*/ på nyt öffuerseet och förmeret (Eine neue geistliche Weise, aufs Neue bearbeitet und vermehrt), s.l., s.t., s.a. (Stockholm: Andreas Gutterwitz, um 1584).
WIJSE, *Een skön Andeligh Wijse* at tröste sigh medh på sitt yterste (Eine schöne geistliche Weise um sich am Lebensende zu trösten), s.l., s.t., s.a.

Forschungsliteratur

Acta Synodica in Concilio Ubsal. Anno 1572, in: O. Ahnfelt (Hg.), Bidrag till Svenska Kyrkans Historia i sextonde århundradet, Lund, *1895*, 21–28.
AGRICOLA, MIKAEL, *Mikael Agricolan teokset*, 3 vols., Porvoo 1987.
AHLBERG, BO, Laurentius Petri och *traditionen*, Kyrkohistorisk årsskrift 1963, 145–199.
—, Laurentius Petris *nattvardsuppfattning*, Lund, 1964.
ÅHLÉN, BENGT, *Ord* mot ordningen: Farliga skrifter, bokbål och kättarprocesser i svensk censurhistoria, Stockholm 1986.
AKIANDER, MATTHIAS, Historiska *upplysningar* om de religiösa rörelserna i Finland i äldre och senare tider, Helsingfors 1857–1863.

Andersen, Niels Knud, Om forholdet mellem de ældste svenske og danske *salmebøger*, in: C.-G. Andrén (Hg.), Reformationen i Norden. Kontinuitet och förnyelse, Lund 1973, 217–240.

Andrén, Åke, *Introductorium* theologicum: studier kring ett dokument om prästerlig församlingstjänst från svensk reformationstid, Stockholm 1950.

Annerstedt, Claes, Upsalas universitets *historia*: Första delen 1477–1654, Uppsala 1877.

Appel, Charlotte, *Printed in Books*, Imprinted on Minds: Catechisms and Religious Reading in Denmark during the Seventeenth and Early Eighteenth Centuries, in: C. Appel/M. Fink-Jensen (Hg.), Religious Reading in the Lutheran North. Studies in Early Modern Scandinavian Book Culture. Cambridge Scholars Publishing, Newcastle upon Tyne 2011, 70–87.

Appel, Charlotte/Fink-Jensen, Morten, *Introduction*: Books, Literacy, and Religious Reading in the Lutheran North, in: C. Appel/M. Fink-Jensen (Hg.), Religious Reading in the Lutheran North. Studies in Early Modern Scandinavian Book Culture. Cambridge Scholars Publishing, Newcastle upon Tyne 2011, 1–14.

Arlund Hass, Trine/Humble, Noreen/Pade, Marianne (Hg.), *Latin* and the Early Modern World: Linguistic Identity and the Polity from Petrarch to the Habsburg Novelists, Renæssanceforum 10, 2016.

Arwidsson, A.I. (Hg.), *Handlingar* till upplysning af Finlands häfder, Bd. 6, Stockholm 1853.

Arvidsson, Bengt, *Naturlig teologi* och naturteologi. Naturen som bild i dansk fromhetstradition omkring år 1600, Studia Theologica Lundensia 45, Lund 1990.

Åsbrink, Gustav/Westman, Knut B. (Hg.), Svea Rikes *Ärkebiskopar* från 1164 till nuvarande tid, Stockholm 1935.

Assmann, Aleida, *Canon* and Archive, in: A. Erll/A. Nunning/S.B. Young (Hg.), Cultural Memory Studies: An International and Interdisciplinary Handbook, Berlin 2008, 97–107.

—, *Geschichte* im Gedächtnis: Von der individuellen Erfahrung zur öffentlichen Inszenierung, München 2007.

Assmann, Jan, Das kulturelle *Gedächtnis*: Schrift, Erinnerung und politische Identität in frühen Hochkulturen, München 1997.

Assmann, Jan/Müller, K. E. (Hg.), Der *Ursprung* der Geschichte: Archaische Kulturen, das Alte Ägypten und das Frühe Griechenland, München 2005.

Bacon, Francis, The New *Organon* and Related Writings, Edited with an Introduction by Fulton H. Anderson, Indianapolis/New York 1960.

Barker, Sara/Hosington, Brenda, Renaissance Cultural *Crossroads*: Translation, Print and Culture in Britain 1473–1640, Leiden 2013.

Barnes, Robin B., Der herabstürzende *Himmel*: Kosmos und Apokalypse unter Luthers Erben um 1600, in: M. Jakubowski-Thessen/H. Lehmann/J.R. Schilling (Hg.), Staat, Jahrhundertwenden: Endzeit- und Zukunftsvorstellungen vom 15. bis zum 20. Jahrhundert, Göttingen 1999.

Beemon, F.E., Poisonous *Honey* or Pure Manna: The Eucharist and the World in the "Beenhive" of Marnix of Saint Aldegonde, Church History, 61, 1992, 382–393.

De Beer, Susanna, The *Poetics* of Patronage: Poetry as Self-Advancement in Giannantonio Campano, Turnhout 2013.

—, *Patronage*, in: Ford, Philip/Bloemendal, Jan/Fantazzi, Charles (Hg.), Brill's Encyclopaedia of the Neo-Latin World, Leiden/Boston 2014, 1124–1126.

Belle, Marie-Alice/Hosington, Brenda, *Thresholds of Translation*: Paratext, Print, and Cultural Exchange in Early Modern Britain (1473–1660), London 2018.

—, *Translation*, History and Print: A Model for the Study of Printed Translations in Early Modern Britain, Translation Studies 10:1, 2017, 2–21.

Belial 1864, Belial ex Inferno, in: Twå hittills outgifna Swenska Mystèrer, Stockholm 1864.

Berg, Tor, *Hogenskild Bielke*, Svenskt biografiskt lexikon (urn:sbl:18165; Datum der Internetabfrage: 05.01.2016).

Bernström, Gustaf, *Nyfunna* danska och svenska 1500-tals tryck, Nordisk tidskrift för bok- och biblioteksväsen 40, 1953, 51–63.

Berntson, Martin, Det förlorade *bibeldramat*: Teater och kyrka i Sverige under tidigmodern tid. En fallstudie", in: M. Hagberg (Hg.), Kyrka, kultur, historia: en festskrift till Johnny Hagberg, Skara 2012, 57–71.

—, En djävulskt bra *lärare*! Didaktiska perspektiv på ondskans inkarnationer i några tidigmoderna svenska teaterpjäser, in: S. Olofsson (Hg.), Den trogne arbetaren i vingården: festskrift till Bo Claesson, Göteborg 2015, 81–99.

Berntson, Martin/Nilsson, Bertil/Wejryd, Cecilia (Hg.), *Kyrka* i Sverige: introduktion till svensk kyrkohistoria, Skellefteå 2012.

Beronius, Johannes, *Rebecka*, en ny och andeligh comœdia [Söderköping, 1674], in: Samlade Vitterhetsarbeten af svenska författare från Stjernhjelm till Dalin, Bd. 21, Upsala 1876.

Bireley, Robert, The *Refashioning* of Catholicism, 1450–1700: A Reassessment of the Counter-Reformation, Basingstoke 1999.

Blair, Ann, *Too Much* to Know: Managing Scholarly Information before the Modern Age, New Haven 2010.

Blakeley, James, *Confronting* the Reformation: Popular Reaction to Religious Change in the Pays de Vaud, in: Th. Kaufmann/A. Schubert/K. von Greyerz (Hg.), Frühneuzeitliche Konfessionskulturen, Heidelberg 2008, 101–118.

Bonenberger, Karl (Hg.), Volkstümliche *Überlieferungen* in Wittenberg, Stuttgart [3]1980.

Bornkamm, Heinrich, Martin *Luther* in der Mitte seines Lebens, Göttingen 1979.

Brask, Samuel P., *Acta* et martyria apostolorum. Thet är een tragico-comoedia om Apostlarnas gärniongar och jämmerliga marteringar [...] och hållin in publico theatro i Linköping vppå Pedhersmesse dagh 1648 (Linköping 1648), in: Samlade Vitterhetsarbeten af svenska författare från Stjernhjelm till Dalin, Bd. 22, Uppsala *1878*.

—, *Mars* Germanicus Victus: Thet är en Comaedia om thet welendade tydske kriget [...] och hållen i Linköping den 29 juli 1649 (Linköping 1650), in: Samlade Vitterhetsarbeten af svenska författare från Stjernhjelm till Dalin, Bd. 22, Uppsala, *1878*.

Braunmüller, Kurt, *Semikommunikation* und semiotische Strategien. Bausteine zu einem Modell für die Verständigung im Norden zur Zeit der Hanse, in: K. Braunmüller (Hg.), Niederdeutsch und die skandinavischen Sprachen, Heidelberg 1995, 35–70.

Brecht, Martin, Einleitung, in: Geschichte des *Pietismus*: Das 17. und frühe 18. Jahrhundert, Bd. 1, Göttingen 1993.

Brilioth, Yngve, *Predikans* historia, Lund 1945.

Brilkman, Kajsa, The *Circulation* of Knowledge in Translations and Compilations: A Sixtenth-century Example, in: J. Östling/E. Sandmo/D. Larsson Heidenblad/A. Nilsson Hammar/K.H Nordberg (Hg.), Circulation of Knowledge: Explorations in the History of Knowledge, Lund 2018, 160–174.

Brodd, Sven-Erik, *Biskopsämbetet* i kyrkoordningen 1571, Kyrkohistorisk årsskrift, 1989, 105–106.

Bruni, Flavia/Pettegree, Andrew (Hg.), *Lost Books*: Reconstructing the Print World of Pre-industrial Europe, Leiden 2016.

Bruun, Chr. (Hg.), *Kong Frederik* den Andens Kronings og Salvings Akt, den 20de August 1559, samt Ceremoniellet for Dronning Sophics Kroning og Salving, den 21de Juli 1572, København 1868–1869.

Burgess, Joseph A., Lutheran *interpretation* of Scripture, in: K. Hagen (Hg.), The Bible in the Churches: How Various Christians Interpret the Scriptures, Milwaukee 1994, 101–129.

Callmer, Christian, Svenska studenter i *Rostock* 1419–1828: redigerad av Maj Callmer, Personhistorisk tidskrift 84, 1988.

—, Svenska studenter i *Wittenberg*, Personhistorisk Tidskrift, 72, 1976.

Carlson, Rachel D., The *Honey Bee* and Apian Imagery in Classical Literature, unpublished doctoral thesis University of Washington, Washington 2015.

Carlsson, Gottfrid, Vår förste lutherske ärkebiskops *Wittenbergsstudier*, Kyrkohistorisk årsskrift, 1915, 41–49.

Chærberus, Josephus Svenonis, Itt gudeligit *samtaal* eller andelig prosopopeiæ dickt, uthi hvilken The Gudhdomlighe egenskaperne, rättfärdigheten, sanningen, barmhertigheeten, fridhen och allwijsheten medh Gudh alzvoldigh om menniskiones fall och vprättelse uthi discurs-wijs införde blifva" [Västerås 1642], in: Samlade Vitterhetsarbeten af svenska författare från Stjernhjelm till Dalin, Bd. 21, Upsala *1876*.

Chartier, Roger, The author's *hand* and the printer's mind, Cambridge 2014.

Cleve, Fredric, Förändringarna i tolkningen av reformationen avspeglade i en *finländsk psalm*", in: K. Ståhlberg (Hg.), Norden och Europa: Språk, kultur och identitet, Köpenhamn, 1999, 59–74.

Collijn, Isak, Gustav Vasas *bibel* 1540–1541, Uppsala 1938.

—, Sveriges *bibliografi: 1600-talet*, Uppsala 1942–1944.

—, Sveriges *bibliografi* intill år 1600, Uppsala 1927–38.

—, Nyfunna tryck av *Torbjörn Tidemansson*", Nordisk tidskrift för bok- och biblioteksväsen 17, 1930, 1–13.

Concept till Inventarium öfver Konung Erik XIV:s Böcker upprättadt den 27 September 1568, in: Handlingar rörande Skandinaviens historia: Nya handlingar, Stockholm 1845, 380–390.

Coroleu, Alejandro/Caruso, Carlo/Laird, Andrew (Hg.), The Role of *Latin* in the Early Modern World: Linguistic Identity and Nationalism 1350–1800, Renæssanceforum 8, 2012.

Crawford, Alice (ed.), The Meaning of the *Library*, Princeton/Oxford 2015.

Czaika, Otfried, Några wijsor om *Antichristum* [1536] samt handskrivna tillägg: Utgåva med inledande kommentarer, Helsinki/Skara 2019.

—, *Elisabet Vasa*: en kvinna på 1500-talet och hennes böcker, Stockholm 2009.

—, *Episode II* – Then Swenska Psalmeboken 1582: Det andra exemplaret, Hymnologi 45, 2017, 43–52.

—, *Gothus*, Petrus Johannis, in: Pettke, S. (Hg.), Biographisches Lexikon für Mecklenburg, Rostock 2001, 92–98.

—, *Melanchthon* und Skandinavien. Die exportierte Reformation, in: M. Dall'Asta/H. Hein/C. Mundhenk (Hg.), Philipp Melanchthon in der Briefkultur des 16. Jahrhunderts, Heidelberg 2015, 237–259.

—, *Metropolen* als Vermittler, Förderer und Akteure von Reformation und Konfessionalisierung in Skandinavien und insbesondere im schwedischen Reich", in: H. Assel/J.A. Steiger/A.E. Walter (Hg.), Reformatio Baltica: Kulturwirkungen der Reformation in den Metropolen des Ostseeraums, Berlin & Boston 2018, 721–734.

—, Det kollektiva *minnet* av reformationen och Mikael Agricola i 2000-talets Finland, Biblis 46, 2009, 15–25.

—, *Plinius* världshistoria med Agricolas ägaranteckning: ett fynd i Roggebibliotekets samlingar, Biblis 51, 2010, 30–39.

—, Then swenska *psalmeboken* 1582: utgåva med inledande kommentarer, Skara 2016.

—, Then Swenska *Psalmeboken* 1582. *Avsnitt 2*: Det andra exemplaret, in: Biblis. Kvartalstidskrift och förening för bokvänner 77, 2017, 60–66.

—, *Sveno Jacobi*: boksamlaren, biskopen, teologen, en bok- och kyrkohistorisk studie, Stockholm 2014.

Dahl, Folke, Bibliografisk Beskrivning av *Reykjavikfyndet*, Nordisk Tidskrift för Bok och Biblioteksväsen 51, 1964, 97–100.

Dahl, Gina, Much More than Luther: *Religious Reading* among the Norwegian Clergy 1650–1800, in: C. Appel/M. Fink-Jensen (Hg.), Religious Reading in the Lutheran North. Studies in Early Modern Scandinavian Book Culture. Cambridge Scholars Publishing, Newcastle upon Tyne 2011, 88–111.

Dahlberg, Ragnar, Sällsynta svenska *skrifter* från reformationstiden i Helsingfors universitetsbibliotek", Nordisk tidskrift för bok- och biblioteksväsen 2, 1915, 111–117.

Darnton, Robert, The Forbidden *Best-Sellers* of Pre-Revolutionaly France, New York 1995.

—, The Kiss of *Lamourette*. Reflections in Cultural History. Norton, New York & London 1990.

—, *History of Reading*, in: P. Burke (ed.), New Perspectives on Historical Writing, Cambridge 1995.

Dewailly, Louis-Marie, *Petri*, Catholicisme 11, 49, Sp. 94.

Dietz, Ludwig, Niels Knud Andersen (Hg.), Ludwig Dietz' *Salmebog* 1536, København 1972.

Dingel, Irene, Historische *Einleitung*, in: J.M. Lies/H.-O. Schneider (Hg.), Der Adiaphoristische Streit (1548–1560), Göttingen 2012.

Eckerdal, Lars, När tillkom *De Officiis*? Omdateringsförslag, Kyrkohistorisk årsskrift, 1984, 117–133.

—, 'Församlingen till *förbättring*': Reformatoriskt bruk av 1 Korinthierbrevet kapitel 14", in: L. Eckerdal (Hg.), Kyrka och universitet: Festskrift till Carl-Gustaf Andrén, Stockholm 1987, 91–112.

—, History of *Reading*, in: P. Burke (ed.), New Perspectives on Historical Writing, Cambridge 1995.

Eisermann, Falk, The Gutenberg Galaxy's Dark Matter: *Lost Incunabula*, and Ways to Retrieve Them", in: F. Bruni/A. Pettegree (Hg.), Lost Books: Reconstructing the Print World of Pre-industrial Europe, Leiden 2016, 31–54.

Ek, Sverker, Våra första *psalmböcker*, Samlaren 39, 1918, 1–24.

Ekholm, R., *Columbus*, Jonas, in: Svenskt biografiskt lexikon Bd. 8, Stockholm 1929, 755–756.

Eklof, Ben, Russian Peasant *Schools*: Officialdom, Village Culture, and Popular Pedagogy, 1861–1914, Berkeley/Los Angeles/London 1990.

Enenkel, Karl A./Laureys, Marc/Pieper, Christoph (Ed.), *Discourses* of Power: Ideology and Politics in Neo-Latin Literature, Hildesheim/Zürich/-New York 2012.

Engelsing, Rolf, Der Bürger als Leser: *Lesergeschichte* in Deutschland 1500–1800, Stuttgart 1974.

Erikson, Leif, *Johann Arndt* und die Finnländische Erweckung des 19. Jahrhunderts, in: Johann Arndt – Rezeption und Reaktion im Nordisch-Baltischen Raum, Hilding Pleijel Symposium III, Lund 1999.

Eriksson, Erik, Kring några nyfunna svenska *1600-talstryck*, Nordisk tidskrift för bok- och biblioteksväsen 59, 1972, 130–140.

—, Några nyfunna äldre svenska tryck som bl.a. justerar den svenska *psalmboks-historien*, Nordisk tidskrift för bok- och biblioteksväsen 62–63, 1975–1976, 81–91.

Estborn, Sigfrid, Evangeliska svenska *bönböcker* under reformationstidevarvet: med en inledande översikt över medeltidens och över reformationstidens evangeliska tyska bönelitteratur, Lund 1929.

Fairclough, H. R. (1999), The *Aeneid*, Loeb Classical Library, Cambridge, Mass./London 1999.

Falck, Erik, Een kort *vnderwijsning* (Stockholm: Amund Laurentzson, 1558), in: M. Hagberg (Hg.), Een kort underwijsning om några aff the förnemligaste Articlar i then Christeligha Läron: Erik Falcks Dogmatik på nytt utgiven med inledande kommentarer, Skara 2010.

Färnström, Emil (Hg.), Laurentius Petris *Kyrko-ordning* av år 1571, Stockholm, 1932.

Flacius, Matthias, Etliche tröstliche *Vermahnungen* in das heilige Wort betreffenden Sachen, in: I. Dingel (Hg.), Controversia et Confessio Digital, (http://www.controversia-et-confessio.de/id/fb12821f-3eb1-4663-9740-bb6d12a267fd) [Datum der Internetabfrage: 29.05.2017]).

Foerstermann, Carolus Eduardus (Hg.), *Album* Academiae Vitebergensis Ab. A. Ch. MDII Usque Ad A. MDLX, Ex Autographo Edidit, Leipzig 1841.

Fransén, Nathanael, *Källorna* till den svenska reformationstidens liturgiska utveckling: en kort översikt, Kyrkohistorisk årsskrift 1936, 147–207.

Garstein, Oskar, *Rome* and the counter-reformation in Scandinavia: until the establishment of the S. congregatio de propaganda fide in 1622 – Based on source material in the Kolsrud collection, 4 Bde, Oslo 1963–1980.

Genette, Gérard, *Paratexte*: Das Buch vom Beiwerk des Buches, 5. Aufl., Frankfurt am Main 2014.

Gilmont, Jean-François, *Printing* at the dawn of the sixteenth century, in: J.-F. Gilmont (Hg.), The Reformation and the Book, Aldershot, 1998, 10–20.

Goeing, Anja-Silvia/Grafton, Anthony T./Michel, Paul (Hg.) (2013), Collector's *Knowledge*: What is Kept, What is Discarded = Aufbewahren oder Wegwerfen: Wie Sammler Entscheiden, Leiden/Boston 2013.

Göransson, Ulf, *Kulturarvsbyten* och den rättsliga utvecklingen från Grotius, in: P. Sjökvist (Hg.), Bevara för framtiden: Texter från en seminarieserie om specialsamlingar, Uppsala 2016, 73–81.

Green, Jonathan/McIntyre, Frank, Lost Incunable *Editions*: Closing in on an Estimate, in: F. Bruni/A. Pettegree (Hg.), Lost Books: Reconstructing the Print World of Pre-industrial Europe, Leiden 2016, 55–74.

Gundersen, Riiser, Memory and Meaning: The *Haugean Revival* (1796–1804) and its Place in the History of Reading, in: Ch. Appel/M. Fink-Jensen (Hg.), Religious Reading in the Lutheran North. Studies in Early Modern Scandinavian Book Culture, Newcastle 2011, 159–190.

Gunneng, Hedda, Biskop Hans Brasks *registratur*. Textutgåva, Uppsala 2003.

Gwynne, Paul, *Epic*, in: Victoria Moul (ed.), A Guide to Neo-Latin Literature, Cambridge 2017, 200–220.

—, Patterns of *Patronage* in Renaissance Rome: Francesco Sperulo: Poet, Prelate, Soldier, Spy, Oxford 2015.

Hagen, Kenneth, The history of *Scripture* in the Church, in: K. Hagen (Hg.), The Bible in the Churches, New York 1985, 1-28.

Hägglund, Bengt, *Arvet* från reformationen: teologihistoriska studier, Göteborg 2002.

—, Trons *mönster*: en handledning i dogmatik, Lund [3]1997.

Hägglund, Bengt/Sjöberg, Cajsa (Hg.), Mattias *Hafenreffer*: Compendium doctrinae coelestis: utgivet med översättning, inledning och kommentarer, Skara 2010.

Hagström Molin, Emma, *Krigsbytets biografi*: Byten i Riksarkivet, Uppsala universitetsbibliotek och Skoklosters slott under 1600-talet, Göteborg 2015.

Häkkinen, Kaisa (Hg.), Mikael Agricola: *Abckiria*: Kriittinen editio, Helsinki 2007.

— (Hg.), Mikael Agricolan *käsikirja*, Turku 2011.

—, *Mikael Agricolan* teokset ja kieli, in: K. Häkkinen/T. Vaittinen (Hg.), Agricolan aika, Helsinki 2007, 84–102.

—, *Spreading* the Written Word: Mikael Agricola and the Birth of Literary Finnish, Helsinki 2015.

—, *Westhin* koodeksin suhde Mikael Agricolan teoksiin, in Kaisa Häkkinen (ed.), Tutkimuksia Westhin koodeksista, Turku 2012, 43–92.

Hansson, Stina, Afsatt på swensko: 1600-talets tryckta *översättningslitteratur*, Göteborg 1982.

Hardie, Philip, The Last Trojan *Hero*: A Cultural History of Virgil's Aeneid, London 2014.

HASSE, HANS-PETER, *Zensur* theologischer Bücher in Kursachsen im konfessionellen Zeitalter: Studien zur kursächsischen Literatur- und Religionspolitik in den Jahren 1569 bis 1575, Leipzig 2000.

HAUSEN, REINHOLD, *Förteckning* öfver hertig Johans af Finland och hans gemål Katarina Jagellonicas lösegendom 1563, Helsingfors/Helsinki 1909.

HAUSLEITER, JOHANNES, Matthias *Flacius* als Herausgeber von Luthers Koburger Briefe und Trostsprüche (1530), Neue Kirchliche Zeitschrift 28, 1917, 149–187.

HAYNES, KEVIN J., A Colonial Woman's *Bookshelf*, Knoxville 1996.

HEDENBORG, SUSANNA, Det gåttfulla folket. Barns villkor och uppfattningar av *barnet* i 1700-talets Stockholm, Stockholm 1997.

HEININEN, SIMO, *Abckirian* sisältö ja lähteet, in: K. Häkkinen (Hg.), Mikael Agricola: Abckiria: Kriittinen editio, Helsinki 2007, 42*–61*.

—, *Mikael Agricola*. Elämä ja teokset. Helsinki 2007.

—, *Mikael Agricola psalmien suomentajana*, Helsinki 2020.

—, *Nuori* Mikael Agricola, Helsinki 1976.

HEININEN, SIMO/HEIKKILÄ, MARKKU, Suomen *kirkkohistoria*, Helsinki 1996.

HEINO, HARRI, *Hyppyherätys* – Länsi-Suomen rukoilevaisuuden synnyttäjä, Helsinki 1976.

HELANDER, HANS, Neo-Latin *Literature* in Sweden in the Period 1620–1720: Stylistics, Vocabulary and Characteristic Ideas, Uppsala 2004.

—, *Metaphors* for the Quest for Truth, in: B. Linde (Hg.), Early Modern Academic Culture, Stockholm 2019, 215–228.

HELLEKANT, BENGT, Engelsk *uppbyggelselitteratur* i svensk översättning intill 1700-talets mitt, Stockholm 1944.

HELLSTRÖM, OLLE, *Laurentius Petri*, in: Svenskt biografiskt lexikon (Datum der Internetabfrage: 14.04.2017).

HESS, GILBERT, *Florilegien*: Genese, Wirkungsweisen und Transformationen frühneuzeitlicher Kompilationsliteratur, in: F. Grunert/A. Syndikus (Hg.), Wissensspeicher der Frühen Neuzeit: Formen und Funktionen, Berlin 2015, 97–138.

HEYWOOD, COLIN, *Growing up* in France: From the Ancien Régime to the Third Republic, Cambridge 2009.

HOLFELDER, HANS HERMANN, *Bugenhagen*, in: Theologische Realenzyklopädie, Bd. 7, Berlin/New York 1993, 354–363.

HOLLINGSWORTH, CHRISTOPHER, *Poetics* of the Beehive: The Insect Metaphor in Literature, Iowa City 2014.

HOLMA, JUHANI, Sangen ialo rucous: *Schwenckfeldiläisten* rukouskirja Mikael Agricolan lähteenä, Helsinki 2008.

HOLMQUIST, HJALMAR, Svenska kyrkans historia. Bd 3, *Reformationstidevarvet*, 1521–1611, T. 1: Den katolska svenska kyrkoprovinsens omgestaltning till en egenartad svensk evangelisk kyrka 1521–1572, T. 2: Den svenska reformationskyrkans fortbildning till ortodox luthersk bekännelse och folkkyrka, 1572–1611, Stockholm 1933.

Holofernes, *Holofernes* och Judit: ett drama från reformationstiden, utgifvet med en inledning om dess utländska förebilder, O. Sylwan (Hg.), Upsala 1895.

Hult, O. T., *Benedictus Olai*, Svenskt biografiskt lexikon (http://sok.riksarkivet.se/sbl/artikel/18477; Datum der Internetabfrage: 08.07.2016).

Ikola, Osmo, *Agricolan* äidinkieli, in: E. Koivusalo (Hg.), Mikael Agricolan äidinkieli, Heksinki 1988, 25–68.

Ilić, Luka, Matthias *Flacius* Illyricus, in: I. Dingel/V. Leppin (Hg.), Das Reformatorenlexikon, Darmstadt 2016, 116–122.

Ingemarsdotter, Jenny, *Ramism*, Rhetoric and Reform: An Intellectual Biography of Johan Skytte (1577-1645), Uppsala 2011.

Ingebrand, Sven, *Bibeltolkningens* problematik: en historisk översikt, Stockholm 1965.

—, *Predikan* under reformationstiden, in: Å. Andrén (Hg.), Sveriges kyrkohistoria: Reformationstiden, Stockholm 2005.

Jackson, Sidney L., *Bodley* and the Bodleian: Collections, Use and Administration, The Library Quaterly 39, 1969, 3, 253-270.

Jajdelska, Elspeth 2007: *Silent Reading* and the Birth of the Narrator, Toronto 2007.

Janzon, Per, Erik XIVs *kröningsritual*", Kyrkohistorisk årsskrift 1959, 175-226.

Johannesson, Kurt, The *Renaissance* of the Goths in Sixteenth-Century Sweden: Johannes and Olaus Magnus as Politicians and Historians, Berkeley 1991.

—, Det svenska *skoldramat*, in: S.Å. Heed (Hg.), Ny svensk teaterhistoria 1. Teater före 1800, Hedemora 2007, 81–101.

Johansson, Egil, Kvantitativa studier av *alfabetiseringen* i Sverige: exempel på källmaterial, metoder och resultat, in: E. Johansson (Hg.), Kunskapens träd: artiklar i folkundervisningens historia II, Umeå 1988, 4–19.

—, The History of *Literacy* in Sweden, in: H.J. Graff/A. Mackinnon/B. Sandin/I. Winchester (Hg.), Understanding Literacy in its Historical Contexts: Sociocultural History and the Legacy of Egil Johansson, Lund 2009, 28–59.

Juusten, Paavali, *Suomen piispainkronikka*, Helsinki 1988.

Kallendorf, Craig, *Virgil*, in: P. Ford/J. Bloemendal/C. Fantazzi (ed.), Brill's Encyclopaedia of the Neo-Latin World, Leiden/Boston 2014.

Kansallisbibliografia, Suomen kansallisbibliografia 1488–1700: Toimittaneet Tuija Laine & Rita Nyqvist, Helsinki 1996.

Kansanaho, Erkki, Wegeliuksen *postillan* lähteet ja teologia, Suomalaisen teologisen kirjallisuusseuran julkaisuja LIII, Helsinki 1950.

—, Suomalaiset yltiöpietistit *Lauri Ulstadius* ja Pietari Schaefer, Suomen kirkkohistoriallisen seuran vuosikirja XLI–XLII, Helsinki 1954.

Kaufmann, Thomas, *1600* - Deutungen der Jahrhundertwende im deutschen Luthertum, in: M. Jakubowski-Thessen/H. Lehmann/J. Schilling/R. Staat (Hg.), Jahrhundertwenden: Endzeit- und Zukunftsvorstellungen vom 15. bis zum 20. Jahrhundert, Göttingen 1999, 73–128.

—, Ohne *Buchdruck* keine Reformation?, in: S. Oehmig (Hg.), Buchdruck und Buchkultur im Wittenberg der Reformationszeit, Leipzig 2015, 13–34.

—, Das Ende der Reformation: Magdeburgs "*Herrgotts Kanzlei*"(1548–1551/2), Tübingen 2003.

—, *Konfession* und Kultur: Lutherischer Protestantismus in der zweiten Hälfte des Reformationsjahrhunderts, Tübingen 2006.

—, Geschichte der *Reformation*, Frankfurt am Main 2009.

Kaufmann, Thomas/Mittler, Elmar (Hg.), *Reformation und Buch*: Akteure und Strategien frühreformatorischer Druckerzeugnisse/The Reformation and the Book: Protagonists and Strategies of Early Reformation Printing, Wiesbaden 2016.

Kick, Remi, The *Book* and the Reformation in the Kingdom of Sweden, in Gilmont (Hg.), The Reformation and the Book, Aldershot 1998, 449–468.

Kiiskinen, Terhi, The Library of the Finnish Nobleman, Royal Secretary and Trustee *Henrik Matsson* (ca. 1540–1617), Helsinki 2004.

— (Hg.), Fem *källor* från den svenska reformationstiden i Finland, Viisi Ruotsin reformaatioajan lähdettä Suomessa, Helsinki 2010.

Kjærgaard, Thorkild, *Genesis* in the longhouse: Religious Reading in Greenland in the Eighteenth Century, in: C. Appel/M. Fink-Jensen (Hg.), Religious Reading in the Lutheran North: Studies in Early Modern Scandinavian Book Culture, Newcastle upon Tyne 2011, 133–158.

Kjöllerström, Sven, *Ärkebiskopsvalet* 1531, Svensk Teologisk Kvartalskrift, 1937, 221–237.

—, *Kräkla* och Mitra, En undersökning om biskopsvigningar i Sverige under reformationstidevarvet, Lund 1965.

—, Svenska *förarbeten* till kyrkoordningen 1571, Stockholm 1940.

—, Den svenska *kyrkoordningen* 1571, jämte studier kring tillkomst, innehåll och användning, Lund 1971.

—, *Striden* kring kalvinismen i Sverige under Erik XIV: en Kykohistorisk Studie, Lund 1935.

Klemming, Gustaf Edvard, Swenska *psalmboken* af 1536 å nyo utgifwen, Stockholm 1862.

Knuutila, Jyrki, *Avioliitto* oikeudellisena ja kirkollisena instituutiona Suomessa vuoteen 1629, Helsinki 1990, 255–279.

—, *Liturgisen* yhdenmukaistamisen toteutuminen Suomessa reformaatiokaudella 1537–1614, Suomen kirkkohistoriallisen seuran vuosikirja 77, 1987, 9–40.

—, *Tukholman* seurakunnan 'messukirja' ja jumalanpalveluselämän muuttaminen evankeliseksi 1500-luvulla, in: J. Hannikainen (Hg.), Facultas ludendi: Erkki Tuppuraisen juhlakirja: Erkki Tuppuraiselle hänen 65-vuotissyntymäpäivänään 15, Kuopio 2010, 79–113.

Koch, Ernst, *Lutherflorilegien* zwischen 1550 und 1600: Zum Lutherbild der ersten nachreformatorischen Generation, Theologische Versuche XVI, 1986, 105–117.

Kock, Ebbe, En svensk *bokkatalog* från 1500-talet, Nordisk Tidskrift för Bok- och Biblioteksväsendet 7, 1920, 146–155.

Köhle-Hezinger, Christel (Hg.), *Alltagskultur*: sakral – profan: Ausgewählte Aufsätze, Münster/New York et al. 2011.

Kolb, Robert, Martin *Luther* as Prophet, Teacher, Hero: Images of the Reformer, 1520–1620, Grand Rapids 1999.

—, Die *Umgestaltung* und theologische Bedeutung des Lutherbildes im späten 16. Jahrhundert, in: H.-C. Rublack (Hg.), Die lutherische Konfessionalisierung in Deutschland, Heidelberg 1992, 202–231.

Kõivupuu, Marju, *Eestlase eluring*, Tallinn 2015.

Komedi, R. H., En svensk 'komedi' för 200 år sedan, Svenska Familj-Journalen, 15, 1876, 227.

Korpiola, Mia, Lutheran *Marriage* Norms in Action: The Example of Post-Reformation Sweden 1520–1600, in: V. Mäkinen (ed.), Lutheran Reformation and the Law, Leiden 2006, 131–169.

Kuismin, Anna/Driscoll, M.J. (ed.), White Field, Black Seeds: Nordic *Literacy* Practices in the Long Nineteenth Century, Studia Fennica Litteraria 7, Helsinki 2013.

Laasonen, Pentti, Die Bücher *Johann Arndts* in Finnland im 17. und 18. Jahrhundert, in: Johann Arndt – Rezeption und Reaktion im Nordisch-Baltischen Raum, Hilding Pleijel Symposium III, Lund 1999.

—, *Johannes Gezelius* vanhempi ja suomalainen täysortodoksia, Suomen kirkkohistoriallisen seuran toimituksia 103, Helsinki 1977.

—, Suomen kirkon *historia*, Bd. 2: Vuodet 1593–1808, Porvoo/Helsinki/Juva 1991.

—, Pohjois-Karjalan luterilainen kirkollinen *kansankulttuuri* Ruotsin vallan aikana, Suomen kirkkohistoriallisen seuran toimituksia 72, Helsinki 1967.

—, *Johannes Gezelius* d.J. und die Rezeption des deutschen Pietismus in Finnland, Wolfenbütteler Beiträge 8, Frankfurt am Main 1988.

—, Vanhan kirkollisuuden hajoaminen *Pohjois-Karjalassa*, Suomen kirkkohistoriallisen seuran toimituksia 83, Helsinki 1971.

Lahtinen, Anu, *Mikael Agricola* aatelisvallan verkostoissa, in: K. Häkkinen/T. Vaittinen (Hg.), Agricolan aika, Helsinki 2007, 24–35.

Laine, Esko M., *August Hermann Francken* teosten kirjallinen vastaanotto Ruotsi-Suomessa 1600–1700-luvuilla, in: Johannes Wallmann: Totinen kääntymys ja maailmanparannus: Pietismi kirkkohistoriallisena ilmiönä, Helsinki 1997.

—, *Iltahetki Tukholmassa* 1700-luvun alussa: Pietistinen konventikkeli Ruotsi-Suomessa, in: Johannes Wallmann: Totinen kääntymys ja maailmanparannus: Pietismi kirkkohistoriallisena ilmiönä, Helsinki 1997.

—, *Pietismi* sairautena, in: Johannes Wallmann: Totinen kääntymys ja maailmanparannus: Pietismi kirkkohistoriallisena ilmiönä, Helsinki 1997.

—, *Pietistit* ennen pietismiä Ruotsi-Suomessa, in: Johannes Wallmann: Totinen kääntymys ja maailmanparannus: Pietismi kirkkohistoriallisena ilmiönä, Helsinki 1997.

—, *Tuomas Ragvaldinpoika* (1724–1804), in: Kansallisbiografia, http://artikkelihaku.kansallisbiografia.fi/artikkeli/357/ (Datum der Internetabfrage 05.04.2017).

Laine, Esko M./Laine, Tuija, *Kirkollinen* kansanopetus, in: Huoneentaulun maailma: Kasvatus ja koulutus Suomessa keskiajalta 1860-luvulle, Suomalaisen Kirjallisuuden Seuran Toimituksia 1266:1, Helsinki 2010.

Laine, Tuija, *Aapisen* ja katekismuksen tavaamisesta itsenäiseen lukemiseen: Rahvaan lukukulttuurin kehitys varhaismodernina aikana, Historiallisia tutkimuksia 275, Helsinki 2017.

—, *Finnish primary religious books from the seventeenth* century, in: H. Assel/J.A. Steiger/A.E. Walter (Hg.), Reformatio Baltica: Kulturwirkungen der Reformation in den Metropolen des Ostseeraums, Bd. 2, Berlin/Boston 2017, 855–866.

—, *Finnish primary religious books from the sixteenth* and seventeenth centuries, in: Luther, reformaatio ja kirja/Luther, the Reformation, and the Book, T. Laine (Hg.), Helsinki 2012, 100–106.

—, *Johannes Gezelius* vanhemman katekismus ja sen lähteet, Helsinki 1993.

—, *Kolportöörejä* ja kirjakauppiaita: Kirjojen hankinta ja levitys Suomessa vuoteen 1800, Suomalaisen kirjallisuuden seuran toimituksia 1098, Helsinki 2006.

—, Bibliografia *Henrik Renqvistin* kirjoittamista ja kääntämistä julkaisuista sekä hänestä kirjoitetuista tieteellisistä ja taiteellisista teoksista, in: Henrik Renqvist julkaisijana ja kirjakauppiaana 1815–1866, Suomen kirkkohistoriallisen seuran toimituksia 198, Helsinki 2005.

—, *Uskonnollisen* kirjallisuuden valvonta, Suomalaisen Kirjallisuuden Seuran Toimituksia 724:1, Helsinki 1999.

—, *Ylösherätys* suruttomille: Englantilaisperäinen hartauskirjallisuus Suomessa Ruotsin vallan aikana, Suomalaisen kirjallisuuden seuran toimituksia 775, Helsinki 2000.

LAITINEN, KAI/SCHOOLFIELD, GEORGE C., New *Beginnings*, Latin and Finnish, in: G.C. Schoolfield (ed.), A History of Finland's Literature, Lincoln 1988, 34–63.

LAMBERG, MARKO, *Jöns Budde*: Birgittalaisveli ja hänen teoksensa, Helsinki 2007.

LAURENTIUS PETRI, *Acta* circa Matrimonium (1552), in: O. Ahnfelt (Hg.), Bidrag till Svenska Kyrkans Historia i sextonde århundradet, Lund 1895, 10–49.

—, Then swenska Kyrkeordning (Stockholm: Amund Laurentzson, 1571), in: S. Kjöllerström (Hg), Den svenska kyrkoordningen 1571, jämte studier kring tillkomst, innehåll och användning, Lund 1971, 3–200.

—, *Oeconomia* Christiana (1559), in: H. Lundström (Hg.), Skrifter från reformationstiden, Bd. 5, Uppsala *1897*.

—, Förklaring på *Ordinantien*, 1533, in: P. E. Thyselius/V. Ekblom (Hg.), Handlingar rörande Sverges inre förhållande under Konung Gustaf I, Bd. 1, Stockholm 1841, 84–101.

—, En forklaring och Uthtydelse på Westeråhrs *Recess*, 1533, in: P. E. Thyselius/V. Ekblom (Hg.), Handlingar rörande Sverges inre förhållande under Konung Gustaf I, Bd. 1, Stockholm 1841, 69–83.

—, Ornatissimo viro ac Domino D. Magistro Georgio *Superattendij* suo in Domino maiorj, 12. 11. 1540, in: P.E. Thyselius/V. Ekblom (Hg.), Handlingar rörande Sverges inre förhållande under Konung Gustaf I, Bd. 2, Stockholm 1844–1845, 240–242.

LAUREYS, MARC (2015), Political *Action*, in: S. Knight/S. Tilg (ed.), The Oxford Handbook of Neo-Latin, Oxford 2015, 345-361.

LAUSTEN, MARTIN SCHWARZ, Den helige stad *Wittenberg*: Danmark og Lutherbyen Wittenberg i reformationstiden, Kopenhagen 2002.

LAVERY, JASON, *Reforming Finland*: The Diocese of Turku in the Age of Gustav Vasa 1523–1560, Boston and Leiden 2017.

LEHTONEN, MIKKO, *Kyklooppi* ja kojootti: Subjekti 1600–1900-lukujen kulttuuri- ja kirjallisuusteorioissa, Tampere 1994.

LEINBERG, K.G., Företalet till P. Jwstens *Postilla*, Historiallinen arkisto 19, 1905, 267–274.

LEMPIÄINEN, PENTTI, *Kastekäytäntö* Suomen kirkossa 1500- ja 1600-luvulla, Helsinki 1965.

LEMPIÄINEN, TERTTU, *Agricola* yrtit: Vanhin suomenkielinen dokumentti mauste- ja lääkekasveista, in: K. Häkkinen/T. Vaittinen (Hg.), Agricolan aika, Helsinki 2007, 48–83.

Lénström, C.J./Gegerfelt, H. G., Lars *Fornelius*: Sveriges första ästhetiker: en litterär-historisk undersökning, Uppsala 1838.

Leppin, Volker, *Antichrist* und Jüngster Tag: Das Profil apokalyptischer Flugschriftenpublizistik im deutschen Luthertum 1548–1618, Gütersloh 1999.

Lewin, Barbro, Johan *Skytte* och de skytteanska professorerna, Skrifter utgivna av Statsvetenskapliga föreningen i Uppsala 100, Uppsala 1985.

Liedgren, Emil, Svensk *psalm* och andlig visa: Olaus Petri-föreläsningar i Uppsala mars 1924, Stockholm 1926.

Lindberg, Sten G., Konung Johan II:s *boksamling* år 1571, ett hittills otryckt bokförteckningskoncept av Rasmus Ludvigsson (Cod. Holm. U201.), Lychnos 1937, 212–220.

Linder, Maria/Thor, Lena, *Trä*, sten och tradition – så formades staden, in: M. Karlsson (Hg.), Den dolda staden: arkeologiska undersökningar i kvarteret Druvan Karlstad, Karlstad 2006, 29–44.

Lindgren, Mereth, Att lära och att pryda: om efterreformatoriska *kyrkomålningar* i Sverige cirka 1530–1630, Stockholm 1951.

Lindroth, Sten, *Johannes Magnus*, in: Svenskt biografiskt lexikon (= https://sok.riksarkivet.se/sbl/artikel/12115 [Datum der Internetabfrage: 15.01.2017]).

—, Svensk *lärdomshistoria*: Medeltiden, reformationstiden, Stockholm *1975*.

—, Svensk *lärdomshistoria*: Medeltiden, reformationstiden, Stockholm *21989*.

Lohse, Bernhard, Philipp *Melanchthon* in seinen Beziehungen zu Luther, in: H. Junghans (Hg.), Leben und Werk Martin Luthers 1526–1546, Göttingen 1983, 404–418.

Loimaranta, Sakari, *Erikssonien* mystillis-separatistinen liike vuoteen 1745, Suomen kirkkohistoriallisen seuran toimituksia XLIII, Helsinki 1941.

Lotz-Heumann, Ute, *Die doppelte Konfessionalisierung* in Irland: Konflikt und Koexistenz im 16. und in der ersten Hälfte des 17. Jahrhunderts, Tübingen 2000.

Lotz-Heumann, Ute/Pohlig, Matthias, *Confessionalization* and literature in the Empire, 1555–1700, in: Central European History 40, 2007, 35–61.

Lundblad, Kristina, *Föreställningar* om förlag: gränser mellan produktion och förmedling i den svenska bokvärlden 1600-tal till i dag, Biblis 72, 2015/2016, 3–11.

Lundstedt, B.V. *Bibliotek*, in: Nordisk familjebok, Bd. 3, Stockholm 1905, Sp. 281.

Lundström, Ruth, Some Notes on the Swedish Neo-Latin Poet *Jonas Columbus*, in: P. Tuynman/G.C. Kuiper/E. Keßler (ed.), Acta Conventus Neo-Latini Amstelodamensis: Proceedings of the Second International Congress of Neo-Latin Studies, Amsterdam 19–24 August 1973, München 1979, 675–681.

Luther, Martin, D. Martin Luthers Werke: Kritische *Gesamtausgabe, Weimar*.

LUUKKANEN, TARJA-LIISA, Mitä maalaiskansa luki? Kirjasto, kirjat ja kirjoja lukeva yhteisö *Karstulassa* 1861–1918, Historiallinen arkisto 143, Helsinki 2016.

MAK, BONNIE, How the *Page* Matters, Toronto 2011.

MAKKONEN, ANNA, Waimot ne laulelit kiitosta pauhelit: *Kaisa Juhantyttären* virsi, 1831, in: T. Nordlund/T. Onikki-Rantajääskö/T. Suutari (Hg.), Kohtauspaikkana kieli: Näkökulmia persoonaan, muutoksiin ja valintoihin, Suomalaisen Kirjallisuuden Seuran Toimituksia 1078, Helsinki 2006.

MALMGREN, ARTHUR/KROON, JOHN, Fyra svenska *reformationsskrifter* tryckta i Stockholm år 1562, Bd. 1–3, Malmö 1965–1966.

MAURER, WILHELM, Der junge *Melanchthon*, T. 2: Der Theologe, Göttingen 1969.

MEDICK, HANS, Weben und Überleben in *Laichingen* 1650–1900: Lokalgeschichte als Allgemeine Geschichte, Göttingen 1972.

MENIUS, JUSTUS, Vom *Exorcismo* [...], Erfurt 1551 [VD16 ZV10865].

METCALF, MICHAEL F., *Scandinavia* 1397–1560, in: T.A. Brady Jr/H.A. Oberman/J.D. Tracy (ed.), Handbook of European History, 1400–1600, Late Middle Ages, Renaissance and Reformation, Vol. II Visions, Programs and Outcomes, Leiden 1995, 523–550.

METZ, DETLEF, Das protestantische *Drama*: Evangelisches geistliches Theater in der Reformationszeit und im konfessionellen Zeitalter, Köln 2013.

MEYER, HANS BERNHARD, Das Danziger *Volksleben*, Würzburg 1956.

MICHEL, STEFAN, Die *Kanonisierung* der Werke Martin Luthers im 16. Jahrhundert, Tübingen 2016.

MISRAHI, JEAN, Beginnings of the Jesuit *Theatre* in France, The French Review 16, 1943, 3, 239–247.

MONTGOMERY, INGUN, Die *cura religiones* als Aufgabe des Fürstens: Perspektive der Zeiten Reformation in Schweden, in: H. Schilling (Hg.), Die reformierte Konfessionalisierung in Deutschland - Das Problem der "Zweiten Reformation": Wissenschaftliches Symposium des Vereins für Reformationsgeschichte 1985, Gütersloh 1986.

—, *Värjostånd* och lärostånd: Religion och politik i meningsutbytet mellan kungamakt och prästerskap i Sverige 1593–1608, Uppsala 1972.

MUIR, LYNETTE R., European communities and medieval *drama*, in: A. Hindley (Hg.), Drama and community: People and plays in Medieval Europe, Turnhout 1999, 1–17.

MÜNTER, FREDRIK/WERLAUFF, E.C. (Hg.), *Aktstykker* vedkommende Kong Christian den Tredies og Dronning Dorotheas, Kroning i Vor Frue Kirke i Kjøbenhavn, den 12te August 1537 af Dr. Johannes Bugenhagen, Kopenhagen 1831.

NEDDERMEYER, UWE, Von der Handschrift zum gedruckten Buch: *Schriftlichkeit* und Leseinteresse im Mittelalter und in der frühen Neuzeit: quantitative und qualitative Aspekte, Wiesbaden 1998.

NEIERMAYER, J. F./VAN DE KIEFT, C., Mediae Latinitatis *Lexicon* Minus: M–Z, Leiden/Boston ^{2}2002.

NELSON, ERIC, The *Jesuit legend*: Superstition and myth-making, in: H. Parisch/W.G. Naphy (ed.), Religion and superstition in Reformation Europe, Manchester 2003.

NIELSEN, LAURITZ, Dansk *bibliografi* 1482–1600, Kopenhagen 1919–1996.

NISSER, PER OLOF, Ett *samband* att beakta: psalm, psalmbok, samhälle, Skellefteå 2005.

NORDSTRANDH, OVE, 1951: Den äldre svenska pietismens *litteratur*, Samlingar och studier till svenska kyrkans historia 26, Lund 1951.

ÖHRBERG, ANN, A *Threat* to civic Coexistence: Forbidden religious Literature and Censorship in Eighteenth-Century Sweden, in: C. Appel/M. Fink-Jensen (ed.), Religious Reading in the Lutheran North. Studies in Early Modern Scandinavian Book Culture. Cambridge Scholars Publishing, Newcastle upon Tyne 2011, 112–132.

OJANEN, EEVA, *Kirkko* ja kansanelämä Länsi-Hämeessä 1800-luvulla, Suomen kirkkohistoriallisen seuran toimituksia 71, Helsinki 1966.

OLAUS PETRI, Samlade *skrifter*, B. Hesselman (Hg.), Upsala [Uppsala] 1914.

OLDANI, LOUIS J./YANITELLI, VICTOR R., Jesuit *theatre* in Italy: its extrances and exit, Italica 76, 1999, 1, 18–32.

OLDEN-JØRGENSEN, SEBASTIAN, Det genfundne originalmanuskript til Peder Vinstrups *kroningstale* 1596, Danske Magazin, 9:1, 1999, 2, 245–270.

OLSON, OLIVER KERMIT, Matthias *Flacius* and the survival of Luther's reform, Wiesbaden 2002.

ÖSTERBLADH, KAARLO, *Laihian* separatismia koskevia asiakirjoja, in: Suomen uskonnollisten liikkeiden historiasta asiakirjoja ja tutkimuksia: Kolmas nidos, Suomen kirkkohistoriallisen seuran toimituksia XII, 3, Helsinki 1938.

OVID, *Tristia*: Ex Ponto, Loeb Classical Library, Cambridge, Mass./London 2014.

PAHLMBLAD, CHRISTER, *Mässa* på svenska: Den reformatoriska mässan i Sverige mot den senmedeltiden bakgrunden, Lund 1998.

PEIL, DIETMAR, Zur konfessionellen Problematik in den *Schuldramen* Georg Rollenhagens, in: D. Breuer (Hg.), Religion und Religiosität im Zeitalter des Barock, Bd. II, Wiesbaden 1995, 643–653.

PERSSON, ROLAND, *Johan III* och Nova ordinantia, Lund 1973.

PETTEGREE, ANDREW, *Brand* Luther. 1517, printing, and the making of the Reformation, New York 2015.

—, *Centre* and Periphery in the European Book World. In: Transactions of the Royal Historical Society 18, 2008, 101–128

—, The *Legion* of the Lost. Recovering the Lost Books of Early Modern Europe, in: F. Bruni/A. Pettegree (Hg.), Lost Books: Reconstructing the Print World of Pre-industrial Europe, Leiden 2016, 1–27.

Philip, Ian, The *Bodleian* Library in the Seventeenth and Eighteenth Centuries: The Lyell Lectures, Oxford 1980–1981, Oxford 1983.

Pihlajamaa, Lauri, *Raamatunlauseet* sielun lääkkeessä," in Kaisa Häkkinen (ed.), Tutkimuksia Westhin koodeksista, Turku: Turun yliopisto, 2012, 93–116.

—, Tukholman suomalaisen seurakunnan ensimmäinen saarnaaja: *Mathias Westh*?, Suomen kirkkohistoriallisen seuran vuosikirja 100, 2010, 71–92.

Piltz, Anders, *Jonas Columbus* självbiografiska elegier, in: A.M.H. Nilsson/A. Damtoft Poulsen/J. Svensson (Hg.), Humanitas: Festskrift till Arne Jönsson, Göteborg/Stockholm 2017, 511–541.

—, *Peder Månsson*, in: Svenskt biografiskt lexikon (=https://sok.riksarkivet.se/sbl/artikel/8088 [Datum der Internetabfrage: 28.2.2017]).

Pirinen, Kauko, *Turun* tuomiokapituli uskonpuhdistuksen murroksessa, Helsinki 1962.

Platen, Magnus von, Djävulens *bländverk*: Om motstånd mot teatern i gamla tiders Sverige, Kungl. Vitterhets Historie och Antikvitets Akademiens Årsbok 1980, 55–82.

Pleijel, Hilding, Der schwedische *Pietismus* in seinen Beziehungen zu Deutschland: eine kirchengeschichtliche Untersuchung, Lunds universitets årsskrift. N. F.1:31:4, Lund 1935.

Pohlig, Matthias, Matthias *Flacius*, Simon Goulart and the Catalogus testium veritatis: Protestant historiography in an age of inner-Protestant struggle, ARG 101, 2010, 263–274.

—, Zwischen *Gelehrsamkeit* und konfessioneller Identitätsstiftung. Lutherische Kirchen- und Universalgeschichtsschreibung 1546–1617, Tübingen 2007.

Proot, Goran, *Survival* factors of Seventeenth-Century Hand-Press Books Published in the Southern Netherlands: The Importance of Sheet Counts, Sammelbände and the Role of Institutional Collections, in: F. Bruni/A. Pettegree (Hg.), Lost Books: Reconstructing the Print World of Pre-industrial Europe, Leiden 2016, 160–201.

Proot, Goran/Egge, Leo, Estimating *editions* on the basis of survivals: printed programmes of Jesuit plays in the Provincia Flandro-Belgica before 1773, with a note on the Book Historical Law, in: The Papers of the Bibliographical Society of America 102, 2008, 149–174.

Psalmboken, Then swenska psalmboken. Med the stycker som ther til höra, och på föliande blad vpteknade finnas, uppå Kongl. Majtz. nådigste befalning

[…] åhr M DC XCIII. Med flit öfwersedd, förbättrad, och förmehrad: och vngdomen til fromma, vti thenne beqwäme storlek åhr 1695. Af trycket vtgången (Stockholm 1695).

Raittila, Pekka, *Tuomas Ragvaldinpoika*: Tyrvään seudun Museo- ja Kotiseutuyhdistyksen julkaisuja XXI, Vammala 1949.

Ranke, Leopold von, Ueber die *Verwandschaft* und den Unterschied der Historie und der Politik, in: Sämtliche Werke, Bd. 24, Leipzig 1872.

Rapola, Martti, *Mikael Agricola* ja suomenkielisen proosan alku, in: M. Rapola (Hg.), Suomen kirjallisuus, Bd. 2, Helsinki 1963, 69–138.

Reinhard, Wolfgang/Schilling, Heinz (Hg.), Die katholische *Konfessionalisierung*: Wissenschaftliches Symposion der Gesellschaft zur Herausgabe des Corpus Catholicorum und des Vereins für Reformationsgeschichte 1993, Münster 1995.

Repgen, Konrad, Über *Rankes Diktum* von 1824: 'bloß sagen, wie es eigentlich gewesen', Historisches Jahrbuch 102, 1982, 439–449.

Repo, Matti, Uskon lahja vai rakkauden päämäärä? *Johann Arndtin* käsitys vanhurskauttamisesta ja uniosta, Suomalaisen teologisen kirjallisuusseuran julkaisuja 206, Helsinki 1997.

Riksdagsakter, Svenska Riksdagsakter [Ser. 1], Under tidehvarfvet 1521–1718, [Afd. 1], [1521–1611], T. 3:1, 1593–1594, Stockholm 1894.

Rimpiläinen, Olavi, *Läntisen* perinteen mukainen hautauskäytäntö Suomessa ennen isoavihaa, Helsinki 1971.

Roberts, Michael, The Swedish Imperial *Experience* 1560–1718, Cambridge-/London/New York/Melbourne 1979.

—, *Gustavus Adolphus*, London/New York ²1992.

Rondeletius, Jacob, *Judas* Redivivus: Thet är: En christeligh tragicocomædia, lärandes huru allom siälfzwyrdigom och öffwerdådigom skalkom, som föräldrars, öffwerheets och lärares förmaningar och agha för achta, sedan the haffwa sins raserijs mått vppfylt, på sidstone til skam wardha; Men the som aff them haffwa warit bedröffwadhe på endalychtene tröstade: Allom, och huarjom och enom vthi huadh stand, eller huadh wilkor the wara kunna, till rättelse, Stockholm *1871*.

Sachs, Hans, Das handschriftliche *Generalregister* des Hans Sachs: Reprintausgabe nach dem Autograph von 1560 des Stadtarchivs Zwickau von Hans Sachs mit einer Einführung von Reinhard Hahn, Köln/Wien 1986.

Salminen, Seppo J., Den finländska *teologin* under frihetstiden, Finska kyrkohistoriska samfundets handlingar 168, Helsingfors 1994.

Savin, Kristiina, Fortunas *klädnader*: Lycka, olycka och risk i det tidigmoderna Sverige, Lund 2011.

Schalin, Olav, Kulthistoriska *studier* till belysande av reformationens genomförande i Finland, Bd. 1, Helsinki 1946.

SCHICKETANZ, PETER, Der *Pietismus* von 1675 bis 1800, Kirchengeschichte in Einzeldarstellungen 3:1, Leipzig 2001.

SCHILLING, HEINZ, *Konfessionalisierung* und Staatsinteressen: Internationale Beziehungen 1559–1660, Paderborn 2007.

—, *Konfessionskonflikt* und Staatsbildung: Eine Fallstudie über das Verhältnis von religiösem und sozialem Wandel in der Frühneuzeit am Beispiel der Grafschaft Lippe, Gütersloh 1981.

SCHILLING, MICHAEL, Katalog Nr. 13 *Lebensstationen* Luthers, in: H. Rössler (Hg.), Luthermania: Ansichten einer Kultfigur, Wolfenbüttel 2017, 160–163.

SCHMIDT, MARTIN, *Wiedergeburt* und neuer Mensch: Gesammelte Studien zur Geschichte des Pietismus, Arbeiten zur Geschichte des Pietismus 2, Witten 1969.

SCHMIDT, STEFFIE, *Professoren im Norden*: Lutherische Gelehrsamkeit in der Frühen Neuzeit am Beispiel der theologischen Fakultäten in Kopenhagen und Uppsala, Göttingen 2018.

SCHNEIDER, HANS, *Johann Arndt* und die Mystik, in: Zur Rezeption mystischer Traditionen im Protestantismus des 16. bis 19. Jahrhunderts, Schriftenreihe des Vereins für Rheinische Kirchengeschichte 152, Köln 2002.

SCHNITZLER, HENRY, Jesuit contribution to the *theatre*, Educational Theatre Journal 4:4, 1952, 283–292.

SCHNURR, EVA MARIA, Religionskonflikt und Öffentlichkeit: Eine Mediengeschichte des *Kölner Kriegs 1582–1590*, Köln 2009.

SCHÜCK, HENRIK, Den svenska förlagsbokhandelns *historia*, T. 1, Stockholm 1923.

—, Petrus Johannis *Gothus*, in: Till Hugo Geber den 30 augusti 1913, Stockholm 1913, 3–81.

SCHWITZGEBEL, BÄRBEL, Noch nicht genug der *Vorrede*: Zur Vorrede volkssprachiger Sammlungen von Exempeln, Fabeln, Sprichwörtern und Schwänken des 16. Jahrhunderts, Tübingen 1996.

SILFVERHUTH, VOITTO, *Kirkon* ja keisarin sensuuri: Uskonnollisen kirjallisuuden valvonta Suomessa 1809–1865, Suomen kirkkohistoriallinen seura 104, Helsinki 1977.

SJÖKVIST, PETER, Om böckernas *ordning* i Uppsala universitetsbiblioteks första byggnad, Biblis 85 (2019), 65–71.

SJÖKVIST, PETER, On the *Order* of the Books in the First Uppsala University Library Building, Journal of Jesuit Studies (2019), 315–326.

SOU 1975:2, *Psalmer* & visor: tillägg till Den svenska psalmboken, förslag avgivet av 1696 års psalmkommitté, Bd. 1:1, Stockholm 1975.

SOU 1975:3, *Psalmer* & visor: tillägg till Den svenska psalmboken, förslag avgivet av 1696 års psalmkommitté, Bd. 1:2, Stockholm 1975.

SOU 1975:4, *Psalmer* & visor: tillägg till Den svenska psalmboken, förslag avgivet av 1696 års psalmkommitté, Bd. 1:3, Stockholm 1975.

SOU 1981:49, Den svenska *psalmboken*: Betänkande av 1696 års psalmkommitté, Bd. 1: Psalmboksrevisionen: inledande redovisning: provsamling för advent, jul och dagens tider, Stockholm 1981.

SOU 1981:50, Den svenska *psalmboken*: Betänkande av 1696 års psalmkommitté, Bd. 2: Förslag angående bearbetning mm av psalmerna i 1937 års psalmbok/1939 års koralbok, Stockholm 1981.

SOU 1985:17, Den svenska *psalmboken*: Slutbetänkande av 1696 års psalmkommitté, Bd. 2: Historik, principer, motiveringar, Stockholm 1985.

SOU 1985:18, Den svenska *psalmboken*: Slutbetänkande av 1696 års psalmkommitté, Bd. 3: Text- och musikkommentarer, Stockholm 1985.

SOU 1985:19, Den svenska *psalmboken*: Slutbetänkande av 1696 års psalmkommitté, Bd. 4: Ackompanjemang, Stockholm 1985.

Stobaeus, Per, *Från biskop Brasks tid*, Skellefteå 2010.

Strömberg-Back, Kerstin, *Lagen*, rätten, läran: Politisk och kyrklig idédebatt i Sverige under Johan III:s tid, Lund 1963.

Sulkunen, Irma, *Liisa Eerikintytär* ja hurmosliikkeet 1700–1800-luvuilla, Helsinki 1999.

Suphan, Bernhard, *Hans Sachs*: Humanitätszeit und Gegenwart, Weimar 1895.

Taipale, Matti, *Rippikoulun* syntyvaiheet Turun hiippakunnassa vuosina 1627–1763, Suomen kirkkohistoriallisen seuran toimituksia 120, Helsinki 1980.

Tala, Yrjö, *Kirkon* vai valtion kirjat? Uskontokuntasidonnaisuuden ongelma Suomen väestökirjanpidossa 1839–1904, Helsinki 2008.

Tarkiainen, Viljo/Tarkiainen, Kari, *Mikael Agricola*: Suomen uskonpuhdistaja, Helsinki 1985.

Thors, Carl-Erik, *Nya Testamentet* 1550, Nysvenska Studier, tidskrift för svensk stil- och språkforskning, 47, 1967, 82–172.

Tiili, Eeva-Liisa, *Kaisa Juhantytär* ja virren poetiikka, Helsinki 2008.

Tiililä, Osmo, *Rukoilevaisten kirjoja*, Helsinki 1961.

Toepfer, Regina, Antike Historiographie im deutschen Südwesten. Das *Übersetzungswerk* Hieronymus Boners, in: F. Luchs/G. linz (Hg.), Humanismus im deutschen Südwesten, Wiesbaden 2015.

Toepfer, Regina/Kipf, Johannes Klaus/Robert, Jörg, Einleitung Humanistische *Antikenübersetzung* und frühneuzeitliche Poetik in Deutschland (1450–1620), in: R. Toepfer/J.K. Kipf/J. Robert (Hg.), Humanistische Antikenübersetzung und frühneuzeitliche Poetik in Deutschland (1450–1620), Berlin 2017, 1–24.

TROELS-LUND, FREDERIK, Dagligt *liv* i Norden på 1500-talet: 14, Livsavslutning, Stockholm 1942.

TRYPUĆKO, JÓZEF (2007), Introduction, in: M. Spandrowski/S. Szyller (Hg.), The Catalogue of the Book Collection of the Jesuit College in *Braniewo* held in the University Library in Uppsala, Bd. 1, Uppsala/Warsawa 2007.

TUNTURI, JANNE, Vielä yksi vallankumous? Lukemisen historian tutkimisen *metodeista* ja mahdollisuuksista, in: E. Kuparinen (Hg.) Työkalut riviin: Näkökulmia yleisen historian tutkimusmenetelmiin, Turku 1997.

TUPPURAINEN, ERKKI (2012), *Westhin* koodeksi reformaatioajan musiikin dokumenttina, in: K. Häkkinen (Hg.), Tutkimuksia Westhin koodeksista, Turku 2012, 29–42.

Ulväng, GÖRAN/MURHEM, SOFIA/LILJA, KRISTIINA, Den glömda konsumtionen: *Auktionshandel* i Sverige under 1700- och 1800-talen, Riga 2013.

UNDORF, WOLFGANG, *Hogenskild Bielke's Library*: A Catalogue of the Famous 16th-Century Swedish Private Collection, Uppsala 1995.

—, *Catalogue* of Books Printed in the 15th Century in Swedish Collections, 2 Bände, Wiesbaden 2012.

—, From *Gutenberg* to Luther: Transnational Print Cultures in Scandinavia 1450–1525, Leiden/Boston 2014.

—, *Lost Books*, Lost Libraries, Lost Everything? A Scandinavian Early Modern Perspective, in: F. Bruni/A. Pettegree (Hg.), Lost Books: Reconstructing the Print World of Pre-industrial Europe, Leiden 2016, 101–121.

VILKUNA, KUSTAA H.J., *Viha*: Perikato, katkeruus ja kertomus isostavihasta, Historiallisia tutkimuksia 229, Helsinki 2005.

Vitterhetsarbeten, Samlade Vitterhetsarbeten af svenska författare från Stjernhjelm till Dalin, Bd. 21, Uppsala 1876.

VOGEL, SABINE, *Kulturtransfer* in der frühen Neuzeit: Die Vorworte der Lyoner Drucke des 16. Jahrhunderts, Tübingen 1999.

VON AMMON, FRIEDER/VÖGEL, HERFRIED, *Einleitung*, in: F. Ammon/H. Vögel (Hg.), Die Pluralisierung des Paratextes in der Frühen Neuzeit: Theorien, Formen, Funktion, Berlin 2008.

WALDE, OTTO, Några böcker ur *Benedictus Olais* bibliotek, Nordisk tidskrift för bok- och biblioteksväsen 20, 1933, 205–213.

—, *Bielkeättens* insatser i svensk bibliofili, Nordisk tidskrift för bok- och biblioteksväsen 1940, 1–45.

—, En svensk *boksamlare* från Vasatiden: Hogenskild Bielke och hans bibliotek, in: Uppsala universitetsbiblioteks minnesskrift 1621–1921, Uppsala 1921, 193–267.

—, Biskop *Erasmus Nicolai* i Västerås och hans bibliotek, Nordisk tidskrift för bok- och biblioteksväsen 28, 1941, 15–33.

—, Doktor *Johann Copps* bibliotek: Några anteckningar, Nordisk tidskrift för bok- och biblioteksväsen 21, 1934, 51–60.

—, Storhetstidens litterära *krigsbyten*: En kulturhistorisk-bibliografisk studie, Bd. 1, Uppsala/Stockholm 1916.

—, Konung *Sigismunds* bibliotek och Gustaf Adolfs donation 1620–21: Ett bidrag till Upsala universitetsbiblioteks äldsta historia, Nordisk tidskrift för bok- och biblioteksväsen 2, 1915, 317–332.

Wallmann, Johannes, *Beziehungen* des frühen Pietismus zum Baltikum und zu Finnland, in: Der Pietismus in seiner europäischen und außereuropäischen Ausstrahlung, Suomen kirkkohistoriallisen seuran toimituksia 157, Helsinki 1992.

—, Totinen kääntymys ja maailmanparannus: *Pietismi* kirkkohistoriallisena ilmiönä, Helsinki 1997.

—, Der *Pietismus*, in: Die Kirche in ihrer Geschichte: ein Handbuch, Bd. 4 Lieferung O 1, Göttingen 1990.

—, *Philipp Jakob Spener* und die Anfänge des Pietismus, Beiträge zur historischen Theologie 42, Tübingen 1970.

Walsby, Malcom, Book *Lists* and Their Meaning, in: M. Walsby/N. Constantinidou (ed.), Documenting the Early Modern Book World: Inventories and Catalogues in Manuscript and Print, Leiden/Boston 2014, 1–24.

Wedow, Christian, Die Rolle des deutschen *Luthertums* für Schweden zwischen 1600 und 1648, Rostock 2013.

Westman, Knut G., Reformationens *genombrottsår* i Sverige, Stockholm 1918.

Wiegelmann, Günter, Theoretische *Konzepte* der europäischen Ethnologie: Diskussionen um Regeln und Modelle, Münster 1991.

Yelverton, Eric, An Archbishop of the Reformation: *Laurentius Petri* Nericius Archbishop of Uppsala 1531–1573, London 1958.

Zedelmaier, Helmut, Karriere eines Buches: Polydorus *Vergilius'* De inventoribus rerum, in: F. Büttner/M. Friedrich/H. Zedelmaier (Hg.), Sammeln, Ordnen, Veranschaulichen: Zur Wissenskompilatorik in der frühen Neuzeit, Münster 2003, 175–203.

Personenregister

Autor*innenverzeichnis

Martin Berntson ist Professor für Theologie mit dem Schwerpunkt Kirchengeschichte an der Universität Göteborg. In seiner Dissertation *Klostren och reformationen. Upplösningen av kloster och konvent i Sverige 1525–1596* (2003) untersuchte er den Prozess der Auflösung der Klöster in Schweden. Er recherchierte anschließend Reformen und Rebellion in Schweden im 16. Jahrhundert. Im Jahr 2017 veröffentlichte er ein populärwissenschaftliches Buch über die Reformation in Schweden, das sich mit den Transformationen der Frömmigkeitskultur befasst. Seitdem interessiert er sich für das Schultheater in Schweden in der Frühen Neuzeit und untersucht, wie diese Theaterstücke als didaktische Instrumente im Prozess der Konfessionalisierung fungieren.
Martin.berntson@lir.gu.se

Otfried Czaika ist seit 2013 Professor für Kirchengeschichte mit Schwerpunkt Reformation an MF – Norwegian School of Theology, Religion and Society. Seine Forschungsinteressen decken u.a. Bildungs-, Buch- und Bibliotheksgeschichte sowie (früh-)neuzeitliche Verfassungsgeschichte ab. Ein besonderer Schwerpunkt liegt ferner auf der Geschichte der schwedischen Gesangbücher im 16. Jahrhundert. Zudem hat er sich mit Fragen von Kulturtransfer und Migration im Ostseeraum gewidmet. Czaika hat zahlreiche Artikel und Monographien in deutscher, schwedischer und englischer Sprache veröffentlicht sowie im Jahr 2017 den Schweden-Teil der Ausstellung "Der Luthereffektäm Deutschen Historischen Museum in Berlin mitbetreut.

Elena Dahlberg, PhD in Latin (2015), Department of Linguistics and Philology, Uppsala University. Her scholarly interests include humanist culture in the Baltic Region, early modern academia and occasional poetry. Between 2012 and 2016 she worked at Södertörn University Library, where she catalogued several thousand early modern dissertations. She is now conducting a project on the ideological applications and uses of neo-Latin poetry produced in Sweden c. 1550–1650.
Elena Dahlberg, Upplandsvägen 56, 186 35 Vallentuna, elena.dahlberg@lingfil.uu.se

Als gebürtiger Straßburger promovierte Remi Kick 1997 in Lund unter Professor B. Hägglund, mit einer Abhandlung zu Laurentius Petris Kirchenverständnis. Diese Arbeit beinhaltet die erste chronologischen Bibliographie des Erzbischofs

und Reformators. Zuvor hatte er am Projekt „Die Reformation und das Buch von Professor Jean-François Gilmont, 1987–1990 geleitet wurde, teilgenommen. 1992 arbeitete er zu den Spuren vom Straßburger Reformator Martin Bucer in der Schwedischen Reformation und den Bibliotheken des Landes. Neben der Reformations- und Buchgeschichte Schwedens im europäischen Kontext, hat er sich den Fragen der theologischen Ethik und Politik und der kulturellen Vermittlung zwischen Skandinavien, Mitteleuropa und Nord-Amerika gewidmet. Seither ist er als theologischer Privatgelehrter, Übersetzer und Fremdenführer tätig.
Remi Kick, 15 rue de la Fecht, 67000 Strasbourg, Frankreich, kick.remi@gmail.com

Dr. Tuija Laine, Professor für ältere Kirchengeschichte, Theologische Fakultät, Universität Helsinki, war in den Jahren 2012–2016 Professorin im Fachbereich Buchgeschichte an der Universität Helsinki. Sie hat über die englische Erbauungsliteratur in Finnland zur Schwedischen Zeit disputiert (2000) und danach verschiedene Themen aus den Bereichen Buchgeschichte und Kirchengeschichte behandelt. Sie ist die Autorin von Monographien über den Erweckungsprediger Henrik Renqvist (1815–1866) als Buchhändler und Verleger (2005), über den Buchhandel in Finnland bis 1800 (2006), über Carl Fredrik Fredenheim als Neuhumanist (2010), sowie über das religiöse Lesen in Finnland im 17. und 18. Jahrhundert (2017). Im Jahre 2018 publizierte sie ein digitales Lehrbuch über Buchgeschichte und buchgeschichtliche Forschung. Zurzeit beschäftigt sie sich in ihrer Forschung mit der älteren protestantischen Missionsgeschichte unter Medien- und Kommunikationsaspekten.
Tuija Laine, Church history, Box 4, 00014 University of Helsinki, Finland, tuija.laine@helsinki.fi

Esko M. Laine ist Dozent in Kirchengeschichte an der Universität Helsinki sowie an der Universität von Ostfinnland. Er ist Vorstandsmitglied im Verband für wissenschaftliche Veröffentlichungen in Finnland. Von 2003 bis 2013 war er Herausgeber der Teologisk Tidskrift. Seine Forschungsintressen erstrecken sich insbesondere auf das 17. und 18. Jahrhundert, im besonderen auf die Geschichte des Herrnhutismus in Finland im 18. Jahrhundert.

Regents Professor Jason Lavery (Ph.D. Yale 1997) ist seit 1997 an der Oklahoma State University tätig. Seit 2010 ist er Dozent für finnische und skandinavische Kirchengeschichte an der Universität Helsinki. Er hat zwei Bücher im Brill Verlag veröffentlicht: *Germany's Northern Challenge: The Holy Roman Empire and the Scandinavian Struggle for the Baltic 1563–1576* (2002) und *Reforming Finland: The Diocese of Turku in the Age of Gustav Vasa 1523–1560* (2017). Im

Jahr 2006 hat er *The History of Finland* beim Greenwood Verlag publiziert. Dr. Lavery hat auch zahlreiche Artikel über den Ostseeraum im 16. Jahrhundert veröffentlicht. Momentan beschäftigt er sich mit den religiösen Konflikten in Finnland in den Jahren 1560 bis 1611.
Jason Lavery, Regents Professor, Dept. of History, Oklahoma State University, 101 Social Sciences and Humanities, Stillwater, OK 74078, USA.

Dr. Wolfgang Undorf arbeitet seit 1995 an der Königlichen Bibliothek in Stockholm, der schwedischen Nationalbibliothek. Dort ist er u.a. als Koordinator für den Fachbereich Alte Drucke zuständig. In seiner Forschung beschäftigt er sich vor allem mit den transnationellen Dimensionen der skandinavischen, vor allem der schwedischen Buchgeschichte. 2012 veröffentlichte er den ersten nationalen Inkunabelkatalog Schwedens. 2014 erschien seine Abhandlung über skandinavische Buchgeschichte zwischen 1450 und 1525, *From Gutenberg to Luther – Transnational Print Cultures in Scandinavia 1450–1525*. Seitdem hat er seine Untersuchungen auf das gesamte 16. Jahrhundert ausgedehnt.
Wolfgang Undorf, Kungliga biblioteket, Box 5039, 10241 Stockholm, Schweden

Kajsa Weber (ehem. Brilkman) ist Historikerin an der Historischen Institution/Lunds Universität und leitete 2016-2020 das Projekt "Mare Lutheranum. The Book Market and Lutheran Confessional Culture around the Baltic Sea 1570-1620". In diesem vom schwedischen Wissenschaftsrat (Swedish Research Council) finanzierten Projekt hat sie zu Buchgeschichte und Luthertum in Nordeuropa geforscht. Sie hat eine Reihe von Beiträgen zur Reformatuon und lutherische Konfessionakultur veröffentlicht, zuletzt "Petrus Johannis Gothus in Rostock und der Konfessionskonflikt im schwedischen Reich: Kompilation, Übersetzung und Paratext in „De christiano Milite" (1592)" (in: Holze & Skottki, *Verknüpfungen des Neuen Glaubens* 2019) und "Confessional Knowledge; or how can the History of Knowledge and the History of Confessional Europe influence each other?" (in: Östling et. al. *Forms of Knowledge* 2020).

